Claude McKay, Code Name Sasha

UNIVERSITY PRESS OF FLORIDA

Florida A&M University, Tallahassee
Florida Atlantic University, Boca Raton
Florida Gulf Coast University, Ft. Myers
Florida International University, Miami
Florida State University, Tallahassee
New College of Florida, Sarasota
University of Central Florida, Orlando
University of Florida, Gainesville
University of North Florida, Jacksonville
University of South Florida, Tampa
University of West Florida, Pensacola

Claude McKay,

CODE NAME SASHA

Queer Black Marxism and the Harlem Renaissance

Gary Edward Holcomb

University Press of Florida
Gainesville * Tallahassee * Tampa * Boca Raton * Pensacola
Orlando * Miami * Jacksonville * Ft. Myers * Sarasota

First cloth printing, 2007
First paperback printing, 2009

Excerpts from the following poems are reproduced courtesy of the literary
representative for the works of Claude McKay, Schomburg Center for Research
in Black Culture, New York Public Library, Astor, Lenox, and Tilden Foundations: "America," "America in Retrospect," "Dreams," "Fez," "Flower of Love,"
"International Spirit," "If We Must Die," "London," "Marrakesh," "Moscow,"
"On a Primitive Canoe," "Paris," "Petrograd," "A Red Flower," "Snow Fairy,"
"Tanger," "White House," "We Who Revolt."

Library of Congress Cataloging-in-Publication Data
Holcomb, Gary Edward.
Claude McKay, code name Sasha : queer Black marxism and the Harlem
Renaissance / Gary Edward Holcomb.
p. cm.
Includes bibliographical references and index.
ISBN 978-0-8130-3049-4 (alk. paper)
ISBN 978-0-8130-3450-8 (pbk.)
1. McKay, Claude, 1890–1948—Criticism and interpretation. 2. McKay,
Claude, 1890–1948—Political and social views. 3. African Americans—
Intellectual life. 4. Jamaican Americans—Intellectual life. 5. African
Americans—Race identity. 6. Blacks in literature. 7. Bisexuality in literature.
8. Communism in literature. 9. Harlem Renaissance. 10. Black nationalism—
History—20th century. I. Title.
PS3525.A24785Z73 2007
811.'529–dc22 [B]   2007001296

The University Press of Florida is the scholarly publishing agency for the State
University System of Florida, comprising Florida A&M University, Florida
Atlantic University, Florida Gulf Coast University, Florida International
University, Florida State University, New College of Florida, University of
Central Florida, University of Florida, University of North Florida, Univer-
sity of South Florida, and University of West Florida.

University Press of Florida
15 Northwest 15th Street
Gainesville, FL 32611-2079
http://www.upf.com

To Kim

"I am an Anarchist! Anarchist! Anarchist!"
A Long Way from Home

". . . ain'tchu one of us, too?"
Home to Harlem

Contents

Preface and Acknowledgments

Claude McKay, Code Name Sasha: Queer Black Marxism and the Harlem Renaissance is intended to be useful to those working in a range of critical studies. As McKay is among the foremost New Negro movement authors, this work should interest those who study and read African American literature, and not only the writers of the Harlem Renaissance. No scholarship in African American studies has addressed the multilayered queer black Marxism in the New Negro author's writings, and I would hope that this study might assist in similar efforts to find common ground in habitually discrete critical spheres. I also hope that the book is of use to those interested in postcolonial and négritude studies, as it proposes new ways of approaching the notion of a black diaspora literature. As no critical work has dealt with the way a black modernist period author's notion of diaspora was linked to sexuality and leftist politics, this book is meant as well to satisfy a want in transnational studies. While touching on transnational and postcolonial studies, I hope that readers of Caribbean literature will find it helpful, particularly those interested in rereading Caribbean writers of the period between the world wars, as McKay is a key Jamaican author. My objective is also that the text will interest those studying twentieth-century transatlantic modernist writers and their literary yield, both poetry and prose. As the work recovers McKay as a radical leftist writer, the text should be of interest to those who are concerned with the history and historiography of the Old Left as well, but also ways in which an Old Left, modernist period author assisted in articulating and challenging assumptions about New Left vocabularies of cultural inquiry. Finally, as the study reexamines his sexuality, I hope it is of use to those who are interested in queer writers—in gender studies and cultural studies—particularly those who are invested in rethinking ways in which race and leftist politics intersect with sexual dissidence. My principal aspiration, however, is to suggest that these allegedly discrete fields of critical taxonomy may find mutual ground in the study of Claude McKay. *Claude McKay, Code Name Sasha* is meant to have a bearing on the "New American Studies" concern with a postnationalist critique and the employment of cultural studies; consequently, I also hope that it will be useful to those working in North American Studies.

For the sake of readability, I have kept my use of abbreviations to a minimum, although the reader should be aware of the following: generally after the initial usage, African Blood Brotherhood appears as "ABB," Industrial Workers of the World as "IWW," Communist Party of the USA as "CPUSA," Communist Party of Great Britain as "CPGB," Communist Party of the Soviet Union as "CPSU," and so on. The word *Communist* generally appears with an uppercase C because I am referring to its proper noun usage, its signing as the Communist Party, whether in the United States, Britain, France, or Russia. By the same token, when I talk of *Anarchism* with a capital A, I mean the political society, but when I give *anarchist* a lowercase a, I mean to indicate its manifestation as a philosophy rather than in its organized form. Moreover, though I have listed in my bibliography the titles of the original publications of the poetry, all citations of McKay's verse will refer to the *Complete Poems* (2004), edited by William Maxwell, and will be abbreviated as *CP* when in parentheses. The *Complete Poems*'s exhaustive annotations and, as its title suggests, comprehensiveness make the text not just an anthology of poetry but indeed a portable archive of McKay's poetry. Finally, each of the epigraphs included herein is taken from the McKay work named in the chapter. A source note in the endnotes provides further documentation.

I am grateful for the assistance of various institutions that supported this endeavor. I thank the New York Public Library's Schomburg Center for Research in Black Study for making me a copy of the microfilmed McKay collection, including the entire manuscript of *Romance in Marseille*, an act of goodwill that made this study possible. I would like to further thank the Schomburg Center, in particular Diana Lachatanere, curator of the Manuscripts, Archives, and Rare Books Division, for generously granting me permission to quote poetry, fiction, memoir, journalism, and correspondence from the collection of the Claude McKay estate. I thank the archivists at the Beinecke Rare Book and Manuscript Library at Yale University for their kind assistance in gaining access to the James Weldon Johnson Collection of Negro Literature and Art, a crucial storehouse of McKay materials. I would like to acknowledge as well that a portion of chapter 2 appeared as "Diaspora Cruises: Queer Black Proletarianism in Claude McKay's *A Long Way from Home*," in *Modern Fiction Studies* 49.3 in Winter 2003, an act which includes my thanks to John Duvall, editor of *MFS*, for his constructive critique. I thank the American Studies Association for allowing me to arrange my panel on "Routes, Roots, and Ruts: Claude McKay and the New Black Transnationalism" for the 2003 ASA Annual Meeting on Violence and Belonging, in Hartford. I further thank the organizers of the European Perspectives in American Studies conference, in particular, Ingrid Thaler, at the John F. Kennedy Institute for North American Studies, Free University in Berlin, for inviting me to speak about my work on McKay in February 2005. I also give thanks to the Hemingway Society for providing me with the opportunity to hold my "Hemingway and the Black Renaissance" session at the 2005 MLA Annual Convention in Washington D.C., where I presented my paper on McKay and Hemingway: "The Sun Also Rises in Harlem." I give my sincere thanks, too, to the U.S. Fulbright Scholar Program, with a special expression of my gratitude to Dr. Barbara Nelson, executive director of the Fulbright Commission in Bucharest, for permitting me to return to Romania in 2004 and 2005, as my second Fulbright in Romania gave me the time to compose much of this book. I am grateful, additionally, to Emporia State University for two annual research grants, time off from teaching that also made it possible for me to accomplish this project.

As this book is intended to be useful to several reading communities, its arrival would be impossible if not for the support of a number of scholars, students, sisters, brothers, friends, and fellow travelers. I would like to offer my sincerest thanks to Amy Gorelick, Nevil Parker, Michele Fiyak-Burkley, Elaine Durham Otto, Diana Wayne, and Ashley Sink at the University Press of Florida. I also would like to offer my deep thanks to T. V. Reed for his encouragement; above all, I thank T. V. and Noël Sturgeon for their friendship. I would like to extend my sincere gratitude to a number of teachers and colleagues for the benevolent gift of time and charitable encouragement of my work over the years: David Anderson, Paul Brians, Bob Brophy, Charles Brown, Joan Burbick, Chris Fox, Susan Kendrick, Elizabeth Locey, Gerry Locklin, Dave Peck, Charlie Scruggs, Carol Siegel, Siobhan Somerville, Edgar Tidwell, and Amy Sage Webb. I would like to acknowledge my indebtedness to the work of Wayne Cooper, Brent Edwards, Michel Fabre, Josh Gosciak, George Hutchinson, John Lowney, Christa Schwarz, Winston James, Tyrone Tillery, John Trombold, and others who have contributed valuable scholarship on McKay. I extend particular thanks to Christa, who, never having met us, gave Kim and me a place to take a breather in Berlin in June 2005. I offer a very special thanks to Sandra Pouchet Paquet and John Carlos Rowe, who as readers for my manuscript offered vital comments for revision. Last in this paragraph but emphatically not least, I would like to thank Bill Maxwell for his support and suggestions, but most of all for his enjoyable comradeship commencing with our meeting at the Future of the Harlem Renaissance conference at the University of Tennessee in 1997, where, following Bill's talk, I first conceived of writing this book.

I taught McKay's queer black Marxism in my course on Radicalism and Black Literature in 2003 and 2004, on both sides of the Atlantic. It was my pleasure to discover that as much as the students were the beneficiaries of my teaching, I was the recipient of fresh ideas. As a result, I found that the act of teaching McKay was instrumental in producing the present volume. I would therefore offer a warm thanks to my most intellectually energetic students, in both the former Communist Central Eastern Europe and the once radical now red-state Kansas. The limitation of space prevents me from identifying all the students who contributed to this effort, but I would be negligent if I did not cite the following for their enthusiasm and lively company: Alice Bardan, Nathan Hall, Taylor Hammer, Jack Hutchens, Matt Lexow, Ruxie Radulescu, Cristina Stanciu, and Agnieszka Tuszynska.

I reserve special thanks for my mother, Toby (aka "Tessie") Rachel (née Brownson) Holcomb. During the late 1930s, teenaged Tessie Brownson (formerly Bronstein, the surname forcibly Anglicized by immigration officers when her father's family, after a stopover in Romania, had fled the Ukrainian pogroms and arrived in Great Britain) stood on a street corner in Manchester and passed out copies of the British *Daily Worker*. We do indeed build our temples for tomorrow.

Finally, I give my deepest thanks to my wife, Kim Holcomb. For years she has listened to my ideas, then read various versions of my manuscript and offered lengthy, detailed, invaluable critical comments. I am indeed fortunate to be united with a superlative writer and an editor with an excellent eye—a life mate with a finely tuned sense of veracity. *Claude McKay, Code Name Sasha* is for Kim.

Just as this book's presumed attributes are largely due to my good luck in encountering such extraordinary, gifted, generous folks, its faults are exclusively and unquestionably my own.

Manifesting Claude McKay

IN VIEW OF the mounting wave of scholarship concerning the Harlem Renaissance author, Festus Claudius McKay (1889–1948) is at last in vogue.[1] Even in his glory days McKay was something of a marginalized figure among various constituencies. During the 1920s, McKay saw himself as the wandering bard of a burgeoning black nationalism, a fugitive poet prowling the transatlantic margins of the modernist fête. Despite his disposition as an expatriate, McKay's fidelity to formal verse forms—and above all being a black Marxist—disqualified him from entrée into the high modernist temple of T. S. Eliot et alia. When he turned to writing prose fiction, he produced *Home to Harlem* (1928), a best seller that marked the climax of his success as a writer. The white press generally received the novel agreeably, while black reviewers almost unanimously treated the publication as scandalous.[2] That both sides regarded it as a sensational narrative of jazz, drugs, sex, and violence among "primitive" blacks is a forceful comment on the wide-ranging misreading of McKay's project even in his own time. The problem that the nomadic McKay and his transnational, aesthetically itinerant writing inevitably posed was where to locate him.

As McKay's transnationalism is reflected by his transatlantic travels, it makes sense at this point to recall his diaspora itinerary. In 1912, under the tutelage of his first patron, Walter Jekyll, McKay published two volumes of groundbreaking Jamaican creole poetry in Kingston. Following this triumph, McKay went abroad. He first traveled to Alabama to attend the Tuskegee Institute, but, dissatisfied with Booker T. Washington's philosophy of compliant adaptation, he moved on to the prairie to attend Kansas State College. In 1914, he made his way to New York to marry Eulalie Imelda Edwards, a union that would end six months later.

In 1918 he met his second supporter, Frank Harris, publisher of *Pearson's Magazine.* Enthusiastic about his poetry, Harris would be among the first to publish McKay in the United States. In 1919 McKay met the Leninist Max East-man, who would publish "If We Must Die" (1919) and several other poems in the *Liberator,* the leading American leftist magazine of the early 1920s. McKay then spent a year in England working for the *Workers' Dreadnought*, a Socialist newspaper. There he published his third book of poetry, *Spring in New Hamp-shire* (1920). Upon returning to New York, he edited the *Liberator* with Michael Gold, and in 1922 he published his final collection of poetry, *Harlem Shadows.* He then promptly hopped back to Europe where on his "magic pilgrimage" to Russia he attended the still new-sprung Soviet Union's Fourth Congress of the Third Communist International in the fall of 1922. He remained in Russia for a year, where he produced his first collection of short fiction and a cultural study of African Americans in the United States. He then resided in France until the late 1920s, where he composed *Home to Harlem.* He lived mainly in Paris, but also spent lengthy intervals in the Côte d'Azur, with a particular interest in the seaport town of Marseilles. In addition, captivated by "savage" Iberian culture, he sojourned in Spain, living mostly in Catalan Barcelona. In the late twenties, he drifted toward North Africa, where he lived for three years. In Morocco, he put the finishing touches on *Banjo* (1929) and produced *Romance in Marseille* (c. 1929–32); he also published his second collection of short fiction, *Gingertown* (1932), and a novel, *Banana Bottom* (1933). He returned to the United States in 1934. Although his movement seems rather erratic, McKay's travels had a kind of logic, from modern America to the historic British Isles, from revolutionary Russia to late-empire France, from pagan Spain to Muslim Morocco. Although each destination enabled a new momentum in his life, his nomadic tendencies contributed to his declining reputation.

For most of the Great Depression, critical interest in the author suffered as much as McKay, who was frequently in poor health. British police and intel-ligence services, law enforcement in France and French colonial authorities in North Africa, and the U.S. State Department and Bureau of Investigation took their turns at harassing McKay for two decades. By the 1940s, almost the only critical attention paid to him and his writings came in the shape of reports in a stout FBI file and "a full record of [his] political and other activities" collected by Her Majesty's Office of Works in the British Foreign Office (Maxwell, Introduction xvii).[3] His fading from the pages of public notice during the purges of the Red Scare ended at last with his nearly unnoticed death in 1948. McKay was resurrected in the Black Power/Black Arts 1960s and 1970s in Afro-American studies curricula, however, once again as the poet of ethnic nationalism and this time justifiably pressed into the service of black pride. In 1968, James A. Emanuel and Theodore L. Gross, in *Dark Symphony: Negro Literature in America*, would write, "More than any of his black contemporaries, McKay converts social polemicism and protest into poems of permanent value" (88). And in *Black Expression* (1969), Addison Gayle would honor McKay for writing "propaganda poetry of the highest order" (78).

Still, even this apposite mark of distinction has brought about critical difficulties. The McKay who now appears in anthology head notes, Web site representations, and other general reference sketches bears the messy traces of assorted retrofittings. Partly as a result of being utilized for various scholarly and general reference ends, he has been catalogued according to somewhat contradictory critical assessments. He is the politically trailblazing black nationalist poet, yet a little mystifying and unacceptable because of his dedication to Communism.[4] Although he is an unquestionably essential New Negro figure, he is perplexing and difficult to classify within the Harlem Renaissance historical chronotope. Unlike Langston Hughes and Sterling Brown, he did not generate folk vernacular verse pieces during the 1920s. His celebration of black "primitivism," moreover, understandably discomfits contemporary views of black essentialism. Furthermore, his lengthy residence abroad still complicates his credentials as a Harlem Renaissance author. Generally speaking, the McKay currently familiar to the world is an anomalous pastiche of frequently incompatible identities. In the late 1980s and early 1990s he reemerged through Caribbean studies, which was engaged in rediscovering black Anglophone writers.[5] But he became a problematic figure in this reassessment as well. Although his early Jamaican "dialect" poetry was composed in Caribbean vernacular speech, his rendering of basilectal creole verse was antithetic to the project of Caribbean "nation language" poetry. According to Kamau Brathwaite, McKay's vernacular poetry of the early 1910s does not articulate Caribbean speech as a linguistic mode that poses a resistance to and destabilization of First World supremacy. The Caribbean nation language disparagement of his Jamaican vernacular poetry performs an ironic postcolonial counter riff on the African American literary studies' difficulty in classifying the New Negro author due to his indifference toward writing dialect verse after the early 1910s.

Postcolonial criticism, extending the early 1990s' Caribbean studies approach, has treated McKay more recently in terms of Africana, transnational, and diaspora studies strategies.[6] Undertaking long overdue approaches, critics have evaluated his négritude transnationalism. Indeed, McKay's contingent, supple, sometimes strategic blackness anticipates Francophone Caribbean philosopher and poet Édouard Glissant's revision of Césairean négritude. Glissant defines "creolization" as a kind of postcolonial phenomenological condition of becoming, an emergence beyond "race" to culture built on the potential for "a new set of possibilities": "There is a difference between the transplanting (by exile or dispersion) of a people who continue to survive elsewhere and the transfer (by the slave trade) of a population to another place where they change into something different, into a new set of possibilities. It is in this metamorphosis that we must detect one of the best kept secrets of creolization" (14). Although the black transnational criticism on McKay has generated valuable scholarship, it has nevertheless engendered some critical attenuation. In an effort to address the predicament of his leftist commitment, critics using black transnational studies modes have substituted the author's obviously contradictory black Marxism with a radical black diaspora transnationalist universalism. The black transnationalist approach has posed a négritude that is set entirely in discord with internationalist, historical materialist engagement.[7]

McKay's radical leftist politics is a topic that was once given scant attention when not disregarded or evidently suppressed.[8] However, where McKay is now being reconsidered in terms of his black transnationalism, scholars of leftist radicalism also are reassessing his effort as part of the collective articulation of the Literary Left. As Alan M. Wald says in *Exiles from a Future Time: The Forging of the Mid-Twentieth-Century Literary Left* (2002), McKay's "literary and political trajectory anticipated aspects of the Black revolutionary Marxist tradition that cohered during the first part of the Depression; as McKay had done, Black writers personally and artistically blended literary trends of the Harlem Renaissance and the new proletarian literature orientation promoted by the Communist Party" (83). Indeed, the radical recovery arm of the New American Studies scholarship has improved our understanding of his role in transnational black Marxist proletarian struggle as it intersected with pluralist leftism. The predicament of the closet, as it presently materializes in McKay scholarship, however, is a little atypical. The radical recovery work on McKay, whether oriented in black transnational diaspora or leftism internationalist studies, has not shown sufficient interest in the question of how his bisexuality bisected his Marxist engagement. In truth, scholarly writings on both his transnational and his radical politics have tended either to ignore or openly scorn speaking to the issue of his sexual distinction.[9]

The general outcome of the critical work retrieving him in view of his gay identified writings also has resulted in valuable readings of the author's works.[10] Even so, inquiries into his divergent sexuality have tended to overlook the evidence of his proletarian radicalism, preferring to isolate sexually indicative passages of his writings in order to verify his gay identity.[11] Not so long ago, authenticating the gay character of Harlem Renaissance authors—Countée Cullen, Alice Dunbar-Nelson, Angelina Grimké, Langston Hughes, Alain Locke, Richard Bruce Nugent, Wallace Thurman, and so on—was a crucial critical act. But the shortcomings in this pursuit when performed in isolation are conspicuous when it comes to McKay's work.

Although a valuable body of scholarly work therefore now exists on McKay, at this stage of the négritude writer's rediscovery, critics still have not navigated the dark, difficult waters of his language, literature, life, and labor, the fluid depths through which the black Atlantic author took up what I have called his "diaspora cruising." The discrete characteristics that critics find noteworthy in his writings when singled out, to put it another way, pose difficulties when his multiplicity is taken into account. The difficulty of his multiplicity requires an approach inflected by a Jamesonian historicization, an engagement with the nexus of modernist stylistics and Marxist polemics. The problem that McKay's poetry poses, for example—his abandonment of dialect, or creole, stylistics—underscores the need to historicize the author. The principal reason McKay abandoned creole verse, a little ironically, was due to his enthusiastic desire to help formulate a New Negro stylistics, a passion that shared in an early Harlem Renaissance reply to questions of authenticity and aesthetic value. When he set out to write his post-Jamaican poetry, his choice of lyrical mode reflected burgeoning American New Negro values, exemplified by James Weldon Johnson's appeal in the introduction to *The Book of American Negro Poetry* (1921) for "a form that is freer and larger than dialect, . . . but also capable of voicing the deepest and highest emotions and aspirations" of the New Negro (44). Johnson's preface calls for a cultural national awakening, as J. M. Synge fashioned for the Irish Renaissance. When McKay began to create his version of the New Negro lyric, writing in vernacular was adverse to the needs of the African American literary renaissance, and this steadfastness to the values established at the birth of New Negro lyricism was formed on and morphologically bound with his dedication to Marxist politics, a commitment that came into being at the same time. Although he would modify his political views, he held fast to his commitment to high-minded lyricism, never adjusting the essential principles of his verse aesthetics. Incessantly moving, both geographically and intellectually, McKay saw poetry as an intensely personal, protected *home* where the poet could gain access to the truth, to the core of language itself. In the concluding pages of his memoir, *A Long Way from Home* (1937), McKay refers to his life as "the distilled poetry of my experience" (354). Bending to current taste would compromise the integrity of his experience.

The scholarly distance when it comes to his troubling anomaly and obscurity—his puzzling range of engagement—is in some measure due to the distance between disciplinary points of departure: the discursive boundaries between literary, historical, philosophical, sociological, political, and related field-driven humanities approaches. At the same time and somewhat contradictorily, the critical reserve when confronted with McKay's boundary crossings is due to a scarcity of dialogue across allegedly interdisciplinary methods of criticism and research that have surfaced over the past twenty or so years. Though multidisciplinary in form, when such modes of historicist and culturally oriented criticism as transnational diaspora studies, radical recovery criticism, and queer studies have been applied to him, they have tended to function in isolation, as if each area of study were a discrete critical subject. The disinclination to interrogate his mixing of anomalous poetics, politics, and proclivities is not only a scholarly oversight. The reluctance to meet McKay's multiplicity is also a consequence of near-institutional, established classes of critical formation. Ironically, each of these is a radical new way of viewing literary labor of the modernist period.

The chief obstacle in the way of discovering a more expanded sense of McKay's writing and travels lies in the way critics still present him—as they continue to present Du Bois, author of the crucial black Marxist study *Black Reconstruction in America* (1935), and Hughes, writer of numerous pro-Communist poems, plays, essays, and stories, and other black Marxist authors—almost exclusively as an early voice of black nationalism. A lingering wisdom, left over from texts like Harold Cruse's *Crisis of the Negro Intellectual* (1967)—the "crisis" being Communist influence—is the idea that white leftists duped blacks into joining the party and engaging in similar actions. It is necessary to articulate a simple if evidently subtle fact. During the 1920s McKay was a cultural nationalist, the strident voice of black self-determination, while he was simultaneously an internationalist, a radical dedicated to Marxist-Leninist-Trotskyist cross-racial revolutionary change. McKay's compound revolutionary views call to mind the thinking of another black Marxist Caribbean author, C.L.R. James, who wrote in 1935:

When I hear people arguing about Marxism versus the nationalist or racialist struggle, I am very confused. In England I edited the Trotskyist paper and I edited the nationalist, pro-African paper of George Padmore, and nobody quarreled. The Trotskyists read and sold the African paper and . . . there were [African] nationalists who read and sold the Trotskyist paper. I moved among them, we attended each other's meetings and there was no problem because we had the same aim in general: freedom by revolution. (qtd. in Callinicos 62)

What are seen today as hostile convictions were not routinely recognized as political polarities during the 1920s and 1930s. Indeed, McKay's 1920s writings verify the telescoping of the distance between positions that are today habitually considered unbridgeable peripheries. In the interwar period, each *difference* could inform the other, if often in vigorously dialectical ways. While insisting that those engaged in the internationalist struggle recognize that race must become a central signifier of revolutionary discourses, black nationalist cultural workers believed that only a collective effort against world capitalism could overcome imperialism and racism. In this way, as Cedric Robinson says in *Black Marxism: The Making of a Black Radical Tradition* (1983; rpt. 2000), blacks participated in the realization and the radicalization of twentieth-century Marxist theory and practice, playing a vital role in revolutionizing leftism during its post-Bolshevik stages. McKay's Leninist Trotskyism set the stage for pivotal black thinkers like Frantz Fanon, author of the Marxist anticolonialist psychoanalytic study *The Wretched of the Earth* (1961), and the poet Aimé Césaire, who identified négritude as a black Marxist aesthetic and philosophical movement. It is noteworthy that these two black transnational Caribbean authors ardently diverged on the issue of négritude but shared a passion for international leftism.

McKay was dedicated to radical socialist action for over fifteen years during his most productive years as a poet. He helped found the radical underground African Blood Brotherhood (ABB) during the late 1910s and early 1920s (James, *Holding* 156, 165–66) and published the iconoclastic "If We Must Die." Among the batch of poems published in the *Liberator*, the sonnet was written in swift response to the events of what James Weldon Johnson called the "Red Summer," when white mobs assaulted black labor protesters across the Midwest and South. As William M. Tuttle recounts in his study of the period, whites rioted against blacks in Chicago, Washington, D.C., and other cities, in some cases assisted by the police, leading to some sixty lynchings of black strikers. At the same time and though for the most part unorganized, following the models of

Ireland's 1915 Easter Rebellion and Russia's 1917 Red October revolution, it was the first instance when blacks materially resisted, acting in effect like an armed insurgency. The Red Summer events must be contextualized and historicized as part of a series of Anarchist, Communist, and Socialist strikes and actions, most notably the Seattle General Strike in February and the Winnipeg Strike beginning in May 1919. Indeed, the Red Summer must be understood in terms of the Red Scare of 1917–20, when the Espionage Act of 1917 was extended by passing the Sedition Act in 1918, bringing about the subsequent assault on "Reds." Taking possession of the Declaration of Independence's inclusive plural voice, "We the People," McKay's sonnet utters the impatience of the tyrannized black Great Migration class along with the cresting tide of besieged cross-cultural American radical socialist action. The poem's first-person plural subjectivity swings pendulously between black and radical voices, finally uniting these two masses while still placing to the forefront black speech, designating *radical* and *black* suddenly synonyms in the American age of modernity. Indeed, the black minority is the most radically disposed: "If we must die, let it not be like hogs / Hunted and penned in an inglorious spot, / While round us bark the mad and hungry dogs, / Making their mock at our accursèd lot" (ll.1–4, *CP* 177).

In fact, his radical leftist politics did not end in the mid-1920s but affected his literary turnout into the early 1930s. McKay's fierce predilection for Communist politics in the early to mid-1920s is corroborated by the publications of *The Negroes in America* (1923) and *Trial by Lynching* (1925), printed by a Russian state publisher. But he produced dozens of radical proletarian poems and prose works right up until the mid- to late 1930s (around the time comrade Caribbean C.L.R. James moved toward Trotskyism). Trotsky's permanent revolution is inscribed through the subversive dialects of négritude and sexual alterity in McKay's first three consecutive, connected novels. Really, focusing so intensely and specially on his mid- to late 1930s rejection of leftism shrinks his radical literary action to a single formal ideological act, as though his repudiation says everything one needs to know about black writers and leftist cultural work. Such a supposition executes the very problematics of ideology that McKay struggled against. Paul Ricoeur's *Time and Narrative* (1983–85) provides an essential challenge to the critical act of reading the past in reverse, of judging the actions of history through the *telos*, the narrative ending. Ricoeur interrogates the idea that all action arrives at a logical, natural, and therefore enlightening endpoint. The significance of McKay's engagement with Communism is not that he finally renounced it.

McKay's intellectual and creative *dis*-position consequently should be weighed in terms of an adaptable black Marxism, an innovatory twentieth-century form of Marxist politics spun out of the aesthetic movement négritude, that is, post–Great War universalist politicized Africanness or blackness. Articulated in the *écoles* and labor unions of France, the négritude movement was itself driven by an early black Marxist anticolonialist politics in Africa and the Caribbean. Black Marxism is principally concerned with colonialism and its cultural productions. As James E. Smethurst points out in *The New Red Negro: The Literary Left and African American Poetry, 1930–1946* (1999), "African-American writers such as Hughes, Frank Marshall Davis, and Richard Wright significantly urbanized and proletarianized the Communist-influenced concept of the vernacular" of black Marxist revolutionary practice (29).[12] In an effort to *re-member* the *new*, to reconstruct the body of black modernity, a new grammar must be brought to an understanding of McKay's even earlier writing and rewriting, during the 1920s, of Marxist politics and proletarian aesthetics.

McKay's late 1910s to mid-1930s writings collectively articulate a Trotskyist-anarchist political aesthetic, and the modernist principles that his most important works inscribe also bear a striking resemblance to Antonio Gramsci's convergence on *culture* as the dynamic of power. Depoliticized blackness is manufactured consent in racist and imperialist cultural hegemony, in McKay's critical discourse. In *The Negroes in America*, a text that qualifies as an embryonic form of "black cultural studies," as William J. Maxwell says, the black organic intellectual, "Marxian pre-critic" McKay probes the idea of a nonaligned blackness (*New Negro* 87). Maxwell's assessment of the Soviet-published document as anticipating "both the expansive horizon and uneven adroitness of cultural studies at its most ambitious" (76) provides an essential reconsideration of McKay's project. Areas of *The Negroes in America* that deal with the sexualized black body and its association with labor Maxwell identifies as "the cultural chapters," investigations into American social forms that "mingle high and low forms, culture, power," and the analysis of "national propaganda." McKay's cultural chapters "insist that the approach to *culture as a site of struggle* over the meaning of race will be impeded or exploited by those capitalizing the [prize]fights, the plays, *and the novels*" (emphasis added, 87). A crucial claim of my study is that the "cultural chapters" of *The Negroes in America* in 1923 were only the beginning of his black cultural studies. McKay's black historical materialist cultural studies, in fictional form, continued for ten years after the publication of *The Negroes in America*, the moment that scholars almost unanimously mark as the end of his love affair with Marxism. His Marxist-Leninist-Trotskyist creative writings of the early 1920s represent a critical moment, the naissance of a counterculture of modernity and dialectical materialism. His black anarchist writings blend the "old" Marxist ideology critique including an interest in commodity fetishism—signing the black body as fetish commodity—with the "cultural materialist" interest in identity construction: sexual/sexist, gender, racist, and nationalist structures of feeling.

In company with and indeed integral to the necessary act of recovering his leftist politics, a second essential critical act is to initiate a new perception of the black author's sexual politics. A good place to start is with the way McKay's sexual difference has been critically classified. McKay has been generally identified as bisexual. The question of what terminology is most appropriate for the author's aesthetic project and racial-sexual dis-position goes to the core of how one may most effectively read the black Atlantic author's poetry and prose. McKay himself supplies ample assistance toward reading his signing of sexual difference. The novel "fragment of Aframerican Life" that he was unable to publish before he died in 1948, *Harlem Glory* (1990), contains a cross-dressing character who anticipates Judith Butler's theory of sexual performativity: "He was formerly a female impersonator of the rough burlesque type and had delighted the hard-boiled patrons of colored cabarets from San Francisco to New York. The big scene of his act used to be a parody of congenitally effeminate female impersonators" (39). In other words, the act of the black "rough burlesque type" was to parody drag artists who emulated the manner of femininity. The female impersonator in *Harlem Glory* performs in his exposure of naive drag queens—cross-dressing men who mistake femininity for womanhood—the concept that drag is a subversive act. The female impersonator does not so much reveal the social construction of sex as lay bare the performativity of the sex-gender system (Butler 231). As gender performativity is both a theory for analyzing ludic sexual ambiguity like drag *and* a critical language for understanding daily, public human intercourse, as Butler says, McKay's imaginative writing may be identified as pioneering the queer critique of gender performativity. In other words, in Butler's contention that gender, beyond its endurance as a social construction, is a "performance," a set of repetitive acts and signs that make up the human subject's daily social actions (181), one may locate McKay's black queer anarchist poetry. Like Butler, he challenges the conception of a "natural" self who exists a priori to the construction of cultural identity. Butler calls into question the very notion of an ontological order through which one may locate essential value, a performance that is "specifically political":

> The mode of sex is neither invariant, nor natural, but is a specifically political use of the category of nature that serves the purpose of reproductive sexuality. In other words, there is no reason to divide up human bodies

into male and female sexes except that such a division suits the economic needs of heterosexuality and lends a naturalistic gloss to the institution of sexuality. (*Gender* 143)

Every human subject functioning under heterosexual social conditions is compelled to perform gender, indeed is policed into doing so by the "heterosexualizing law and its expropriability" (232). Any act of resistance against the law of gendered identity formation risks harsh punishment, a point that builds on the work of sociologist Gayle Rubin, who theorizes the resistant alterity of the "sexual dissident," a kind of sexual outsider whose social presence speaks against dominant gender/sex codes.

A crucial component of my study is the recognition that in McKay's writing sexual variation and racial difference are formed on shared discourses. As Foucault says in *The History of Sexuality* (1978), the modern episteme's Victorian regime of power invented the language that made possible the scientific treatment of sex, classifying as abnormal all sexual activity outside of the married and heterosexual. This forced other sexual practices to be dispatched to the brothel or mental hospital, thereby effecting their ostensible disappearance, yet the evidence of their existence remained as a set of coded, covert discourses. In his theory of biopower, Foucault thereby links the history of sex to repression, power, and knowledge, and the "truth" is bound up with politics, linking the repression of sexuality to capitalism (*History* 140). Exploited workers aren't permitted access to pleasure except in the service of reproduction. McKay's black queer proletarian characters defy the enforcement of capitalist-nationalist reproduction, of biopower.

Following Foucault's historic and Butler's indispensable contributions to queer studies, scholars like Robert Reid-Pharr, E. Patrick Johnson, and Mae G. Henderson have begun to study the relationship between racial difference, divergent sexuality, language, and power. Siobhan Somerville's *Queering the Color Line: Race and the Invention of Homosexuality in American Culture* (2000) discusses the ways "that questions of race—in particular the formation of notions of 'whiteness' and 'blackness'—must be understood as a crucial part of the history and representation of sexual formations, including lesbian and gay identity and compulsory heterosexuality" (5). As with Butler's theory of gender as an unstable category of being, in Somerville's assessment "whiteness" and "blackness" are volatile signifiers. Such social markers are signifiers in a culturally porous semiotic system: "One's sexual identity, while at times linked directly to one's sexual activities, more often describes a complex ideological position, into which one is interpellated based partly on the culture's mapping of bodies and desires and partly on one's response to that interpellation" (6). Moreover, the "term 'race' . . . refers to a historical, ideological process rather than to fixed transhistorical or biological characteristics: one's racial identity is contingent on one's cultural and historical location" (7).

In spite of the critical advances made in queer studies, inquiries into McKay's literary expression of sexuality as well as his representation of sexual difference have generated a limited critical discourse. If we read his writings with a methodology calculated to *divulge* the gay or bisexual constituent, to decode closeted signs of *the life,* then we pursue an incomplete study. When it comes to considering McKay's life and labor in the 1920s and 1930s, *queer* is the ideal terminology. In the genealogy of queer, one may trace a subject agency that refuses to submit itself tractably to questionings of identity. The transgressive idiom of queer resists succumbing to an interrogation that would make the primary focus on a literary artist unambiguous—understandable, redactable, attainable—according to clinical or sociological taxonomies. Queer does not merely articulate a sexual orientation or preference or even a social identity or classification. Queer countersubjectivity repudiates the notion that sexuality is limited by social practices and classificatory systems, that the human subject is reducible to scientific and therefore ideological arrangements. The consequence of this concept is particularly necessary to recognize where Claude McKay is concerned. He may be clinically described as bisexual, but precisely because of its use in medical science classification systems (and taxonomies designed to determine subcultural criminal behavior), such a term renders unworkable questions of how his sexual difference unites with Marxist-Trotskyist revolutionary internationalism and radical ethnic nationalism to be articulated as a transgressive force against reactionary, imperialist hegemony. McKay's black Marxism cannot be disentangled from his queer resistance.

One may assert that *queer* is too current a term to be of use when coming to an understanding of a figure like McKay, that *queer* is too abundant with its own presentism to bring into play in a study that covers an author of the modernist period. However, employed to signify sexual outlaw positionality, the term *queer* was in common use by the early 1920s, and no current conception of it would be possible without its antecedent. Indeed, the current language of queer counterhegemony may be traced to its origins in the 1920s, and McKay's writings are among those that first inscribe the "odd" idiom. Indeed, some of the earliest expressions of queer counterspeech are present in McKay's black radical leftist writings.

The vernacular of queer, moreover, goes to the core of modernist anastrophe. In *Libidinal Currents: Sexuality and the Shaping of Modernism* (1998), Joseph Boone "takes up the diverse Modernist practices originating within nonmainstream, mainly homosexual subcultures of the 1920s and 1930s," and argues "that the literally and figuratively perverse fictions of sexuality they produced cannot be separated from the uniquely twentieth-century urban topographies that these sexual subcultures inhabited and represented" (28–29). Boone suggests that queer creators of the New Negro Renaissance contributed to shaping the very language of modernism. Signifying a sexualized anarchist counterhegemony, that is, queer as counteridentity, reaches back to the beginnings of modernist revolutionary rhetorics; the idiom of the avant-garde is itself a corollary of queer speech genealogies. It is necessary to add that during the modernist moment avant-gardism and radicalism united in political resistance:

> Across the country, when radicals went to jail for fulminating against capitalist injustice, they gained support from local . . . editors . . . and progressive thinkers. Writers, theater people, and sex radicals became involved, because of an 1873 federal law—one of the famed "Comstock Laws". . . . The Comstock law was used to suppress birth control literature and sex information, but from 1910 on, agents also went after novels, and eventually avant-garde literature. (Stansell 76)

In *New Negro, Old Left: African-American Writing and Communism between the Wars* (1999), Maxwell argues that the birth of the New Negro language of the "new" may be traced to the 1920s' twin nativities of the New Negro movement and the U.S. Communist Party. Boone similarly argues that one may trace queer to the crux of the modernist moment, inscribed onto radical expression of the 1920s and early 1930s. Boone's prime mover of black queer art is Bruce Nugent, author of the initiatory bun-burying short story "Smoke, Lilies and Jade" (1926), published in the one-off Harlem Renaissance literary arts magazine *Fire!!* But while Nugent is a major early black queer presence, McKay is its ardent progenitor and passionate philosopher. He is the revolutionary writer who would clear the bookshelf for both Bob Kaufman's 1950s and 1960s black queer, radically political, caustic bebop Beat "Abomunist" manifestos and Essex Hemphill's 1980s and 1990s enraged, tribal, outlaw "ass-splitting truth" poetry. As his notion of *Negro* confronts even revolutionary Harlem Renaissance conceptions of blackness as centered in black American national identity formations, the *post* identity queer challenges all stable notions of sexual identity.

Referring to studies by scholars like Lauren Berlant and George Mosse, Somerville says: "The emphasis on affective, 'primordial,' and familial bonds in models of the nation has made it a visible site of queer critique" ("Notes" 660). As a form of counterhegemonic defiance to heteronormative ideology, queer is therefore fundamentally transnational, positioned to apply a postnationalist critique. In other words, it is not so much that *queer* is the more suitable term for interpreting his writings as that the subcultural, transgressive idiom articulates the essential character of McKay's black-red-black (that is, négritude anarchist) nomadic wanderings at taxonomic boundaries. One may not grasp his black Marxism without perceiving the author's radical dis-position toward the use of the sexualized black male worker's body in capitalist production and colonialist mastery. Queer resistance authorizes the act of uncovering the intimate relationship between sex radicalism, race resistance, and leftist anarchism, as the queer—repudiating, indeed politicizing the already received rhetoric of stable sexual identity—must inhale and exhale anarchy, or permanent revolution. Queer must resist all forms of ideological imposition of the nation's repressive and ideological apparatuses. Fred Moten's *In the Break: The Aesthetics of the Black Radical Tradition* (2003) encourages a concentration on the "space-time separated coincidence and migrant imagination, channels of natal prematurity as well as black rebirth, modernism as intranational as well as international location, and the politico-aesthetics of a surplus of content irreducible to identity in or for itself, but held, rather, in identity's relation to a general upheaval, ... the force that animates and awaits release from texts ... that represent the itineraries and locales of modernism and modernity" (35).

The U.S. Bureau of Investigation's interest in McKay ironically plays an essential role in responding to "the force that animates and awaits release from" McKay's texts. The present discussion of modernism informs this history. Claire A. Culleton's discussion of J. Edgar Hoover's paranoia about modernist literature, in *Joyce and the G-Men: J. Edgar Hoover's Manipulation of Modernism* (2004), assists in illuminating McKay's condition regarding state apparatuses: "Hoover feared that the modernist writers were participating in a movement to destabilize American democracy; that modernism was seditious; that it could spoil everything that was good and clean about the nation and hasten the nation's devolution; and that it was filthy, vulgar, and radical" (91). In McKay's particular case, the essence of the bureau's apprehension was that as a result of his sojourn for over a year in the Soviet Union, the black leftist author would return to the United States under Bolshevik orders to program suggestible Negroes to follow Communist directives. Along with the detection of his revolutionary Communist politics was an identification of his queer sexuality; it is ironic that the government justifiably assumed that these attributes were radically allied. While the Bureau of Investigation (later the FBI) saw McKay during the early 1920s as threatening to force his way through the back door of manly white America, they also located him as a shadowy figure haunting the underground. Indeed, almost invisible, he was a man existing several strata beneath the topsoil. Claude McKay, code name Sasha, was the deepest mole, a diaspora undercover agent of queer black Marxism. Looking for queer Claude is a search for the true identity of code name Sasha.

It is appropriate that he was the government's ultimate target of black Red queer terrorism, because McKay's target was ultimately state nationalism, the modern western state's ideology of ancestral exclusionism: the incestuous relationship of racism, imperialism, and fascism. For McKay, state nationalism, particularly in imperialist nations like the United States, Britain, and France, was the panoptic malevolent twin of ethnic nationalism. State nationalism was a simulacrum of authentic species unity manufactured by the state to maintain order, wage war, and criminalize the Other. It qualifies as another form of biopower, Foucault's notion of a political technology that fabricates the human subject living in the modern episteme into the discourses of classification and discipline. The Negro, however, resists being merged into disciplinary discourses because he or she is prevented from entering the linguistic and legal domain except as criminal.

In the 1921 article "How Black Sees Green and Red," published in the *Liberator*, McKay states that blacks and Irish share a common struggle: "I suffer with the Irish. . . . My belonging to a subject race entitles me to some understanding of them" (59). The black proletarian author and militant activist asserts that the ethnic and ancestral nationalisms of black chauvinism and Irish separatism sets in motion a shared understanding of oppression. Social groups like African Americans and native Irish are able to take up the consciousness of Marxist internationalist struggle against capitalism, imperialism, and state nationalism: "it is with the proletarian revolutionists of the world that my whole spirit revolts. . . . The yearning of the American Negro can only find expression in the class struggle" (58). By this statement McKay does not mean to suggest that blacks should subordinate their ethnic difference to class struggle. Such an undertaking would not be viable in his view, as being black is fundamentally and sometimes even biologically innate, a genetic disposition. Despite white supremacist attempts at eradicating black primordial genealogies, being black carries a vigorous, tenacious hereditary memory. Négritude is not a condition that may surrender to a vertical taxonomy like class structure. Class and race/ethnicity are categorically dissimilar in this way. Rather, at a time when African Americans are becoming politically conscious, only just organizing for radical action on a global scale, black laborers, like white American workers, must learn to embrace solidarity with other peoples who suffer under capitalism and class-consciousness. Blacks must learn to take up shared aims with whites, even while the white underclass is manipulated by racist supremacist ideology. By the same sign, whites must learn to welcome blacks into the common struggle: "white workers must accept him [the black worker] and work with him, whether they object to his color and morals or not" (58–59). Racism and classism are linked in the American Imaginary, employed as innate values in order to police subaltern peoples and maintain economic and political power. McKay essentially never stopped believing in the imperative of racial solidarity against the ideological and repressive apparatuses of state nationalism.

At the root of McKay's queer black Marxism is the compound predicament of national identity and making literary art. Theorist of the "New American Studies," John Carlos Rowe offers a radical revision of literary studies in terms of postnationalist critique: "Among other cultural products of modern capitalism," literary products like the novel have "been especially important in representing such powerful economic and political interests as the 'nation,' 'people,' 'government,' or 'way of life'" (*Literary* xi). Rowe's postnationalist critique demonstrates a fundamental concept of postcolonial studies; iterating Edward Said's theory of Orientalism for the service of North American Studies, Rowe asserts that western literature played a leading role in manufacturing the imperialist ideology of the nineteenth and early twentieth centuries. Yet while the canonical American novel has participated in disseminating the formation of an exclusionary, or "exceptionalist," American nationalism, Rowe's postnationalist critique suggests a method for reading the minority, alternative novel, the avant-garde of fugitive writing. McKay's three key novels collectively articulate a postnationalist critique of state nationalist hegemony and imperialist ideology. For McKay, the art of the Negro novel could perform the function of ideology critique; in this way the black novel could revolutionize the art form. Although he was intensely focused on producing for a U.S. literary marketplace, McKay always positioned himself materially in opposition to the metropolitanism of modern America. His detachment manifested itself through his representation of black peoples throughout Africa and the diaspora, his passion for recording the experience of subaltern diaspora communities in localities like Harlem and Marseilles. For McKay the struggle of black people and the allied effort to bring into being a black "national" literature required an advocating of black multiplicity, a Negro worldliness—a consciousness that was antithetic to the aims of a homogeneous national renaissance. McKay was profoundly influenced by Du Bois's critique of double consciousness, a theory that articulated the condition of the New Negro: the black subject must constantly reinvent him- or herself in order to maintain the artificial ideology of double consciousness imposed by white racist American hegemony. The theory of double consciousness exposed the hypocrisy that policed blacks to make ends meet between the polarities of an Americanness that denied them access and a black social status that could not claim even the paltriest rights of citizenship. McKay promoted a Negro political attitude that both retained ethnic distinction and grew beyond the boundaries of any form of prescriptive chauvinism. This is how black transnationalism or postnationalism and Communist then Trotskyist internationalism were connected in his writings to sexual dissidence. Because they were forced into the shadows, different sexuality, négritude, and anarchism could not form an allegiance with imperialist ideologies; all were congenitally incapable of conforming to nationalist stabilization. Collectively, they generated a revolutionary force. In *A Long Way from Home*, McKay identifies himself to penal authorities as a "bad nationalist" (300). Anticipating Althusser's bad subject, McKay's bad nationalist subjectivity is positioned so that the queer, the anarchist, and the Negro refuse to be interpellated. Bad nationalist agency constitutively poses a vital challenge to manufactured chauvinist and imperialist consent, authorizing a martial opposition to state nationalism. Queer black permanent revolution is synonymous with being a bad nationalist.

McKay was drawn to the idea of generating cycles of works in related sets of three, and my study considers the way in which his novels *Home to Harlem*, *Banjo: A Story without a Plot*, and *Romance in Marseille* mutually perform an innovative form of black cultural studies. The three novels cooperatively invent and articulate a black modernist fiction aesthetic, that is to say, reinventing the inherited blueprint for Negro novel writing as a means for black cultural revolutionary work—another inflection of diaspora cruising. In this way, McKay is generating what Deleuze and Guattari call a "minor literature." A minor literature is seditious, pioneering, and probing, standing in opposition to "majoritarian" literature, which proposes to render a known world through reputable literary modes. Rather than being an expression of an existing order and assumed human subjectivity, a minor literature is an art of "becoming." Best expressed in the novel by a minority author, such an art, laboring from the margins, reveals literature's immanent difference, thus releasing the resistant potential of literature to authoritarian ideologies. Moreover, only through a reading of McKay's queer black anarchist trilogy of novels may one observe the emergence of a nascent form of creolization.

The first novel, *Home to Harlem*, articulates the perspective of the emergent New Negro laboring class and its revolutionary promise, in effect chronicling in prose the Great Migration; the emergent experience of southern migrants and Caribbean immigrants occurs simultaneously with the burgeoning black queer subculture. When these collectivities meet, they begin to shape a nascent queer black anarchy. *Banjo* enlarges the focus, staging the creolized experience of the black diaspora proletariat—African, African American, and Caribbean—collected on the soil of imperial power, France, giving a new inflection to the meaning of expatriate subjectivity. Beneath *Banjo's* "story without a plot" exists a queer black anarchist counterplot. His third, unpublished—and until now unread—dispatch, *Romance in Marseille*,[13] adds to the diaspora assemblage the open experience of a queer proletarian subculture, where the fusion of black and white radicalism is most intensely achieved. Partly because almost nothing has been written on the novel, the various critical communities concerned with his work have not been aware that *Romance in Marseille* is as intimate a companion text with *Banjo* as *Banjo* is with *Home to Harlem*. Most important, *Romance in Marseille's* candid intercourse of queer black and white proletariat unifies the project of the three black queer revolutionary novels. Without a cognizance of the third novel's presence, a critical understanding of the coupling of *Home to Harlem* and *Banjo* is incomplete. But McKay's fiction tetralogy does more than articulate an embryonic black cultural studies. Léopold Sédar Senghor and Aimé Césaire's crediting of *Banjo* with being a kind of négritude manifesto (Hones 32–39) signifies that McKay not only helped fashion the underpinning for the American New Negro movement but also played a significant part in inspiring black literary art and liberation struggle beyond the United States. The recovered letter in the chain, *Romance in Marseille*, is a document that articulates dramatic intelligence about the character of radical fiction during the late 1920s and early 1930s. The narrative of this key unpublished novel manuscript presents a gay white radical character who imparts to black workingmen and Communists—African, African American, and West Indian—the emancipatory power of queer anarchist possibility. Like *Banjo*, *Romance in Marseille*, in its enunciation of black radical becoming, of *coming out* beyond race to contingent *new mergings*, anticipates Glissant's theory of creolization. McKay's three successive novels need to be read as narrative articulations of radical intrigue, of both political and literary subversion. *Home to Harlem*, *Banjo*, and *Romance in Mar-*

seille manifest a literary form of black Trotskyist permanent revolution, primers for insurrection, collectively a black queer ABC of anarchism. The three novels jointly fashion McKay's queer black Marxist prolegomena, a three-volume manifesto—in other words, a cluster of three little black bombs to be hurled into the discourses of state nationalism, racism, capitalism, and imperialism.

With respect to the author's contradictory character, McKay warrants reimagining in all his multiplicity, through every part of his difficulty. He merits a revisioning of his compound confrontation with received categories of literary being. In *A Long Way from Home*, his meaning both materialist and metaphorical, he expresses his motivating logic: "I had wandered far and away until I had grown into a truant by nature and undomesticated in the blood.... I desired to be footloose, and felt impelled to start going again" (150). My purpose is not so much to resolve the contradictory nature of the author's life and writing as to engage with the multiplicity of his diaspora traveling, following the circuitous paths in my subject's truant, undomesticated wanderings. In pursuing this course I consequently provide a critical discourse that bridges Caribbean and postcolonial studies, the New American Studies and radical recovery criticism, and queer and race studies. My object is the innovation of an analytical language that collectively assists in mounting a more inclusive critical representation of McKay and writers like him who, due to the fusion of ostensibly discrete trajectories, present difficulty and anomaly. Among the fundamental assertions of my study is that queer disobedience licenses the act of disclosing the closeted close relations between sex radicalism, black insurgency, and leftist anarchism.

Although my analysis includes some discussion of his life experience, it is not my intention, however, to provide a critical biography. My project is a critical study of four crucial texts, extended prose works that until now have not been read in terms of their queer black permanent revolution. Consequently, it is not my aim to achieve "coverage" of his prose publications, to present a text that analyzes all of the author's work in uniform detail. Although my analysis is supplemented by referring to stories collected in *Gingertown*, the short story collection is not part of the black queer Trotskyist manifesto trilogy. The same principle applies to his last complete novel, *Banana Bottom*. It does not play a role in the queer black Marxist novel ménage a trois. I am interested in how each of his first three novels is dependent on the other dialectically to enunciate the author's revolutionary literary program.

Before I can adequately articulate the project of his transgressive black anarchist triptych, however, it is necessary to examine McKay's memoir, *A Long Way from Home*, written a decade after the first of the trio, *Home to Harlem*, and five years before *Romance in Marseille*. The three brotherly novels enact his sexually dissident diaspora radicalism in an unruly manner, while his autobiography attempts to efface his queer black permanent revolution. Yet under its anticommunist whiteout the memoir nonetheless sustains the masked veracity of his queer black anarchism. The arrangement of chapters and their content may strike some readers as unorthodox, as I begin with two chapters devoted to McKay's life-writing and then move back in time, as it were, to discuss his three earlier novels. The reason for this, I believe, will become clear, though I would say here that considering how little has been written about the memoir and how much it has been relied on as an accurate expression of his life, the text warrants extensive discussion. My reordering of the historical chronology—starting with his autobiographical wrap-up and then retracing my way from the beginning through his fictional musings—stresses some crucial concepts. My arrangement not only underscores that this is not a biography but also demonstrates that my analysis must confront on his own terms my subject's deliberate reorganization of his past. At the same time, I would like to emphasize my own deviating, admittedly somewhat heterodox motive. Through a reading of his FBI file and autobiography together, chapter 1 establishes how the author artfully re-created his radical past, while chapter 2 investigates the way that McKay's memoir fulfills an anxious need to control textual awareness of his sexuality. To find my way into the interior of McKay's black anarchist novel tetralogy, I must first pay a sustained visit to his autobiographical performance, the cunning rendering of the life in art that produced the three novel manifestos that make up his black queer anarchist prolegomena. My intention, in other words, is not to offer a monograph whose goal is to put to bed the study of Claude McKay. My aim is to open the black diaspora author's confidential interior space—closeted not only by his own sometimes deceptive rescriptings but more effectively by the critical treatment applied to him, including the government's critical apparatus—for a more expansive conversation with the dead than has been possible until now. Ultimately, my purpose is to propose how the tactic of queer black Marxism suggests a way of reading problematic black Atlantic texts, while recognizing that all diaspora texts may challenge received critical and ideological apparatuses.

DEPARTMENT OF STATE
WASHINGTON
May 12, 1973.

Dear Mr. Burns:

Please refer to your letter of February 10, 1923, initialed
TFB:CA regarding an inquiry of the Translation Section of your
Department concerning the identity of the delegate to the Fourth
Congress of the International, Sasha or Sayesh.

I have recently been advised by the Legation at Riga that a
great amount of confusion has been caused by various ways of
spelling the name of this delegate, due to the variations which
can occur in transcribing the name from Russian to English script.
It has been rendered Sasha, Sayesh, and Sascha. From all the
information gathered, it appears that all these renderings refer
to the same person, who is listed as an American delegate.

The fact that he spoke about the necessity for propaganda
among the American negroes, would make it seem most likely that
he spoke as an American.

Very truly yours,

W. L. Hurley.

William J. Burns, Esquire,
Director, Bureau of Investigation,
Department of Justice.

190-1781-6

1. Memorandum, Agent Hurley to Director Burns, March 23, 1923, clarifying identity of
"Sasha." Federal Bureau of Investigation, FOIA Claude McKay FBI file, no. 61–3497.

JFP:GAJ

May 11, 1940

Dear

      With further reference to your letter of May 1,
1940, addressed to Mr. Harold Nathan of this Bureau, please
be advised that I am transmitting a copy thereof to Mr. E. A.
Soucy, Special Agent in Charge, Federal Bureau of Investigation, U. S. Department of Justice, 600 Court Square Building, Baltimore, Maryland.

      It would be very much appreciated if you would furnish
the papers referred to in your letter to Mr. Soucy at the above
address.

      I am indeed grateful for your courtesy and cooperation
in making this material available to this Bureau.

                Very truly yours,

                John Edgar Hoover
                Director

61-3497-78X outgoing

2. Memorandum, Director J. Edgar Hoover, May 11, 1940, requesting Claude McKay papers. Federal Bureau of Investigation, FOIA Claude McKay FBI file, no. 61-3497.

Code Name Sasha, "My Real Name"

[A] great amount of confusion has been caused by various ways of spelling the name of this delegate, due to the variations which can occur in transcribing the name from Russian to English script. It has been rendered Sasha, Sayesh, and Sascha. From all the information gathered, it appears that all these renderings refer to the same person, who is listed as an American delegate.

Claude McKay FBI file 61–3497

She hinted even that there was something suspicious about my use of my real name in Moscow. For all the American delegates had secret names. Mrs. Stokes's own was Sasha.

Claude McKay, *A Long Way from Home*

THE FOLLOWING INVESTIGATION places Claude McKay's first and unques-tionably most important memoir, *A Long Way from Home* (1937), next to his FBI file in order to demonstrate that in certain respects the once classified dossier is a more dependable portrayal of his years in Europe and North Africa than his own autobiography. My purpose is to confront the question of whether, when it comes to McKay's queer black Marxism, *A Long Way from Home* is a completely reliable resource and, more important, why it isn't. I inquire into the text's pas-sionate denunciation of Communism and the resultant generally complacent view of the memoir, prefiguring the Communist repudiations of writers like Richard Wright, Ralph Ellison, and James Baldwin, to serve as the archetypal African American refutation of international leftism. For over half a century, critics have counted on *A Long Way from Home* when a black repudiation of Communism was needed, and indeed, this is understandable because the au-tobiography, read in comparative isolation, delivers the message that its author was never truly a committed Marxist and has long since suspended his onetime association with subversives. My aim is to search into the core of McKay's mem-oir and to locate the still smoking residue of his queer black Marxism, made manifest by the survival of McKay's "real name": Sasha.

Among the final communiqués collected in his FBI file is a succinct memo-randum, dated May 11, 1940, requesting that a bureau agent deliver the "papers" of one Claude McKay. The signature on the order to take delivery of the docu-ments—the correspondence and other materials that would become his 119-page classified dossier—is "John Edgar Hoover, Director." If by the early 1940s McKay was on the verge of being all but forgotten in the world of black literary arts, his historical and literary memory is preserved by the grim fact that even as late as 1940 Hoover placed an order for the collected prose not *of* but *on* Claude McKay. Right-wing zealots like Hoover thought of Red and black as furtively interconnected, assembled in order to stage "a Communist war on whiteness" (Maxwell, *New Negro* 92). But another identity category may be added to the union of the Red and the black in the aroused imagination of the Right. For Hoover and his ilk, Communists, Negroes, and homosexuals formed a degen-erate, subversive ménage à trois whose united aim was to overthrow the white heterosexual nation. Moreover, this profane threesome did not at all times form discrete classes of identity. Under the racist and anti-Red propaganda apparatus of the late 1930s and within the government's undertaking to purge Communists from the Federal Writers Project (FWP), the organization that made the writing of his 1937 autobiography possible, the designation "Communist" was habitu-ally tantamount to "queer" (D'Emilio 40–53). And the combination of "Negro" and "political" was instinctively synonymous with "Communist," as McKay's dossier validates. The mania for seeing Communist, Negro, and homosexual as interchangeable, with each side of the tripartite mind of Evil goading the other toward new deeds of iniquity, attained its most fanatical expression by the mid-1950s, even in, and perhaps most intensely in, the minds of frustrated, closeted homosexuals like Hoover. But the postwar fever pitch of the McCarthy witch hunts during the cold war period, fed by the FBI's ferocity in nailing radicals like Wright, Langston Hughes, and Paul Robeson, was the historical waste product of the interwar period Red Scare, the unambiguous correlation between leftist rebellion, African American resistance, and homosexual revolution. Though not generally among the items catalogued when his *firsts* are inventoried, McKay was the prototype for the unholy union of Red, black, and queer.

The origins of the file may be traced to the period when McKay sojourned in Russia in 1922–23, as at this time he attracted the scrutiny of the U.S. Bureau of Investigation. The bureau had been formed in 1910 to enforce the Mann Act, the "white slave law," put into use in order to carry out the United States' most sensational manhunt of the early 1910s, the pursuit of the black heavyweight champion and demolisher of the "Great White Hope," Jack Johnson. But during the late 1910s and early 1920s, the bureau began investigating domestic radicals. On June 2, 1919, Anarchists purportedly bombed the house of A. Mitchell Palmer, Woodrow Wilson's attorney general; Congress subsequently gave the crusading right-wing attorney free rein to rid the nation of subversives. Assisted by Hoover, Palmer dispatched an army of five hundred bureau agents, acting without warrants, to arrest scientists, antiwar protesters, leaders of the Industrial Workers of the World (IWW), and members of other unions. Assisted by the *New York Times* and *New York World*'s sensational praise of Feds cleaning out the Reds, the campaign mounted against radicals and those identified as radical is notable for being among the most brutal, terrifying, and disgraceful periods in American history. As Edwin Hoyt recounts in his study of the Palmer Raids, agents also seized 249 resident aliens, including the Anarchists Emma Goldman and Alexander "Sasha" Berkman, and forced them to set sail for the Soviet Union.

Palmer took an individual interest in McKay, discussing the black radical's poetry "in his lengthy report to the *U.S. Senate, Investigation Activities in the Department of Justice*" (Maxwell, Introduction xvi). Federal interest in McKay's stay in Russia for over a year was intensified by the appearance of poetry and prose publications before, during, and after the period he resided there. When it looked into the black Bolshevik's past, the bureau found that before setting out for the Soviet Union McKay had published militant poetry in the *Libera-*

tor, including "If We Must Die" (1919), "The Tired Worker" (1919), and "To the Entrenched Classes" (1922). While in England, he also penned articles on blacks and internationalism. "Socialism and the Negro" (1920), a piece that urges black participation in the establishment of radical internationalism, appeared in Sylvia Pankhurst's radical socialist newspaper, the *Workers' Dreadnought.* And "How Black Sees Green and Red" (1921), his declaration that black autonomy and Irish home rule should organize under the auspices of international leftism, was published in the *Liberator.* His speech in Moscow appeared under the title of "Report on the Negro Question" in *International Press Correspondence* in 1923, and the pro-Communist article he wrote for the NAACP's *Crisis*, "Soviet Russia and the Negro" (1923–24), came out after he had departed Russia.

The bureau's anxiety over McKay was that the Soviets were sending him to lure susceptible blacks into joining the U.S. Communist Party (CPUSA). When he was thought to be returning from Russia, the file both comically and grimly reveals, agents kept up an anxious watch at key contact points, exchanging communications full of redundancies and inaccuracies, one agent after another apparently trying to lay claim to the earliest intelligence on McKay's radical activities. The following communication originating in Copenhagen and dated March 1923 expresses the Feds' anxiety, as agents believed that "Claude Mackey" would come back to the States by way of the Hague:

> The Honorable
> The Secretary of State,
> Washington.
>
> Sir:
>
> I have to report, confirming my telegram, No. 6, March 8, 3 p.m., that my French Colleague, Vicomte Fontenay, informs me, from official information received by him, that one Claude Mackey [*sic*], an American negro, who has just graduated from the Bolshevik school at Moscow, has been especially delegated by the Soviet Government for propaganda among the North American negroes. In an open letter, which recently appeared in IZVESTIA, Trotsky has published the official instructions given to Mackey for the organization of the black race in the United States against their "American oppressors." I am informed that Mackey is sailing at once for the United States.
>
> I have the honor to be, Sir,
> Your obedient servant,
> John [unreadable] Prince.

The file is a record of the flurry of interest in the black traveler during the early 1920s. In a December 13, 1922, letter dispatched to Hoover's predecessor, Director William J. Burns, Agent Edward J. Brennan passes on information about a black Communist in Moscow named Claude McKay who goes by the designation "Saysch." In the same correspondence, Brennan also calls McKay "Sashsa" or "Saesha," and he refers to "J. Billings," whom the "special agent in charge" identifies as "Housewood" (that is, Otto E. Huiswoud, who sometimes went by the name Frank Billings, the CPUSA's genuine black delegate). Other documents in the file refer to a code name similar to these permutations, including "Sayesh." The documents take on even more opacity, however, when statements identify one "Sayesh Johnson," a black American Communist, because in other correspondence intelligence suggests that Sayesh and Johnson may be two different "negroes." A February 1923 memorandum classifies McKay as "a confidential man for Sylvia Pankhurst" when he wrote for the *Workers' Dreadnought* in London, an identification that accentuates the way bureau agents were keen on feminizing their object of scrutiny, as the black male McKay is a subordinate of a former suffragette. The bureau agents find the idea of a black American male envoy going by the name of a sexually indeterminate Russian name highly stimulating, exactly the sort of radio show alias a Communist agent would be expected to take up. The FBI's "interest in McKay's sexuality is distinct, of a piece with its tendency to criminalize temperament along with dissident creeds," William J. Maxwell observes. "Frozen to McKay's bureau reputation as a 'notorious negro revolutionary' was a fixed identity as a bohemian reprobate" ("F.B. Eyes" 47). Meanwhile, in the shape of additional spelling incarnations of Sasha, more misinformation turns up in the now distended dossier, as an agent passes on the information that McKay is thought to be using "the alias of . . . Saisha" while in Russia. As if the intention were to make all of the intelligence utterly useless, according to a report of March 23, 1923, Sayesh may be "Sascha" or possibly "Johnson." And finally one encounters the memo dated May 12, 1923, "concerning the identity of the delegate to the Fourth Congress of the International, Sasha or Sayesh." Hurley writes to Burns: "[A] great amount of confusion has been caused by various ways of spelling the name of this delegate, due to the variations which can occur in transcribing the name from Russian to English script. It has been rendered Sasha, Sayesh, and Sascha. From all the information gathered, it appears that all these renderings refer to the same person, who is listed as an American delegate": Claude McKay. McKay, *code name Sasha*, seems to be omnipresent, lurking at every port-of-call cavity—in one communiqué entering from

Canada, in another from the Caribbean. A Communist Caliban, he is a one-man political tempest, an ominous force crossing the wide black Atlantic and bearing straight for America. But McKay never arrived to foster a new radical black nation.

Even more than by "If We Must Die," the filers are captivated by McKay's "America" (1921); the file contains a typed copy of the complete poem. Apparently the agents see in the sonnet all that is immoral and illicit about McKay. The date of the poem is vital. In 1921, while still in the United States and getting ready to make his way to Communist Russia—and a year before T. S. Eliot published *The Waste Land*—McKay penned a sonnet that presented a bitter offering to his adoptive country, a poem that lyricized the black radical poet's rendering of twentieth-century dissipation, though a manifestly different take than Eliot's fragmented, ghostly voices of yearning for more stable times. Like black abolitionist James M. Whitfield's 1853 169-line poem with the same title, McKay's "America" is a piercing critique of the conventional allegory of mother country as fostering freedom, though modernized through anarchist antinationalism. The sonnet alleges that America is the feral, pitiless jungle big-cat mother: "Although she feeds me bread of bitterness, / And sinks into my throat her tiger's tooth, / Stealing my breath of life, I will confess / I love this cultured hell that tests my youth!" (ll.1–4, *CP* 153). Considering McKay's passion for the poetry of the Romantics and Victorians (Gosciak 10), the reader would be justified in picking out vampire succubus imagery in the poem—the "stealing" of the victim's "breath of life," as in Coleridge's *Cristabel* (1797). But distinguishing the maternal wild animal imagery throughout the poem is crucial. Written during a period of lynching mania, the poem's upsetting of received sex/gender conditions invalidates the racist representation of the uncontrollable black male, characterized by the blackfaced Gus in *The Birth of a Nation* (1915), whose single-minded desire is to sexually assault patriarchal America's most valued possession, the white woman. The poem undoes the racist sexual certitude by making the white female the antagonist. The primal jungle beast, America, is a creature that retains absolute sway over the black son. In the discourses of nationalism, race, and sexuality, America is represented as female according to the convention of the white goddess Columbia, America's alias popularly identifiable in the shape of the Statue of Liberty, the imposing, stony-eyed lady in New York Harbor whose lamp lights the way for immigrants crossing the Atlantic. In a left-wing toppling of the hegemonic verticality, capsizing the positions of the righteous Palmer agent and Anarchist infiltrator suspected of plotting to overthrow the government, America is obliged to sit in the hot seat, as McKay rotates the harsh light of interrogation in the direction of Columbia's countenance, forcing the truth torch to shed its light on the impassive face of America. This act of Mencken's "American language" illuminates America as the animal mother whose instinctual violence takes the shape of exclusionist, ironically tribal nationalism. Charily portioning out her passions, America nourishes her fair-haired children with the sweetest morsels, but to her despised brood, her lesser offspring, she spoons out the "bread of bitterness," effectively starving the black minority. A maternal creature that consumes the flesh of her own unwanted young, moreover, America is ironically a savage cannibal, the embodiment of darkest Africa in the Western Imaginary. In this way the poet versifies black irony: what it means for the black subject both to taste the fruits of America and at the same time to be devoured alive by her. That is, from the point of view of her desperate black foundling, Mother America, the loving nurturer of all, is a cold-blooded wild animal, ripping into the flesh of the African American minority. A few years later, the image of sitting down to the family meal signifying a metaphor for the national exclusion of the ethnic minority would appear in Langston Hughes's "I, Too" (1925), a New Negro vers libre that claims the right to participate for the hard-pressed black underclass, made flesh as the "darker brother" (l.2, *Collected* 46). The black brother of Hughes's poem refuses to assume the position of servant anymore, declining to wait on America. Echoing the nationalist optimism of Whitman's inclusive "Song of Myself" (1855), Hughes conveys that black pride means joining the white family in the opulent feast that is America.

In McKay's "America," however, the black population is the casualty of the thanksgiving cannibal feast—the New Negro is faced with the predicament of whether he or she will consume or be consumed. And all black people, not only the Caribbean immigrants, are refugees in the *pays natal*. His ambivalence is shaped by the fact that the child who has been grudgingly taken in nonetheless is devoted to his or her unwilling protector: "I will confess / I love this cultured hell that tests my youth." The lost, abused "youth" cannot refrain from adoring the adoptive mother because America after all presents the possibility of ameliorative change, as she embodies the promise of the new, of birth. While the masses of the black minority must reconstruct an obliterated past, retrieve their disregarded, buried black history, and try to build a culture in the teeth of a sadistic social order, racism—in other words, achieve the paramount aim of the Negro Renaissance—blacks must simultaneously, paradoxically embrace the *new*, the promise of the future. The speaker is still in his formative years of American literary history because the Harlem Renaissance's New Negro, the photonegative unintended issue of modernity, is a being who has risen from the ashes of blackface minstrels, Uncle Tom and Jim Crow, figures who have been made extinct by the collective African American defiance to racist hegemony. With its headlong surge toward the modern, America is the collective performance of phenomenological becoming itself and is therefore the stage for a fresh, fierce revolution. Although, like the New Negro, America is a figuration of the new, the form that the transformation may take is yet unknown. America's modernity, in other words, is both the solution and the problem for its hard-pressed black underclass, as *the modern*, American-style, is the kissing cousin of capitalism and imperialism, the close ideological relations of nationalism and racism. A resolute survivor of the early twentieth-century lynching frenzy, the budding black offspring has no alternative but to act as revolutionary, as justly disobedient child.

The next six lines once more suggest America as a life form incarnated as a vampire. But again it is necessary to discern the image of the cannibalistic animal mother, as the youth, locked in a cage with America, is compelled to perform the act of big-cat tamer: in other words, of insurgent. Where the succubus draws the lifeblood from her victim, Mother America feeds existence to her newborn. That is to say, mother country America, through an inexorable regurgitation of the scraps of freedom—an act of nature that America, in her "vigor" and abundance, cannot refrain from performing—supplies the sustenance. Consequently, she supplies the sexually "erect" potency that is vital for regenerating the revolution that will cause her own downfall:

> Her vigor flows like tides into my blood,
> Giving me strength erect against her hate.
> Her bigness sweeps my being like a flood.
> Yet as a rebel fronts a king in state,
> I stand within her walls with not a shred
> Of terror, malice, not a word of jeer. (ll.5–10)

The final quatrain puns on the darkness of the black speaker, the besieged dissenter, as he *darkly gazes* into the future—as in Corinthians' child who must finally grow up. The black son foresees America's masterful experiment in modernity ultimately collapsing, its Lady Liberty granite promise ultimately going the way of Shelley's nearly obliterated "Ozymandius" (1818), "king of kings." And though one might think that this would cause the insurgent to exult, to look forward to dancing on America's grave, it has the opposite effect: "Darkly I gaze into the days ahead, / And see her might and granite wonders there, / Beneath the touch of Time's unerring hand, / Like priceless treasures sinking in the sand" (ll.11–14). In the future, all that will be left of Lady Liberty is the pedestal.

The idea of America's annihilation makes the black anarchist mournful because America, distinguishing the horizons of Whitman's lyrical democratic vistas, holds the promise of fulfillment. Nonetheless, its course, invested in capitalism, imperialism, and state nationalism—the combined cultural Imaginary that jointly produces racism—seems destined, in a world engaged in bitter conflict, for disintegration. It is crucial that McKay generated "America" while planning to travel to Communist Russia, America's dark Other, because it is necessary to understand that his existence in the Leninist Bolshevik nation, something of a second adopted country, helped shape his thoughts on his previously adoptive motherland. As he hesitantly consents to the prospect of Whitman's optimism for America (an optimism Whitman nearly lost for the same reasons McKay verbalizes, as the black poet knows), he is also ambivalent about Eliot's millenarian vision of modernity. His signing of modern America does not evoke the image of a desolate zone, a cultural waste, where alienated human subjects live fragmentary existences. America, particularly for the politically disenfranchised and socially alienated, has the potential to become, to give birth to, Whitman's ideal. But McKay must queerly regenerate and, in verse ideology critique, reconceive Eliot's wasteland imagery. A constituent of this postnationalist critique is an interrogation of Whitman's sanguine patriotism, radical though the "Good Gray" American poet's democratizing verse vision was. But the genuine critique is directed at Eliot's longing for a more refined age. Although the black queer poet envisions a wasteland, the atrophy is localized in the nation, antithetic to the Eliotic modernist and ageless angst. The prospect of America's dissipation, its waste of possibility being inherent in its action—becoming a wasteland is written onto capitalist, imperialist America's future—is a revolutionary Marxist view.

The inclusion of "America" in McKay's FBI file demonstrates that the bureau grasped what was vitally rebellious about their target—what a mere poet could do to their dominance. Despite the farcical accumulation of inaccuracy, its Keystone Kops ineptitude and idiocy, McKay's FBI file is a chilling artifact of interwar right-wing fanatical obsession, the sinister reminder of reactionary hegemony. In other words, McKay's file, even bearing in mind its sometimes laughable manifestation of the banality of evil, is in some ways a more reliable representation of his life during the 1920s than his own 1930s autobiography. Yet critics have relied for the most part on *A Long Way from Home* as a dependable source for his life. The attribute of the autobiography that critics have found most compelling is its ardent rejection of Communism, and as a result, the critical community has disseminated an untroubled reading of the narrative as a model African American repudiation text. The view that has been propagated for nearly sixty years—abetted most effectively by *A Long Way from Home* itself—is that McKay came to his senses, realizing that white Communists were deceiving black cultural artists. Critics have recognized that the aim of his autobiography was to expose this deception, while simultaneously chronicling the engaging moments of his remarkable life. One need go no further than St. Clair Drake's introduction to the 1970 Harvest paperback reissue of *A Long Way from Home*. Acknowledging Harold Cruse's virulently anti-leftist *Crisis of the Negro Intellectual* (1967) as influential (if contradictorily opinionated and unreliable), Drake suggests that McKay's political apostasy serves as a cautionary tale for later black authors. One should observe the unmistakable note of gratification: "He [McKay] must have felt vindicated when younger Negro writers who did join the Party, such as Richard Wright, left it during World War II and defined the object of their former devotion as 'the God that failed'" (xiv). A compilation by former supporters of Soviet socialism, *The God That Failed* (1949) was Richard Crossman's collection of essays organized around the principle of condemning Stalinism; the anthology included Wright's "I Tried to Be a Communist," published first in the *Atlantic Monthly* in 1944.

Still, not everyone has accepted McKay's autobiography as free of difficulty. Biographer Wayne Cooper notes the inadequacies of the memoir as a portrayal of an individual's lived experience, saying that McKay "failed to convey the complexity of his life": *A Long Way from Home* is "a pleasantly impressionistic book, a seemingly effortless account of his travels and his encounters with the great and near-great of international communism and the literary world of Europe and America," but he "actually revealed very little about his personal life" (318). When placed next to McKay's queer black Marxist novel writing of the late 1920s and early 1930s, moreover, more may be said about the defects of the memoir. Most crucial is that the autobiography's lack of willingness to be forthcoming with the personal is inseparable from the question of its authenticity.[1] All three of McKay's first three published novels draw freely from his life to adapt his personal experience to fictional representation. Consequently, considering the outspoken honesty, the confessional spirit, of his first three published novels, the reticence and textual absences in his autobiography may be read beyond its compositional flaws. In fact, the entertaining character of McKay's memoir serves as an instrument in his endeavor to rinse his life of radical contamination. The memoir neglects to mention the pro-Communist texts he produced in Russia, *The Negroes in America* (1923) and *Trial by Lynching* (1925), easily excluded because both books were virtually impossible to attain outside of the Soviet Union by the late 1930s, when he wrote his autobiography. But among its most dramatic absences is the narrative's conspicuous omission of his fourth novel, *Romance in Marseille* (c. 1929–32), a manuscript that, conveniently for McKay the autobiographer, never made it to press. The queer black proletarian manuscript never seeing light simplified the task of writing the repudiating autobiography. *Romance in Marseille*'s material presence on library and bookshop shelves would have illuminated the fact that McKay's black queer historical materialist intensity came to its fullest realization in the early 1930s, a full decade after his memoir claims he had abandoned radical politics. In other words, as well as reading what the text says directly, focusing solely on its presences, it is necessary to read what is implicit, concentrating on the autobiography's voluble lacuna. McKay's 1937 memoir is in fact a creative, playful—if fatally serious—invention. It is true that *A Long Way from Home* is among the most vital archives of the black modernist interwar period. But the irony is that this discolored message in a bottle, which has floated on the black Atlantic for sixty years, this stimulating if muted conversation with the artful dead, has been neglected as a creation of the imagination. The "distilled poetry of my experience" (354), as McKay portrays his memoir in its final pages, *A Long Way from Home* is in its way his most completely realized work of art.

As the details of his personal life are intimately bound with the particulars of his public existence, it is essential to trace the contours of the grim and dangerous reality that McKay's mixture of obscurity and cheerfulness masks in his memoir. D. A. Miller's argument in *The Novel and the Police* (1988) that Victorian novels participate in law enforcement work is worth revisiting in this context, as the present analysis follows McKay through the panoptic looking glass he was compelled to enter, performing a search into the interior of his anxiety about being outed as a Communist. Where his first three published novels engender radical defiance toward authority, his episodic memoir may be understood according to Miller's theory of the realist novel submitting to social control. His autobiography does not so much conceal his sexual difference and black anarchism as wrap up these features of his past in a picturesque, carefree form of bohemianism. McKay designs a charming nonconformity that rewrites sexual difference and leftist dissidence so that such elements of his personal history do not infect his present. In this way the anarchic, queer elements of his 1920s life could not be used against him. The genuine import of *A Long Way from Home* is that of a queer black anarchist communiqué, a confessional capitulation to crushing hegemony (if a mostly unintentional confidentially resistant counterdossier). The way into the text's rhetoric of obscurity lies in tracing McKay's sexual diversity,

but this is made more challenging because his sexual difference is also guard-
edly revealed. The two reticences in the text arise from the same desire to be
vigilant and therefore function in concert. Fused with the necessity to (charily)
divulge to the reader his sexual difference, the autobiography, presented as an
anti-Stalinist repudiation text, proportionately endeavors to tame the still very
much vital inflection of his radical leftism. The text is, in Derridean terms, a
writing that engages in the *erasure of clues*. Yet McKay the self-absolving autobiographer—and on some level understandably—does not wish entirely to closet
his authentic past. The traces of both McKay's sexual politics and the authentic
history of his Communist and Trotskyist cultural work could not be expunged
entirely from *A Long Way from Home*. My interest is in tracing the shadowy imprints beneath McKay's attempt to suppress the entangled presences of "the love
that dare not speak its name"[2] and his very recent and persistent dedication to
radical leftism.

Given the contradictory ways scholars have presented his commitment
to leftism, it is necessary first to attend closely to the radical author's political
trajectory. In *A Long Way from Home*, McKay indicates that reading Marx in
the Reading Room of the British Museum during the early 1920s challenged
his understanding of radical socialism. The Marx he read while writing for the
Workers' Dreadnought did not resemble the social movement forms found on
"street-corners from which I heard [Marx's] gospel preached" (69). McKay is
apparently describing *Capital* (1867–95), the multivolume work that theorizes
commodity fetishism, expands the discussion of the alienation of the worker
under industrial capitalism, and rearticulates the philosophy of the need for creating an international revolutionary society. In Jamaica he read major German
philosophers under the tutelage of his first patron, Walter Jekyll, but he was not
initially educated in radical Socialism by Marx, as he indicates. He was encouraged toward a Marxist view by the radical social movements and organizations
that encompassed his world in London, including Pankhurst's Workers' Socialist
Federation and the London-based International Socialist Club. As Josh Gosciak
has discussed, he was influenced by Fabian Socialism, going back to his years in
Jamaica and a familiarity with the writings of Edward Carpenter, then later a
camaraderie with George Bernard Shaw. Consequently McKay's classical education in Marxian theory did not start until well after his own Marxist social activity. Before going to London, he was a member of the underground union, the
IWW, while practicing a form of clandestine radical black Marxism as a kinsman
of the African Blood Brotherhood (ABB). In his "Harlem Intelligentsia" section

of *A Long Way from Home,* he records his friendship with "Hubert Harrison, the Harlem street-corner lecturer and agitator" (108–9). Following Harrison come the rest of the black Marxist group, most of whom, like McKay, hail from the Caribbean: "Grace Campbell, one of the pioneer Negro members of the Socialist Party; Richard Moore and W. A. Domingo, who edited *The Emancipator,* a radical Harlem weekly; Cyril Briggs, the founder of the African Blood Brotherhood and editor of the monthly magazine, *The Crusader;* . . . and one Otto Huiswood [*sic*], who haled from Curaçao" (109).

When he demonstrates his puzzlement as a result of encountering the source of radical leftist philosophy, Marx, McKay is describing his own provisional, street-corner leftist line of flight—an articulation of black anarchism.

One purpose of McKay's autobiography was to rewrite the narrative of his own radical affiliation, so it is necessary to encounter the central myth apparatus of the autobiographical artifice. Throughout this study I focus on the significance of titles in McKay's writing. Like the names of his novels, *A Long Way from Home* is a title that says much about his situation in 1937, as it is a solemn citation of the African American sorrow song as well as an ironic play on the forlorn condition of diaspora: "Sometimes I feel like a motherless child / A long way from home." Though as a black man he is constrained to endure an inherited estrangement from "home," McKay, the restless wanderer, portrays himself as anything but a "motherless child," a lost exile, eternally alienated from Mother Africa or any site of origin, any median compass location or political affiliation. His radical agency defies the literal denotation of the title, as he presents himself as able to travel wherever he pleases, territorially and intellectually, an articulation that is not quite true in material terms but is confirmed by metaphorical expression. Yet the memoir's title intimates another connotation. Intrigue abounds in *A Long Way from Home,* the title even hinting at the outer perimeters he finds himself hungrily prowling, the far-flung edges of the black Atlantic. The question—a query McKay invites the reader to pose—is what this "black face, intruding into the holy places of the whites," this "specter" who would "haunt the pale devils" (*Long Way* 145), is doing there. When he asks rhetorically, "How can they bear your presence, Blackface, great, unappeasable ghost of Western Civilization?" (145), McKay poses the same question to the reader who contemplates his "presence" in Europe, his existence as a subaltern who refuses to be silenced in the modern world. McKay is describing, if covertly, his anarchist dis-position.

McKay's portrayal of the treatment his intellectual guru Max Eastman receives in Moscow at the Soviet Congress reveals his anxieties about divulging his anarchist tendencies. In the following quotation, despite the transparent "unlike me" qualifier, he may be recognized as the blackface "specter" (145) in his portrait of a patron:

> I said to Eastman, "Why don't you speak?" He said he would like to if they would ask him. Certainly the American Communists had in Max Eastman the finest platform personality to present. Unlike me, he was as pure a Marxist as any of them there and had given the best of his intellect to serve the cause of Communism and extol the Soviets in America. But because of petty jealousy they cold-shouldered Eastman in Moscow. Perhaps if they had been a little diplomatic about him, he probably would be one of them instead of a Trotskyist today. (173)

The account is technically accurate, although it leaves out a few salient details. As early as 1922–23, Eastman was growing more critical of the Russian Communist Party of the Soviet Union (CPSU), as he saw it moving away from internationalist Leninism. In 1925 Eastman published *Since Lenin Died*; the study exhibited an internal Communist Party criticism of the social democratic, or state nationalist, course of the Soviet Union. McKay's enormous gratitude to his mentor stems from Eastman first publishing "If We Must Die" and a handful of other poems in the *Liberator*, then naming him coeditor, with Michael Gold, of the *Liberator* in the early 1920s, before he made his way to Russia. As is apparent by the quotation, Eastman dazzled McKay.[3] A decade later, Eastman, the former American champion of international Communism, published *Artists in Uniform: A Study of Literature and Bureaucratism* (1934), a book that condemned the CPSU for its persecution of the "Left Opposition": the Trotskyists and Anarchists. And in the same year that McKay published his autobiography, a book that is decidedly hostile toward Communists, Eastman translated Trotsky's book *The Revolution Betrayed: What Is the Soviet Union and Where Is It Going?* (1937), three years before Trotsky's inevitable assassination in exile. Like other leftists of the period, Eastman denounced the CPUSA for its silence about the Stalinist tyranny, and his attitude enacts McKay's anarchism. Eastman's influence on his black protégé cannot be underestimated; the white intellectual and his sister, the Marxist-feminist Crystal Eastman, personified all that was good in radical politics, in McKay's view. (McKay's impact on Eastman should be reconsidered as well. Eastman implicitly trusted in his comrade's confidence in Trotsky and distrust of the Stalinists.) My purpose, however, is not to divide up the interwar left wing between those who saw through Stalinism and those who did not. Alan Wald's scholarship shows that the leftism of the between-the-wars period was as compound as the leftist views of the postwar period and that to perpetuate a narrative of the farsighted and the suckered would be to simplify a complex history. My point is that although he represents a recognizable divergence from party politics, McKay's deviation of the late 1920s/early 1930s was one of numerous heretical dis-positions, a line of flight that was consistent not so much with a black-nationalist retreat from the Left as it was a vanguard advancement through the tangled corm of interbellum period leftism. A revisioning of this sort should not be confined to McKay's case. Despite the nearly universal representation of Richard Wright as a black author who rejected leftism, sustained by a narrow reading of his writings from the mid- to late 1940s, to characterize the author of the black Marxist novel *Native Son* (1940) so simply is flawed. Hazel Rowley's *Richard Wright: The Life and Times* (2001) argues that Wright's 1940s dispute with Communism was more a wrangle with American Communism and Soviet Stalinism than a rejection of leftism (291–95). Indeed, when Wright moved to Paris, his dedication to radical politics intensified and increased, looking toward the internationalization of subaltern black peoples in anticapitalist, antiimperialist struggle. Similarly, McKay's late 1920s to early 1930s confrontation with leftism was fundamentally an internal counterrevolutionary critique, not an assault from without.

McKay's FBI file, ironically, is again informative. One of the most pertinent features of the file is the portrayal of McKay's interaction with the Ukrainian Jewish philosopher Leon Trotsky (formerly Lev Davidovich Bronstein). Trotsky submitted to an interview with McKay, and then he wrote an *Izvestia* piece titled "Answers to Comrade Claude MacKay" [*sic*], published February 15, 1923. A significant portion of the dossier is a bureau operative's translation of the entire article into English; in fact, duplicate copies of the translation were stored in the dossier. In effect the doomed commissar formulates the concept of a Bolshevik-sponsored black Leninist vanguard, articulating the need "to have a small number of class-conscious negroes, young and devoted [who are] capable of connecting morally . . . with the fate of the international working class." In *A Long Way from Home*, McKay reports on his meeting with Trotsky, and the Russian leader expresses the idea that blacks should be educated about international proletarian struggle and encouraged to move toward organizing with other members of the oppressed classes. He remarks that Trotsky wrote an article about their conversation and published it in *Izvestia* or *Pravda*, but he can't recall which (208). The memoirist is again being sly. *The Negroes in America,* a text that was until the 1970s unfamiliar to all who read McKay, contains a letter from Trotsky addressed to him in which the commissar declares that "when the hand of capitalism or even sooner the hand of militarism . . . forces them [blacks] to stake their lives for the sake of new and complicated questions and conflicts," then what will logically follow is a situation where embracing "revolutionary ideas" will become essential (7). In other words, the universal crisis for blacks ultimately will reach a head, and Communists can organize a Leninist internationalism among the black proletariat and colonial subjects.

Trotsky insists and, the article suggests, McKay agrees that a vital aspect of the propaganda campaign is the need to promote international struggle over the appeals of "black chauvinism." For all intents and purposes, the two-man team of Trotsky and McKay invents the idea of a Soviet-backed Black Marxist vanguard:

> [I]t is important now, at the present moment, to have a small number of class-conscious negroes, young and devoted, interested in the improvement of the economic and moral level of the black race and at the same time capable of connecting morally its fate with the fate of the whole world and, in the first place, with the fate of the international working class. (McKay FBI file)

This agent-translated passage is followed by the next section of Trotsky's *Izvestia* article, subtitled "The Training of the Black Agitators in the Most Important Revolutionary Problems of the Moment." In chapter 19 of *A Long Way from Home*, "A Great Celebration," McKay talks about his hope of meeting V. I. Lenin: "I had been amazed in 1920, when I received in London a message from John Reed informing me that Lenin had brought the Negro question before the Communist Congress and inviting me to visit Moscow" (206).

Like Eastman's impact on him, Trotsky's influence from the mid-1920s up until the mid-1930s on the black revolutionary author cannot be underestimated, a sway that his autobiography, despite its adjustments, cannot purge. This is why, in some respects, very likely due to his anxiety during the 1930s about how the United States regarded his actions during the 1920s, when it comes to his radical commitment of the 1920s and early 1930s, his FBI file with its obsessive collecting of minutiae is in some ways more reliable than his own 1937 memoir. In Russia, Trotsky gave McKay a new logic for how blacks could employ and indeed expand Marxist engagement. When he interviewed Trotsky, the Bolshevik leader was commissar of war. It is crucial that Trotsky effectively supplied McKay with the assurance that Russia would support blacks in the diaspora in their actions; the commissar then sent the black guest of the state on a sponsored tour of Russian military sites, a conclusive indication of their intimacy and the trust Trotsky put in McKay. Before meeting with Trotsky, McKay had attended the Third International as an envoy of the ABB, as he says in a letter to Comintern General Secretary Vasil Kolarov in 1923. His intention was to attain the kind of pledge of support he received from the commissar of war. Technically his repeated assertion that he is not a delegate sent by the CPUSA is true, but the ABB's intimate relations with the CPUSA make McKay's claim slippery.

All this fell apart, however, and the disintegration was beginning to take place at the moment when McKay and Trotsky were collectively articulating the project of black Marxism. In 1923, as he was interviewing Trotsky and the commissar was publishing his article on recruiting blacks into the international revolutionary project (and the Bureau of Investigation was earnestly, frantically collecting data on all this), Stalin was initiating his four-year move to seize power in the CPSU and ultimately in the Soviet state itself. By the mid-1920s, the Stalinists were in power and Trotsky was out. When Trotsky was expelled from the CPSU in 1927, then forced to flee the Soviet Union the following year, McKay, a perpetual fugitive himself (though a deserter who generated much of his own dislocation), lost faith in the promise of the Soviet state. By the late 1920s Trotsky lived in exile on the Turkish island of Büyükada, or Prinkipo, where he remained for four years. At the same time, McKay lived in Morocco and was prevented from returning to the United States. In exile Trotsky rearticulated his "permanent revolution" theory, published in a text that expands on *Results and Prospects*, issued more than twenty years earlier. The later text is an updating so that the earlier theory may be refitted to the situation of the Stalinist Terror. A concept originally articulated by Marx and Engels, the theory of *Permanent Revolution* (1928) proposes the need for unremitting radical transformation, both within state borders and without. The permanent revolution theory poses the assertion that a Leninism that is true to its original Marxian sources, and the only form therefore that may prevent the gradual return of capitalism, is a worldwide revolution, one that goes beyond the frontiers of Russia to both the metropolitan heart of capitalism, the western nations, and their colonized territories in Latin America, Asia, and Africa. Eventually the Stalinists, ironically, would adapt Trotsky's theory, if in more brutally recognizable and traditionally imperialistic forms. But the permanent revolution notion persisted outside of the Soviet Union for decades, adapted for assorted purposes and appearing in various permutations. The permanent revolution theory found a place in the idiom of the Black Arts/Black Power movement of the late 1960s, as in, for example, the conclusion to Ron Maulana Karenga's manifesto, "Black Art: Mute Matter Given Force and Function" (1968), which calls for a black art that participates in a "permanent revolution."

The date of *Permanent Revolution*'s publication, 1928, is crucial for the present study, as this theory is performed, adjusted through the idiom of négritude and sexual dissidence, in McKay's three consecutive novels of the late 1920s and early 1930s. It is ironic that during the early 1930s the French colonial authorities in Morocco identified and harassed him as a Russian-sponsored Communist spy and provocateur (*Long Way* 300). Rowley's biography of Richard Wright examines the possibility that while residing in Paris Wright was the target of a successful assassination plot carried out by the U.S. State Department. Scholars have discussed for decades the question of whether Wright's purported heart attack was in fact a political execution. Although Rowley cannot prove it conclusively, she clearly indicates a conviction that U.S. agents engineered his unexpected, mysterious death. Likewise, McKay almost certainly used Morocco to duck American surveillance, if not worse. Yet, among the reasons he dwelled in French North Africa very likely was to dodge the Stalinists' ruthless crusade to purge the world of Trotskyites. Indeed, McKay was an agent provocateur, inciting acts of radical black proletarian agency through his three novels. Following the rise of nationalist Stalinism, both McKay and Trotsky believed that the inheritance of the permanent revolution was in the hands of colonized and exploited peoples, workers and peasants not only in Europe and North America but also in Africa, Asia, and Latin America. As Lenin had articulated in 1917, "the Negroes (and also the Mulattos and Indians)" should be recognized as an "oppressed nation" within the American national formation, and therefore they potentially formed a critical popular front (*Collected* 275).

Even his autobiography, a text that takes measures to hide his history as a Leninist-Trotskyist, does not veil his ardor for the two Communist leaders, nor does it conceal his passion for Communist Russia. McKay sings Trotsky's praises several times, including a comment about the Ukrainian Jewish commissar's lack of racist belief:

> When Trotsky, the chief of all the Bolshevik fighting forces, talked to me about Negroes he spoke wisely. Trotsky was human and universal in his outlook. He thought of Negroes as people like any other people who were unfortunately behind in the march of civilization. (182)

Moreover, Trotsky says,

Negroes should be educated, should receive not merely academic education, but a broad spreading-out education in all phases of modern industrial life to lift themselves up as a group to a level of equality with whites.
... he urged that Negroes should be educated about the labor movement.
Finally, he said he would like to set a practical example in his own department and proposed the training of a group of Negroes as officers in the
Red army. (208)

Such comments indicate the black author's highest regard for a white, as one
can see throughout the memoir. As well as observing the social, political, and
economic changes of Russian Communism, McKay is interested in the situation
of ethnic minorities in the Soviet Union, believing that a country's essence lies
in how it behaves toward minorities. Hughes chronicles his 1930s approbation
in the "South to Samarkand" section of his second autobiography, *I Wonder as
I Wander* (1956). A decade earlier, McKay is favorably impressed by what he
sees, marking a striking contrast between the handling of African Americans in
the United States and the treatment of ethnic minorities in Russia: "What the
Bolsheviks had accomplished was to put a stop to the vicious political exploitation of group and race prejudice. I don't think the saintliest human being could
ask more" (194). This may strike the reader as a singular comment for an anti-
Russian-Communist text, but McKay means to contrast the situation of two
phases of Russian/Soviet history. A page before his favorable comments about
Trotsky's aim to back up blacks in their struggle, he remarks that Stalin "was
chairman of the Committee on National Minorities" (207), a bitterly ironic
comment meant to emphasize not only Stalin's mistreatment of the Jews, after
the fashion of the Nazis, but also the fact that the Jewish Trotsky, who constructed a plan to champion blacks in their struggle, would be pursued relentlessly by
cold-blooded assassins dispatched under Stalin's orders.

In McKay's *Nomenklatura*, Lenin is worthy of even more enthusiasm than
Trotsky, his praise bordering on idolization. His honoring of Lenin comes in
a rather complicated comment on the Soviet Union's renaming of Petrograd
as Leningrad, a national gesture toward venerating the Russian leader posthu-
mously: "there is no magic in the name of Leningrad. There is magic in the name
of Lenin, as there is splendor in the word Moscow" (157). Lenin's "life was devoted to the idea of creating a glorious new world," so McKay believes that "the
spirit of Lenin might have been more adequately expressed in the erection of a
brand-new city, rising out of that system to which he dedicated his life, Lenin

without suffix—like a perfect ball of pure gold—a city called Lenin" (157). He had written various poems on the theme of life in the urbanscape before the "Cities" cycle, including the mournful "Tropics in New York" (1920) and the bitter "White City" (1921), "Dawn in New York" (1920) and "When Dawn Comes to the City" (1920), "The Desolate City" (1926), and the angry "Song of New York" (1926). By the mid-1930s, the poet decided that the theme deserved exclusive attention, which led to his collecting the "Cities" poems in a notebook. Most of the cantolike sequences until recently went unpublished.[4] A few of McKay's "Cities" assortment on the subject of urban life show his despair in a particular city. "Paris" (c. 1934) is "cynical and serpent-wise" (l.9), a place "To build the Frenchman and make his mind complete / And fit him for his civilizing part" (ll.7–8, *CP* 231–32). "London" (c. 1934) is "A city without light and without heat, / Whose color was like iron in my breast / And freezing through my body to the bone: / Oh blessed was the fog that veiled me blind!" (ll.5–8, *CP* 232)—a bone-aching chill that metaphorizes the frosty political environment, the inner struggle among British leftists. But most of the poet's lyrics dedicated to the metropolitan are paeans, the capital in question sometimes even rendered as a comely lover. A Baudelairean *flâneur* swelling prosaic as he trips across the urban metroscape, the author of *Home to Harlem* was a keen explorer of the metropolae, seeing in their marble and steel the concrete expression of the modern, both base and beautiful. As Walter Benjamin says, "The reader, the thinker, the *flâneur*, are types of illuminati just as much as the opium eater, the dreamer, the ecstatic. And more profane" ("Surrealism" 190). A "profane illumination" is the performance of shedding light on the potential for revolutionary art, in Benjamin's vision. McKay's "profane," rapturous poems include "Petrograd: May Day, 1923," evidently written in Russia during the early 1920s but included in the mid-1930s "Cities" notebook, then published in *A Long Way from Home*.

One of his homoerotic 1935 "Cities" notebook poems subsequently published in his autobiography is "Moscow." The sonnet portrays the capital as "A glory painted on the Eastern air / Of amorous sounding tones like passionate lyres; / And colors laughing richly their delight / And reigning all over the color Red" (*Long Way* 158). While he may be successful in washing the red-blooded politics from other parts of the text, the presence of the sonnet in his 1937 memoir visibly signifies McKay's still-vital passion for organized internationalist socialism during the mid-1930s, when he generated the "Cities" notebook. "Moscow" ends with a show of fealty to the deceased Lenin, who appeared in 1922, when McKay himself was in Moscow, before the Communist leader was made iconic and lay in state: "And often now my nerves throb with the thrill / When, in that gilded place I felt and saw / The simple voice and presence of Lenin" (*Long Way* 158). Moreover, the sonnet sustains a homoerotic element when joined to another part of the text. In *A Long Way from Home*, he reports that "the people" saw that "Lenin was in the place of the Czar and that he was a greater Little Father," in addition to being a kind of mystical symbol (159). The veneration for Lenin is linked to McKay himself becoming iconographic to the Russian masses: "I was like a black Ikon in the flesh. . . . I was the first Negro to arrive in Russia since the revolution, and perhaps I was generally regarded as an omen of good luck! . . . I was like a black Ikon" (168). Lenin's "magic" mystical aura informs—indeed integrates with—McKay's own black iconography, his own magic pilgrimage. In coming close to becoming a black Lenin, McKay forms a kind of ecstatic sexual union with the Communist leader. The veneration for Lenin and his philosophy is dramatically articulated by McKay's three black Marxist manifestos, *Home to Harlem*, *Banjo*, and *Romance in Marseille*. Faced with the task of inventing a black proletarian fiction, McKay adopted (and refashioned) Lenin's encouragement of *partinost* and the Socialist Realist idea of *narodnost*. Articulated in "Party Organization and Party Literature" in 1905, *partinost* is the notion that politically engaged literature must demonstrate a commitment to Party values, and *narodnost* is the idea that literature should have a popular appeal, that it should be accessible to the masses, and therefore typically concern itself with celebrating the "folk" (Selden, Widdowson, and Brooker 85). Although McKay would reject the subsequent Party application of Lenin's promotion of *partinost*, which became translated into the enforcement of state-controlled aesthetics, he would put to use the spirit of Lenin's aesthetic philosophy.

The presence of Lenin in *A Long Way from Home* militates against the memoir's stated position—that the author never truly subscribed to radicalism, whether materially or aesthetically—and his bureau dossier substantiates the predicament of the autobiographical performance. To begin to unpack McKay's personal textual belongings as they appear, or appear indistinctly, in his life-chronicle it is necessary to articulate his "long way from home" rhetorical performance: that is, the act of narrativizing concealed activity. *A Long Way from Home* is composed of looping narratives of spying and secrecy, subterfuge and surveillance, denouncing and divulging, being renounced and being revealed. The narrative presents such scenes as illuminating, as moments in the text where the narrator demonstrates candor and implies imposing order over chaos. Ultimately, however, these passages, as isolated moments accumulate over the terrain of 350-plus pages, accrue to create a form of extensive obscurity. That is, although McKay's stated intention is transparency—he is willing to cooperate—the inward-arcing narratives achieve an ambiguity that ultimately creates a dimension intended to shield him from the high-wattage exposure of the third-degree lamp, from being unjustly accused of once being a provocateur. The looping of spy narratives is embedded by his use of the locution "spy mania" along with his mocking and ironic mimicking of spy discourse, the cultural language of espionage.

The phrase "spy mania" appears twice in independent parts of the narrative, first in "The Dominant Urge," the first of the seven chapters making up part 4, the "magic pilgrimage" in Russia section. The compound noun occurs when he meets the American Communist Rose Pastor Stokes while in Moscow. McKay sketches a portrait of her from a previous encounter in Harlem: "I remembered Mrs. Stokes's spy mania, when I was on the *Liberator*. She was doing secret radical work. She used to tell me stories of being followed by detectives" (160–61). The recollection provokes one of his many narratives meant to mock the target of the account. He reports that Stokes "was also working with a radical Negro group," the ABB, "and thought she was followed by Negro detectives in Harlem" (161). One night McKay was visiting his friend Grace Campbell when Stokes appeared "breathless, and sank into a chair, exhausted" (161). Stokes explained that "a colored man had been watching her suspiciously while she was riding up on the subway, and when she had got off the train he had attempted to follow her"; she then "hurried and dodged through the insouciant Harlem crowd and gone round many blocks to evade the spy" (161). McKay recruited Campbell in the fun at Stokes's expense, as "Comrade Campbell" informed "Comrade Stokes" that "there aren't any Negroes spying on radicals in Harlem. That colored man, maybe he was attempting—kind of—to get friendly with you" (161). But Stokes is shocked at such a comment, he reports, and in "her voice, in her manner, was the most perfect bourgeois expression of the superior person" (161).

In "Social Interest," the fifth chapter that makes up the magic pilgrimage section, he tells the tale of coming across the Scottish Socialist Arthur McManus in Moscow. Portrayed as an unstable, noxious character prone when intoxicated to accusing those around him of spying—and depicted as often appallingly plastered—McManus takes a dislike to McKay's comrade and interpreter, Venko (198). He defends his Russian "constant companion," dismissing McManus's allegation by saying, "I think I can nose out a secret agent whether he is red or white," asserting that his year as a Jamaican police officer in 1912 equipped him for scrutinizing underhanded motivation (198–99). Sometime afterward, he is at a party with the dreadfully drunk "Wee Arthur," who denounces the large and also exceedingly inebriated Venko as an OGPU, or Russian secret police, agent. In a rage, Venko "knocked McManus down with one blow and kicked him straight across the room." Venko then cries out, "Go back home and make your own revolution and don't stay in Russia and insult a real Communist!" (201). McManus responds, "I am not a Communist! I am an Anarchist! Anarchist! Anarchist!" Immediately following this dangerous declaration, "A comrade clapped his hand over McManus' mouth . . . and carried him out of the room" (201). McKay says that he does "not understand the meaning of McManus' outburst," reasoning that the Scottish radical, reeling through "his drunken anarcho-communist nightmare" (202), must have been "afflicted with spy mania" (201).

Spy mania materializes in several more guises. Later McKay learns that the Russian national police have arrested "one of the youthful Indian delegates" to the Communist international congress. And still later in Berlin, after leaving Moscow, he encounters the leading British Communist, William Gallacher, author of his own autobiography, *The Chosen Few* (1940). He identifies Gallacher as a member of the Pankhurst organization (*Long Way* 87) who eventually would become "a Communist member of Parliament"; Gallacher was elected to the House of Commons in 1935, two years before McKay's autobiography. Willie Gallacher's becoming a "parliamentarist" was a radical turnaround that the memoirist must have still regarded as betrayal, as the British Communists were divided on the question of whether the Communist Party of Great Britain (CPGB) should attempt to place rank and file in political positions or (following the "antiparliamentarist" column—Pankhurst's orientation until she interviewed Lenin in Moscow) work toward total revolution, which would mean remaining outside of political structures.[5] Acting on behalf of the distressed young Indian delegate, McKay inquires into the facts of the Indian student's case, to which Gallacher replies, "He was a spy, . . . and he was fixed" (200). McKay himself was compelled to flee London because he had become embroiled in factional disputes among the British leftist groups during the early 1920s. In the midst of the poisonous air of betrayal, he suddenly found himself being denounced: "One evening, when I visited the International Club the secretary showed me an anonymous letter he had received, accusing me of also being a spy. I declare that I felt sick and was seized with a crazy craving to get quickly out of that atmosphere and far away from London" (*Long Way* 87). Although he disparages Pankhurst in his memoir, saying she was ineffectual as a radical leader (87), he still retains a sense of loyalty to her as he maintains an antipathy for the parliamentarist, or "right-wing" British Communists, whom he characterizes as scheming crackpots, fanatics for spying and treachery. Understandably, he sustains hostility toward those who fingered him as a counteragent. Now in Moscow, safely removed from the lethal environment of radical London, and recalling his own disagreeable experience in England, he demands Gallacher give an explanation of what the "little British Communist Party" has "to spy on." The answer occasions a "mysterious nod," a turn of phrase that will appear later in the text: "'More than you think,' said Gallacher, with a mysterious nod of his friendly head" (200). The story is taken up some forty pages later. While in Berlin in 1923, McKay comes across a number of fellow travelers he had met in Moscow, including the same "Hindu youth" who had been denounced by the Indian Communist delegation and then detained by the Russian secret police (242). The Indian student says that he escaped, but McKay relates to the youth that he is of the opinion that the young man has been allowed to get away. McKay's "inside information" intrigues the student, who presses McKay, but the black author, mimicking Gallacher, nods and looks "mysterious," informing the reader that the Soviet police had released the young man because they "were convinced that he was not a spy, but merely a perfect specimen of a moron" (242).

The narratives of Stokes, McManus, Gallacher, and the Indian student appear to be transparent, as simply unambiguous scenes with little left to the imagination. Indeed, the contrary is taking place, as the interlocking incidents assemble several levels of obscurity. The idea that McKay could "nose out a secret agent whether he is red or white" because of his period as a Jamaican policeman is a singular explanation in view of his experiences beginning with the late 1910s, when he began writing for the *Liberator*. His underground interaction with revolutionaries in the United States, Britain, Russia, Germany, and Morocco—his own activity as a kind of "spy"—prepared him with the skills necessary to smell out undercover agents, as he implies several times elsewhere in the memoir. When he tells the "Hindu youth" that the student was most likely permitted to escape, the young man assumes that McKay has "inside information." Although he gestures mischievously to the reader, suggesting that his privileged intelligence is the rather pitiful knowledge that the Indian is insignificant and was therefore allowed to get away, the reader has witnessed McKay's conversation with Gallacher. The reader knows that the author is in fact in a position to receive confidential information, however inconsequential the young Indian Communist is. McKay's mischievousness is an aspect of his personality that he delights in remarking on. He describes himself as "impish" three times in *A Long Way from Home*. When he encounters the journalist and race leader Walter White, he gets "a weird and impish feeling of the unreality of phenomena" because White, whose surname McKay repeats several times for effect, has a light complexion (111). He later concocts "a plan to ask some impish questions" of H. G. Wells, who has made offensive comments about the Japanese (124); among McKay's closest friends was Sen Katayama, the organizer of the Japanese Socialist Party. And when his girlfriend Manda walks in on him and Michael in Harlem, McKay says, "I felt like saying something impish to stir up Manda's suspicion" (51).

Finally, McKay may be able to renounce Communist Russia by the time he publishes his autobiography in 1937, but he still draws a vivid distinction between Western Anglo-American and British Communists and the Russians, vividly favoring his hosts in Moscow: "To the Russians, spying was real menace. It meant sabotage of revolutionary property, attempted assassination of officials, and working to overthrow the Soviets. They could not understand that when an English or American Communist accused certain persons of being spies, his idea of spying was romantic and akin to eavesdropping" (164). He distrusts the American and British contingents because of the way they perceive him, and he has faith in his Russian hosts because they appreciate his views. McKay is disposed toward the Russian Communists because they see the necessity, stemming from Lenin's design and continued by Trotsky, for taking up the question of the black laboring classes in the United States, following Lenin's identification of the African American minority as an "oppressed nation," a question, the memoirist suggests, that the CPUSA leadership is negligent in addressing (208). When Gallacher nods his head mysteriously and tells McKay that the British Communists have "More than you think" to spy on, he very likely means to insinuate that McKay himself, the former Pankhurst follower and now ambiguously affiliated envoy, is an object of CPGB scrutiny.

As for his sketch of "Wee Arthur," it is important to consider McKay's spelling of the surname of his subject. Arthur *Mac*Manus had been a member of the Socialist Labour Party and an antiwar agitator during the Great War, an extremely dangerous undertaking. In 1920, two years after he painted his dramatically unbecoming portrait, MacManus had become the first president of the CPGB. McKay's "McManus" asserts that he is not a Communist but an Anarchist, and McKay then declares that he does "not understand the meaning of McManus' outburst," saying that the smashed Scot must be "afflicted with spy mania" (201). In terms of British Communist genealogy, the Scottish MacManus could be classified reasonably as an "Anarchist," as he was affiliated with the antiparliamentarist wing of a blistering debate within the CPGB during the early 1920s. Saying that McManus, or MacManus, identified himself as an Anarchist is still a serious matter, even as late as 1937, long after the British CP's bitter disputes over either entering conventional political structures to reform from within or maintaining its distance in order to work toward full-blown revolution. McKay was unquestionably familiar with the Kronstadt rebellion, moreover, which took place just one year before his arrival in Russia. As the Russian-Belgian Anarchist journalist Victor Serge chronicled in his own *Memoirs of a Revolutionary* (1963), the Kronstadt rebellion represented the Russian Anarchist "Third Revolution," ruthlessly crushed by the Bolsheviks in March 1921. The Anarchist revolution's brutal containment effectually meant the violent end of Anarchism in Soviet Russia, and anyone identified as an Anarchist after 1921 was exposed to mortal peril. Somewhat ironically, Trotsky led the suppression of the Kronstadt rebellion, as Emma Goldman documents in her own 1931 autobiography, *Living My Life*, published six years before McKay's memoir. Goldman was still furious with Trotsky ten years after he put down the rebellion.

It is reasonable to speculate how in the noxious environment of so much cloak-and-dagger activity and political infighting, as he portrays Moscow in 1922 and 1923, anyone could avoid becoming manic about spying. McKay was certainly aware of the meaning of McManus's "outburst," his public outing of himself as an Anarchist, as McKay when he wrote his memoir had only just begun to closet his own decade as a Trotskyist, an identity during the mid-1930s that was just as hazardous as being an Anarchist. In the minds of the Stalinists, Trotskyist was effectively synonymous with Anarchist, and in the Imaginary of capitalist imperialist nations, Anarchist was tantamount to terrorist, to employ an expedient anachronism. Indeed, the context for Anglo American anxiety about Anarchism during the time McKay depicts came in the shape of frantic rightist political and juridical engagement, as Michael M. Topp shows in his work on the Sacco and Vanzetti case. The Red Scare began with the Red Summer of 1919 and came to a head when the Italian Anarchists Nicola Sacco and Bartolomeo Vanzetti were arrested for the murder of Frederick Parmenter and Alessandro Berardelli. Sacco and Vanzetti's linguistic and national differences figured crucially in the government's and mainstream news media's manufactured consent against radicalism. And their intensely disputed case became the Left's cause célèbre of the 1920s, led by intellectuals like John Dos Passos and Dorothy Parker. As Sacco and Vanzetti were executed in 1927, their trial, portrayed sensationally by news media, played a central role in defining the way that Americans perceived Anarchism throughout the decade. By laying the *Mc*Kay-like cognomen *Mc*Manus over *Mac*Manus, the memoirist's own anarchism slides behind the Scottish Communist's designation. McManus dramatically insists that he is "not a Communist," and this is precisely what McKay wishes to proclaim in his memoir. In truth, McKay was a Communist at the time when his magic pilgrimage narrative takes place, the early 1920s, despite his protestations to the contrary, and following his period as a Communist he was a Trotskyist and a kind of unaffiliated anarchist. McManus's "anarcho-communist," overly stimulated alcoholic dream of *spy mania* supplies McKay with a rhetorical diversion, like Rose Pastor Stokes's tactic of turning Harlem corners to avoid the imaginary Negro spy. The depiction of Wee Arthur offers a means, in other words, for swinging the third-degree lamp away from McKay's own "anarcho-communist nightmare"—the truly bad dream brought to life by the FBI and the State Department.

As for his comic, massaged representation of "Comrade Stokes," what McKay does not say is that her presence in Moscow represents a threat to his status there as an unofficial black delegate. Stokes is a part of the CPUSA leadership, the American Communists who have traveled to Moscow to participate in the Fourth Congress. McKay made his way to Moscow without the institutional support of the CPUSA. Two radicals helped McKay get into Russia: Edgar Whitehead, secretary of Pankhurst's Workers' Socialist Federation in London; and Crystal Eastman, McKay's friend from the *Liberator* (*Long Way* 155–57). Sen Katayama made it possible for him to attend the Communist Congress (166). As he describes it in his memoir, unpredictably the Russians responded to the black diaspora revolutionary far more demonstrably and favorably than they reacted to Otto Huiswoud, the unnamed "mulatto delegate" (*Long Way* 173), in part because McKay was darker in complexion. As he describes it, he showed up and effectively stole the thunder of the American Communists, which caused rancor between him and the American Communist deputation. When he insists at the beginning of his "Dominant Urge" that he was not a member of the Communist Party while in Russia (153), and later in the chapter titled "The Pride and Pomp of Proletarian Power" he asserts that he "could never be a disciplined member of any Communist party" because he "was born to be a poet" (173), McKay fails to mention that *The Negroes in America*, his first book published in Russia, identifies him as a member of the IWW, the secret, mixed-race anarchist labor society affiliated with the Socialist Party of the United States. He also neglects to say that while in Russia he was a confidential envoy of the ABB, the radical underground black wing of the CPUSA. McKay is certainly telling the truth, however, when he avows that he could never be a "disciplined" member of the Party.

After these complicated narratives of political arrangement, McKay discusses his role among the "white expatriates" in Paris as a "sympathetic fellow-traveler." *A Long Way from Home* requires another perception of context: the perspective of the autobiographer's enigmatic activities in Europe, his flight from British authorities and surveillance by the U.S. Bureau of Investigation, then detainment in and ejection from Fez, Morocco, and ultimately his forced emigration from French colonial Morocco and dejected return to the toxic atmosphere of anticommunist, racist America. The United States was the only nation left that would allow McKay entry and shaky residence, and it was where he wrote this autobiographical account of his travels. It is through this context that the reader is invited to speculate on the diaspora trotter's "inside information." Generally the more transparent McKay appears, the more cautious he is being. Like the young Indian Communist, the reader, faced with the book's sketchy narratives of subterranean conspiracy and subversive counterplotting, cannot help but wonder what else he refuses to say—or wishes to communicate—when he nods and looks "mysterious." The Indian student may be "a perfect specimen of a moron," but McKay does indeed possess inside intelligence. On some level McKay, the "impish" and spectacularly imaginative author of his own existence, encourages the reader to speculate on whether caches of intelligence survive beneath the surface of his buoyant prose, his seemingly effortless diaspora cruise back across the black Atlantic.

In the final chapter of the magic pilgrimage section, "Regarding Radical Criticism," the least agreeable portion of his self-avowedly upbeat memoir, McKay desires to set the record straight—to ensure that no uncertainty about his actions in Russia or his present disposition should linger in the reader's mind: "Thus ended my adventure in Russia. This detailed account should clear up any 'mystery' that is entertained about my going and remaining there. I left Russia with one determination and one objective: to write" (226). In other words, the writer was not in Moscow in order to be trained in disseminating propaganda among blacks in the United States or other noncommunist nations. "I was not received in Russia as a politician, but primarily as a Negro poet" (226). One might pass over the qualifier *primarily* and take the passage as a reliable accounting of the author's actions. But he is not finished: "I had no radical party affiliations, and there was no reason why I should consider myself under any special obligations to the Communists. I had not committed myself to anything. I had remained a free agent" (226). McKay is responding theatrically to "the head-in-the-butt Communist critic" (229) who published an article in the *New Masses* attacking the "retired radical" author, as he refers to himself, of failing to generate truly proletarian literature (along with getting fat, another capitalist sin). Eastman had run the *Masses* from 1911 to 1917 before launching the *Liberator*. After Gold and McKay served as editors, the *Liberator* was taken over by the CPUSA and Robert Minor, thus making it a party organ. In 1926 Gold and John Sloane, distressed over the change, began the *New Masses*. It is necessary to inquire into the meaning of his status as "a free agent."

Public abjuration did not protect McKay from the state's open examination. His last novel manuscript, *Harlem Glory* (1990), the "fragment of Aframerican Life" for which McKay could not find a publisher before he died in the late 1940s, contains the protagonist Buster South. Like McKay, Buster returns to New York from living abroad: "He was like an underworldling living arrogantly a clandestine existence, . . . who at last was trapped in the net of the law, and after being third-degreed, physically or psychically, could never again regain his egoistic spirit of self-confidence" (33). Hounded by the FBI when he returned to the United States, McKay was called before Martin Dies's House Special Committee on Un-American Activities in 1939, two years after his memoir, to be interrogated about his subversive history. If Buster South, like several of McKay's black protagonists, is at all autobiographically drawn, it is reasonable to conclude that McKay was aware of being watched by the authorities from the time when he returned to the States in 1934 to the time when he was hauled before the special committee five years later. In the middle of this five-year period he wrote *A Long Way from Home*, evidently hoping to convince the reader that he had traveled indeed a long way from his past. Ironically, his autobiography very likely motivated the special committee to call him to testify, knowing full well that he would have nowhere to go if classified as an undesirable and ejected from the country. To be sure, McKay's declaration that the Soviets "could not understand that when an English or American Communist accused certain persons of being spies, his idea of spying was romantic and akin to eavesdropping" (164), poses a striking contrast to the author's predicament with the U.S. state. Though they held in a kind of religious awe their own schemes and worshipped leaders like Hoover, the actions of the American surveillance community suggests little in the way of the "romantic" in its pursuit of McKay or American Communists. A year after being questioned, McKay wrote *Harlem: Negro Metropolis* (1940), also composed while he was under the employ of the FWP, and the social analysis is even more severe than his memoir in its condemnation of Communism. In other words, *A Long Way from Home* not only is less reliable in some ways but also holds an intriguing conversation with McKay's FBI file, particularly when it comes to locating the true identity of the author, which lies somewhere between the location of "*Tovarish*" McKay (186) and his position as "a free agent" (226). While poking fun at "Mrs. Stokes," McKay recounts her belief that "we were living through the new Inquisition against radicals in America" (161)—a warranted conviction, as may be seen in the state's crackdown on him only three years later, despite his dismissive view. The presence of McKay's fat FBI dossier substantiates Stokes's suspicious opinion of nationalist powers, and McKay himself would have agreed with Stokes in the early 1920s when he was a member of the two secret Communist organizations, the IWW and the ABB. He communicates her view that "those who did not believe that [America was staging an inquisition] were traitors to the cause" (161–62); the former McKay would have had a similar view of the need for solidarity in international anticapitalist, anti-imperialist struggle. He then reports the following curious piece of intelligence: "She hinted even that there was something suspicious about my use of my real name in Moscow. For all the American delegates had secret names. Mrs. Stokes's own was Sasha" (162).

"My use of my real name": the repetition of the possessive modifier *my* may be distinguished beyond merely a stylistically awkward moment in the text. In view of his FBI file's obsessive effort to identify him by the same code name, his act of naming Stokes "Sasha" is indeed a "mysterious" textual act. Dubbing Stokes Sasha is a crafty move on McKay's part. For Russian-American Alexander Berkman, disciple of German Anarchist philosopher Johann Most, the alias "Sasha" was a naturally assumed name, as Sasha is the standard informal Russian designation for the name Alexander. In the early 1890s Berkman was convicted of the attempted murder of the industrialist Henry Frick, who with Andrew Carnegie launched a brutal campaign to crush the Amalgamated Iron and Steel Workers Union, an action that led to the establishment of the Homestead Law, the right of the federal government to impose martial order. The most prominent subversive in the United States during the early twentieth century, Berkman spent twelve years in prison. After leaving prison in 1906, Berkman published his *Prison Memoirs of an Anarchist* (1912); with Emma Goldman he published the Anarchist periodical *Mother Earth* and circulated the Anarchist journal *The Blast*. Eventually Berkman would publish *The ABC of Anarchism* (1929), regarded as the essential Anarchist manifesto.

For McKay, however, the gender-indeterminate Sasha is particularly edifying given his sexual difference. It is instructive to take an example from modernist fiction. The initially female character Sasha, the Russian princess in Virginia Woolf's 1928 transgender/androgynous novel *Orlando*, verifies intertextually the sex-interchangeability of the Russian name. A character meant to mock Woolf's former lover, popular novelist Vita Sackville-West, Orlando wakes up and discovers, evidently as a result of residing in "Oriental" Constantinople—England's national and racial Other—that he has become female. At the same time Sasha switches sexes to male, becoming a Russian-Orientalist inversion of Woolf's title/titled Englishman/woman. As the novel progresses, each character switches back and forth to suit the circumstances. McKay's reporting that Rose Pastor Stokes went by the alias, merged with the file's identifying him by this name, demonstrates another way in which Sasha may designate either male or female. In view of the bureau agents' near incapacity to get right the spelling of McKay's last name, it may not be a peculiar coincidence that the autobiographer misspelled Arthur MacManus's paternal name. More to the point for the present discussion, it is not certain that when keeping track of him the filers are always talking about the independent radical, as generally reports render his last name "MacKay," along with a few other variants, though occasionally the agents do spell it correctly. The presumption that Sasha was truly McKay, however, is unquestionably not the consequence of right-wing paranoia or unreliable intelligence. In view of his propensity for assuming names, a nom de guerre, perhaps especially a Russian sexually ambiguous code name, seems probable. McKay was Rhonda Hope when he submitted poetry to William Stanley Braithwaite's *Evening Transcript* in 1916. (Two years later, McKay's wife would give birth to Rhue Hope, a daughter the author would never meet.) He turned into Eli Edwards, a contraction of his mother's maiden name, when he sent his verse to James Oppenheim, Waldo Frank, and Van Wyck Brooks's *Seven Arts* in 1917 (*Long Way* 26). He became a mob of generally gender-ambiguous pseudonyms—E. Edwards, C. E. Edwards, and Ness Edwards as well as Hugh Hope (a version of Rhonda Hope)—for his later articles in the *Workers' Dreadnought*, being justifiably anxious about being made by everyone from the British penal authorities to rival radical groups.

"Free agent" McKay was accustomed to living underground, to going for stretches as an invisible man. So his comment about Stokes's belief that he should assume an alias takes on a deeper irony than he lets on. An agent of the Red and the black, Sasha is the subterranean emissary—a spy lurking in the darkest shadows of the black Atlantic. The quest for Comrade Claude is the pursuit of queer Sasha.

The "Distilled Poetry" of Queer Black Marxism in *A Long Way from Home*

I have nothing to give but my singing. All my life I have been a troubadour wanderer, nourishing myself mainly on the poetry of existence. And all I offer here is the distilled poetry of my experience.

A Long Way from Home

"I guess when the gang sees me with these here, . . . they'll be thinking that I'm turning queer."

A Long Way from Home

IT IS NOTEWORTHY that in *A Long Way from Home* (1937), Russia's sensational "Byzantine" effect on McKay is simultaneously "Oriental" (159). Throughout the text, the memoirist weaves a web of narratives and observations that generate linguistic and epistemological confrontations between native and foreign, state nationalism and cultural chauvinism, sex and art. In order to follow the traces in this network of imagery, one must explore the narrative's plotting of its course through Byzantine passages—how it not only obscures and reveals his political past but also bares and buries his queer history. Focusing on *A Long Way from Home,* with calls on writings going back to his Jamaican verse and other works, in this chapter I offer an examination of how his leftism merged with his sexual difference. It is crucial to contemplate where McKay situates his sexual identity vis-à-vis the discourses and apparatuses of state nationalism and other forms of identity policing. I examine his difficult disposition toward the New Negro movement, emphasizing how his multiplicity should be recognized. I also look at his attitude toward patronage and its link to radicalism and proletarianism. But first I consider the importance of his three years in North Africa in terms of how same-sex culture in Tangier and other Moroccan locales informs Communism, anarchism, anticolonialism, queer struggle, and related forms of dangerous dissidence. Ultimately I consider how all of these strands meet on the problematics of state chauvinism and imperialism, McKay's critique of power at both the cultural and national levels. By laying bare the subtle poetry of memory, my intention is to show that McKay's queer black Marxist voice is very much alive, if surviving several levels beneath the surface of his ironic simultaneous effort to conceal (and reveal) his past.

In 1930, without divulging his destination to anyone in Paris, McKay suddenly migrated to Morocco, where he resided for three years. After finishing up *Banjo* (1929), he also produced three books of fiction in Morocco: the still unpublished though extant late 1920s/early 1930s novel manuscript *Romance in Marseille* (c. 1929–32); his second collection of short fiction, *Gingertown* (1932); and his last published novel, *Banana Bottom* (1933). McKay did not even visit the United States for twelve years, from 1922 to 1934—absent, in other words, for most of the American New Negro Renaissance by any analogue—and much of this time he spent in Morocco. His critics have never sufficiently taken up why this anomalous black *littérateur* decided to settle in French colonial Tangier, where the author of *Home to Harlem* (1928) by his own account would inhabit his first and only domicile. To put it another way, why would Claude McKay, the prototypical Pan-African nationalist author, not travel south to black Africa since he was so close? Hughes visited the Gold Coast, Nigeria, and the Belgian

Congo during the 1920s,[1] so why didn't McKay cross the diaspora frontier and make tracks for his hereditary homeland?[2]

Such questions reflect the inheritance of a long-standing supposition that would benefit from another interrogation. No scholarship has considered the significance of McKay's choice of early 1930s Tangier for an expatriate retreat. No study has adequately contemplated the significance of his tarriance in Tangier with respect to his return to the United States in 1934. In his memoir, he refutes the notion that North Africa and sub-Saharan Africa are binary opposites, thus rejecting the idea that he never made it to the genuinely black Africa: "divided into jealous cutthroat groups, the Europeans have used their science to make such fine distinctions among people that it is hard to ascertain . . . when a Negro is really a Negro. I found more than three-quarters of Marrakesh Negroid" (304). Among his "Cities" poems are several that fondly remember Moroccan cities: "Fez," "Marrakesh," "Tetuan," "Xuaen," and "Tanger," the poet preferring the French spelling in his title of three interrelated, sequenced sonnets. Even the international colonial city of Tangier is solidly part of the African continent, as the third "Tanger" sonnet reinforces the notion of Morocco as incontestably "Africa": "While, on your bosom asleep, I heard the drum / Of Africa upswelling from the dense / Dim deeps to stir you far upon the height" (ll.6–8, *CP* 226). As a result of Moroccan society being basically black, McKay insisted that he felt culturally sustained in the French colony, at ease in a way that no other environment granted him: "For the first time in my life I felt myself singularly free of color-consciousness. I experienced a feeling that must be akin to the physical well-being of a dumb animal among kindred animals, who lives instinctively and by sensations only, without thinking" (*Long Way* 300). Although he thought of Morocco as an African country like any in sub-Saharan Africa, he perceived, somewhat paradoxically, the special situation of Tangier, recognizing that the international port was yet another black diaspora harbor. Africans, or "Gueanoua" (*Long Way* 296), to use the term McKay picked up in Morocco, made up a kind of nonnative class assembled, like blacks throughout the diaspora, as a result of the centuries-old slave trade. He maintained that this fringe subjectivity permitted a kind of latitude, a form of social *authorization* and pursuit of personal pleasure unavailable to those who functioned under the hegemony of more licitly stable cultural environments, black or white. His view was recognizably Rousseauist: that civilization is inimical to the individual's happiness. So it is understandable why he exhibited so robust a warmth for Saharan Morocco—and particularly Tangier—and deserted other favored black diaspora sites, including the black colonies in Paris, Marseilles, and even Harlem. McKay was persuaded that Tangier's relatively open international zone society tolerated forms of spontaneous genuine experience, a geniality that was less feasible for those black subjects who lived in white controlled environments.

Given his ardor for Russia, therefore, it is not surprising that the memory of its "eastern" flavor reminds McKay of Arabic North Africa: "all that Byzantine conglomeration of form and color, shedding down its radiance on the proletarian masses[,] . . . like an *Arabian Nights* dream transforming the bleak white face of an Arctic waste" (159). As he enjoys Tangier's refreshing lack of capitalist conscientiousness, he takes pleasure in the "Oriental" authenticity of Moscow, sounding a bit like a black inversion of Sir Richard Burton: "There was so much of that Oriental raggedness that one does not see in New York and London and Berlin" (159). A few pages later, the Russian "magic pilgrimage" image takes shape: "Oh, I remember that magnificent cartoon in colors," painted by a Russian artist, "picturing me sailing on a magic carpet over the African jungles to Moscow. It was the perfect interpretation of my adventure in Russia. An *Arabian Nights* fantasy transformed into reality" (170). Even the Russian food he eats brings to mind the piquancy of Morocco: "I asked for *kasha* and was grandly served . . . an elaborate and most appetizing dish comparable to . . . Moroccan *cous-cous*" (210). Red Russia takes on some of the "form and color" of black Africa. And *Arabian Nights* (1850) indeed: the lesson of the looping narratives of Scheherazade—the Orientalism of Rimsky-Korsakov's symphonic suite would influence modernist composers like Stravinsky—is that one wins life by relating stories. Red Russia gave McKay the inspiration to tell his best tales: *Home to Harlem*, *Banjo*, and *Romance in Marseille*.

The facts of his sojourn in Russia, however, seem less enchanting, as the American Communist delegation in Moscow became incensed when the Russians responded so favorably toward him, preferring the darker McKay to the "Negroid delegate, a light mulatto" (*Long Way* 159). He does not identify the African American Communist Otto Huiswoud by name, as he sometimes takes care even in his mid-1930s Communist repudiation memoir not to expose himself by disclosing the identities of too many fellow travelers. In other words, it is likely that McKay, the black Trotskyist, was holing up in remote Fez, Marrakech, and Tangier, lying low in an effort to stay below the Stalinist radar—anxious that if exposed he would experience the same deadly fate that his idol Trotsky was destined to suffer while in exile. In addition to likely Stalinist interest in his whereabouts, ironically North Africa was also a good place to dodge American and British surveillance. In other words, because he had gone to Russia and tasted its Oriental delights in the early 1920s, he may have had to disappear into the Oriental labyrinthine lanes of Moroccan cities ten years later, a fugitive from both the Right and the Left. Or would living beyond the zone boundaries have made the adventurous McKay feel even more secure, in view of the "spy mania" (*Long Way* 160, 201) that Tangier sustained during the early 1930s? He generally enjoyed himself in unstable environments, and the spy-infested international zone was among the most lawless urban milieus in the hemisphere during the 1930s. Jointly administered since the Great War by several European nations, including France and Great Britain, Tangier continued to remain culturally a part of Morocco (Vaidon 192–229). Spanish, French, Italian, and British subjects were protected—or just as often, like McKay, policed—by their respective colonial power. Because no central authority controlled the multicolonial society, Tangier became a tangle of intrigue and transgression. Whether McKay was hiding out or not, he surely does not perjure himself when he voices his pleasure with Tangier. His three-year residence in Morocco suggests that he had settled happily in a locale that, next to other diaspora destinations, did not systematically need to interfere with black social motility. Most important, however, he encountered a Tangier that was permissive toward sexually radical Europeans and Americans: it was a queer refuge. What is most significant is that his pleasure in the racial openness of Tangier was mingled with his delight in the sexual latitude of the diaspora port. Indeed, the social openness that licensed black freedom engendered the conditions for sexual immunity. In fact, the diaspora cruiser was very likely going underground while simultaneously taking pleasure in the intrigue.

Rather than proceeding as though McKay were marooned in Morocco, prevented from journeying into the heart of ancestral Africa, one could more persuasively argue that the peripatetic writer desired to be in Tangier chiefly because it was a queer refuge. This could be persuasively argued even though French colonial police forcibly escorted him there, chucking McKay, a known radical, out of Fez because French president Gaston Domergue was en route (*Long Way* 327). French authorities inadvertently introduced McKay to his most cherished "home."

It is time to contemplate McKay's evident desire to spend several years in a city known to gay Europeans and Americans as a queer refuge. In his biography of McKay, Wayne Cooper notes that his subject lived in Tangier, that he socialized with gay expatriates, and that Tangier had a manner of "homosexual" colony (277). But Cooper does not venture that McKay remained in Tangier for the culture of open homoerotic society. As Jonathan Fryer discusses in *André and Oscar: The Literary Friendship of André Gide and Oscar Wilde* (1998), Arabic

North Africa's attraction to queer white artists and writers commenced with Wilde's visit to Algeria in 1895, where he happened on Gide at the Grand Hôtel d'Orient. Although Richard Burton blazed the trail of homoerotic society in Arabic culture, Wilde may be credited with opening up to western visitors North Africa's "Oriental" spirit, as he introduced Gide to the same-sex trade in Arabic Algiers. When it was made into a "free" or "international zone," neighboring Tangier, with its easy access to southern Spain, became a magnet for gays, including the American bohemian writers Charles Henri Ford and Paul Bowles. Later the Beats—Allen Ginsberg, William Burroughs, and Jack Kerouac—came for the same reason, as did Tennessee Williams, Truman Capote, Gore Vidal, and English playwright Joe Orton.[3] McKay records the world that white writers found in Morocco in his poetry, as in "Marrakesh" (c. 1934), a poem that acknowledges Saint Wilde's act as queer trailblazer in North Africa and alludes to his notorious 1893 one-act play, *Salomé*:

> The Berber youngsters pitch their little tents,
> And skip gazelle-like for the approving throng
> Of nomads purchasing the city's joys—
> African drum beat, oriental song,
> Salome-sensual dance of jeweled boys,
> Amidst the ruins of austere monuments. (ll.9–14, *CP* 227)

His breezy yet reticent memoir reveals nothing straightforwardly about this question. Still, one may observe that McKay's private life in Tangier was occupied with two sets of social groups. These gatherings were made up of two almost exclusively male societies, assemblages that indeed often merged. His acquaintances included Bowles and Ford. It is interesting to consider the context with which McKay would have assumed his more in-vogue readers to be familiar. With Parker Tyler, Ford was coauthor of "America's first unashamedly homosexual novel" (Watson 136), a semiautobiographical 1933 *roman* about two gay writers, set in Greenwich Village. McKay says that Ford's novel is "a queer book of adolescence . . . under the puritan title of *The Young and the Evil*" (37). The critique may be well taken, as McKay's titles endeavor not to acquiesce to any imposition of authoritarian morality. And it obviously did not help Ford's relationship with McKay that the white writer was a "protégé of Gertrude Stein" (337), as McKay detested Stein. Ford is too flamboyant for the unaffected McKay, as one sees in a letter Ford sent after McKay had published *A Long Way from Home*, a text that contains an unflattering portrayal of him. Ford may be responding to one of McKay's surly letters, as the black author did have the habit of firing off crabby missives, but it is also likely that the white author is responding to *A Long Way from Home*'s "charge of homosexuality, with moral implications," against him. In other words, Ford is piqued by McKay's literary handling of their time in Morocco. Ford turns the tables on the black autobiographer by suggesting that McKay hides his own sexual proclivity, an accusation that contains some truth in view of the care McKay sometimes took in representing his own penchant. Although *A Long Way from Home* paints an unsympathetic portrait of Ford, the memoir shows also that the novelist mixed with McKay and his Moroccan friends, so it seems plausible that during the early 1930s McKay did not hold such a disapproving view of the white writer. In stark distinction to Jake Brown's detestation of his fellow Arab seamen at the beginning of *Home to Harlem*, McKay indicates that he prefers his Arabic comrades to the white pansy author, though the image of the lily is a bit contradictory in light of McKay's transparent antipathy for Ford: "He was like a rare lily squatting in among the bearded and bournoused natives" (337). The lily suggests an allusion to Oscar Wilde, like Lenin (another one of McKay's idols), almost an honorary gay white patron to the black queer writer.

The portrait of the white queer writer is, as Ford's rejoinder suggests, part of a dance McKay performs behind the narrative's veils. When his Moroccan friends comment that Ford "looked wonderfully like the cinema portraits of Marlene Dietrich" (*Long Way* 338), McKay's Arab companions are referring to Josef von Sternberg's film *Morocco* (1930). Dietrich portrays the café chanteuse Amy Jolly, who takes up with a French Foreign Legionnaire played by Gary Cooper. Cooper's emblematic feature is a set of silent film star eyelashes, elongated after the fashion of Rudolph Valentino, Hollywood's original seductive "Sheik of Araby." At the film's climax, as critics have noted, in arguably Hollywood's first drag scene, Dietrich drones a provocative melody while decked out in top hat and tuxedo mufti. The character portrayed by the German *Blue Angel* Dietrich merges the gender ambiguity of the Weimar-period Berlin cabaret with the sexual anarchy of the Harlem dive, taking a turn in the style of Gladys Bentley, the black lesbian Jazz Age cabaret diva. But Cooper is the more sexually ambiguous figure, his erotic elasticity desirable to both sexes. Where Dietrich is ironically mocking and self-consciously impersonating sexual ambiguity, Cooper is playfully performing gender trouble, a far more radical act on sexual identity. By entering the forbidden zone, Cooper's legionnaire, like Sir Richard Burton, becomes the most erotically charged, sexually indefinite figure of all because he is removed from his context, released into a kind of heart of darkness to move freely between polarities.

The impression of obscure Arabic society as an esoteric site of sexual border crossing was a component of 1920s and 1930s western popular exotic imagination. The white adventurer in Arabic society surveys the Oriental other side in drag, wishing to go undetected so that he may, like Burton, visit the holes behind the holy sites and then translate the debauched eroticism of the *Arabian Nights* for western eyes. McKay, conversely, is the photonegative colonial explorer, a black man of ambiguous nationality who travels in his own adaptation of drag mufti. He playfully performs the in-between spaces of gender trouble beneath the sheets of the text palimpsest.

Although he socialized with western visitors like Ford, McKay mixed much of the time with Moroccan friends—all are clearly represented as young men in *A Long Way from Home*—staying overnight at their houses while celebrating Ramadan, for example, enjoying the life of a "native." The young Moroccan Arab men lived outside of the international zone, as McKay eventually did. He says of neighboring Fez, "I thought that the antique African city was the unaware keeper of the cup of Eros containing a little of the perfume of the flower of the passion of ancient Greece" (*Long Way* 299). The great "lover" of cities, McKay consistently personifies the city as a queer capital. His sonnet titled "Fez" (c. 1934) swells ecstatically on the city itself as homoerotic:

> The houris of the sordid Paradise
> Of Moulay Abdullah, the nights exotic,
> And one dear night upon my memory warm,
> Sweet and enthralling like a dream erotic
> Of beauty African in shape and form,
> With glowing fire of Andalusian eyes. (ll.9–14, *CP* 226)

It is essential to note that McKay's most fecund period as a writer transpired while he was residing in Morocco, and this period marks the moment in his life when sexuality as a point of divergence directed him toward his most tangible challenge to the discourses of colonialism. Throughout his poetry McKay disrobes the elemental language performance, the immanent deconstruction, in the hierarchy of white-black color codification, turning inside out the surface notion of color classification in an effort to shift the manner of racial representation from one of biological to discursive signification. McKay's poetry forces linguistic hierarchies to submit to color as a language signifier rather than as a biological category, and in this way he is able to turn the tables on racist and colonialist discourses. In *A Long Way from Home*'s ludic morphology of Tangier, color takes on an even wider angle, encompassing other forms of cultural vitality.

For queer intellectuals and artists, the attraction of Tangier was freedom from social constraints, apparently something like the "pagan delights" and "orgies" of Ray's dream in *Home to Harlem*: an interaction with the Oriental, homoerotic Other (158). McKay was a subject of the British Commonwealth—like his principal fictional characters, a bad subject. Faced with such an extraordinary display of social dissent within the sphere of colonial power, a delighted McKay "goes native," as he remarks, celebrating the various meanings of "color" that he finds in Tangier (299). A form of tolerance and an unfettered gay spirit dwell in his Tangier that vex other forms of social control. The unregulated spirit of Tangier is exhibited in poetry, specifically evoked by the ecstatic, sensual lyrics of the sixth-century black Bedouin warrior bard Antar, McKay's ideal black lyricist, whose homoerotic verse merges love with war. He devotes several pages to Antar in *A Long Way from Home*:

> The Negro child, born into an inferior position in the overwhelming white world, . . . should know something of the Antar who was born a slave, who fought for his liberation, who loved so profoundly, passionately and chastely that his love inspired and uplifted him to be one of the Arabian pleiades. (90–91)

Although McKay credits the Moroccan philosopher and cultural nationalist Sidi Abdallah (Si Abdallah Guennoun, among the initiators of a trans-Saharan Arab renaissance) with making Antar known to him (332), he probably first became acquainted with the ancient Arab poet while reading the *Crisis*. In 1924, Maud Cuney Hare published an essay titled "Antar, Negro Poet of Arabia." It is just as likely that he was familiar with Russian composer Rimsky-Korsakov's Symphony No. 2, based on the legend of Antar. Still, McKay certainly located the spirit of Antar in Morocco. In both Tangier's expatriate community and much "native" society, sexual difference was a far more fluid category of social interplay than anywhere McKay had inhabited or frequented, including London, Paris, the Village, or Harlem.

Yet this clarification raises another set of questions. Why then would McKay risk repatriation from his North African enclave? Why run the risk of ejection from Morocco just to live outside of the Tangier international zone? Indeed, during the political turbulence of the early 1930s, the Left movement toward anticolonialism and anti-imperialism, how safe a port was Tangier? While residing in Fez McKay is "accosted" one day by a *chaoush*, a "native doorman and messenger" who has been dispatched by the British consulate in Morocco to question the black expatriate about his identity (300). The authorities are confused about his nationality—is he an American citizen or a British subject? This is a good question in light of McKay's indistinct classification as a Jamaican journeyer, Harlem Renaissance luminary, diaspora cruiser. In terms of national identity, is he an African American or a West Indian? He lived for over a decade in Europe, including Britain (and Russia), moreover, during most of the Harlem Renaissance, so in terms of actual social identity, is he neither American[4] nor British West Indian but something else? In response to the *chaoush*'s inquiry, he laughs—McKay laughs quite a bit in *A Long Way from Home*, his mirth sometimes enigmatic—and replies: "I preferred to think of myself as an internationalist" (300). He reports that his Moroccan inquisitor doesn't understand what an internationalist is, and McKay expresses amusement once again, informing the courier that "an internationalist [is] a bad nationalist." Declaring oneself a "bad nationalist" is an understandable comment for one of the world's most eminent black nationalists, even acknowledging that McKay is mocking the Moroccan "messenger," the British colonial authorities, and perhaps even his readers. Certainly, he means that he is a bad nationalist with respect to American and British chauvinism—McKay continually demonstrates how nationalism is the intimate ideological relation of racism and imperialism—but his insistence that he is an internationalist and a poor chauvinist may not mean only a disowning of imperialist forms of nationalism. *Internationalist* was synonymous with *Marxist* and *Communist* in the late 1920s, and this is what McKay means to deny being. Imperialist chauvinism and ethnic nationalism are not, however, opposites, if the cultural form of chauvinism polices authentic identity. For Rousseau the danger for the individual lay in the enforcement of the "social contract," the imposition of society and civilization; for Nietzsche the threat inhered in the actions of the modern state, the policing of mindless national order. It is interesting, moreover, that through parody and satire homoerotic Arabic poetry played a complex political role as Moroccan "poets used . . . symbols to recall pre-Islamic tribal mores or to challenge political mandates and theological edicts" (J. W. Wright 2). McKay blends these philosophical and poetic strands with Lenin's dialectical materialist call for the end of state nationalism and Trotsky's post-Bolshevik cry for "permanent revolution." Ultimately, in response to the Moroccan's tedious if treacherous interrogation McKay glibly—and remarkably—comments: "I had said I was an internationalist just by way of a joke without thinking of its radical implications" (300). In other words, when he informs those he encounters in Morocco that he is an internationalist, he does not mean to say that he is a Communist—he means only to be joking! A black modernist, he possesses the right to lay claim to the identity of *citoyen du monde,* like the other expatriate moderns: Fitzgerald, Hemingway, Joyce, Lawrence, Stein.

His explanation is unconvincing—and not only to the authorities who hounded him until he was forced to leave Morocco. Going to Tangier turned out to be a fortunate arrival. After residing in Kingston, Harlem, London, Moscow, Berlin, Paris, Antibes, Marseilles, and Barcelona, McKay finally found his ideal environment in Tangier. The intrigue of Tangier was a function of its allure for him, the underground goings-on making possible the equally subterranean and accommodating queer society. But beyond that, it is interesting to speculate on what McKay, a known radical shadowed by both British Intelligence and the U.S. State Department, would be up to in the international zone, the concentrated gathering place of undercover activity in Africa, cozily congregated in a few square miles. The intersection of his queer black anarchist proletarianism is not merely literary and phenomenological. Although he signs off at the end of the novel "Marseilles-Barcelona, 1927–28," McKay finished *Banjo: A Story without a Plot* in Morocco, and indeed the environment in which he completed the manuscript informs the novel's subtitle. That is, one is encouraged to consider the likelihood of his diaspora intelligence work, to rearticulate Gramsci's notion of intellectual work to fit the circumstances. In Fez, he was accosted by a courier. Was McKay himself a courier, a kind of intelligence agent, who operated in Tangier, and if so, for whom?

In 1933, McKay found himself a colonial without a Commonwealth. He asserts throughout his oeuvre the idea of the white dog hunting down the fugitive Negro, and it resurfaces in his narrative of being expelled from North Africa: "even in Africa I was confronted by the specter, the white terror always pursuing the black. There was no escape anywhere from the white hound of civilization" (304). The circumstances that led to his dispossession of national identity are familiar to few who have studied black modernist authors.[5] The Tangier international zone police, directed by the French administration and assisted by the British consular authority, detained him as an anticolonial "radical propagandist" and seized his passport. As well as being denounced as a Communist revolutionary—the imputation was inaccurate, as he was not a Communist but a Trotskyist by the early 1930s—he was accused of living outside of the zone, an allegation that was true. McKay resided outside of the zone boundaries, in a "Dar Hassani (native house)" (328) that was located in a sector where only Moroccans were permitted to live. The international zone statutory arrangement in Tangier forbade non-Moroccan nationals the privilege of residing outside of the zone, and the punishment for doing so could be expulsion from the country. The fact that he briefly lived clear of colonial borders gave the authorities the excuse to pursue their investigation of the black revolutionary author as an international subversive. His small rental house was located beyond the boundaries of the international zone, which meant academically that he dwelled outside of the protection of the British colonial administration. But more to the point for imperialist control, McKay was situated legally free of the imperious reach of the western colonial authority.

How the authorities learned of his house beyond the boundary is a narrative that is informed directly by his sexual marginality. McKay knew Paul Bowles well enough to accuse the author of *The Sheltering Sky* (1949) of being responsible for causing his effective expulsion from the North African colony. When Bowles first came to Tangier, he found McKay entangled in one of his curious occasional, ephemeral, and chronically unsatisfactory heterosexual relationships, a liaison that was complicated by the intrusion of the third party—McKay being the interloper. Bowles met him through his friendship with the other two participants in the "lovers' triangle" (Cooper 277). Although ultimately Bowles did not cause McKay to be chased out of Morocco, he blamed Bowles, with considerable justification, for his troubles with the French administration. Bowles himself corroborates the story in his own curiously aloof autobiography, *Without Stopping* (1972), which is more of an upbeat travel narrative than a self-searching memoir. Like *A Long Way from Home*, Bowles's text is often informed more by what it is *without* than *with*. McKay invited Bowles to his house outside the zone for a carouse, where the white tourist observed how the black expatriate lived. Bowles describes McKay's quarters as having something like a harem quality, complete with a dancing girl who appears when McKay claps, then disappears when he claps again. A boy also lives in the house, evidently the brother of the girl. While later engaged in procuring opium from a Moroccan who showed a mysterious interest in McKay, Bowles imprudently revealed where McKay was living. The opium merchant was in the covert employ of the zone police, it turned out, almost certainly the native *chaoush* in the earlier narrative, thus McKay's harassment by colonial authorities. Bowles composes a comic portrait of the affair, with McKay showing up at Bowles's squalid hotel in Tangier brandishing a cane and threatening him (*Without Stopping* 147–49).

Eventually the French authorities returned his passport. A Jamaican colonial subject, McKay thereupon discovered that the British consular authority, evidently at the request of the French colonial rule, had barred him from traveling to any of the British Crown's colonial territories (Cooper 279). He was forced to return to the United States. Because of the severe anti-immigration laws that had been enacted by the mid-1930s, however, West Indians faced formidable difficulties when they appealed to gain entry into the United States—above all those who were known Communists. Even so, galled and embittered by the institutionalized racism in American society, McKay was not eager to return to the United States.[6] Consonant with his demonstrated lyrical nostalgia for his *pays natal*,[7] he longed to return to Jamaica, at that time a Crown Colony remotely governed by Great Britain. Perhaps his homesickness was partly the consequence of being prohibited from returning to his native land.[8] Notwithstanding, knowing that he could no longer set foot in any part of the British Commonwealth, he had little choice but to petition to return to the United States. The British and French principally wanted to keep the radical author out of Africa, but this injunction also prohibited him from returning to Jamaica. With the aid of James Weldon Johnson and Walter White, McKay was obliged to abandon his house beyond the Tangier zone boundary and come "home" to Harlem (Cooper 288–89). Although the colonial ascendancy technically didn't deport him, their manifest objective was to force him to withdraw from Morocco. And in truth they were instrumental in effecting his banishment, if chiefly more through psychological assault than tangible action against him. A consequence of this act was to prevent the author of *Home to Harlem* and *A Long Way from Home* from ever returning home.

Prohibiting him from going back bodily to Jamaica did not mean, however, that he could be prevented from returning textually. McKay may be a long way from home by the mid-1930s, but he nevertheless finds his way back to his homeland by a circuitous route, an indirection whose dust tracks in the road are even more indistinct than his representation of his Communism and Trotskyism. While McKay's autobiography is sly about his past as a radical, it appears to impart a more frank delineation of his different sexuality. Like Foucault in *The History of Sexuality* (1978), McKay rejects western "scientia sexualis" and its imposed identity as, in Foucault's words, "Perverse Adult" for the psychoanalytic category of non-reproductive sexual behavior. For example, when he communicates his lack of sexual inhibition in the "Berlin and Paris" section of the memoir, the comment seems unambiguous:

> sex was never much of a problem to me. I played at sex as a child in a healthy harmless way. When I was seventeen or eighteen I became aware of the ripe urge of potency and also the strange manifestations and complications of sex. . . . I never made a problem of sex. . . . I became intellectually

cognizant of sex problems. But physically my problems were reduced to a minimum. And the more I traveled and grew in age and experience, the less they became. (245)

This section of the life-chronicle is indeed sweeping in its collection of memories and meditations. The chapter begins by describing the atmosphere of wide-open Weimar-period Berlin, with its move toward National Socialism and the gathering of an assortment of radicals who, like McKay, are traveling through the German capital after attending the Third International in Moscow. It is interesting that elsewhere he notes spotting Stalin: "a strikingly big man wearing high black boots. . . . It was the first time I heard the name of Stalin, and the information was extremely important" (207). Portraying Stalin through the synecdoche of the sadomasochistic image of the "high black boots" is McKay's indication to the mid- to late 1930s reader to associate the Soviet leader with Mussolini's and Hitler's severe martial dress. The photographic image of Stalin as transposable with Hitler underlines the palpable failure of Stalinist socialism.

The Paris section also expresses his views on expatriate writers and modernist literature and thereby articulates aspects of his own black modernist aesthetic. One may question why a chapter on black aesthetics situates itself first in Weimar-period Berlin, locates itself in the center of the advent of National Socialism, removed now from Communism. Along with a form of Communist state nationalism, the abolishment of the possibility of the permanent revolution philosophy, Stalinism also brought about a change McKay no doubt found distressing. As Daniel P. Schulter discusses in his study of gay life in the USSR, among the legal adjustments of Stalinism was the criminalization of homosexuality as a form of bourgeois degeneracy. As a result, queer leftists found themselves in a position where their radicalism was no longer acceptable as part of the Communist international effort. The effect of the Soviet criminalization of homosexuality cannot be underestimated in the history of Left politics, as leftist bohemianism and party Marxism contained practically interchangeable lexica during the 1920s and 1930s. Progressive-minded Bolsheviks and western Marxists of the bohemian persuasion like McKay who considered homosexuality a form of resistance against capitalist mastery over the revolutionary human body were left out of the party. The black queer author reacted against ideologized Communism at the moment when Stalinism beset sexual liberation.

The criminalization of homosexuality was a feature of a greater predicament in leftist politics and modernist art, one that Trotskyism and Anarchism conveyed. For McKay, the reactionary reform taking place in the Soviet Union, including the persecution of Anarchists and other counterrevolutionary dissidents, represented the return of a state nationalist politics in Russia and therefore the loss of the Bolsheviks' most valuable weapon against imperialism and capitalism: Leninist internationalism. Stalin's "high black boots" indicate that Russian socialism has been co-opted by a form of extremist nationalism that best resembled fascism, as the Nazis classified homosexuality as degenerate, forcing gays into concentration camps and eventual extermination. Indeed, by 1933 the Nazi Party described modern art interchangeably as "Jewish," "Bolshevik," and "degenerate," elevating instead Romantic, heroic, and nationalistic works. Demonstrating a characteristic incoherent muddle, the Nazis found the source for their theory of degeneracy in writings of the Zionist philosopher Max Nordau, author of *Entartung* (Degeneration) (1892). Nordau theorized that the connection between criminal behavior, sexual degeneracy, and anticlassical artistic production was traceable and verifiable through scientific methodology. Illicit actions, in other words, resulted from biology. Although the idea of tying degeneracy with new modes of art was nothing new by the late nineteenth century, Nordau contributed the idea that anti-Semitism was the result of moral disintegration; along with Nietzsche, Wagner, and Ibsen, his targets were Walt Whitman and Oscar Wilde. As Hellmut Lehmann-Haupt discusses in *Art under a Dictatorship* (1973), the Nazis organized the mammoth 1937 art show *Entartete Kunst* ("degenerate art") in Munich in order to reveal to the masses the decadence of modern artists—like McKay's admired acquaintance George Grosz (*Long Way* 240). Similarly, as Igor Golomstock recounts in his discussion of totalitarian art in the Soviet Union and the Third Reich, the Stalinists harshly punished those who generated art that did not replicate Socialist Realist principles. In their 1938 "Manifesto: Towards a Free Revolutionary Art," former Surrealist André Breton, embattled muralist Diego Rivera, and hunted insurgent Trotsky avow: "Every progressive tendency in art is destroyed by fascism as 'degenerate.' Every free creation is called 'fascist' by the Stalinists. Independent revolutionary art must now gather its forces for the struggle against reactionary persecution" (483). Their manifesto would assert the need "to develop an *anarchist* regime of individual liberty. . . . No authority, no dictation, not the least trade of orders from above! . . . Marxists can march . . . hand in hand with anarchists, provided both parties uncompromisingly reject the reactionary police-patrol spirit represented by Joseph Stalin" (483). But it is important to note the distinction in the minds of many Marxist modernists between Stalinism and the potential for revolutionary Communism, as Lukács describes it. Walter Benjamin's "The Work of Art in the Age of Mechanical Reproduction" (1936), stimulated by the influence of

Brecht's Epic Theater, illustrates my point: "Mankind . . . now is one for itself. Its self-alienation has reached such a degree that it can experience its own destruction as an aesthetic pleasure of the first order. This is the situation of politics which Fascism is rendering aesthetic," as in branding modernist art degenerate and celebrating ritualistic and mythic nationalism (252). "Communism," conversely, "responds by politicizing art," Benjamin says (252). Communism exposes the political content in art, compelling the appreciator of art to be cognizant of its relation to ideological function while achieving an aesthetic appreciation that only revolutionary consciousness can generate.

The idea of comprehending McKay's literary output through the radical politics of his sexuality necessitates an inquiry into the cataloguing of his location in literary studies. It is time to question how useful it is to continue positioning him within the discursive field of Harlem Renaissance studies without at least acknowledging a few difficulties with this chronotopic taxonomy. Here is where a review of McKay's cultural identity and aesthetic classification as Harlem Renaissance author is so crucial. As well as a historical chronotope, the Harlem Renaissance may be understood as an affirmation of nationalist structures of feeling. I do not mean cultural or ethnic nationalism, an often useful kind of strategic essentialism. I mean that the Harlem Renaissance risks enforcing an American exceptionalist ideology, to perpetuate the received privileged position of language arts generated within American national limits.

Paul Gilroy's *Black Atlantic: Modernity and Double Consciousness* (1993) most dramatically challenged the tendency toward nationalism in black discourses by locating the center of black modernity in the middle of the "black Atlantic," the site of the Atlantic Slave Trade—equidistant between the Americas, Africa, and Europe. It is a simple matter first to recount a bit of relevant historical data. McKay did not live in Harlem during most of its renaissance, spending almost all of his time in Europe and North Africa, and this detail is important not merely because of what it says about him as a *diaspora* cruiser but also because of what it says about him as a diaspora *cruiser*. It must be stated finally that to continue characterizing him as exclusively a Harlem Renaissance author is to persist in failing to attend to the négritude writer's import in the New Negro modernist export. Although he incontestably was a New Negro writer, to position him primarily within the Harlem Renaissance constellation means eliding other, in many ways more dynamic features, characteristics that are as compelling to his critics and readers as they were to McKay himself. His positioning is multiple. But the predicament is not only one of how he is situated historically and critically. The Harlem Renaissance that currently endures may itself be distinguished as a product of historiographic narrative discourses.

The Harlem Renaissance, or the rendition that has been passed on to current study, is fundamentally a literary-historical chronotope[9] created by the "Niggerati," as Zora Neale Hurston termed the gifted gathering of second-generation writers collected around "Niggerati Manor" (Boyd 116). The group included Hughes, Hurston, Countée Cullen, Wallace Thurman, Gwendolyn Bennett, and Bruce Nugent—the brilliant circle involved in bringing out the intentionally inflammatory 1926 cultural journal *Fire!!* Scholars and anthologists have understandably disseminated the useful Harlem Renaissance chronotope, although they have wrestled with McKay's singular disposition toward its most prominent personalities. Steven Watson says, "When he ran into members of the generation of New Negroes, McKay recalled, 'I was an older man and not regarded as a member of the renaissance, but more of a forerunner'" (81). But more should be said on this subject. McKay served as an inspiration to the Harlem Renaissance notables, but he was never truly a member in any unproblematic way. Ironically, though much of what has been written about his politics reflects a reductive view of his affiliation with the Communist Party, critics have never satisfactorily assessed his renunciation of his association with the Harlem Renaissance movement. His rejection of the Harlem writers as a unified, stable school can no longer be depicted as solely an idiosyncratic, contradictory feature of his role as a particularly prickly Harlem Renaissance author.

McKay not only distanced himself from the younger generation of Harlem writers who identified as part of a cultural movement; he was positively hostile toward the older generation of Harlem intellectuals, the "mid-wives" of the renaissance nativity, as he contemptuously called them. Du Bois "is a great passionate polemic" but "possessed of a cold, acid hauteur of spirit" (*Long Way* 110), and Jessie Fauset is "prim, pretty," and conservative (112). Although the editor of *The New Negro* (1925) had published some of McKay's poetry, Alain Locke and he did not even encounter one another until they met in Berlin in 1923. For decades McKay held a low opinion of "Professor" Locke as "the animator of the movement as well as," probably mistakenly, "the originator of the phrase 'Negro renaissance'" (313). Because of "a kink in Dr. Locke's artistic outlook, perhaps due to its effete European outlook," the Howard University academic was unfit to "lead a Negro renaissance" (313). McKay clearly disagreed with Locke's statement in the introduction to the foundational anthology *The New Negro* that "fundamentally for the present the Negro is radical on race matters, conservative on others, in other words, a 'forced radical,' a social protestant rather than a genuine radical" (8). But McKay's hostility toward the Rhodes scholar and Howard University professor, his sketch of the black critic as having aesthetic intestinal troubles, also had a personal feature to it: Locke had altered the title of McKay's sonnet "The White House" to "The White Houses" when he published it in *The New Negro*.

Indeed, his personal attacks on the first generation signify more than bad temper. He articulates his decision to desert Harlem for the second time, in 1922, a trip that turned out to last twelve years, as being brought on by his antipathy for the African American awakening centered there, culminating three years later with the publication of *The New Negro* collection, the amassing and perceived leveling of diverse black voices in a single text. McKay is ambivalent toward his role in the renaissance, his inability to "distill" poetry from his experience:

> now that I was legging limpingly along with the intellectual gang, Harlem for me did not hold quite the same thrill and glamor as before. Where formerly in saloons and cabarets and along the streets I received impressions like arrows piercing my nerves and distilled poetry from them, now I was often pointed out as an author. I lost the rare feeling of a vagabond feeding upon secret music singing in me. (*Long Way* 114)

For McKay, the older generation personifies the closing down of Harlem speakeasy, transgressive culture. Being "pointed out" as one of the Talented Tenth, a set that embodies to him a dull crowd of wet blankets, "the intellectual gang" enforcing conformity to rigid renaissance values, portends the passing of Harlem as a site for revelry and its materialization as a fetish commodification of black difference. According to McKay, at the moment when he was poised to benefit from recognition as the foremost writer of a major movement, after so many years of struggle and relative obscurity, he abandoned Harlem for Europe. And the motivation to flee was the collective countenance of the writers of the Harlem Renaissance. Indeed, the reason for his flight, he insists, was due to being interpellated by the African American literary community as a Harlem Renaissance author. Once an external designation is given to his insurgence, the revolution dies and the motivation for the poetry grows stale. An apposite Prohibition image, he is no longer able to *distill* poetry from his Harlem experience.

In light of his spending most of the 1920s and a third of the 1930s living in Europe and North Africa, it is useful to consider how his existential understanding of and orientation in sexual subculture were as informed by interaction with British, French, and American expatriates and natives and African diaspora same-sex society as they were enlightened by the doings of Harlem Renaissance gay folk. In *A Long Way from Home*, by way of commenting on his preferences and aversions for certain kinds of modernist writers, McKay declares that even though Gertrude Stein's salon at 27 rue de Fleurus was open to Negroes, he intentionally stayed clear of her regular soirées due to his "aversion to cults and disciples" (248). McKay's antipathy for the illustrious Jewish American avant-gardist is a result of his reaction to her novella *Melanctha*, one of Stein's *Three Lives* (1909), which "seemed more like a brief American paraphrase of Ester Waters than a story about Negro life" (248). In one lacerating critique—there are two rebukes in *A Long Way from Home*, and several curt passing references—Stein is "the high priestess of artless-artful Art" that "identifies Negro with Nothingness" (348). His problem with Stein is of the same variety as his criticisms of Alain Locke and Carl Van Vechten, whose *Nigger Heaven* (1926) he disparages. In contrast to making Stein his bête-noir, McKay's recollection of his acquaintance with Edna St. Vincent Millay in Montparnasse during the 1920s is near rapturous (*Long Way* 258–59). In fact, he witnessed the sexual and political transformation cultivated by bohemian lesbianism in the Paris of the 1920s, the women of the Left Bank, including literary lesbians in "the Amazon" Natalie Clifford Barney's crowd and beyond: Millay, Collette, Djuna Barnes, Radclyffe Hall, Alice Toklas, and Stein. Ray's spirited defense of the "bulldyker" (129) in the late 1920s novel *Home to Harlem*, a document he produced while living in France, articulates McKay's view that the transgressive literature of the literary lesbian revolution presents a momentous challenge to bourgeois conformity.

McKay's European queer commerce, however, journeyed beyond the Rive Gauche expatriates, white and black. He interacted on a daily basis with British Socialists while in England, then Bolsheviks in Russia, and white and black comrades of the proletariat while in France, and all three of these revolutionary assemblages were peopled with queer radicals. McKay's stopovers in Germany are of interest to this query as well. Using the city as a gateway for his trip to and from Russia, he resided twice in Berlin in the early 1920s, first in 1922, then in the following year. Five years later Christopher Isherwood lived in the capital and then chronicled his experiences in fictional form. *Goodbye to Berlin* (1939) indicates the kind of uninhibited queer subculture McKay experienced in the Weimar-period capital, with the fluid interaction between the gay cabaret and the "'communist' café," as Isherwood calls one of the Berlin retreats. McKay's description is brief but consistent with Isherwood's: "I visited many of the cabarets . . . , some of which seemed to express the ultimate in erotomania. The youngsters of both sexes, the hectic pleasure-chasers of the Berlin of that epoch . . . were methodically exploiting the nudist colony indoors" (*Long Way* 156). As James T. Sears chronicles in *Behind the Mask of the Mattachine* (2005), the foundations of the Gay Rights movement were laid in Berlin in the early 1920s by the social-ist revolutionary Benedikt Friedländer, the socialist Jewish sexologist Magnus Hirschfeld, and the conservative businessman Friedrich Radszuweit, whose aim was to attract members of the proletariat to join in the repeal of the sodomy law.

As it was located across the Atlantic, the Harlem gay literary subculture was for McKay the most remote—and least counterhegemonically engaged—ho-mosexual development of the 1920s. After 1922, McKay's experience with the Harlem Renaissance notables occurred through intermittent encounters in Paris (Fabre 92–113; Stovall 60–61). His awareness of gay society in the Village and Harlem was attained almost exclusively through correspondence, gossip, and whatever journalism friends would send or bring to the diaspora expat. It is sig-nificant that, though they carried on an extensive, generally affable correspon-dence, in spite of Hughes's extensive European travels and near idolization of McKay, they did not meet personally until McKay was back in the United States during the mid-1930s, long after the headiest climax of the Harlem Renaissance (Cooper 296). The queer experience he had in Europe was shaped by interac-tions with bohemian intellectuals and with constituents of the British, Russian, and French revolutionary proletariat.

In other words, yet another aspect to McKay's anarchist tendencies may be identified. It is instructive that at the moment when the Soviet Union outlawed homosexuality and other "bourgeois" bohemian forms of social interaction as degenerate, black leaders in the United States were calling for the cleaning up of homosexuality among the black society in Harlem. During the late 1920s, Adam Clayton Powell, who was pastor of Harlem's First Abyssinian Baptist Church, commenced a campaign to eradicate homosexuality once and for all in black Manhattan (Chauncey 253–56); the attitude of black cultural leaders was that black homosexuality signified a criminal subculture. McKay did not only vent an antipathy against Communism at the moment when the Soviet Union insti-tuted a sexually reactionary politics. He also recognized that a totalizing black struggle policed the lines of cultural identity, particularly as it viewed different sexuality and masculinity. His later radicalism is both a confrontational black revolutionary Marxist-Leninist Trotskyism—in other words, vigilant of hege-monic discourses in their manifold forms—as well as an autonomous anarchist confrontation with narrow color politics. For McKay revolutionary intellectual work must transpire at the level of cultural discourses; radical literary militancy must not only stage a counterrevolutionary demonstration but also articulate the hegemony, as Gramsci says, and he would not submit his own liberation politics to an ideologized redaction. Permanent revolution is universal, a transformation that touches on all levels of social intercourse. McKay's Harlem shadows—the traces of his free agency—take on another hue when it comes to his memoir's portrayal of his sexuality. Where he playfully portrays the experience of operating underground as a black Bolshevik, Leninist, and Trotskyist, he must charily obscure the truth of his past; otherwise, he risks an exposure that would be dangerous indeed. But when it comes to representing the experience of being queer, McKay must borrow from his postcommunist rhetoric to fashion a new language. Bhabha's theory of colonial liminality, of the Third Space, is useful:

> How are subjects formed "in-between," or in excess of, the sum of the "parts" of difference (usually intonated as race/class/gender, etc.)? How do strategies of representation or empowerment come to be formulated in the competing claims of communities, where despite shared histories of deprivation and discrimination, the exchange of values, meanings and priorities may not always be collaborative and dialogical, but may be profoundly antagonistic, conflictual and even incommensurable? (2)

In a telling passage of his memoir McKay declares "the Oscar Wilde case" to be a conspicuous instance of injustice (43). This is an illuminating moment in the text because, as a result of his relationship with his first patron, Walter Jekyll, the Wilde trials and the white Anglo-Irish author's imprisonment and exile played a central, if oblique, part in the black Jamaican's formation as a radical author. A British homosexual, Jekyll relocated to Jamaica during the late nineteenth century. An aristocrat with the credentials of the voluptuary, Jekyll withdrew from England after Wilde had been tried under the Criminal Law Amendment Act of 1885. The law enacted Henry Labouchère's attack on those he labeled "Snob Queers," aristocratic aesthetes who corrupted manly, liberal English youth (Dellamora 202).[10] The Wilde trials influenced anxieties over identifiably homosexual public figures in Britain, particularly those who hailed from the aristocracy (Sedgwick 217). Gay Englishmen of Jekyll's class felt obliged to flee England during the late Victorian assault on "deviant" sexuality occasioned by Wilde's scandalous trials; the late Victorian "Pansy Craze" posed a threat to the construction of masculinity propagated for empire maintenance (Weeks 18). According to McKay's article in *Pearson's Magazine* in 1918, McKay the pupil and Jekyll the mentor explored the work of three literary masters in their intimate literary salon. These three writers framed the principles and aesthetic values of nineteenth-century English and American gay writing: Edward Carpenter, Socialist author of the pioneering proto-gay manifesto *Homogenic Love and Its Place in a Free Society* (1894);[11] Wilde, martyr of sexual autonomy; and Whitman, both Carpenter's and Wilde's ideal of the sexually emancipated national poet.[12] Moreover, Robert Louis Stevenson chose the name Jekyll for his famous character who leads a secret sexual life (Cooper 23). The historical Jekyll was an authority on culture and language, thus Stevenson's use of his friend's name. The fictional split personality of Dr. Jekyll/Mr. Hyde characterizes late Victorian anxiety over a crisis of masculinity, the Sex Panic of the 1880s. But the most significant aspect of the persecution of Saint Wilde is in the resemblance to the state's hounding of McKay as a queer black Communist. Before considering this aspect of the memoir, it is necessary to examine McKay's origins and his versifying of social control while a police officer in Jamaica, the years that shaped the political ideals that would later become his queer black Marxism.

Constab Ballads (1912), McKay's second collection of poems published in Jamaica and issued under Jekyll's guidance, openly portrays the expatriate Englishman's lessons in valuing "homogenic love." Jekyll discouraged his pupil from writing the sort of classically metered lyrics that, in a desire to be seen as a genuine poet, McKay wished to compose, and convinced him instead to write more of his "dialect" or, to be more precise, creole poetry. For Jekyll, the euphony of the Afro-Jamaican male voice vocalizing creole speech was a quality that could arouse what amounts to sexual stimulation, an aspect of the Jekyll-McKay relationship that deepens the meaning of interaction within the colonial contact zone. Remarks in Jekyll's 1907 study, *Jamaican Song and Story: Annancy Stories, Digging Tunes, Dancing Tunes, and Ring Tunes*, impart a sexual preference for and homoeroticism of black Jamaican creole:

> The [black Jamaican] men's voices are of extraordinary beauty. To hear a group chatting is a pure pleasure to the ear, quite irrespective of the funny things they say; their remarks are accompanied by the prettiest little twirks and turns of intonation, sometimes on the words, sometimes mere vocal ejaculations between them. (6)

An awareness of this aspect of Jekyll's desire to see McKay write dialect poetry, therefore, sheds meaning on the situation between the two men. Several of the vernacular poems in *Constab Ballads* deal with a same-sex love affair or perhaps multiple affairs. In other words, for Jekyll, whose influence on McKay can be traced judiciously, two marginal expressions—black Jamaican basilectal English creole and sexual difference—were linked, and his influence on the young black poet was to see this idea realized, to hear "vocal ejaculations" in McKay's verse.

Constab Ballads also documents the poet's first black proletarian social experience. Black Jamaicans filled the ranks of the Royal Jamaican Constabulary, and nearly all of the *Constab* poems celebrate the "peasant class" Jamaican. Accordingly, the text also represents McKay's first experience with the ingenious technology of colonial hegemony. The British ascendancy populated the colonial constabulary force with Jamaican "colonials," motivating the colonized bourgeois class to police their underclass kinsmen, thereby fashioning a military police class that perceived of itself as aligned with the colonial power—a shrewd articulation of colonial hegemony. But the *Constab* poems demonstrate another strain in McKay's trajectory as well. Some of McKay's *Constab* rhymes describe or refer to the painful separation the speaker experiences when a comrade is suddenly relocated to another district. "Bennie's Departure" is perhaps the most helpful because, though its voice employs what seems an acceptably heterosexed convention—the recognizably Kiplingesque jaunty, homosocial, imperialistic esprit de corps diction and cadence—its message of taboo sexuality is unambiguous:

> Once his cot was next beside me,
>   But dere came misfortune's day
> When de pleasure was denied me,
> For de sergeant moved him 'way:
> I played not fe mind de movin'
> Though me heart wid grief be'n full;
> 'Twas but one kin' o' de provin'
>   O' de ways o' dis ya wul.' (ll.129–36, *CP* 91)

Passages of *Constab Ballad*'s poems make perfunctory attempts at dissembling their queer meaning by offering alternative readings: representations of asexual homosocial relationships, manly comrades in arms. But the stanza above does not attempt such a pretext. One may contextualize the narrative's subject. Although we cannot be sure why the two black proletarian-class gay constables were separated, we can speculate judiciously, considering how colonial authorities operating under the consensus of late Victorian imperial assumptions about sexual "inversion" would have looked on a same-sex relationship. One should note the stanza's withering conclusion: "de ways o' dis ya wul.'" McKay's "special friend"[13] Jekyll, an influential Englishman, was able to help him. He intervened

with colonial authority, and McKay was transferred to a constabulary unit located in the district where Jekyll resided; in this way the two were able to spend
more time together. Eventually Jekyll was able to have McKay, unhappy as a colonial police officer, released early from his term with the constabulary (Cooper
34). *Constab Ballads* autographs the colonialist-imperialist policing of queer
black proletarianism at the outset of McKay's vocation.

McKay felt indebted to his first patron and even felt that Jekyll was his only
sympathetic comrade in Jamaica. Still, he shows signs throughout his life of ambivalence toward Jekyll's influence. Many years after publishing *Constab Ballads*
he restages the conditions of Jekyll's patronage in *A Long Way from Home,* but
this time the roles are inverted, with McKay as the protector and a young white
male as the patronized. At the beginning of the memoir, McKay follows a chapter titled "White Friends" with one titled "Another White Friend." The chapter
offers a critical moment in his work, a performance that permits access to his
sometimes open closet, if the language within is coded. In contrast to one of his
most celebrated angry sonnets, "To the White Fiends," the *white friends* were important literary people and patrons like Max Eastman and Frank Harris. But the
"other white friend" is a young pickpocket McKay meets, Michael. The modifier
"another" in "Another White Friend" signifies both the marginalization of unnamed "friends" as well as a recognizably McKayesque impish irreverence for
respected white patrons. It is important to note, in addition, that he composed
A Long Way from Home during the mid-1930s, ten years after the events that he
depicts here. In other words, the performance the reader experiences in the first
part of the book, in which he relates his experiences with Michael—events that
took place before he went abroad—is colored by his experiences in Tangier and
even experiences before coming to Harlem, particularly in Jamaica.

Early in the text, McKay finds himself one night in downtown Manhattan,
a kind of black sightseer touring the White Belt, and he meets Michael, one of
the single-name-only personalities, or characters, in the memoir. Michael is fleeing from the police and, becoming "confidential," asks McKay not to give him
away; he has "escaped by a ruse that cannot be told" (46). Appreciating Michael's
refreshing honesty about his transgressive activities, the black cruiser brings the
small-time malefactor back uptown to his modest apartment in Harlem. Much is
revealed in a brief section involving McKay's girlfriend, Manda. Accustomed to
entering his room without knocking, Manda barges in on the boys and exclaims,
"Foh the land's sake! I wonder what will happen next!" (46). The narrative vol-
unteers no more than this, specifically to what spectacle Manda is reacting in
such an "excitable state" (46). His representation of his relationship with Man-

da exhibits a legerdemain that McKay frequently demonstrates when depicting his heterosexual, nominally genital relationships: "There was always a certain strangeness between Manda and me" (46). He indicates that essentially Manda, a southern migrant and "a real peasant type," cleaned and cooked for him, and their affiliation seems to have no other feature to it (48). Like a code laid out for the reader to crack, here he remarks, "I felt like saying something impish to stir up Manda's suspicion" (51). McKay, with his devilish sense of humor, is tempted to encourage Manda to believe that he has thrown in with a white lawbreaker, that the two form a secret, intimate gang. But the scene is not so simply read. Later in the text he will go out of his way to deny being a spy while encouraging the reader to infer that he is a radical agent. Certainly, the implication here is that Manda would suspect something else is going on between the two men.

Secrecy is the rule. Everyone in Harlem who encounters McKay and Michael together is puzzled: "Whatever they really thought of him I never knew, for they never said. But they were aware that our relationship was not a literary one; they knew that he was not one of those white folks who were interested in the pattern of words I was always making" (50). Although in "appearance he was like a nice college student" (52), Michael "made no pretense of being intellectual" (50). Those who come across the pair together uptown "never imagined that he was what he was. And it would never have occurred to them that I could be friendly with a crook. One never can tell about appearances, and so we all make mistakes by it" (50). The explanation turns on several "confidential" turns of phrase, where those who are outside of the "relationship" are not in a position to imagine "that [Michael] was what he was." On the surface Michael is a "crook," but at the moment when McKay clarifies, he leaves the door open for interpretation, for the imagination: "One can never tell about appearances." The "patterns of words" McKay makes are "literary," poetic, and poetry is the language of multilayered meaning. He ends his memoir by saying: "I have nothing to give but my singing. All my life I have been a troubadour wanderer, nourishing myself mainly on the poetry of existence. And all I offer here is the distilled poetry of my experience" (354). The "distilled poetry" of McKay's "existence" and "experience" lies in his black queer anarchism.

The narrative of Michael is complicated, as McKay demonstrates what could be an aversion for white male sexual contact in his memoir. At one point one of "Gertrude Stein's young men" in Paris tells the black cruiser, "J'ai le béguin pour toi" [I've got a crush on you] (328), and McKay's reply is, "Merci, mais je n'ai pas" [Thanks, but I don't for you], adding, "His bloodless white skin was nauseating. He had no color" (329). "A Red Flower" (1922) typifies McKay's wish for color in a lover: "Your lips are the red symbol of a dream. / What visions of warm lilies they impart, / That line the green bank of a fair blue stream" (ll.9–11, *CP* 184). He has several white male friends whom the text hints are gay. He possesses enormous fondness for Lucien, the young French sailor, who seems to be bisexual; Lucien is a radical proletarian character who is keen to read Marxist literature (259–61). And "the American lad" he met "at the American Express office . . . professed a liking for" McKay because of the black writer's poetry (241). The memoir is scattered with various other white males with whom McKay keeps company, some of whom are also signed as gay, if a bit discreetly. Just as he intends to retain command of the discourse of spying, the "bloodless white" man's pickup line in French is not translated, giving the sly author a modicum of control over who gets exactly what point he wants to make. It is likely that Michael is "The Snow Fairy" (1922), one of the poems suitable for retrieval from McKay's poetically open closet. Or Michael is among the synthesis of white lovers who constitute the image: "I made room for you in my little bed, / Took covers from the closet fresh and warm, / A downful pillow for your scented head, / And lay down with you in my resting arm" (ll.9–12, *CP* 188). The reader may locate an intimate link between "spy mania" (160, 201) and "erotomania" (156).

This is made traceable by a fascinating scene in the memoir. Most intriguing is how the autobiographer stages a way to consider sexuality, work, and the male body. One day McKay and Michael are in his room, and the narrator is dressing to go to work as a waiter on the Pennsylvania Railroad. McKay "was suddenly made self-conscious by Michael remarking: 'If I had your physique, I wouldn't work.'" Michael also tells McKay that he finds it "*queer*, you liking a woman like Manda," because she is "so homely, she couldn't do any hustling to help you out" (emphasis added). Evidently Michael wishes to suggest that McKay procure, and then the underprivileged black man could acquire the finer things in life, like the services of "a pretty woman." When McKay declares, "Every man has his style and limit," Michael, offended, assumes that his companion does not approve of his own vocation, which seems to be petty theft. Michael then throws back McKay's obliging attitude toward menial labor for blacks, his willingness to be a Pullman waiter, serving white folks: "But ain't it hell to be a slave on a lousy job?" (53). As he does in Tangier, in Harlem he ludically performs in mufti.

As Siobhan Somerville says, "sexual identity . . . often describes a complex ideological position, into which one is interpellated based partly on the culture's mapping of bodies and desires and partly on one's response to that interpellation" (*Queering* 6). The circumstances of the bedroom scene suggest the need for critical attention. The passage seems to present the reader with an acceptably heterosexed, nongenital homosocial situation, though somewhat iniquitous. Yet the frame of the dialogue stimulates certain questions; the reader is presented with imagery charged with sexual meaning. One man watching another dressing remarks on the shape of the other's body and the way that such a matter relates to physical work. Although the text informs the reader that Michael is asserting McKay should become a pimp and pay for a female sex worker, the young white man's comment about the black man's "physique" sends a different signal. The intimation is that McKay himself should engage in financial exchange for sex, which thereby suggests that this is a form of "work" Michael engages in. The reader discovers later that McKay is incapable of engaging in sex work:

> When I was working as a [nude] model in Paris a handsome Italian model brought me an offer to work as an occasional attendant in a special *bains de vapeur*. The Italian said that he made good extra money working there. Now, although I needed more money to live, it was impossible for me to make myself do such things. The French say "*On fait ce qu'on peut.*" I could not. The very idea turned me dead cold. My individual moral was all I possessed. I felt that if I sacrificed it to make a little extra money, I would become personally obscene. I would soon be utterly unable to make that easy money. I preferred a menial job.
>
> Yet I don't think I would call another man obscene who could do what I was asked to do without having any personal feeling of revulsion against it. And if an artistic person had or was familiar with such sordid experiences of life and could transmute them into literary or any other art form, I could not imagine that his performance or his thought was obscene. (315–16)

Michael relates accounts that imply he is a hustler. Each story he tells conveys an act of extortion, in which he coerces a male victim into giving him money (52). The "big-time representative of an ancient business" (52) is shaken down in a subway toilet: "[Michael] said it was down in the subway lavatory, when he was attempting to pick a man's pocket" (45). The anecdote summons the record of Wallace Thurman's arrest for public indecency in a men's washroom. But the image of *underground* activity resurfaces when Rose Pastor Stokes testifies that "a colored man had been watching her suspiciously while she was riding up on the subway" and that "when she had got off the train he had attempted to follow her." Implied in the relating of the stories is McKay's suggestion that Michael's comic situation, prolonging the act of *robbing* the men, means accompanying them somewhere so that he may be given an amount of cash. Yet each man negotiates with Michael over the money that he seems to owe the "little pickpocket"

(46). Although he is a bantamweight in a physically hazardous occupation, Michael nonetheless refuses to carry a weapon because it will only cause complications with the "bulls," or undercover police (54). But how he manages to force victims—all clearly inscribed as males—to hand over their money is left unexplained, a substantial lack. In each comic story Michael relates, or each story of the smalltime lawbreaker that McKay relays, the gag turns on the suggestion that the delinquent will expose his victim. The respected businessman—"the big stiff!"—is anxious that he not be implicated in a "scandal" (52). One pauses over how being robbed could provoke scandal against the victim, as well as the implications of "pick[ing] a man's pockets" (45).

McKay himself was intimately familiar with the occupations of the undercover police. While working as a Pennsylvania Railroad waiter, he relates in *A Long Way from Home,* he received a message from Frank Harris to meet in New York on a specified date: "I was intent on my own role—as a waiter—waiting for recognition as a poet" (4). McKay is laid up overnight in Pittsburgh, like Ray and Jake in *Home to Harlem*'s chapter 11, the "Snowstorm in Pittsburgh" episode, and anxious to get back to New York to meet Harris. When he stays out all night at a speakeasy, he is taken as a vagrant because he has forgotten his papers: "Bulls! … As I had no papers, the detectives arrested me" (7). On the verge of success, he is anxious about being arrested for a reason beyond possible incarceration. The waiter-poet is in a panic because his detention in Pittsburgh may prevent him from keeping the date with Harris, the publisher of *Pearson's Magazine,* and the sponsor who will give him his first big break.

Years later, McKay has begun to enjoy some success as a writer, his direction having taken a radical turn, and Michael looks him up in his *Liberator* office. This is a point in the autobiographical narrative where sexual difference and political disposition converge. It is 1922, the year of McKay's coeditorship of the magazine with the memoir's "other" Michael, Mike Gold. Michael's career as a petty criminal has been replaced by more grave criminal activities, and he has fallen in with a "rotten gang" (106–7). Before assuming coeditorship of the *Liberator,* McKay had fled London and its "Socialists, Communists, anarchists, syndicalists, one-big-unionists and trade unionists, soap-boxers, poetasters, scribblers, editors of little radical sheets," any number of whom are depicted as potentially spies (28). Michael has the same problem: "I'm in with a rotten gang. We'se all suspicious of one another" (107). But it is "too late" for the small, smalltime criminal to take flight: "I can't get away or escape. I'm not like you" (107). Feeling sorry for Michael, McKay gives him two volumes of poetry, one of which is his most recent, *Harlem Shadows* (1922). The other is "a pocket edition" of

Francis Thompson's "The Hound," one of the poet's favorites, a poem about the consequences of fleeing from God: "I fled Him, down the labyrinthine ways / Of my own mind. . . . / I stand amid the dust o' the moulded years—/ My mangled youth lies dead beneath the heap" (107–8). Moved, Michael says, "I guess when the gang sees me with these [the books of poetry] here, . . . they'll be thinking that I'm turning *queer*" (108; emphasis added).

McKay also feels "queer" at one point. In the chapter titled "Marseilles Motley," on his second visit to Marseilles in 1926, he witnesses a debate between a black café owner and the black Communist labor organizer Lamine Senghor about Communism and racial intermarriage. The café owner criticizes "this" Senghor for being married to a white woman because marriage between the races does not set the appropriate example for black leadership. Senghor defends himself by asserting that black and white legal union offends "white chauvinists," so intermarriage is a political act like other forms of cultural work (279). Senghor is in essence articulating a Marxist internationalism against black nationalism, a position McKay would have rejected in 1926, as he believed that it was possible to be a supporter of internationalist revolution while recognizing the exceptional predicament of ethnic minorities and promoting their need to preserve cultural difference. When Senghor points out that the café owner is also keeping the company of a white woman, the owner concedes that this is true, but he asserts that, unlike the union organizer, he does not aspire to be a black political leader (279–80). The white female "French companion" of the proper-minded proprietor then enters the café, and the couple demonstrate their fondness for each other. McKay says that he is puzzled by his own reaction to the candid expression of black and white heterosexual affection: "It was a strange scene, after that strange conversation, and it made me feel queer. Sentimentally, I was confused; intellectually, I was lost" (281). The "strange scene" suddenly discloses to McKay his own dis-position, his tendency to "feel queer." In one of the few moments coming close to self-confession in *A Long Way from Home*, the passage unveils how he is positioned "a long way" from heterodox discourses of racial, sexual, and national knowledges. This passing moment of revelation hints at one feature of McKay's free agency.

So it is not surprising that, despite the faint signals directing readers toward challenging the essential meaning of what they are reading, McKay attempts to present his relationship with Michael once again according to certain acceptable autobiographical discourses when they meet in the *Liberator* offices. One discursive frame is that of homosocial, manly camaraderie, the acceptability of the hearty, muscular workingman of the 1930s, a characterization closely bound to the meaning of being masculine and leftist. For example, Michael Gold, wishing to settle once and for all the conflict between himself and McKay over the editorship of the leftist magazine, challenged McKay, the memoir reports, to a boxing match (140). Beyond the masks he slips on in order to permit his reader to be comforted by a permissible homosocial masculine relationship, however, the persistence of unsettling questions is written into the text that, on some level, necessitate answers. What most distinguishes the scene is that the reader is compelled to consider the idea of Michael exhibiting—or unveiling?—himself as "queer," an identity his "gang" evidently would not tolerate. Attacked by black cultural leaders for writing an obscene novel, *Home to Harlem*, McKay could sympathize with Michael. McKay's "gang" also would not permit him to be queer, for the exemplary black author must be a respectable representative of the race: healthy, normative—in a word, heterosexual. McKay took a similarly disparaging view of the other former "gang" he had belonged to, if obliquely, the Communist Party, while a member of the IWW. Michael wishes that he could flee from his mob, so McKay gives him a poem about escaping from God or oneself—or from the authorities or Communists? McKay, like Jekyll, was also required to flee, hounded by the FBI.

Michael has more in common with McKay and others in the narrative than is at first observable. The young man's status as "another white friend" is meant to mark him as antithetic to "white friends" like his second gay patron, Frank Harris, yet he seems to intimate that Harris and Michael have something in common after all: "some of the readers of [Harris's] marvelous biography of Oscar Wilde imagined that there is something more than a platonic relationship between the two men," Harris and Wilde (267). McKay does not reject this idea. He even reports rumors that Harris, like Michael, had a bit of larceny in him, as the Irish author "pos[ed] as an art connoisseur," then "palm[ed] off fake pictures as old masters" (128). Another aspect of McKay's merging of Harris and Michael is connected with his wariness of white support. His distrust of white patronage is most vivid when he complains bitterly about the English aristocrat Nancy Cunard's intention to publish an article of his in "her strange, heavy and ineffectual giant of a Negro anthology" (345). Cunard expects contributors to donate material to *Negro* (1934) without compensation, and McKay remarks: "if I were composing an anthology of the white hell, it never would have occurred to me that all sympathetic white writers and artists owed me a free contribution. I suppose it takes a modern white aristocrat to indulge in that kind of archaic traditional thinking" (344). So it is understandable that he takes a dim view of the possibility that Harris did not pay for literary material, that the white publisher used pieces for his magazine and then did not compensate the writers (128). Evidently, Harris shares some of Michael's propensity for illicitness as well as licentiousness. And Harris has something else in common with Cunard. When McKay comes across Harris in Nice, Harris tell him that he is "thinking of doing a book of contemporary portraits of Negroes only," and among the portraits would be a section on McKay (270). McKay is unenthusiastic about the idea: "I resent that kind of patronizing criticism" (270).

Indeed, resentment toward the guidance of white former benefactors, even the likes of Walter Jekyll, form a kind of undercurrent in *A Long Way from Home,* a hostility that the memoirist may not be fully aware of himself. By the early 1930s, as the autobiography reveals, McKay was still reflecting on his relationship with the aristocratic Jekyll. The way in which the autobiographer re-presents his memories indicates his hesitant feelings. In *Banana Bottom* (1933), Squire Gensir, based on Jekyll, helps Bita Plant regain her Afro-Jamaican culture's hereditary, rhythmic folkways. *Banana Bottom* is a positive autobiographical portrayal of McKay's relationship with Jekyll, and its act of presenting the Jekyll-McKay story in fictional form makes the narrative permissible, able to avoid risking the revelation of hidden truths. In *A Long Way from Home,* however, he sets an epicene, coded restaging of his relationship with Jekyll, suggesting his ambivalence toward white patrons who, like Jekyll, navigated his life for a lengthy period. In this case, McKay becomes the patron, first making sure, as Jekyll did for him, that Michael is able to pursue his choice of profession by providing sustenance and a place from which to work. Not only may Michael eat at McKay's boardinghouse. He also allows Michael to use the Harlem apartment for his "hideout" while the petite offender performs his "petty tricks" downtown (50). And he later provides Michael with literary material meant to promote his spiritual growth, a coded reworking of the Jekyll-McKay literary salon focused intensely on Whitman, Wilde, and Carpenter: the value of "homogenic love" and homoerotic aesthetics. It is not surprising that among the triumphs on the London stage during McKay's sojourn in the early 1920s was George Bernard Shaw's recycling of Ovid's *Metamorphoses*, the playwright's *Pygmalion* (*Long Way* 60). The passages devoted to Michael suggest Shaw's comic portrait of a linguist, a social scientist analogous to an ethnographer—Jekyll's occupation—who takes in an underclass pupil and refashions her into the simulacrum of a civilized Victorian lady. The farce for McKay, however, was in the illicit nature of Michael's career, at the very least a pickpocket, with cues suggesting that he was a male hustler.

The prime difference between the two situations, however, is that McKay and Michael are both underclass (or, in Marxist critical terms, constituents of the lumpenproletariat). In Jamaica, Jekyll was upper class and McKay was peasant middle class. In America, Michael is *lumpen* because he is a miscreant and queer, McKay because he is black, queer, and a part of Harlem's hard-pressed laboring majority, his criminality inscribed onto his black body. But in this case, McKay becomes a kind of proletarian patron, and Michael becomes his underclass or *lumpen* prole rehabilitation project. As Michael Gold sentimentalized proletarianism (139), according to *A Long Way from Home*, a "European woman" romantically misconstrues the single-name Michael as a "significant symbol of the unity of the white and black [American] proletariat" (56). Although he enjoys the irony of a white petty criminal using Harlem as his hideout while he performs his "tricks" downtown, and though he savors the idea of a white sexual delinquent living in Harlem during a time when white tourists visit Harlem for its attractions as a sexual contact zone, McKay is nonetheless ambivalent about what Michael *symbolizes* or, more fittingly, embodies. Although he is mistaken as a member of the proletariat by some of McKay's crowd, who romanticize Michael without knowing anything about him, the young white lawbreaker is decidedly *not* a card-carrying member of the principled proletariat, the memoir implies. In this passage McKay demonstrates that he sees the proletariat in classical Marxist terms, as the politically informed working classes, cognizant of their oppression and alienation from labor, working toward dialectical materialist praxis. The knowledgeable proletariat is the antithesis of the lumpenproletariat because the criminal subculture's illicit activities impersonate capitalism.

Key to understanding McKay's disposition toward the young man and what Michael embodies is the text's autobiographical representation of masculinity. The pansy is vital to Jazz Age Harlem as he portrays the Black Belt in *Home to Harlem,* but McKay's autobiographical persona demonstrates a vexation with the idea of the typical gay man being represented as effeminate. The present discussion warrants returning to *Harlem Glory*'s cross-dresser: "formerly a female impersonator of the rough burlesque type and had delighted the hard-boiled patrons of colored cabarets from San Francisco to New York," whose "big scene . . . used to be a parody of congenitally effeminate female impersonators" (39). In his lived experience, McKay's idiosyncratic queer identity was inflected by a recognizably 1930s homosocial complexion, including an absorption in blood sport, a technical interest in boxing—generally, a vigorous, muscular, masculine outlook. Echoing Ray in *Home to Harlem*, McKay indicates his assent to the Nietzschean antipathy for "civilization." Discussing the reception of *Home to Harlem*, McKay responds to an unnamed "peeping critic"—an apt depiction of concealed sexual surveillance into his literary output—who assumes that the protagonist Jake Brown is autobiographical. McKay denies this, restating Ray's invective against the hypocrisy of "civilized" behavior: "I couldn't indulge in such self-flattery as to claim Jake . . . as a portrait of myself. My damned white education has robbed me of much of the primitive vitality, the pure stamina, the simple unswaggering strength of the Jakes of the Negro race" (229). The gesture reveals the frayed edges beneath the top folio of McKay's life palimpsest. On one level McKay is suggesting that his actual autobiographical semblance is Ray, not Jake, the closeted homosexual in *Home to Harlem.* On another level, one may conclude that the memoirist wishes to conceal his sexual orientation by performing a recognizably hard-boiled masculinism, and certainly there is something in this. Yet he genuinely was interested in prizefighting and other manly arts, and he did value primitive instincts and reject purposeless, refined behavior, psychological encumbrances that he saw as a form of social conditioning. But he does not demonstrate the need to choose between heterosexual and homosexual masculinity. McKay's proletarian queer black male anarchist exemplar—as much Jake as Ray—is both unsentimental and primitive, manly and intractable toward anything that would place limits on his "simple unswaggering strength."

McKay's autobiographical persona being constructed on a kind of casehardened masculinism lies at the heart of his ambivalence about Michael as a model of proletarian harmony. In fact, it is the author himself, or *A Long Way from Home*'s autobiographical, somewhat dressed-up impersonation of McKay, who qualifies as the model for "the unity of the white and black proletariat," not a constituent of the lumpenproletariat like Michael. Despite its anticommunist revisioning, *A Long Way from Home* retains the traces of its author's radicalism, elevating the worker and denigrating capitalism, the modern economic by-product of "civilization." Throughout the memoir McKay takes pains to point out that he has lived the life of the common worker, without the benefit of financial peace of mind or a middle-class background to fall back on, supported only by the encouragement of other proletarian men. Gramsci says, "All men are intellectuals," but he adds, "all men" must have the opportunity to be intellectuals. McKay may have had to be "a slave on a lousy job," but he is a true organic intellectual worker, aware of his enslavement, ennobled by participating in the international proletarian struggle. Resembling Gramsci, McKay says, "Every man his style and limit." In a sense, he ironizes his patronage of Michael. Yet there is the suggestion as well that he sees his role as Michael's sponsor as an earnest undertaking, for he believes that he may help the young white man forswear his criminal life and begin to contribute to and participate in the radical proletarian cause. When he sees McKay's name over a poem in a newspaper—probably

"If We Must Die," reprinted in black newspapers—Michael "surprised" him "by saying that he was thinking of getting a job" (56). By implication, chief among the changes McKay suggests he would like to see includes Michael no longer prostituting himself and promising to become a clean-living, healthy proletarian gay man. As he demonstrates in texts like *Home to Harlem*, McKay drew no lines between proletarian society and transgressive sexuality; indeed, each informed the other at fundamental echelons. The needs of the proletarian included sexual emancipation, a revolution against sexuality as commerce. Prostitution and pimping are activities that are counterintuitive for a liberated proletarian black man. Sexuality unencumbered by the boundaries of civilization and the exigencies of capitalism, however, is necessary. McKay's pre-Stonewall queer proletarian man must be queerly manly. That is, he must not act as a sign for the received, standard image of femininity, an identity given to passivity.

Still, one must pause over the idea of McKay's Harlem apartment serving as a place to hide out. He must have seen himself as also needing sometimes to hide out from certain tyrannical communities, those who would police his own transgressive, anarchic tendencies. Moreover, the echo of Ray's comment about "pimps" and "civilization" in *Home to Harlem* must be heeded. Ray proclaims that civilization is "rotten" and that he would prefer the company of pimps to that of "dictees." McKay was intolerant of those who buried their sexual impetus in the name of decency and being civilized. Following Leninist values, the proletarian, particularly the black worker, was virtuous. And though the pimp and prostitute only served capitalist and colonialist ideology, below such figures, in McKay's estimation, was the black man who, through the act of embracing the "civilized" and "educated," had divested a necessary native primitive vitality. The proletarian black man, embodied in characters like Jake Brown and Banjo, in his perfection and purity, never faced such absence. Race leaders envisioned the New Negro as married, with children, of the professional class, and, above all, manly, which meant that such a male was endowed with integrity, stability, and rationality. McKay claims the same sort of manly virtues for the queer proletarian black male, thus at once laying open the deconstruction inherent in the myth of black manliness while attempting to construct a more inclusive black masculinity.

Finally, written deep into McKay's portrayal of his relationship with Michael are hints at ambivalence over such patrons as Walter Jekyll. Significantly, though Jekyll introduced him to a world where being a celebrated poet was possible, he was at the same time the patron responsible for initiating McKay into western modes of inquiry, the kind of education Ray impugns in *Home to Harlem* and he himself gainsays in *A Long Way from Home*. Moreover, the aristocratic flourish of directing McKay to write "dialect poetry," although the young poet wished to write in traditional form, must have generated in him some hesitant feelings about white guidance, considering that he never again wrote dialect verse. Nor did McKay choose vers libre; he almost invariably composed in traditional, or "classic," form, as he termed it. The circumstances also suggest issues surrounding white patrons insisting that their black disciples write in dialect form. Paul Laurence Dunbar's relationship with William Dean Howells offers the archetypal example. Yet in McKay's case, laid atop such matters is the issue of his dialect poems staging almost entirely open themes of queer sexuality. At the very least, Jekyll recognized what his pupil was doing in *Constab Ballads*. It seems likely, moreover, that Jekyll encouraged his project to write sexually charged dialect poems. Jekyll was denied participation in late Victorian and British Empire constructions of masculinity, yet Jekyll's version of control over McKay's literary product mimics the colonial relationship, a relationship that is au fond gendered and sexualized.

McKay's *A Long Way from Home* subverts the colonial relationship by staging the colonial contest. First he controls the level of information about sexual difference in the passages dealing with Michael. As Jekyll no doubt needed to be careful in Jamaica, McKay was cautious in the United States. But McKay wrote both works: *Constab Ballads* and *A Long Way from Home*. Representing divergent sexuality in autobiographical form forced him to consider the risk of doing so openly, as he had done in *Romance in Marseille* and *Constab Ballads*. In addition, he not only directs the portrayal of patronage and sexuality but also determines the form it takes: an autobiography, where the writer shapes personal history according to his or her terms. And he controls not only the form but also what is being said about transgressive sexuality, directing his own well-turned-out persona to be the patron. When McKay came "home to Harlem" in the mid-1930s, he produced *A Long Way from Home*, a text that restages his beginnings and visits some old antipathies.

McKay's autobiography is a communication that has indeed drifted *A Long Way from Home*. He wanted to redraft his radical bohemian 1920s life through his more judicious—and judged—late 1930s experience. As a result, his travelogue-autobiography re-*presents* his unacceptable past in pleasing terms. Where his memoir wraps up his past in a form that is meant to give the impression of a buoyant joie de vivre, the effect is to conceal the anarchic, riotous, queer components of his life during the New Negro Renaissance, his sojourns on the margins of the black diaspora in Europe and North Africa. Through these means

McKay hoped that his militant past—his participation in establishing the African Blood Brotherhood, his commitment to the Communist Party, then his Trotskyism and articulation of a black queer anarchism—could not become evidence that would be put to use against him. Indeed, the self-suppression in the memoir made things easier for the memoirist when faced with the undertaking of writing *A Long Way from Home*. Yet, notwithstanding his ambition to censor his passionate radicalism, the filtrate of both his Marxist intellectual work and sexual dissidence resides in his autobiography. Even Claude McKay the artful memoirist did not succeed fully in rinsing out the dark discoloration of his past. Yet what is most remarkable about the memoir is that on some level the failure was deliberate, as *A Long Way from Home* is after all the "distilled poetry" of the author's queer black Marxism. The following chapters investigate the equally complex character of his queer dis-positionality as it appears in three novels.

"Dark Desire All Over the Pages"

Race, Nation, and Sex in *Home to Harlem*

Races and nations were things like skunks, whose smells poisoned the air of life. Yet civilized mankind reposed its faith and future in their ancient, stilted channels. Great races and big nations!

Home to Harlem

... literature, story-telling, had little interest for him now if thought and feeling did not wrestle and sprawl with appetite and dark desire all over the pages.

Dreams of making something with words. What could he make ... and fashion? Could he ever create art?

Home to Harlem

ALTHOUGH SEVERAL valuable readings of McKay's first novel have appeared over the past ten years or so, it is my view that because nothing has been said about *Home to Harlem*'s assemblage of queer black Marxism, no criticism on the novel has met the text's merging of multiple subjectivity and therefore radical cultural work. *Home to Harlem* is a dialogical act of Great Migration ethos that verbalizes the diverse dialects of Marxist cultural work and different sexuality, anti-imperialism and antiwar dissent, Socialist Realist regard for the "folk" and esteem for Bergsonian-Laurentian essential "knowledge," New Negro race work and a budding négritude—an early critique of global capitalism formed on historical materialist comradeship. Through the conventions of the novel, *Home to Harlem* discloses how diverse identity-making arrangements may unite to create an instrument for envisioning the need for full-scale political and social transformation. McKay's novel, "a long way from" its classification as solely a rowdy Jazz Age chronicle, envisages *being* at the frontier of social insurgency. As well as a Harlem Renaissance novel, his first extended publication—released the year following the execution of Sacco and Vanzetti—is more completely appreciated when recognized as a queer black anarchist manifesto. Like his next novel, *Banjo* (1929), his first novel is "without a plot," and in this one may ascertain how the best seller revolutionizes the novel. *Home to Harlem* summons the queer black proletarian class laboring at the peripheries of society, yet the novel's most noteworthy accomplishment is to visualize the intellectual work of the black Trotskyist full-blown revolution as already taking place, in the form of *dreaming* queer black transformation. McKay's diaspora cruising text is a document with, as the novel itself articulates, "dark desire all over the pages."

The way into McKay's novel as queer black Marxist manifesto is to be found in "Snowstorm in Pittsburgh," the crucial eleventh chapter. The African American southern migrant Jake Brown and Raymond, the Haitian immigrant comrade he has recently befriended, are working as part of a restaurant crew on the Pennsylvania Railroad. Flung far from their New Negro Mecca home, Harlem, the two Pullman crewmembers have a stopover in bitterly cold Pittsburgh—a cold layover due to both the weather whiteout and the rail company's policies for segregating the black personnel. Nimble Jake meets a willing waitress in a "basement eating-joint," then tracks down Ray in "the big Wiley Avenue poolroom" and informs his comrade that he is "gwine to the colored show" with his pickup (141–43). Not interested in accompanying Jake and his date, Ray buys the Negro newspapers—"*The Pittsburgh Courier, The Baltimore American, The Negro World, The Chicago Defender*"—and makes his way to the "wretched free quarters" where the Pennsy puts up the black workers (143–44). Well after midnight, when Jake reaches the boardinghouse, he finds that Ray is still awake, his grubby sheets flung on the floor (144–45). In place of the bedding Ray sits on a pile of the Negro newspapers that he has arranged on his mattress, occupied with a disagreeable job: "By the thin flame of the gaslight he was killing bugs" (145). Jake and Ray are done in, but the vermin in their beds are so abundant that they head out again, accepting the invitation of a Pullman crewmember named Happy for a carouse in a nearby "barrel-house speakeasy" (148). In the backroom of the dive, the aptly named "hophead" invites Jake and Ray to try some cocaine (149). Ray begs off, but Jake, always up to "try anything once," buys a few packets of the crystalline stimulant (149–51). When the pair return finally to the "bug house" (147), Jake, notwithstanding the copious arthropods, "fell asleep as soon as his head hit the filthy pillow," but Ray lies sleepless on the newsprint-covered mattress, tormented by the parasites and the snores of his fellow Pullman workers (151).

As Ray tosses and turns, vexation develops into insomnia, which causes the Haitian to begin probing familiar thoughts of isolation and alienation. He wishes he could be as free and easy as his new companion: "Perhaps love would appease this unwavering angel of wakefulness. Oh, but he could not pick up love easily on the street as Jake . . . " (ellipsis in original, 152). He then reminisces about his true home, Haiti, hoping that warm thoughts of the island will "snare sleep":

> All the flowering things he loved, red and white and pink hibiscus, mimosas, rhododendrons, a thousand glowing creepers, climbing and spilling their vivid petals everywhere, and bright-buzzing humming-birds and butterflies. All the tropic-warm lilies and roses. Giddy-high erect thatch palms, slender, tall, fur-fronded ferns, majestic cotton trees, stately bamboos creating a green grandeur in the heart of space . . . (152–53)

But as the closing ellipsis signifies, meditating on home doesn't achieve the desired result either: "Sleep," like *love*, "remained cold and distant" (153).

In any case, a concentrated meditation on home cannot be sustained in the present atmosphere. Discordant snoring and "masticating noises" that sound "like animals eating" disrupt his imaginings of home. The reader discovers that much more afflicts Ray than the biting pests and the cacophonous effects of collective sleep apnea. In spite of a conviction that black people throughout Africa and the diaspora share a psychic bond, "the keen ecstatic joy a man feels in the romance of being black" (154), Ray admits to himself that with the exception of his companion Jake, he does not much like his fellow Negroes: "These men claimed kinship with him. They were black like him. Man and nature had put them in the same race. He ought to love them and feel them (if they felt anything). He ought to if he had a shred of social morality in him. They were all chain-ganged together and he was counted as one link" (153). Lying there analyzing this contradictory aversion, he finally concludes that any form of collective identity arranging is false because the essential categories of racial and national authenticity are enforced by master narratives and the master class: "Races and nations were things like skunks, whose smells poisoned the air of life. Yet civilized mankind reposed its faith and future in their ancient, stilted channels. Great races and big nations!" (153–54). Only the privileged class, whites, he decides, benefit from racial and national formations; anticipating Fanon's *Black Skin, White Masks* (1952, trans. 1967), Ray is "conscious of being black and impotent" (154). The policing of collective identity arranging inhibits the happiness of the individual human subject, whether the identity formation takes the shape of national or racial solidarity: "Race. . . . Why should he have a love of race?" (ellipsis in original, 153). *Love* is one of the disobedient signifiers in *Home to Harlem*, assembled as it is throughout the novel alongside supposedly stable master—and mastering—signifiers like *race* and *nation*, while partnered with other almost equally unruly signifiers like *labor* and *comradeship*.

Desperate now with insomnia as he lies in the darkness, and feeling devoid of racial brotherhood, Ray is troubled most by his own cultivated intellectual faculty. Iterating Hamlet's act 3, scene 1 soliloquy about the predicament of consciousness itself—"And thus the native hue of resolution / Is sicklied o'er with the pale cast of thought," Ray is tormented:

> Thought was not a beautiful and reassuring angel, a thing of soothing music and light laughter and winged images glowing with the rare colors of life. . . . thought was a terrible tiger clawing at his small portion of gray substance, throttling, tearing, and tormenting him with pitiless ferocity. Oh, a thousand ideas of life were shrieking at him in a wild orgy of mockery! (156)

The image also iterates the imagery of McKay's sonnet "America" (1921):

> Although she [America] feeds me bread of bitterness,
> And sinks into my throat her tiger's tooth,
> Stealing my breath of life, I will confess
> I love this cultured hell that tests my youth. (ll.1–4, *CP* 153)

That is to say, hostile thought is related to questions of race and nation. Thought is antagonistic toward everything "soothing," like memories of warm Haiti, with its "winged images," or the "bright-buzzing humming-birds and butterflies," and the "rare colors of life," or "the tropic-warm lilies and roses" of the lush island. Like America in the 1921 sonnet, thought is "a terrible tiger clawing" at his brain, a notion inspired by the "masticating noises" his fellow Pullman workers make in their sleep that sound like "animals eating," sounds that torment him "with pitiless ferocity."

Unaware that cocaine is a stimulant, Ray ingests a packet of Jake's white powder in desperate hope that it will cause him to fall asleep, and when nothing happens, he finishes off the rest of Jake's supply (157). The effect of having overdosed is to make Ray immediately drift off, and evidently because he has ingested a euphoric stimulant, he experiences a sequence of spectacular, revealing reveries—the confessions of a black cocaine dreamer, however insensible of their substance the dreamer himself may be when conscious. Only in dreams, the Surrealists argued, may one locate the essential self, or to put it in Bergsonian terms, primitive "pre-knowledge." Later McKay would recollect this inspiration for his poem "Dreams": "Oh I have even drugged myself to dream / Of dear dead things, trembling with hope to capture / The sunlit ripples laughing on the stream / That bathed my boyhood days in foamy rapture" (ll.9–12, *CP* 219). The diaspora dreamer first travels back to his homeland, Haiti, experiencing a nostalgic, vivid night vision of his green *pays natal*, unmediated by Superego "thought," where his body takes the shape of a Freudian-inflected, free-floating "gay humming-bird, fluttering and darting his long needle beak into the heart of a bell-flower" (157), transmuting into dream imagery the "bright-buzzing humming-birds" of his waking reminiscences of Haiti. His chemically enhanced unconscious then briefly returns Ray to the United States to call on Howard University where because of his straitened financial situation, he is only able to attend as an intermittent student (137). As Ray experiences the classic cocaine symptom of paranoia, thought now intrudes on his REM cycle, and the black college in the nation's capital materializes, in contrast with Edenic Haiti, as a nightmarish, panoptic "prison with white warders" (157).

But the paranoia phase passes, and Ray's id cruises onto uncharted territory. Drifting between the surreal polarities of the unconscious, Ray dreams finally of neither home nor exile; his imagination drifts onto an exotic dreamscape. He dreams of being "a young shining chief in a marble palace," a dreamscape vision fittingly evoking the imagery of the palatial sanctuary of *Kubla Khan*. However, in Ray's dream, Coleridge's laudanum-induced pleasure palace is converted into a sensual citadel geographically situated on the other side of the "Orient," a Near Eastern Alcazar where, along with "slim, naked negresses" and "courtiers on cushions," a crew of "gleaming-skinned black boys bearing goblets of wine and obedient eunuchs" wait on the young black waiter's carnal desires (157–58). Or, in spite of the identification with the "Orient," Ray is an Ashanti king. As all three surreal landscapes merge, Ray as restive "gay" hummingbird, his phallic beak thrusting into every blossom in his path, has found a nesting place that exists beyond racial and national boundaries. That is to say, Ray's "thousand ideas of life," like phantoms "shrieking at him in a wild orgy of mockery" while suffering from insomniac self-doubt, have been transformed into an emancipating queer orgy.

In this white marble dream realm, moreover, "the world was a blue paradise." People and animals assume an azure hue. The tinting of human bodies coupled in homoerotic orgiastic union the color blue is an act that joins up several seemingly remote metalinguistic acts. Blue evokes the idiom of staged illicit sex, as in the enactment of blue laws in nineteenth-century New England, and by the 1920s the color blue brings to mind *blue movies*, the first phase of the raunchy cinematic pornography during the social revolution of the interwar period. The roots for the vernacular of the blues itself are tangled up with these forms of prohibited expression, and a possible link survives between pornography and black migrant music, as blues lyrics and even the music's tempo and notation were seen by anxious conservatives as openly vocalizing indecency.[1] The discursive act of relating the color blue to performed sex acts was so integrated into American culture by the time he composed *Home to Harlem* that even mainstream Hollywood talky period filmmakers busied themselves exploiting such subjects as the rousing world of transvestitism, endeavoring to utilize motion picture pornography—the competing underground mode of cinema—for culture industry consumption. It is notable that in *A Long Way from Home* (1937), McKay cites Josef von Sternberg's scandalous *Blue Angel* (1930), the film that presented Marlene Dietrich's disorienting, sensational performance of gender-bending (338). Indeed, *Banjo*, the novel that followed *Home to Harlem*, contains a chapter entitled "The Blue Cinema," which begins with a discussion of René Maran's African novel *Batouala* (1921) and ends with Ray and other black characters checking out a Marseilles pornographic film. An argument erupts between Ray and another character over the merits of film as art. The entire art of filmmaking is written off, and Ray takes up its defense: "You can't condemn an art wholesale because inartistic people make a bad business of it." The chapter, giving a nod to the sensational outlawing of Joyce's *Ulysses* (1922) for obscenity (Law 219–39) and thereby hoping to preempt its own possible banning by black critics, as *Home to Harlem* was critically proscribed, permits McKay to comment on the difference between pornography and an art that honestly portrays human experience: "The same condition exists in the other arts. . . . It's a crazy circle of blue cinema people, poor conscientious artists, cynical professionals and an indifferent public" (216). The "other arts," of course, include the modern novel.

But in *Home to Harlem* McKay is doing more than simply exploiting the recognizable color of public sexual performance by lowlighting the bodies of his dreamscape orgy blue: "And life was all blue happiness. Taboos and terrors and penalties were transformed into new pagan delights, orgies of the Orient-blue carnival, of rare flowers and red fruits, cherubs and seraphs and fetishes and phalli and all the most-high gods" (158). Siobhan Somerville discusses the way that whiteness and blackness act as social signifiers, discursive registers operating at the level of linguistic referentiality that pose as existentially identifiable signs (*Queering* 7). Whiteness in McKay's symbolic order is the absolute absence of color, so as the snowstorm symbolically engulfs all blackness in its whiteness, and as the *white snow*, cocaine, controls his black body's nervous system, thereby swallowing up blackness in the absence of whiteness, Ray dreams in color, his reveries transforming his "thoughts" of Haiti into symbolic referentiality. Indeed, McKay's poetry frequently employs lush imagery to perform the semiotic link between the homoerotic and *color* aesthetics. The openly homoerotic, Whitman- and Wilde–inflected poem "To O.E.A." (1920), its male muse described as "a flower, a fairy" (l.11 and l.14, *CP* 185), begins with the image of the lover's "voice" being "the color of a robin's breast" (l.1). "Flower of Love" (1922) also merges queer and color imagery:

> The saffron petals tempt my amorous mouth,
> The yellow heart is radiant now with dew
> Soft-scented, redolent of my loved South;
> O flower of love! I give myself to you. (ll.6–9, *CP* 187)

Blue, as *Banjo* illustrates throughout the narrative, is the color of proletarianism, as French laborers are recognizable by their blue uniforms. Human beings are proletarian blue in *Home to Harlem* because when Ray is released from the Howard University confinement into this de Chirico address, he enters a world no longer arranged according to the racially man-made, monochromatic world of race. Compelling bodies to correspond to slave taxonomies, to the totalitarian vocabulary of racial colorlessness, disseminates and sustains the absence of imagination, the defect at the center of racism itself: the newsprint world in black and white. McKay exposes the irony that the racial language of color in fact enables its antithesis: colorlessness, the incapacity to imagine beyond binary categories. The "Orient-blue carnival" imparts something about the complexity of Ray's discordant thoughts about race, sexuality, and nation. At the fore of his waking consciousness, Ray bears his rage at racism and, like a kind of living embodiment of McKay's enraged New Negro sonnets, at the ideology of race itself, assisted by its evil twin, state nationalism. Yet when his unconscious plumbs its depths, Ray does not see the world in black and white, according to either the requisites of race or the speech acts of sexuality.

Dreaming in color means the recognition of neither social nor terrestrial nor corporeal boundaries. Black Howard University was like a white-controlled detention center, but the carnivalesque "Orient-blue" pagan paradise admits no "taboos and terrors and penalties." If human bodies are no longer regulated according to the classification system of black and white but transformed into proletarian blue, then the *terra cognita* of manifestly heterosexualized bodies deconstructs, as in a *drag blues*. Dreaming in blue also contravenes the assimilationist ideology which asserts that black and white may be merged into gray (matter). It recognizes that the solution to the crisis caused by racist ideology is *not* in merely mixing the binaries to generate another level of colorless haze, an opacity that obscures the ideology of binarized racial and national systems. As Derrida insists, the critical reader does not impose a deconstructive act on the text; the text's binaries are composed of their own deconstruction. The text of race and nation falls apart in the hands of the reader at the moment when she or he tugs on the loose threads tying ideology to language. On this diaspora dream cruise across the black Atlantic, in other words, all identity and ideological couplings fall to pieces in the wake of the wreckage of racial and national binaries. Racism and nationalism are reterritorialized, toppled by a dream-blue other-logic.

The obscurely heterosexual Ray eventually tumbles toward consciousness, and as he reluctantly awakens, feasted on by the swarming race of bedbugs, the frenzied dream imagery of being repeatedly pricked blends the euphoric state of the enraptured medieval saint—clad in a chest full of arrows and bearing a blissful coital smile, literally loved by the Supreme Patriarch—with the entranced though emphatically stimulated Sufi dervish bopping toward worshipful and orgasmic oblivion. The image also iterates the phallic "Giddy-high erect thatch palms," the "slender, tall" vegetation of his Haitian home, as well as the id's gay hummingbird's darting phallic needle beak, though now Ray is the recipient of the penetration instead of agent of dissemination. McKay integrates all of these racially and ostensibly discrete ancestors in an orgy of tropes by concluding with a unifying, transporting sadomasochistic homoerotic vision: a "thousand pins were pricking Ray's flesh" (that is, the bedbugs are biting); and on this limp journey back to consciousness, "he was shouting for Jake" (158), his "beautiful and reassuring angel."

Theorist of the novel M. M. Bakhtin stated that the self is positioned within a social web made up of different memories, dreams, and voices demanding attention and response, inviting accommodation and negotiation. Identity is the result of such negotiation, a process that is never easy. Among *Home to Harlem*'s many iterative acts, toward the end of the novel, the frustrated Ray onanistically "wrap[s] himself darkly in self-love" (264). When at the moment the Haitian shifts from the inability to sleep due to the snoring and bedbugs to insomnia induced by "thoughts" of alienation, Ray considers "love": "Perhaps love would appease this unwavering angel of wakefulness" (152). He then envies Jake's facility for finding love: "Oh, but he could not pick up love easily on the street as Jake . . ." (152). The ellipsis signifies Ray's incapacity—or reluctance—to complete the *thought*. The locution itself is linguistically obscure: Ray could be envious of Jake's ability to effortlessly find love, or he could desire to love Jake and feels frustrated because he can't. Either way, Ray is unable to pick up women on the street because his middle-class social encoding prohibits him from engaging in casual sexual encounters. Yet on a deeper level, a plane that Ray is unaware of himself, the available *love* for the Haitian in the general society is limited to the heterosexual. Although cells of same-sex society have come into being (like the circle of black intellectuals in Harlem McKay participated in during the early 1920s), the wide-ranging, all-embracing culture of queer cruising has not yet developed, as such activity would be as dangerous as the appearance of biracial couples, the circumstances of the prizefighter Jack Johnson underscoring the risk. Jake is Ray's "beautiful and reassuring angel," moreover, linking the African American proletarian to Ray's desire for a "love" that "would appease this unwavering angel of wakefulness," a "love that dare not speak its name" in Lord Alfred Douglas's 1894 poem "Two Loves." Jake is the recipient of the West Indian's deepest affection, however aware of this forbidden desire Ray may be: "but his voice was so faint he could not hear himself" calling Jake's name as he crosses the threshold of the waking state (158). Evidently Jake can hear Ray just fine, however, because the African American wrestles his Caribbean comrade into consciousness: "Jake had him in his arms," trying to get Ray to stand on his own two feet, but Ray "crumpled. . . . All his muscles were loose, his cells were cold, and the rhythm of being arrested" (158). Ray's diaspora cruising vision of blue love and repeated "pricking" is a queer wet dream. As *Home to Harlem* is the first of the three manifestos that make up McKay's queer black Marxist prolegomena, it appropriately must first *dream* black queer solidarity before the reverie can become a reality.

The circumstances under which McKay wrote his novel provide necessary understanding of its counterhegemonic positionality. He composed *Home to Harlem* while living in France, much of the time dwelling in Toulon, the hometown of his French proletarian friend Lucien, supported by one of America's renowned radicals, Louise Bryant, and a Garland Fund grant of fifty dollars a month (*Long Way* 257). McKay reports in his autobiography that, fearing the authorities would become suspicious that he "was making political propaganda," he did not let on even to his friends in Toulon that he had spent an extended period in Communist Russia, much less that while a guest of the state, the Comintern had honored him as a leader of the black internationalist movement (260). But evidently spending time among the French proletariat involved cultural work in 1920s France. *A Long Way from Home* recounts that at a bash McKay gives in his room a sailor begins singing the "Internationale," and he joins in with the rest, "singing in English." This activity initiates the inevitable revolutionary oration on solidarity among workers: "One sailor jumped on my writing table and said: 'After the world revolution there will be no more white and black and yellow; we shall all be a fraternity of men.'" McKay is incensed by the comment: "My sense of the distinctive in the difference of color was outraged, and I said, 'We can still be a fraternity of men and guard our complexions'" (260). The next day two plainclothes policemen appear at his door. Under questioning McKay tells the investigators everything except that he visited the Soviet Union. But they are aware that guests at the party sang the "Internationale," and McKay remarks to the reader: "I am not sure, but I think that there is a government ruling which forbids French sailors and soldiers from singing the 'Internationale'" (260). McKay knows that he is in danger of deportation when the "English-speaking inspector smiled and asked me whether I was a Communist," further remarking that he would not be surprised "if a Negro-American had advanced ideas" (260). Warned, he henceforth is even more circumspect while in France, and soon he departs for Morocco.

The scene paints a sketchy portrait of his experience in Toulon. To start with, one wonders why McKay would think that the authorities might be suspicious that he "was making political propaganda," particularly when he says he is behaving circumspectly. The friends he says he does not let on to about his radical activities seem to be of the same political disposition, as all sing the "Internationale" with the sailor. Yet it seems that his anxieties are well founded, as apparently someone has recounted his behavior to the authorities. Just as interesting, McKay's being angered about a white Communist ignoring color "difference" in radical politics seems to indicate his total dedication to black nationalism.

But in fact it suggests that he is capable of retaining a sense of ethnic integrity while embracing the "international spirit," to use the title of a poem he wrote in the same year as *Home to Harlem*: "We can still be a fraternity of men and guard our complexions." Is it likely, moreover, that in 1937 McKay was unaware of the French restrictions against demonstrating Communist sympathies for those serving state duty? *Romance in Marseille* (c. 1929–32) indicates that he was acutely aware of the constraint and its consequences. Most chilling is the black radical's recognition of the possibility of repatriation. He had to flee Britain in 1921 when embroiled in a radical conspiracy, and then he was watched closely by federal agents because he was suspected of plotting against the U.S. government.

It is worth pointing out that the novel generally recognized as the first black queer textual outing, James Baldwin's *Giovanni's Room* (1956), was published some three decades after McKay's first novel. Two crucial differences exist between the two books. Baldwin's novel investigates the meaning of the interaction between white gay characters, and *Home to Harlem* is peopled with a company of black queer characters. And whereas Baldwin disparaged "everybody's protest novel," McKay embraces a prose fiction of explicit dissent. Indeed, the literary model for the three novels, *Home to Harlem, Banjo,* and *Romance in Marseille,* was the manifesto. The inspiration for his ménage a trois of radical romances is informed by the foundational revolutionary call, the *Communist Manifesto* (1848), which proclaims, "A specter is haunting Europe—the specter of communism." But McKay's three novels were more immediately inspired by the manifesto-writing vogue of the prewar and interwar periods. As the editors of *Modernism: An Anthology of Sources and Documents* (1998) say in their introduction, "the manifesto develops a status of its own, embodying rather than explicating the aesthetic gesture of the new—even while exploding the very category of the aesthetic" (Kolocotroni, Goldman, and Taxidou xix). Despite his aversion to modernist aesthetics, McKay's writing evinces the kind of rules against decorative writing generated in such manifestos as *Some Imagist Poets* in 1915. However, he was much more responsive to arguments over art as a social tool. McKay's writing reflects the avowal of protoanarchist John Dos Passos's "Against American Literature," published in the *New Republic* in 1916, a manifesto calling for an American literature that engages in historical materialist critique, with Dos Passos taking his ideal from socially conscious Russian literature.

Following the 1917 Bolshevik revolution, American and Russian intellectuals produced urgent art manifestos, prolegomena aimed at articulating an aesthetics that matched the sudden, massive social transformation. The major debate occurred over the schism between avant-garde and proletarian art. During McKay's brief tenure with the *Liberator*, Michael Gold, McKay's coeditor, published the American Communist literary manifesto, "Towards Proletarian Art" (1921). Despite the disagreement with Gold over the merit of proletarian literature in his 1937 memoir—his criticism of Gold's objective to make the *Liberator* "a popular proletarian magazine" (*Long Way* 139)—McKay was during the early twenties the foremost architect of black proletarian poetry, and the evidence of this may be located in the record of his time in Russia. According to the diary of the distinguished writer of socially responsible children's literature Korney Chukovsky, McKay read his poetry, in Russian, while attending literary parties at the Moscow home of Vladimir Mayakovsky (238). During this period, Mayakovsky and other Bolshevists framed the *Lef* manifesto in 1923, a proposal calling for an international proletarian art. McKay participated in the debate between the advocates of a proletarian aesthetic and the proponents of a politicized avant-garde art. During the early stages of Russian Communist vanguardism, the proletarian was not the only model for radically political art. While McKay was in Russia, an alternative Russian literary collective generated *The Eccentric Manifesto* (1922), a document that promoted an avant-garde art for the new Soviet state.

Meanwhile, beyond American and Russian borders, German Kurt Schwitters, rejecting Tristan Tzara's apolitical 1918 "Dada Manifesto," generated the Antidada movement's commentaries in *Merz* in 1924. Schwitters and German artist George Grosz, whose *Ecce Homo* (1923) McKay extols in *A Long Way from Home* (240), contended for a Dadaism that fused avant-garde aesthetics with Marxist revolutionary consciousness, thus "Antidada." Also composed as a reaction against Dadaism came the Surrealist movement's tenets, especially André Breton's first *Manifesto of Surrealism*, also published in 1924. Although Surrealism was originally articulated to proceed from a position that was deliberately aloof from political concerns, eventually the rift between Breton, who moved toward Communism in 1927, and Antonin Artaud, who averred to preserve the apolitical strain of Surrealism, would express the fundamental tension of the modernist avant-garde.

One may find it difficult to see the consistency between McKay's traditional stylistics and such experimentalist proclamations. However, in spite of his later denunciations of both experimentalist high modernist and proletarian literary stylistics, his first three extant novels in effect demonstrate the impact of avant-garde and proletarian aesthetics, indeed a kind of fusion of these two perceived polarities. The Freudian-inflected proletarian-blue dream sequence in *Home to Harlem* owes much to the Surrealist imagination, the notion that only in dreams may one catch a glimpse of the Real, of essential existence. The source of this complex merging lies in McKay's enthusiasm for Trotskyist philosophy. As early as 1923, Trotsky, in *Literature and Revolution*, sided with the avant-gardists against proletarian art. Trotsky was not the only major political thinker who advocated modernist experimental modes, however. Several years earlier, in "Marinetti the Revolutionary" (1916), Gramsci praised the revolutionary avant-gardism of the Futurists (not knowing that Marinetti would turn toward the Right) while disparaging the Socialists' lack of interest in cultural production (*Cultural*). For a twentieth-century Marxist art, Gramsci argued in favor of a principled avant-garde proletarian aesthetics. And in 1929 Walter Benjamin would write:

> The Surrealists . . . are the first to liquidate the sclerotic liberal-moral-humanistic ideal of freedom, because they are convinced that "freedom," which on this earth can only be bought with a thousand of the hardest sacrifices, must be enjoyed unrestrictedly in its fullness without any kind of pragmatic calculation, as long as it lasts. ("Surrealism" 189)

Though apparently "traditional" in style, the content of McKay's prose and poetry is radical—in its way as radical as more recognizably revolutionary art—the link between avant-gardism and Leninist vanguardism lying in innovative expressions that lead to the articulation of "freedom," according to Benjamin. It is worth noting that Benjamin, also intrigued with prewar Marseilles, apparently read *Banjo* (Edwards 189). Benjamin's notion of the articulation of freedom occasions being motivated by diverse ideas, models, and styles, even those that are ostensibly mutually exclusive. Benjamin's conceptualization of freedom and art excellently applies to McKay's first three published novels.

An even more dramatic manifestation of McKay's modernist insurgence lies in his hot opposition to Locke's programmatic introduction to *The New Negro* (1925); McKay considered the document an argument for the literary homogenization and deradicalization of color aesthetics. He categorically rejected Locke's attempt to soothe white worries about black radicalism being aligned with antinationalist, Russian-related revolutionary action, Locke's pronouncement that "the Negro is . . . a 'forced radical,' a social protestant rather than a genuine radical" (*New Negro* 5). Locke's introduction to *The New Negro* was widely regarded as *the* manifesto of Negro Renaissance literary art, an essay that kindled the second generation's comparatively avant-gardist rejoinder, *Fire!!* in 1926. The jointly authored introductory essay published in *Fire!!* qualifies as the final black arts manifesto until the arrival of *Home to Harlem* two years later.

Knowing the history of *Home to Harlem*'s immediate critical reception, its orientation vis-à-vis Locke and the New Negro movement, is important in understanding the novel's significance and place among the 1920s literary archive. *Home to Harlem*'s historical intertextuality may be noted, for example, in the similarities it shares with Eugene O'Neill's 1921 Expressionistic play, *The Emperor Jones*, a stimulating depiction of Pullman porters, jazz, intoxication, knife fights, and gunfights—the sort of elements critics noted in McKay's first novel. But the most controversial intertext was Carl Van Vechten's *Nigger Heaven* (1926). Writing for the black press, African American reviewers during the late 1920s condemned *Home to Harlem*, most drawing either overt or implicit comparisons between McKay's novel and Van Vechten's, published two years earlier. Written by a well-established novelist, as well as one of the Harlem Renaissance's most ardent champions—one of the "Negrotarians," as Zora Neale Hurston dubbed white promoters like Van Vechten (Lewis xvii)—the "Nordic" author's novel indicates that the lived experience of the black underclass embodied the modern social revolution of the 1920s. While Van Vechten's New Negro friends like Langston Hughes and James Weldon Johnson defended the novel, most black critics, including W.E.B. Du Bois, assailed *Nigger Heaven*, arguing that the book perpetuated crude stereotypes of black people (Worth 461–73). For some African Americans, the title alone was enough to cause outrage; Hughes suggests in his somewhat faint-praise apologia for Van Vechten's novel in *The Big Sea* (1940), his first memoir, that evidently a fair share of black people reacted against the imprudently titled *Nigger Heaven* by actually refusing to read it (270). In an article published in the scandal-broadcasting *Inter-State Tattler*, Du Bois declares that McKay "out-niggered Mr. Van Vechten."

As to the question of whether McKay was simply riding the crest of success that had greeted Van Vechten's book, archival evidence demonstrates that this claim is difficult to assert without at least acknowledging some complexity. Van Vechten's book contains characters who, like Ray, wrestle with their "color." The librarian Mary Love, for example, feels alienated from authentic feeling:

> she had lost or forfeited her birthright, this primitive birthright which is so valuable and important an asset, a birthright that all the civilized races were struggling to get back to—this fact explained the art of a Picasso or a Stravinsky. To be sure, she, too, felt this African beat—it completely aroused her emotionally—but she was conscious of feeling it. This love of drums, of exciting rhythms, this naive delight in glowing color—the color that exists only in cloudless, tropical climes—this warm, sexual emotion, all these were hers only through a mental understanding. (89–90)

Still, McKay's novel cannot be dismissed as a black-behind-blackface impersonation of Van Vechten's minstrelsy, if blackface accurately characterizes what Van
Vechten was up to. The critics reacted strongly against McKay's representation
of what they saw as the perpetuation of nasty stereotypes of blacks—namely,
not being much interested in self-improvement, and instead being absorbed
in blues, booze, and Eros. The accusation against McKay was partly the criticism against a black writer who is reproducing racist stereotypes, an even worse
transgression than Van Vechten's appropriation of Negro life. During the 1920s,
black critics encouraged Negro writers to produce literature of the "Talented
Tenth," as Du Bois in *The Souls of Black Folk* (1903) designated the 10 percent of
African American society who made up the professional middle class. Whites
had generated enough portrayals of blacks as indolent and ignorant, so it was
time for more positive images. Moreover, if the renaissance was going to improve
the situation of African Americans—among the often-stated intentions of the
New Negro movement—then the art it produced should elevate rather than
denigrate Negroes. It would be incorrect to suggest that Du Bois enforced black
bourgeois aesthetics. Yet his own novel, published in the same year as *Home to
Harlem*, focuses on the African American middle class. *Dark Princess* (1928) ex-
emplifies the need to tell the story of the Talented Tenth. (Although he helped
articulate it in his way, Du Bois would part with this tendency on the part of the
black bourgeoisie to push for respectability in the arts.) The African American
social exemplar was referred to as the representative of the race, a recognizable
figure among African Americans during the 1920s. The representative of the
race was upright, moral, a church deacon, a professional man, and a family man,
categorically not one of the black migrant, proletarian characters of *Home to
Harlem*—and certainly not a homosexual.

McKay was the most famous black radical poet of the 1920s, moreover, and
therefore had a duty to live up to. Inherent in the African American critical ad-
monishment of him is a rebuking of the author of "If We Must Die" (1919) for
selling out his ardent black radical proletarian poetic talent by producing a sensational book that would appeal to white fantasies of black sexuality and violence.
More than ten years earlier, Du Bois had pounced on a white poet for carrying
out the same transgression, Vachel Lindsay, who published *The Congo and Other
Poems* (1914), a collection that includes verse employing the jazz idiom and portraying black folk expression. Du Bois recognizes that Lindsay's poetry "is well
meant," that is, not deliberately racist, but ultimately "Mr. Lindsay knows little
of the Negro, and that little is dangerous" ("Looking" 182). Lindsay, Du Bois
indicates, is performing a kind of literary blackface, a performance of race that

is potentially as deceitful as minstrelsy's vaudeville performance of blackness. And twelve years after Du Bois demonstrated his exasperation with Lindsay, the younger generation of Harlem writers, of all people, got together to publish a surprise magazine whose stated objective was to generate a new black literature that would achieve high art principles but whose ulterior purpose was to offend race leaders like Du Bois. *Fire!!* had the desired effect (Wirth 47). It was bad enough for a white poet like Lindsay to commit the offense of perpetuating the racist myth that blacks were innately licentious and unprincipled; it was far worse for black writers.

After *Congo, Fire!!,* and *Nigger Heaven,* Du Bois was in no mood for appreciating the finer points of McKay's black proletarian novel. Delaying comment on the book for a few months, Du Bois eventually published an influential joint review of Nella Larsen's *Quicksand* (1928) and McKay's best seller in the *Crisis,* the NAACP's cultural magazine. As editor of the *Crisis,* Du Bois was in the position to consider the two novels as the hottest competitors for 1928's most valued award for best novel by a black author, the Harmon Gold prize. Du Bois praised Larsen's Talented Tenth first effort. Then, on McKay's novel, after acknowledging that the author of "If We Must Die" was "too great a poet" to produce a book without merit, he indicted McKay for gratifying the "prurient demand on the part of white folk for a portrayal in Negroes of that utter licentiousness which conventional civilization holds white folk back from enjoying" ("Browsing" 202). Du Bois comments witheringly: "Claude McKay's 'Home to Harlem' for the most part nauseates me [in comparison with Larsen's novel], and after the dirtier parts of its filth I feel distinctly like taking a bath" (202). Du Bois's now well chronicled choice of words[2] is remarkably indicative of the sexual assault victim, feeling the need to bathe in order to remove the psychological stain of sexual assault—and this is also interesting in light of his progressive endorsement of a then promising black woman novelist. Du Bois seeing himself after a get-together with McKay's book in the condition of the object of sexual violation places an interesting turn on the narrative of McKay's predicament. In other words, although in his *Crisis* review Du Bois dismisses *Home to Harlem* on the grounds that McKay's novel contradicts and undermines his role as the radical black poet of the New Negro, another all but implied level of criticism is present in Du Bois's public writing off of the novel. *Home to Harlem*'s literary cannibalism and imaginative act of racist deconstruction seemed to go unnoticed, while its transvestitism did not.

As well as the interesting aspect of his promoting Larsen, Du Bois had an investment in running down *Home to Harlem* that may be traced closer to home.

In the same year that McKay published his hit, Countée Cullen's marriage to Du Bois's daughter Yolande took place in Harlem. The wedding was the event of the 1928 season, seen as the great "coming out" of black Mecca society (Watson 80). A few weeks after the nuptials, however, Cullen boarded a cruise bound for France, setting sail across the black Atlantic. Cullen fled on his own diaspora cruise with his companion, Harold Jackman, and the most famous African American poet of the 1920s stayed in Europe for several months—among other things initiating a close relationship with McKay in Montparnasse—while Yolande remained stateside (Watson 81). The marriage dissolved in a few months. Du Bois must have been cross indeed when McKay took the Harmon Gold.

As well as his personal reason for disliking McKay's novel, Du Bois's revulsion against *Home to Harlem* must be understood as a reaction against the novel not chiefly as a representation of the Great Migration 90 percent. The moral rejoinder against the novel was not confined to arguments in critical commentaries. Although he later became a defender of gay folk, Du Bois's late 1920s reaction against McKay's novel reflected a universal unease among the black middle class during the late 1920s. In 1929, the year after *Home to Harlem* appeared, Adam Clayton Powell, influential pastor of the First Abyssinian Baptist Church of Harlem, launched a crusade to wipe out all homosexuality in Harlem (Chauncey 253–56). Powell and other black social leaders were distressed over such "spectacles in color," to use Hughes's term, as the Hamilton Club Lodge Ball at the Rockland Palace Casino, Harlem's annual mid- to late 1920s drag ball, a sensational event attended by many of the Harlem Renaissance elite, including Locke, Cullen, and Hughes, who describes "the queerly assorted throng on the dance floor" in the "black Renaissance" section of *The Big Sea*: "males in flowing gowns and feathered headdresses and females in tuxedos and box-back suits" (273).

Hughes is most interested in the combination of black and white males and their competition for an award that is quite different than the Harmon Gold. Hughes notes that the "males" appear to masquerade femininity until closer inspection. His narrative shifts from past to present verb tense, swinging from the rhetoric of the past to the vernacular of artistic depiction—to the immediacy of the image:

For the men there is a fashion parade. Prizes are given to the most gorgeously gowned of the whites and Negroes who, powdered, wigged, and rouged, mingle and compete for the awards. From the boxes these men look for all the world like very pretty chorus girls parading across the raised platform in the center of the floor. But close up, most of them look as if they need a shave, and some of their evening gowns, cut too low, show hair on the chest. (273)

On closer scrutiny the drag queens' camping, particularly as it is inflected by the integration of black and white, bares the ultimate effect of the drag ball, the *spectacle in color* itself: to stage the way in which gender is performed through costume and expression, to parody gender and sexual identity in order to expose the gender binary's intrinsic deconstruction.

Judith Butler reasons that gender consists of "citational repetitions," or the miming or imitating of hegemonic gender-related conventions, and this theory leads to her analysis of drag as a subversive act (231). Drag provides a critical language for understanding daily, public human experience. Every human subject functioning under heterosexual social conditions is compelled to perform gender, Butler argues, and is policed into doing so by the "heterosexualizing law and its expropriability" (232). The appearance of McKay's novel was but one of several causes for black middle-class anxiety over the scourge of homosexuality in Harlem during the late 1920s. In this belief structure one may locate McKay's revolt against the influence of conservative black leadership. Drag threatened the attempt on the part of black leaders to stabilize notions of normative codified black behavior because not only did drag expose gender and sex as identity performance but, even more threatening to conservative control, the parody of miscegenation enacted by the spectacle of the black and white queens queried the notion of a secure color code itself.

As for the accusation against McKay that he was rather cynically permitting himself to be transported by the success following *Nigger Heaven*, documentation contradicts this view, as McKay himself says. Responding to criticism that his blues vernacular poetry came about as a result of Van Vechten's encouragement, an irritated Hughes indicates in *The Big Sea* that he wrote the "dialect and folk-poems" (271) published in *Fine Clothes to the Jew* (1927)—a book that Hughes acknowledges was also probably given an "unfortunate" title (270)—well before he became friends with white promoter Van Vechten. In the same vein of claiming pre–Van Vechten authenticity, McKay points out in *A Long Way from Home* that despite its purported resemblance to Van Vechten's novel, *Home to Harlem* started as a piece of short fiction before *Nigger Heaven* came along, and he began developing the story, called "Back to Harlem," into a novel at the urging of his publisher (282–83). He does not acknowledge that his publishers apparently encouraged him to develop the story because Van Vechten's

Nigger Heaven was livening up the New Negro literary vogue in 1926. Nonetheless, though McKay was cognizant of the excitement and resentment stirred up by Van Vechten's novel when he published his own novel, and it may be argued that in this way he profited from the controversy, the idea that he cynically attempted to replicate *Nigger Heaven's* alleged sensational representation of black primitivism for *Home to Harlem* is unconvincing. In fact, McKay's novel carries on an adversarial dialogue with Van Vechten's, sounding the depths of its black characters as a means of confronting what he unmistakably sees as *Nigger Heaven's* incapacity for rummaging among prickly ideological questions of race, class, sex, nation, and power, despite the white author's inclusion of earnest-sounding, naturalistic passages devoted to the sociology of being black.

It is instructive when the expression "nigger heaven," used for the segregated upstairs section of a theater where African Americans were forced to sit, appears in *Home to Harlem*. Acknowledging that blacks are compelled to sit in its nigger heaven, Gin-head Susy declares that the white downtown theater is nonetheless superior to any form of entertainment available in Harlem. When she designates Harlem "nigger hell" (98–99), the reader recognizes in Susy's comment a view that *Home to Harlem* vigorously disavows. Early 1920s Harlem is nearer to Negro heaven, not hell, as the medieval symbolic perception of celestial heaven being above and black hell below is inverted. Harlem is in the vicinity of heaven because the farther the black subject travels from Harlem's heart—as in the appositely named *Pitts*burgh—the further he or she penetrates glacial Negro Perdition, the heart of whiteness. Intended to be a revolutionary novel, *Home to Harlem* is meant to poke around relentlessly in the deep structures of feeling at the other extreme from the white ceiling of *Nigger Heaven*. In McKay's inverted dream world, Paradise may be located in the nether region, not the upper reaches of the firmament.

Following this observation, it is important to be acquainted with the openness of queer culture during the generation of the New Negro in Harlem, to recognize the viability of a kind of resistant alterity of the sexual dissident during the 1920s. Social historian George Chauncey's *Gay New York: Gender, Urban Culture, and the Making of the Gay Male World, 1890–1940* (1994) suggests that Harlem queer society, the other Harlem Others, was anything but concealed or secret:

> Although Greenwich Village's gay enclave was the most famous in the city, even most white gay men thought gay life was livelier and more open in Harlem than in the Village—"Oh, much more! Much more!" the artist

Edouard Roditi declared. "Harlem was wide open," a white female impersonator recalled. The clubs would "be open all night long. Some of them
didn't *open* until midnight".... black gay men ... turned Harlem into a homosexual mecca. Denied access to most of the segregated restaurants and
speakeasies white gay men patronized elsewhere in New York, they built
an extensive gay world in their own community, which in many respects
surpassed the Village's in scope, visibility, and boldness. (244)

Calling on the renaissance's most out queer figure, Bruce Nugent, Steven Watson reiterates this view:

Advertised largely by word of mouth to those in the "life," homosexual and
lesbian nightlife thrived in Harlem. Greenwich Village and Harlem were
[New York City's] main areas that countenanced homosexual gatherings,
and homosexual Richard Bruce Nugent recalled that the two bore many
similarities. "You didn't get on the rooftop and shout, 'I fucked my wife
last night.' So why would you get on the roof and say 'I loved prick.' You
didn't. You just did what you wanted to do. Nobody was in the closet.
There wasn't any closet." (134)

Those of us who confront the archive of the New Negro Renaissance may gain
from such scholarship a vital point of departure for our own scholarly labor.
Namely, different sexuality was customary enough among many New Negroes
that declaring its existence—or even talking about it as something anomalous—
would have been utterly pointless and redundant to an insider like Nugent. To
put it in theoretical terms, the queer life was so prevalent in 1920s Harlem that
to strive to prove its existence would be an attempt to certify the presence of the
New Negro awakening itself.

From this juncture it is useful to consider Chauncey's statement that during
the 1920s "black gay men ... turned Harlem into a homosexual mecca" (244)—
in other words, as well as being the New Negro Mecca, to use James Weldon
Johnson's label,[3] Harlem was an enticement for black queer pilgrims—and how
such a comment relates to *Home to Harlem*. Queer sexuality saturates the narrative of *Home to Harlem*, permeating other ostensibly discrete systems of social
transformation, political change, and historical becoming. As McKay's is an eminent Jazz Age novel, it is useful first to consider how the text's use of black migrant music touches on issues of sexual difference. The novel twice paraphrases
a popular blues performance of sexual ambiguity sung by Bessie Smith, "Foolish

Man Blues" (1927). *Home to Harlem*'s version of Smith's lyrics are only slightly different than Smith's "drag" blues (36): "And there is two things in Harlem I don't understan'[:] / It is a bulldyking woman and a faggoty man" (36, 129).[4] In Smith's recording of the song, the speaker is "puzzled" by "two things" in Harlem: a "mannish actin' woman" and a "skippin', twistin', woman actin' man." McKay includes the pointed refrain: "Oh baby, how are you?" which transforms into the play on words, "Oh, baby, *what* are you?" (emphasis added, 36–37), chanted by dancing couples, straight and queer.

The term *drag blues* suggests the deliberate slow blues tempo and the crawl-like dance such music engendered, though in *Home to Harlem* the use of the locution *drag blues* takes on a mischievous double meaning, given the propensity of cabaret singers like Gladys Bentley, the "bulldagger who sang the blues."[5] The ample, masculine Bentley played piano at the crowded Clam House, improvising off-color lyrics to contemporary tunes hour after hour in her distinctive low growl while decked out in a white tuxedo and top hat. Alberta Hunter evidently married in order to dispel rumors of her lesbianism, and although Bentley was considered the only openly lesbian bulldagger blues singer, Ma Rainey, the Mother of the Blues, "was known to take women as lovers," and her "Prove It on Me Blues" "speaks directly to the issue of lesbianism." In "Prove It on Me Blues," she "admits to her preference for male attire and female companionship, yet dares her audience to 'prove it' on her" (Garber 331). Although one may hear the drag blues performed in the Congo Club, "Foolish Man Blues" is proscribed elsewhere: "In all the better places it was banned. Rumor said it was a police ban" (36). In "Foolish Man Blues," Smith portrays the bewilderment of the representative heterosexual, a "square," to use the "hep" Harlemite idiom of the 1920s,[6] who encounters the photonegative world of Harlem gay culture. In this new world, men and women perform sex-gender role "switchin'" as in Fats Waller's rent party tune "The Joint Is Jumpin'." In Waller's stride song, a buffet flat rent or "social whist"[7] party being "ten more times than gay" includes eating pig's feet, cutting a rug, getting loaded on bathtub gin, smoking reefers, sniffing cocaine, flaunting loaded weapons, and engaging in transvestitism. In Waller's spoken refrain, the speaker notes that someone has just entered the party, observing: "Just look at the way he's switchin'!" Through these images, the song's listener ascertains what it means to be "hep" to the "Harlem way." Smith's act of speaking for the sexually disoriented outsider in "Foolish Man Blues" is an ironic articulation to be sure, considering the blues monarch's own zest for lesbian love[8] (and McKay's appetite for Homeric male-male ardor). Within the resistant strains of the music of blues musicians like Smith and Rainey, one may discern the traces of multiple insurrectionary exertions. In *Blues Legacies and Black Feminism: Gertrude "Ma" Rainey, Bessie Smith, and Billie Holiday* (1999), Angela Davis proposes that 1920s blues women like Rainey and Smith generated a body of music that conveyed a mode of emergent black feminist counterdiscourse against masculinist violence and primacy. I would argue, moreover, that Smith's "Foolish Man Blues" parodies naive views of variable and insurgent sexuality.

Home to Harlem's queer terrain isn't limited to the referentiality of modes of cultural expression like drag balls and drag blues, however. In *Home to Harlem,* queer folk are anything but banished to the shadowy corners of the narrative. Pansies, fairies, and dandies openly attend the nightclubs in *Home to Harlem*. As well as being a fundamental work of Jazz Age literature and Harlem Renaissance writing, McKay's queer carnivalesque is among the most important chronicles of Harlem's Pansy Craze of the 1920s. The pansy, or drag queen, is so vital to Jazz Age Harlem that to leave the pansy out in reimagining the cultural landscape—as in the injustice of expunging the node of black and Red during the 1920s—is to demonstrate indifference to the lived experience of the New Negro movement, and *Home to Harlem* is the document that gaily broadcasts this bulletin. One pansy is intimately acquainted with a palace that is far from Ray's subterranean, Oriental marble dreamscape citadel: a "straw-colored boy . . . was a striking advertisement of the Ambrozine Palace of Beauty. The boy was made up with high-brown powder, his eyebrows were elongated and blackened up, his lips streaked with the dark rouge so popular in Harlem, and his carefully-straightened hair lay plastered and glossy under Madame Walker's absinthe-colored salve 'for milady of fashion and color'" (91). The cabarets that Jake, his pal Zeddy Plummer, and other straight black proletarian men and women spend their time and money in are filled with giddy queer folk, dizzy with the freedom to express themselves, and the ostensibly straight characters don't seem to be bothered greatly by this company: "All round the den, luxuriating under little colored lights, the dark dandies were loving up their pansies. Feet tickling feet under tables, tantalizing liquor-rich giggling, hands busy above" (30–31). The gay characters openly croon to one another, "Honey gal! . . . What other sweet boy is loving you now?" (31). The pansies are admittedly a bit troubled by Jake's comely presence, but not because they are fearful of being exposed among straight folk: "The pansies stared and tightened their grip on their dandies. The dandies tightened their hold on their pansies. They looked the favored Jake up and down. All those perfection struts for him. Yet he didn't seem aroused at all" (32). Jake isn't "aroused" by the pansies and dandies, but he has an arousing effect on everyone, from the women who pursue him—"the girls liked to make an argument around him"—to his straight pals: "Buddies, on the slightest provocation, were ready to fight for him" (103). Even the generally disinterested omniscient narrative finds him "beautiful": "Jake was a high favorite wherever he went. There was something so naturally beautiful about his presence that everybody liked and desired him" (103).

If he is unquestionably straight, why does Jake enter this field of colored and painted "pansies": "chocolate, chestnut, coffee, ebony, cream, yellow, [where] everybody was teased up to the high point of excitement" (32)? Jake is on the prowl: "he was going crazy. A hot fever was burning him up" (32–33), as he desperately searches for his "tantalizing brown" (27), Felice, the young sex worker he got together with in chapter 2. In Harlem, straight and queer patronize the same dives, so as Jake searches for Felice, the reader is treated to a pub crawl of Jazz Age Harlem speakeasies, juke joints, cabarets, and buffet flat social whist parties, any of which may be peopled by The Folk. Indeed, the Congo Club, with its "real throbbing little Africa," prohibits whites, but its "African spirit and color" and its queer culture function reciprocally (29).

Such imagery demonstrates how the political culture permeates the sexual, how all political and social arrangements in the text's narrative are porous, receptive to being penetrated from tacitly isolated ideological positions. Consider the minor character Billy Biasse, a gambler known as "Billy the Wolf": "Billy boasted that he had no time for women," but Billy describes himself as the "'happiest, well-feddest wolf in Harlem'" (88). Billy, "who loved to indulge in naked man-stuff talk" (324), may characterize himself so, Zeddy wryly observes, because Billy "eats his own kind" (92). Billy Biasse does communicate a *bias*, an illuminating comment the novel makes, given the ascendant society's racial bias. Although he interacts intimately with pansies, dandies, and fairies, however, Billy does not noticeably perform ludic sexual ambiguity. The tough gamer Billy Biasse is a proletarian butch queer, a black man with a gun who (like McKay) is willing to use it when he thinks he must.[9] Billy is wary of intervening in the affairs of others because he must vigilantly protect the confidentiality of his bias, and attention would jeopardize his privacy. But when "a bad nigger" attacks "that spade prof that's always there on the Avenue handing out the big stuff about niggers and their rights . . . and bolschism" near the end of the novel, Billy intercedes by landing a solid punch in the hoodlum's face and then chasing him away with his pistol (286). Whenever he appears in the novel, Billy Biasse asserts that he minds his own business, and the rest of his actions substantiate this claim. So what makes him insert himself into a risky situation, acting on behalf of someone he barely knows—as Jake steps in to help the beleaguered black scab—to defend the black Bolshevik against the thug?

In *A Long Way from Home*, McKay comments about his reading of Marx. The Marx he read while living in England and writing for the radical socialist *Workers' Dreadnought* during the early 1920s did not resemble the social movement forms found on Harlem "street-corners from which I heard [Marx's] gospel preached" (*Long Way* 69). In 1928, following up on Lenin's notion of African Americans qualifying as an "oppressed nation," the Communist International in Moscow proclaimed that blacks in the United States constituted a distinct nation, and as such they had the right to national self-determination. Communists developed the "Black Belt Theory," as Mark Naison recounts in *Communists in Harlem during the Depression* (1983), which insisted that African Americans should be provided with a separate state in the South and that blacks should secede from the United States. McKay's influence in the early 1920s in Russia contributed to this result. This is somewhat ironic because by 1928 McKay had broken with Communism to follow Trotskyism. The history of McKay's complex involvement with Communism is reflected in his portrayal of Billy. Although not as prominent as Jake and Ray, Billy may claim a share of McKay's *Home to Harlem* compound subjectivity. The reader can only surmise why Billy thinks it is his duty to come to the aid of the street-corner black Communist. The street-corner black Bolshevist is a fictional representation of "Hubert Harrison, the Harlem street-corner lecturer and agitator," one of the "Harlem Intelligentsia"—along with Cyril V. Briggs, Grace Campbell, W. A. Domingo, and Richard B. Moore—whom McKay admires in *A Long Way from Home* (108–9). The black Bolshevik provokes revolutionary transformation, as Billy Biasse, "who swerved at a different angle and was always absorbed in the games and winnings of men" (237), sets store by the insurgent nature of his own anarchistic sexual subculture.

Although Billy inhabits a substantial part of McKay's imagination, Jake and Ray collectively form the primary field of interplay in McKay's multipart mind, merging the focal position of protagonist, the "first actor," or the *agonist*—thus dialogizing the novel's central voice—into two characters. Each plays off and sings to the other, in effect creating a black proletarian duet. They express their author's views on the value of sexual freedom. It does not require an ornate decoding instrument to tease the Haitian's sexual difference out of the textual closet. In chapter 13, "One Night in Philly," Jake takes Ray to a brothel, with "cheerful and coquettish girls in colorful frocks" (190), and tells his old friend Madame Laura: "Mah friend's just keeping me company. . . . He ain't regular—

you get me?" (191). Although Ray wishes he could "be touched by the spirit of that atmosphere and, like Jake, fall naturally into its rhythm" (194), he cannot: "some strange thing seemed to hold him back from taking the girl [that Madame Laura assigns him] in his arms" (195). Plainly, spontaneous sex with a stranger does not appeal to the West Indian, and Ray, with his understanding of how capitalism consumes black workers, opposes black women being forced to trade sexual favors. But when his comrade sees that "something was between" (196) Ray and the woman, Jake observes, "Youse awful queer, chappie" (200). If this comment is not clear enough, the chapter ends with Jake volunteering the following statement: "the next Saturday night we lay over together in the big city Ise gwine to show you some real queens" (203). In light of the novel's gathering of pansies, or drag queens, and the context of Harlem's Hamilton Club Lodge drag ball, McKay clearly hopes to provoke a query in the mind of the reader who is hep to Harlem ways.

But the inversion in Harlem culture is reflected by straight society as well, particularly in the depiction of women in heterosexual relationships. With the exception of the black bourgeois Agatha, McKay's novel may be occupied exclusively with sex workers and sugar mamas, but their financial independence demonstrates the potential for self-determination available to women in New Negro culture, the freedom that Davis locates in women's blues lyrics. Susy, who belongs to "the ancient aristocracy of black cooks" (77), boots out the "cocky sweetman" (90) Zeddy when he stays out all night; in effect Zeddy has refused to abide by her command over the situation (100). Even the story within a story of Jerco and Rosalind demonstrates the gender turnaround; when Jerco is faced with the possibility of finding a job to save the sex worker Rosalind's life, he is feminized: "I ain't no good foh no job. . . . I wish I was a woman" (257). *Home to Harlem*'s frank representation of what is available to young black female migrants indicates that some women would prefer to solicit sexual favors than become domestics. Felice may have to survive as a sex worker, but at least she controls her own pecuniary and therefore social condition. Not only does the novel portray the sexual inversion of 1920s Harlem culture. It also depicts the gender role reversal of Great Migration labor and life—and through this shows another side to the opportunity for full-blown revolution among the transplanted African American minority.

Following this revolutionary potential, the narrative's representation of Ray's need to break off his engagement with Agatha, and his departure from the text, necessitate inquiry. Ray loathes Agatha's dream of marriage and children in metaphorically familiar terms: "Soon he would become one of the contented hogs in the pigpen of Harlem, getting ready to litter black piggies" (263). The imagery of hogs as being manipulated by social forces occurs throughout McKay's writings, starting in 1919:

> If we must die, let it not be like hogs
> Hunted and penned in an inglorious spot,
> While round us bark the mad and hungry dogs
> Making their mock at our accursèd lot. (*CP* 177)

To be porcine in this trope is to be held in bondage to bourgeois values: "he and Agatha were slaves of the civilized tradition" (263). Marriage, indeed heterosexual union, is slavery for Ray, and the "escape" from this enslavement is "self-love," masturbation being linked psychosocially to homosexuality (264). Agatha's aspiration to heterosexual coupling dramatically contrasts Ray's reverie of queer blue abandon: "He saw destiny working in [Agatha's] large, dream-sad eyes, filling them with the passive softness of resignation to life, and seeking to encompass and yoke him down as just one of the thousand niggers of Harlem. And he hated Agatha and, for escape, wrapped himself darkly in self-love" (264). An observation about Ray in a previous chapter sheds light on his discontent: "Ray was not happy. The sudden upset of affairs in his home country," Haiti, "had landed him into the quivering heart of a naked world whose reality was hitherto unimaginable. It was what they called in print and polite conversation 'the underworld'" (224), that is, the black underclass. Ray's disgust with heterosexual legal union is tangled up with his antipathy for the institutionalized racism in and imperialism waged by America, so he takes flight. Like McKay himself, who left his spouse at around the same time that *Home to Harlem* is set, Ray ships off on a freighter (275), departing the pages of the novel in the same way that Jake entered them: as a laborer crossing the wide black Atlantic sea to Europe. In becoming a European émigré, Ray, like McKay, enters the field of the modernist expatriate author.

In view of Ray's transatlantic passage, it would be beneficial to return to the predicament posed by the presence of *Nigger Heaven*, or the Marxist problematic presented by the black author entering the stage that is discursively occupied by the white. It is instructive that Scott Fitzgerald detected the influence of McKay's friend Sinclair Lewis on McKay's novel (*Long Way* 259) because McKay was certainly drawing on ascendant American literary resources. John Trombold has discussed *Home to Harlem*'s unmistakable sampling of Dos Passos's newsreel-like, lost generation "collective novel" (and bordering on Anarchist manifesto), *Manhattan Transfer* (1925), a fiction that is, like McKay's, also somewhat autobiographical. Most germane is the novel's Francophone black Anarchist, Congo Jake, who proclaims, "*Moi je suis anarchiste*" (193). The bootlegger's compound name designates a rejoinder to American nationalism and racism: being named "Congo" metonymizes blackness, and being "Jake" signifies feeling good, *feeling jake* (192). Both novels paint graphic, expressionist portraits of New York City as the center of the clash between international radicalism struggling for progressive change and American capitalist interests striving to undermine it.

But my interest is in retrieving the way that *Home to Harlem* bears a salient and historically significant resemblance to another lost generation literary document of the mid-1920s: Ernest Hemingway's modern expatriate novel of ritualistic primitive revelry, *The Sun Also Rises* (1926). McKay reports in *A Long Way from Home* that he met Hemingway on the Left Bank, introduced by their mutual friend, Max Eastman (249). He also says that though he lived as an émigré in Paris, he did not share the experiences of the "white expatriates," who are described as "radicals, esthetes, painters and writers, pseudo-artists, bohemian tourists": "I was a kind of sympathetic fellow-traveler in the expatriate caravan. ... Their problems were not exactly my problems. They were all-white with problems in white which were rather different from problems in black" (243).

Recent inquiries into the complexity of black literary expression during the modernist period have expanded the discussion started by Houston Baker's *Modernism and the Harlem Renaissance* (1989). Edward M. Pavlic's *Crossroads Modernism: Descent and Emergence in African American Literary Culture* (2002) argues in favor of recognizing two interconnected varieties of black modernism: "Afro-modernism" utilizes recognized modernist stylistics to elucidate black psychological experience, and "diasporic modernism" identifies importance in collective culture, developing customs inherited from West African traditions. Pavlic's work is significant, but my interest is in the radical, internationalist disposition at the center of black modernism, an innovation that even Baker underestimates. As I said in the introduction to this book, Fred Moten's study of the "aesthetics of the black radical tradition" salvages the vital memory of black Marxist modernism by offering a theory of "black modernism as intranational as well as international location" while promoting the need for adjusting the critical focus on "the politico-aesthetics of a surplus of content irreducible to identity in or for itself, but held, rather, in identity's relation to a general upheaval" (35). An analysis of the way McKay's novel responds to Hemingway's ultimately occasions a means for seeing how *Home to Harlem* ransacks Hemingway's novel, simultaneously adulating the modern/primitive play in *The Sun Also Rises* while revealing the inherent deconstruction in its (white) fleshed-out/minstrel-marginal binary hierarchy, an act of intertextual cannibalization that expresses much, as George Hutchinson's work inaugurated, about the interchange between white and black modernist literature. The black author's novel expropriates the modern master narrative to perform a radical act of black queer literary anarchism.

Like *Nigger Heaven*, Hemingway's hit appeared two years before McKay's best seller, but *The Sun Also Rises*'s cozy parallels with *Home to Harlem* are much more tangible than the intimate relations that McKay's novel had with *Nigger Heaven*. Both men's novels follow the experiences of leading characters named Jake, and their last names, designations of their *be*-ingness, are remarkably analogous, one reverberating meaningfully with the other. That is, both reveal something *essential* about the two Jakes: the midwestern white expatriate Jake Barnes in Hemingway's novel; the southern migrant man of color Jake Brown in McKay's. Both protagonists joined to fight in the Great War, signifying their roles as early twentieth-century males as historically significant, their actions as existentially consequential. Both novels chronicle the social revolution of the postwar period, an investment in a decidedly Bacchic zeal for material existence, Hemingway's away from the constraints of Prohibition, McKay's smack in the middle of the American defiance to Prohibition's restrictions.

What did McKay think of Hemingway and *The Sun Also Rises*? The answer to this inquiry requires a consideration of McKay's view of modernist literature, specifically D. H. Lawrence's novels. In one chapter of *A Long Way from Home*, McKay says that although he admires "*le maître* of the ultra-moderns" (248), James Joyce, he expresses his preference for Lawrence's fiction above writings by the avant-garde literary moderns, even saying that Lawrence is "more modern than . . . Joyce" (247). Lawrence is more modern because in the English author's writing the black writer "found confusion—all of the ferment and torment and turmoil, the hesitation and hate and alarm, the sexual inquietude and the incertitude of this age, and the psychic and romantic groping for a way out" (247), the same sort of innovation with subject matter that McKay aimed for in his own fiction. One need go no further than the co-protagonist of *Home to Harlem*, Ray, a latent writer himself who admires Lawrence as much as his creator (227). The effect of Lawrence on McKay's work is indisputable: the Laurentian disclosure of western society's hypocrisy respecting the nature of sexuality and primitive instinct, Lawrence's "blood-knowledge":

> My great religion is in a belief in the blood, the flesh, as being wiser than
> the intellect. We can go wrong in our minds. But what our blood feels
> and believes and says is always true. The intellect is only a bit and a bridle.

... We know too much. No, we *think* we know such a lot.... And we have forgotten ourselves.... We cannot *be*." (qtd. in Steele xxi)[10]

Lawrence's idea of blood-knowledge reflects Henri Bergson's "vitalist" theory of primal "*élan vital*," in *Creative Evolution* (1907):

> memory . . . is not a faculty of putting away recollections in a drawer. . . . These memories, messengers from the unconscious, remind us of what we are dragging behind us unawares. . . . What are we, in fact, what is our *character*, if not the condensation of the history that we have lived from birth—nay, even before our birth, since we bring with us prenatal dispositions? (70)

But it also exhibits Edward Carpenter's application of socialist philosophy to sex and marriage (Delavenay 99–110). McKay, who discussed Carpenter with Walter Jekyll in Jamaica, reworks Lawrence's adaptation of Carpenter.

Respecting Hemingway's writing, McKay both venerates and satirizes the white American writer, his view fluctuating with the text and even depending on the passage in a text; indeed, sometimes he does both simultaneously. In the 1937 *A Long Way from Home* he slyly mocks Hemingway's 1935 safari chronicle, *Green Hills of Africa*.[11] In a Marseilles African bar, McKay has a conversation with an unnamed Senegalese acquaintance about taking a holiday, and the African expresses a preference for Paris, an act that the Jamaican clearly interprets as colonial mimicry: black skin, white camouflage. As one who has exhausted the amusements of the expatriate bohemian Left Bank, McKay writes: "I said I didn't feel attracted to Paris, but to Africa. As I wasn't big and white enough to go on a big game hunt, I might go on a little one-man search party" (*Long Way* 295). Like Hemingway, McKay is "attracted" to Africa, but as he is a black Atlantic cruiser, the desirability is in the opportunity to make a spiritual quest, a voyage within the primal self as well as a journey without maps—not a "big game hunt." But in the same chapter that singles out Lawrence as a foremost influence on his writing, McKay confesses his "vast admiration" (250) for Hemingway (*Long Way* 249). Where the Jamaican speaks of Lawrence as suggesting to him in a general way the valuing of primitive sensation as the subject of his writing, McKay expatiates on Hemingway's impact on his understanding of the existential condition: "He has most excellently quickened and enlarged my experience of social life" (252). As for Hemingway's mid-1920s novel of modern primitives and their riotous behavior in France and Spain, McKay impersonates the World Heavyweight Champion rhetoric: "When Hemingway wrote *The Sun Also Ris-*

es, he shot a fist in the face of the false romantic-realists and said: 'You can't fake about life like that'" (251). McKay later reiterates the Hemingwayesque pugilistic image, mingling it with an earnest *afición*, sounding very much like a passage in *Death in the Afternoon* (1932), when he sets off for Barcelona accompanied by a "Senegalese boxer, who had a bout there":

> The magnificent spectacle of the sporting spirit of the Spaniards cap-
> tured my senses and made me an *aficionado* of Spain. I had never been
> among white people who gave such a splendid impression of sporting im-
> partiality, and with such grand gestures. Whether it was boxing between
> a white and black or a duel between man and beast in the arena, . . . the
> Spaniards' main interest lay in the technical excellencies of the sport and
> the best opponent winning. (295–96)

Charles Scruggs is unquestionably on the mark about McKay's use of Hemingway's novel for black radical purposes:

> McKay's sexually potent "Jake" deliberately signifies upon Hemingway's
> sexually wounded "Jake," but McKay's point is not to rewrite Hemingway.
> Rather McKay shows that "The Great War" that hovers over Paris also
> manifests itself in the racial war(s) in Harlem. Imperialism in Europe, the
> cause of the "The Great War" and the basis of its peace process, takes the
> form of colonization back home, and thus Harlem is no safer for McKay's
> Jake than the minefields in Europe were for Hemingway's. (319)

Indeed, the black expatriate author's avowed admiration mixed with his desire to satirize the white big game hunter–writer metaphorically surfaces, generating a significant intertextuality in the novel. That is to say, *Home to Harlem* carries on a metanarrativistic conversation with *The Sun Also Rises*, and unlike his whole-sale dismissal of *Nigger Heaven*, McKay, setting out on an imaginative "little one-man search party," simultaneously idolizes and lances Hemingway's mod-ernist master narrative. Jake Barnes is wounded in the war, leaving him sexually impotent, the imagery reflecting western male, late modernist dissipation, the modern dispossession of access to species regeneration—the hero Jake Barnes cannot procreate with Lady Brett Ashley—as well as spiritual renewal, in effect putting into fictional form, while itself ironically also parodying, Eliot's poem *The Waste Land* (1922). Hemingway's novel depicts the experiences of bourgeois Anglo-American and British expatriates who feel morally bereft and psychologi-cally devitalized following the momentous, intense, and therefore self-defining experience of war, its collection of characters therefore existing at the exhausted closing stages of a history reduced to rubble. Consequently, the wine-soaked lost generation of *The Sun Also Rises* must seek out in a foreign location moments of authentic, ritualistic, primitive, Dionysian stimulation as a pungent tonic against the festering consequences of modernist, bourgeois capitalist alienation: an estrangement from true sensation and a recoverable origin. During the 1920s Anglo-American expatriate intellectuals like Hemingway and Gertrude Stein, who urged her young apprentice to visit the Iberian country, romantically thought of Spain as a savage, blood-obsessed society, observably executed by the ritual of the *corrida* (series of bullfights), as the site of the linguistic, national, cultural, and even racial Other. The pure moment in *The Sun Also Rises* is the San Fermín bullfighting *feria* in Iruña, or Pamplona, with its testosterone-charged running of the bulls, set in the untamed Basque region of Navarra, a fiesta that is depicted as a magnificent debauch and engagement with death—and therefore an opportunity for the vital retrieval of the almost totally vanished instinctual. While McKay conveys in *A Long Way from Home* his sarcastic critique of Stein as a writer who "identifies Negro with Nothingness" (348), he cannibalizes Hemingway's idiom of meaninglessness under modernity, as in "A Clean, Well-Lighted Place," the story in *Winner Take Nothing* (1933) that articulates death as *nada*.

In contrast with Jake Barnes's sexual (and modern) impotence, Jake Brown's lusty libido figures as the antithesis of teleological modern disintegration—of Hemingway's *nada*. For McKay, the condition of being a constituent of the black proletariat itself provides the means for dodging the bullets of modern impotence and its inexorable masculine incapacitation. Moreover, Brown deserts the war because as a black man he was prevented from participating in the fighting according to institutionalized racist policy. Indeed, the Great War was for Jake "a white folks' war" (107). Brown's frustration marks a dramatic contrast with Barnes's emasculating war wound—the signs of history and ideology are scored on the bodies of the two protagonists in radically different typographies. Mimicking the *agon* of whiteness, Ray is "conscious of being black and impotent" (154), a political condition, as Fanon says. This impotence signifies his incapacity to make contact with the instinctual, the essence of blackness, due to the infection of the modern world, the cultivation of the intellect, an act that results in the civilizing of and therefore obliteration of the primitive life force. Ray's incapacity is also articulated through his closeted sexual difference, as Jake Brown, in contrast with Jake Barnes, has no psychological complex, whereas Ray is prevented from consummating his desire for happiness by his sexual tendency, thus engendering a different take on modernist impotence.

Indeed, with the exception of the intellectually smothered and ambivalent

Ray, McKay's black proletarian characters in *Home to Harlem* experience genuine emotions; they are nearly impervious to modern angst. Their daily lives are absorbed in gambling, jazz, brutality, alcoholic indulgence, the use of narcotics and stimulants, and an emancipated, distinctly post-Victorian, Laurentian devotion to Eros and *jouissance*. The biggest problem that blacks have is white oppression and repression: "white folks can't padlock niggers outa joy forever" (336). In order to experience authentic sensation, the constituents of Hemingway's *génération perdue* must relocate themselves among the foreign Other, where they find genuine instinctual feeling in the novel as open-ended travelogue, the modernist act of reviving the narrative of exploration for the modern western subject's tourism, in the manner of Gauguin, experiencing life among the savage Other (Holcomb, "Travels" 297–300). McKay's central characters, conversely, are the visited exotics, from the point of view of the white majority, inhabiting the alien site, Harlem, visited by whites looking for a bargain-priced thrill among the racial Other. White women are especially enamored of Harlem: "They were wearied of the pleasures of the big white world, wanted something new—the primitive joy of Harlem" (109). And this takes place within the pages of a picaresque narrative. Whereas for alienated Anglo moderns, the sun only rises in foreign lands, for McKay's black characters, home as nocturnal Harlem signifies the voyage toward realizing genuine feeling among one's own kind. What makes Harlem heavenly is its "colorful" diversity: "All the various and varying pigmentation of the human race were assembled there: dim brown, clear brown, rich brown, chestnut, copper, yellow, near-white, mahogany, and gleaming anthracite" (289). But it is also a matter of safety in numbers. When Jake intervenes to help the black scab being attacked by white strikers, he says, "Come on, let's haul bottom away from here to Harlem" (47).

The two novels ultimately present fundamental differences of race and racism, nation and nationalism. Replying radically to the assumed racist superiority written into the anxiety of influence, McKay's strategic mimicry engages trenchantly with Hemingway's carnivalesque novel, cannibalizing from the perspective of the essentialized authentic primitive. Two black characters emerge in Hemingway's text. It is fitting that the shatterer of the "Great White Hope" myth, Jack Johnson, appears in a list of "big niggers" (66) in *Home to Harlem*, as the second black figure in *The Sun Also Rises* is the "noble-looking nigger" prizefighter, a kind of Jack Johnson figure who is chased out of Vienna by early fascists. But the first black character in *The Sun Also Rises*, Joe Zelli's "nigger drummer" who plays for Brett Ashley and her *bal musette* crowd, concerns me here, as Hemingway's literary performance acts as a form of Jazz Age minstrelsy.

The narrative conveys the black drummer's minstrelsy by the economical modifier "all teeth and lips." Whether or not Hemingway based the caricature on an actual drummer at Zelli's Jazz Club in the early 1920s (Svoboda 1), practically the same percussionist shows up in *Home to Harlem*, perhaps before he made his way across the black Atlantic to the Rive Gauche watering hole of Brett Ashley and her retinue. Eric Lott in *Love and Theft: Blackface Minstrelsy and the American Working Class* (1993) says, "The black mask offered a way to play with collective fears of a degraded and threatening—and male—Other while at the same time maintaining some symbolic control over them" (25). Yet Lott also identifies a singular form of "love" in many whites' response to blackface minstrelsy. *Love and Theft* relies quite rightly on Ralph Ellison's elucidation of the meaning of blackface, but McKay is also a valuable, earlier source on the subject of minstrelsy. His essay "He Who Gets Slapped," published in the *Liberator* in 1921, is a review of the 1915 play by the Russian playwright Leonid Andreyev, *He, the One Who Gets Slapped*. (Diarist Korney Chukovsky, an acquaintance who noted McKay's presence at the Russian home of Mayakovsky in the early 1920s, authored a book on Andreyev.) A sardonic turn on Andreyev's incessantly slapped clown, McKay's "Blackface" is the author himself, "shunted upstairs" by a stammering manager (*Long Way* 144). McKay, "apart, alone, black and shrouded in blackness," is compelled to sit in the balcony, "nigger heaven," while reviewing a comic play for a respected American periodical. A paragraph of the essay is reprinted in *A Long Way from Home*: "Poor, painful black face, intruding into the holy places of the whites. How like a specter you haunt the pale devils! . . . How can they bear your presence, Blackface, great, unappeasable ghost of Western Civilization!" (145). In *Home to Harlem,* McKay converts Hemingway's *bal nègre* musician from a blackface minstrel, performed like a string-puppet by a white literary master, into a Harlem luminary: "What a place Conner's was from 1914 to 1916 . . . ! And the little ebony drummer," like an African work of art, "beloved of every cabaret lover in Harlem, was a fiend for rattling a drum!" (28).

Du Bois faulted *Home to Harlem* for idealizing primitive instincts among the black proletariat of the 1920s. But it may be vaunted as well as an act of responding to and mocking the assumption of modernist authors like Eliot and Hemingway that the modern subject suffers a fait accompli estrangement from authentic experience. For the white modernists, the modern subject is categorically white and bourgeois. But the ideology of savagery and primitiveness is a two-way street. In the end, Hemingway's desperate, spiritually spent characters are lodged in history's Hotel Terminus, where McKay's Great Migration becoming-souls are impatient to get history on the road, its home, its grand central station, being Harlem. Yet it is important to understand that McKay's literary parody and critique of Hemingway is not a retaliation taken against a racist white writer. McKay certainly did not shrink from exposing literary racism and cultural imperialism among white authors, including writers whose work he admired, like H. G. Wells. When he asserts that Hemingway "most excellently quickened and enlarged my experience of social life" (252), he is not demonstrating the predicament of mimicry, of absorbing white hegemony. In fact, he is doing the opposite: articulating and marking out territory for his own voice, his own modern subjectivity. *The Sun Also Rises* achieved one of his own aims, to discredit "the false romantic-realists," insisting: "You can't fake about life like that" (251).

McKay's narrative of being in Spain with the "Senegalese boxer" samples with approbation Bill Grady's story of being in Vienna and the "noble-looking nigger" fighter, and McKay loots Hemingway's representation of Spanish society as having "a splendid impression of sporting impartiality, and with such grand gestures." McKay takes his direction from Hemingway's south-pointing compass. Spanish culture is, as in Hemingway's novel, antithetic to Germanic, or "Nordic," to use a word McKay employed: "The magnificent spectacle of the sporting spirit of the Spaniards captured my senses and made me an *aficionado* of Spain." And like Hemingway's romanticizing of the Spanish, he "had never been among white people" who showed such "impartiality" (296). He cannibalizes Hemingway's carnivalesque in order to write his own narrative of modern primitives, or primitive moderns—his own manifesto on experiencing authentic feeling while compelled to exist under the effects of modern civilization. It is instructive that, after Spain, Hemingway wrote about British East Africa as a site for the white hunter to track down a sense of the authenticity, to contact the primal core of the self. McKay also traveled to Africa, though ironically he did not make it to *Black Africa* in his search for authenticity but instead contented himself with exploring the outer reaches of the black diaspora, North Africa: "As I wasn't big and white enough to go on a big game hunt, I might go on a little one-man search party."

Finally, although Hemingway is instinctively identified as the personification of masculinist, homosocial literary art, the most significant way in which *Home to Harlem* draws on *The Sun Also Rises* is in plundering Hemingway's blurring of sexual and gender identity, *The Sun Also Rises*'s deconstruction of sex/gender structures as *natural*. This includes Brett Ashley's androgyny and expropriation of masculine traits; Robert Cohen's cowardly machismo; Pedro Romero's obsolete masculinism; and the novel's thoughtful comment on Jake Barnes's lack of

identifiable heterosexual relationship signaling the alarming possibility of homosexuality. *Home to Harlem*'s wide array of queer characters—from the most
marginal pansies to Ray's feelings of sexual anxiety—may outstrip Hemingway's
racy novel, but their very advent validates the manifestation of *The Sun Also Rises*. Thus is McKay's novel an embodiment of, a manifesto on, the art of sex radicalism. The act of appropriating and inverting Hemingway's bracing bohemian
novel of existential hopelessness ultimately makes it possible for McKay to over-
turn the race hierarchy built into the white modernist blackface minstrel literary
act, revolutionizing the modern novel by seizing the stage without makeup. His
literary act attempts to perform the authenticity of the New Negro by presenting
a complex black co-protagonist, Ray, a queer black anarchist whose "dream" is to
write the novel the reader is reading. No more subversive act could be conceived
than to produce a little black bomb camouflaged as a racy modernist novel fashioned by a black man.

    In addition, it is useful to linger over McKay's representation of the white
expatriates as "radicals, esthetes, . . . bohemian tourists" and his location as "a
kind of sympathetic fellow-traveler in the expatriate caravan" (*Long Way* 243).
McKay's choice of words—"fellow-traveler"—iterates his narrative about Berlin
and Paris and his departure from Moscow, where he participated influentially in
the Communist International's 1922 congress. The political feature of being a fellow traveler among the Left Bank expatriates is an intriguing aspect of McKay's
queer black Marxist writing, most radically detectable in his character Ray.

    The extratextual feature of McKay's other co-protagonist adds another level to
Home to Harlem's multilayered metanarrativistic intensity. Whereas Jake Brown
resonates intertextually with Jake Barnes, "pure ebony" (127) Ray is the most recognizable self-representation of McKay himself in the novel, as the assonance of
Mc*Kay* and *Ray* indicates. Other appreciable similarities loom apparent, beginning with Ray being from the Caribbean and immigrating to the United States.
As for the difference in their Commonwealth or national background, Ray is a
Haitian, not a Jamaican or a subject of the British West Indies, like McKay, for
literary and historical reasons. Jamaica was a "Crown Colony," its affairs administered by Great Britain, while Haiti was the target of U.S. imperialism against
blacks in the Caribbean, which led to the loss of its independence as a result of
the U.S. invasion in 1915 and subsequent occupation. What's more, Haiti was the
site of the San Domingo slave rebellion and effort to establish the first black republic in the late eighteenth and early nineteenth centuries, an undertaking that
was ruthlessly crushed by the Napoleonic government, thus historicizing slave
resistance and emergent black separatist nationalism and tying these strands to-

gether with modern black anticolonial struggle. As for their parallels as West Indian immigrants, McKay came to America for two reasons: to attend college and to strive as a poet in a major literary market. The first endeavor was only marginally successful, as McKay spent two months at Booker T. Washington's Tuskegee Institute in 1912, then moved to Kansas State College. In this history one may locate Ray, who attends Howard University, a black college, and is unable to finish, just as McKay left Tuskegee and did not complete a degree program at Kansas State. As McKay was disappointed in Tuskegee's capitulation to white supremacy, Ray thinks of Howard University as a black penal complex run by white keepers. And like McKay, who remained married for many years after abandoning his spouse, Ray flees from his relationship with Agatha, boarding a ship, again like McKay, bound for Europe.

As McKay did during the early 1920s, Ray yearns for success in the second endeavor, becoming a writer: "Ray had always dreamed of writing words some day. Weaving words to make romance, ah!" (225). As Ray ponders the literature that shaped his consciousness, including the abolitionist manifesto *Uncle Tom's Cabin* and several socially conscious Dickens novels, then the free-thinking radical writers, Shaw, Ibsen, Anatole France, and H. G. Wells, and finally the world-shattering moderns, Joyce and Lawrence, the reader discovers his enthusiasm for Bolshevism: "He had lived on that brilliant manna that fell like a flame-fall from those burning stars. Then came the great mass carnage in Europe," the Great War, "and the great mass revolution in Russia," the Bolshevik Revolution's "ultimate splendor" (225–26). But Stalinism shattered the potential for a new Russian literary revolution: "Only the Russians of the late era seemed to stand up like giants in the new. . . . When he read them now he thought: Here were elements that the grand carnage swept over and touched not" (228). What Ray and McKay admire about America is its manufacturing of modernity, its strapping vision of the future and impatience with the dross of the past: "Thank God and Uncle Sam that the old dreams were shattered" (228). Ray's awe reiterates McKay's sonnet "America": "Her vigor flows like tides into my blood, / Giving me strength erect against her hate" (ll.5–6, *CP* 153). In view of his bitterness over the Marines invading Haiti and killing his brother in the street, along with his rage against domestic American racism, Ray's admiration for America is mixed with the bite of irony. McKay's "A Capitalist at Dinner" (1919) establishes early his Marxist revolutionary view of western economics:

> Great God! if creatures like this money-fool,
> Who hold the service of mankind so cheap,
> Over the people must forever rule,

Driving them at their will like helpless sheep—
Then let proud mothers cease from giving birth;
Let human beings perish from the earth. (ll.9–14, *CP* 136)

A capitalist order cannot offer a solution to racism because it is regulated by a brotherhood that imposes imperialism and nationalism.

The dream imagery imparts a language of transformation. Ray's thoughts of becoming a writer come in the way of two fragments that make a thread of nouns: "Dreams of patterns of words achieving form" (227), and "Dreams of making something with words" (228). The fragments unite the formless act of writing "something" with the Haitian's hazy (indistinct to him if not the reader) queer dream of the blue citadel. Ray's dream is to write a novel with "dark desire all over the pages" (228). That is, he would like to achieve what his hero Tolstoy and other literary masters accomplished for their time—a literature that explores the reality of *dark desire*, in all of its signings: the appetites of the prerational, primordial self; the aspirations of black proletarian struggle; and the ardor for the sexual fulfillment that unifies the signings. The following passage from *Home to Harlem*, its depiction of the jazz pianist's "sacred frenzy of phallic celebration" and "remote scarce-remembered past," illustrates my point, the link between art and the primeval:

> The piano-player had wandered off into some dim, far-away, ancestral source. . . . Far, far away from music-hall syncopation and jazz, he was lost in some sensual dream of his own. . . . These notes were naked acute alert. Like black youth burning naked in the bush. Love in the deep heart of the jungle. . . . Simple-clear and quivering. Like a primitive dance of war or of love. (196–97)

For McKay, the romantic rapture of writing was linked to the ecstasy of radical socialist revolution as it interconnected with, indeed, was inseparable from, the interwar sexual insurrection, and this integrated thrill thrives in Ray. In 1929, the year following *Home to Harlem*, Walter Benjamin wrote, "as we know, an ecstatic component lives in every revolutionary act. This component is identical with the anarchic" ("Surrealism" 189). In the shared dialectical of modernism, the rhetorics of art, the speech of the primordial, and the idiom of anarchic revolution cannot exist independently.

Brought into being as a result of his exile and anger at U.S. imperialism, Ray's Marxism is oriented in intellectual and romantic notions of the intersections of writing and revolution, elevated ideals that the southern migrant Jake, as a member of the black working class, does not have access to. Yet, because of his lifetime of laboring in black toil, Jake engages in cultural work that Ray is not sufficiently prepared to undertake. When Jake takes a short job as a longshoreman only to find that he has been duped into scabbing, he finds that the situation is complicated by the fact that the whites' own corrupt union does not support its striking workers. Jake has belonged to a union in Philadelphia, moreover, but New York unions disregard the needs of black workers. When a white organizer carrying a little red book invites Jake to join the strike, Jake responds, "I won't scab, but I ain't a joiner kind of fellah [either]. I ain't no white folks' nigger and I ain't no poah white's fool" (45). McKay himself was a member of the Industrial Workers of the World "Marine Transport Workers Industrial Union 510, whose Philadelphia leader, Ben Fletcher, was the best known of the IWW's black organizers" (Cowl 7). Until white workers and their labor institutions in New York are ready to accept blacks as equals, as the IWW did when McKay joined their ranks in 1919, Jake will not submit himself to their authority. Yet, at the same time, and not in contradiction to this need, the black Marxist street-corner orator, the "prof," hopes to persuade blacks to ally themselves with Marxist internationalism, and this action must be safeguarded, as Billy demonstrates with a fist and gun. It is necessary to add as well that the union in Philadelphia that Jake belonged to was probably the radical, secret Wobblies. Jake is not anti-union; he is against a labor organization that excludes or makes subalterns of black workers.

It is instructive that, although Jake is intolerant of lesbianism, his most spirited criticism is aimed at sanctimonious "educated 'dicktees,'" the black professional class, for their hypocrisy toward liberated sexuality. Jake agrees with Miss Lavinia Curdy, who says, "They [educated dicktees] all talks and act as if loving was a sin, but I tell you straight, I wouldn't trust any of them after dark with a preacher" (164). Though educated and therefore disturbed by modern-world anxieties, Ray, as an autobiographical version or face of McKay himself, shares this view:

> modern education is planned to make you a sharp, snouty, rooting hog. A Negro getting it is an anachronism. We ought to get something new, we Negroes. But we get our education like—like our houses. When the whites move out, we move in and take possession of the old dead stuff. Dead stuff that this age has no use for. (243)

McKay's two core characters become acquainted on the same provisional territory. When Jake and Ray first meet, Ray is reading Alphonse Daudet's *Sapho* (1884). Talking about the French naturalist's novel leads to Jake quoting Smith's

"Foolish Man Blues" (128–29). In contrast with *Home to Harlem*'s frank delineation of queer characters, Daudet's novel must diplomatically hint at sexual divergence, its female protagonist, Fanny, having had a lesbian affair before the novel's recounted narrative takes place. The novel must muffle lesbianism by forcing the lesbian background of its principal female character to lurk in the narrative's past. At the moment when Jake encounters Ray, "The waiter was reading the scene between Fanny and Jean when the lover discovers the letters of his mistress's former woman friend and exclaims: 'Ah *Oui . . . Sapho . . . tout la lyre . . .*" (ellipsis in original, 128), thus the use of Sappho in the title of a novel set in Belle Époque France. Fanny's lesbianism is present through her past, thereby disturbing the stability of the present heterosexed narrative, slyly informing the forbidden heterosexual passion between Fanny and Jean.

The novel was familiar to the bohemian crowd during the 1920s, most likely influencing the controversial lesbian love poetry of Edna St. Vincent Millay (Burch 277–79), a white modern whose acquaintance McKay made in Montparnasse during the 1920s (*Long Way* 258). In *Home to Harlem* Jake expresses his distaste for lesbians: "Tha's what we calls bulldyker in Harlem. . . . Them's all ugly womens" (129). But Ray ardently disagrees: "'Not *all*. And that's a damned ugly name. . . . Harlem is too savage about some things. *Bulldyker,*' the waiter stressed with a sneer" (129). At this moment Jake recalls the controversial lyrics of Smith's "Foolish Man Blues." This is Ray's first lesson for the African American proletarian. Examining the French-text *Sapho*, Jake is "like a child that does not know its letters" (129). Consequently, the sexual and political revolution immanent in 1920s bohemian lesbianism—the reminder of such literary lesbians as Millay, Collette, Gertrude Stein, Djuna Barnes, Radclyffe Hall, and Natalie Clifford Barney[12]—sets the complexion of their comradeship, the pair's union, for the remainder of the novel. Sappho's "story gave two lovely words to modern language," Ray instructs: "Sapphic and Lesbian" (129). The very language that Ray and Jake speak is made pleasurable and political by the insertion of the lesbian.

This exchange, where Ray corrects Jake's unenlightened view of divergent sexuality, sets in motion Ray's—and the text's—didacticism: his teaching of Jake, the unlettered African American. Jakes incarnates the green heterosexual character in Smith's drag blues, the very drag blues he quotes, perplexed by the gender "switchin'," the "mannish actin' woman / and . . . woman actin' man"—or in *Home to Harlem*'s paraphrase, the "bulldyking woman and a faggoty man." And though he is unquestionably aware of the meaning of being black in U.S. society, he is uninformed about the historical and political constituents of being black. That is, Jake is as mystified by Ray's being both a foreigner and black as he is by the specter of Harlem homosexuality: "ain'tchu one of us, too?" (131). In actual fact, Ray both is and is not "one of us."

Ray sits Jake down and starts at the beginning, with modern black history, lecturing on how the "universal spirit of the French Revolution" propelled the Haitian slave rebellion during the late eighteenth and early nineteenth centuries (131). Jake learns of Jean-Jacques Dessalines and Toussaint L'Ouverture, and Ray even recites verbatim Wordsworth's protest sonnet devoted to preserving the memory of the dead San Domingo slave general, whose spectral persistence of memory evokes the spirit of Romantic revolution (132–33). Ray also enlightens Jake on the history of Africa and the Caribbean, replacing Jake's cultural hegemonic nationalist "yankee contempt for poor foreigners," like West Indians, or "monkey-chasers," with a newfound Pan-Africanism. As Ray lectures, Jake feels "like a boy who stands with the map of the world in colors before him" (134). Africa takes shape in his eyes; Jake learns of the "black kings" and their struggle for independence: "Premphreh of Ashanti, Tofa of Dahomey, Gbehanzin of Benin, Cetawayo of Zulu-land, Menelik of Abyssinia" (135), royals and realms that will be summoned forth later in the form of Ray's ecstatic blue dream, notwithstanding its express Orientalist setting. The education of Jake Brown returns to more recent history—Liberia, "founded by American Negroes," and Abyssinia, "besieged by the hungry wolves of Europe" (135)—thus stirring up in Jake an awareness of the modern horrors of colonialism and imperialism, exhibitions of white domination and brotherly toil in faraway lands that touch on his own struggles as an African American worker. In the opening pages of the novel, as Jake is making his way home to Harlem on a tramp steamer, he feels contempt for Arab fellow seamen (2). His disdain reflects an internalization of western superiority, the very ideology of racial hierarchy that impedes his right to equal pay and position in labor unions. Ray's cultural lecture provides Jake with the means for probing his own arrogance toward foreigners, particularly brown and black ones.

Ray concludes his lecture with a comment on how history impinges on the life of the individual subject, himself, how "Uncle Sam put me here" in America: the 1915 and 1916 U.S. military invasions and then ongoing occupation of Haiti. Ray's father, "an official down there," protested, as did his brother, for which the "American marines killed him in the street" (138).[13] Ray's narrative of Manifest Destiny–motivated violence against his family resembles the story of the assassination of a popular Haitian insurgent organizer: "To break the back of the resistance, Marines in blackface surprised and killed the rebel leader Charlemagne Péralte" (Black 29). The anxiety over blacks governing themselves is reflected in the white American racist Imaginary, the mythic memory of the Haitian slave revolution of the late eighteenth century: "Southerners spoke of a 'second Haiti'" (Black 38). It is not coincidental that Haiti was invaded in the same year as the appearance of D. W. Griffith's film *The Birth of a Nation* (1915), as the blackface epic melodrama portrays black political involvement in the Reconstruction-era South as corrupt and unnatural. Because U.S. military occupation forces imprisoned his father, Ray was forced into exile in the country that caused his deracination, the United States, a bitterly ironic situation given assumptions about American democracy and Manifest Destiny. Learning of the hypocrisy of American racism and imperialism occurs following the revelation of sexual freedom in *Home to Harlem*, connecting the value of political insurgency with sexual liberation. Jake enters Ray's gorgeous "dream" of "varied colors":

> Jake felt like one passing through a dream, vivid in rich, varied colors. It was a revelation beautiful to his mind. That brief account of an island of savage black people, who fought for collective liberty and was struggling to create a culture of their own. A romance of his race. . . . How strange! (134)

Engaged in an encounter with a didactic novel, a black anarchist manifesto, the reader of *Home to Harlem*, whether black or white, is put into the position of Jake, illuminated by suppressed history, knowledge forced into the shadows, like homosexuality—like radical socialism. Jake is already disposed toward anarchic behavior, his "primitive passion for going against regulation" (44), and the dream provides him with the means for imagining ways to merge the condition of being black with that of the anarchic. Though discontented with the way that the white union treats black workers, Jake supports syndicalist action. When Zeddy refuses to observe union rules about scabbing and Jake reprimands his friend for his behavior, Zeddy accuses Jake of "gettin' religion," of supporting black-white solidarity (49).

Considering the blending of queer, black, and anarchist proletarianism in his first published novel, it is useful to consider what else McKay was producing when he brought out *Home to Harlem*. Almost all discussions of McKay's poetry concentrate on verse written during the late 1910s and early 1920s, largely because it was during this period that he nearly exclusively wrote poetry, and the lyrics he produced include his most recognized. Poems like "If We Must Die," "America," and "The Tropics in New York" are among his best. Although he published the short story collection *Trial by Lynching* (1925) in the Soviet Union, it was not until the mid-1920s—urged by friends like Louise Bryant

(Lewis, *When Harlem* 140)—that he seriously decided to write fiction. In 1926 he wrote and then destroyed a manuscript he referred to as "Color Scheme." But the archival record disproves the assumption that he stopped writing poetry in the early 1920s (Maxwell, Introduction xxii–xxiii). Most notably, he wrote the cycle of poems he called "The Clinic," circa 1923, produced while he was laid up for a syphilis treatment. Included in this extraordinarily grim but inspired batch of Baudelairean lyrics is "The Desolate City," a poem inflected by wasteland imagery but more explicitly resembling the Victorian poet James Thomson's Dantesque "City of Dreadful Night" (1882). McKay singles out Thomson's poem in his memoir: "it was one of the first books of poems that Mr. Jekyll presented to me and . . . for a long time I was haunted by the spirit of the strange music of the desert song and the pessimistic feeling of the whole poem, which acted like a damper on my naturally happy disposition" (*Long Way* 19). "The Desolate City" anticipates McKay's next poetry cycle, "The Cities" (c. 1934), including such poems as "Berlin," "Moscow," and "Harlem." In 1943 McKay wrote the aptly titled sequence "The Cycle," and indeed continued to write poetry virtually up until his death in 1948.

It is enlightening to look at verse McKay was producing around the time he was moving toward and then writing *Home to Harlem* for what the poems say about another shift McKay was supposed to be making: away from Marxism. What is most interesting about "The Years Between" (*CP* 208–22),[14] his mostly missing poetry from 1925 through 1934, is indeed the way the poems reveal McKay's capacity for finding the bonds *between*: the mingling of sexual difference, black struggle, and, during a time when by his own account he was supposed to have disavowed leftist politics, a devotion to Marxist revolution. "We Who Revolt" (1925) takes the first-person plurality of "If We Must Die" and once more gives it a Leninist vanguardist pluralism, the *we* being a group of bohemian cultural workers living, as homosexuals must, at the edge of existence: "We who revolt against life's iron bars, / And teach the world's unthinking how to think, / . . . And urge the multitude toward the brink / Of freer worlds—what do we hope to gain?" (ll.1–5, *CP* 208). The "we" of this poem "live" like saints—that is to say, bohemian poets—"careless of clothes or victuals, / And of all things that tend to blind and bind" (ll.9–10). And being revolutionary bohemian poets means practicing the proletarianism one preaches: "We who make hymns, high music of revolt, / Who work at words like sailors at the ropes, / So that they strike men like a thunder bolt" (ll.21–23). By the conclusion of the poem, the objectives of revolution seem hopeless, "Yet we must sound the call and onward press, / For tyranny eternal must be fought" (ll.34–35, 209).

In the same year that McKay published *Home to Harlem*, 1928, he found the time to write a poem that invokes "The International Spirit," the final stanza approximating the best of Wordsworth or Shelley:

The nations shall be stricken at thy word,
And grand old prejudices crumble down,
That ancient pride in warring breasts has stirred.
The noblest men shall work for thy renown.
Thy truest heralds do not fear the frown
Of legioned bigots leagued by fear and spurred
To crush thy truth, but more the shouting clown,
That standard-flocking of the sheeplike herd. (ll.17–24, *CP* 216)

Three years after the melancholy romanticism of "We Who Revolt," he is more optimistic about international radical transformation, despite the anxiety about the double trouble of capitalist manufactured consent and fascist repressive state apparatuses: "That standard-flocking of the sheeplike herd." R.J.B. Bosworth's biography of Benito Mussolini delineates the succession of events. Two years after Mussolini became premier of Italy in 1922, he outlawed all labor unions except those that were fascist, and two years after that he dissolved the parliament. By March 1928 Il Duce had abolished the right to hold free elections, and in May he ended women's rights in Italy. It is significant that the last item in Ray's outline of history is the Italian aggression against Haile Selassie's Ethiopia, or Abyssinia, "besieged by the hungry wolves of Europe." Although it would not be until 1935 that Italy invaded Ethiopia, by 1928 it was clear what the fascists truly intended as they began to move into Ethiopia to establish military posts, manifestly flouting a friendship treaty Mussolini had signed with Selassie. In 1938 C.L.R. James would also unite the struggle of the Haitian slave rebels Toussaint L'Ouverture, Jean-Jacques Dessalines, and Henri Christophe with those of modern anticolonialism and international leftism in a "classic of Marxist historiography, *The Black Jacobins*" (Callinicos 63).

Like *Home to Harlem*'s Ray, McKay in "The International Spirit" is made jubilant by the idea that the "nations" would quake in the presence of Communist revolution, but he is simultaneously apprehensive about the turn that mass social movements have taken in Europe, where he has been living for the past six years. The "standard-flocking of the sheeplike herd" includes the rise of Stalinism, to McKay's Left Opposition thinking circa 1928 a potentially equal threat to world revolution as the development of fascism. As James would assert nearly ten years later in the black Trotskyist *World Revolution, 1917–1936: The Rise and Fall of the Communist International* (1937), Stalinism was a perversion of revolutionary history. In "Petrograd: May Day, 1923," a "Cities" poem written to commemorate not just May Day but the day he departed Russia, armed with revolutionary ideas, McKay voices his love of the Soviet nation: "in the years, the wondrous years to come, / The heart of youth in every land will leap / For Russia that first made national the day—/ The embattled workers' day—the first of May" (ll.37–40, *CP* 231). By the late 1920s his commitment to Mother Russia has not abated; his hostility toward its distortion of socialism is a later expression of his dedication to the USSR.

It is imperative to consider how McKay developed the idea that "the international spirit" would effect the end of nationalist mystical and political power and its manufactured hegemony, racism ("grand old prejudices" and "legioned bigots"). A means toward exhuming this buried intelligence lies in dusting off the author's Bureau of Investigation dossier. In light of the present literary discussion, it is instructive that a running fretfulness in McKay's FBI file is the conviction that the black author will return from Russia in 1923 to indoctrinate uneducated blacks into Communist politics. What these records reveal about McKay's life corresponds to his fiction; the organic intellectual Ray provides Jake with a Marxist cultural education, the new "education" that New Negroes "ought to get" (243), revealing how African Americans are linked historically and politically with their African brothers and sisters. He does not follow Trotsky's dictum, however, that the appeal of Communism must be made against "black chauvinism," if indeed the idea of blacks participating in world revolution was primarily Trotsky's and not McKay's five years before *Home to Harlem*. Ray blends the history and struggle of African and diaspora people with the international struggle against imperialism, promoting in Jake's mind the idea that he belongs to a great race as well as a global struggle of workers.

But the relationship between Ray and Jake is more complex than that of "professor" and pupil. Ray suffers from deep ambivalence about his brother migrant-class Negroes, as chapter 11's insomniac night reveals: "These men claimed kinship with him. They were black like him. Man and nature had put them in the same race. He ought to love them and feel them. . . . They were all chain-ganged together and he was counted as one link" (153). As a result of American imperialism, Ray has been cast into the world of the black lumpenproletariat, a fate he laments several times in the narrative. Yet in his ambivalence he also wishes that he could overcome this aversion to his black brothers—and Jake is Ray's *underground* contact. It is vital to recognize that Jake's presence triggers Ray's orgiastic dream of human concert, of overcoming the void between self and Other. Jake is Ray's dream of "love," of devotion beyond boundaries of class, education, geography, nationality, and even within race. Jake is also Ray's access into his own blackness, his négritude made flesh, and therefore Ray's radical *agent* of salvation, as Jake saves the black strikebreaker. Reflecting Bergson's notion of "preknowledge," while also reflecting McKay's version of the Socialist Realist regard for the "folk," the southern migrant African American *primitive* lives naturally, uncontaminated by bourgeois neuroses, the existential embodiment of the extolling of Communist folkways, and for this Ray envies Jake. Moreover, the warrior Jake, prevented from fighting in the Great War, is capable of engaging in cultural work at a level that the cerebral Ray is unsuited to perform: physically fighting the race war, made evident by Jake's intervention in the white assault on the black scab in the back alley. Together, the two black protagonists form the ideal of Communist collective work: Ray, the organic intellectual worker, lighthouse keeper of knowledge beyond institutional forms; and Jake, the cultural worker, the *prize* fighter, the incarnation of armed resistance. Jake's belt is his weapon—in "If We Must Die": "O kinsmen! we must meet the common foe! / Though far outnumbered let us show us brave" (ll.9–10, *CP* 177–78). Collectively Ray and Jake unite the two hemispheres of McKay's imagination.

The gambler Billy Biasse's act of interceding to help the soapbox black Bolshevik validates that the struggles of the black labor class and Marxist revolution function as vitally in *Home to Harlem* as the political emergence of divergent sexuality. Black proletarian effort and sexual radicalism in the narrative cannot be discussed in isolation because the two identity formations don't exist independently. Once on the loose, tolerance recognizes no limits in *Home to Harlem*. Jake's very name points to his "straight" arrow sincerity, everything *being jake* where Jake is concerned. Above-board Jake expects that whites be the same, that those who control labor unions accept blacks as equals, and nothing less is satisfactory. But his expectation enables the next obvious step of tolerance—the straight Jakes of the world, black and white, are obliged to confront their own intolerance of homosexuals. Far from policing isolationist ideologies, the Marxist insistence on inclusiveness in *Home to Harlem* entitles enunciations of difference. Such articulations are only possible as a result of the universalizing articulation of Marxism, if made up of compound and sometimes even competing communisms, thus enacting the union and laboring of difference: black and white, African American and West Indian, nativist and foreign, then straight and queer, gay and lesbian.

The conclusion of *Home to Harlem* reinforces its position as a queer black Marxist manifesto. With Ray's guidance, Jake may see that the war he needs to take up would not place him in the world contest between capitalist nationalist interests—the campaign he abandoned in Europe. Rather, he should take up the struggle of black workers, an act that confronts the very legitimacy of imperialist world war. Charles Scruggs identifies this aspect of the novel: "Imperialism in Europe, the cause of the 'The Great War' and the basis of its peace process, takes the form of colonization back home" (319). Near the end of the novel, Zeddy, who served with Jake in military service and is now suffering a fit of jealousy over Felice, threatens to reveal to the authorities that Jake deserted his post in Europe (327). This moment in the text is related to an earlier one, when Zeddy breaks a strike and Jake expresses his disapproval because Jake expects him to show solidarity with fellow workers (48). The chapter on the Pennsylvania Railroad dining car incident, "The Treeing of the Chef," makes the same point about the need for black solidarity: sabotaging a black man in authority who has internalized white supremacist ideology and employs it for his own benefit is the only solution to racist labor inequity (160–85). Zeddy's act of threatening to report Jake to state authorities not only directly reflects McKay's problems with an assortment of law enforcement agencies but also shows how black solidarity may be imperiled. The greatest menace to black unity is the destructive by-product of racist ideology: self-interestedly resorting to white supremacist, American nationalist hegemony.

Another way in which white hegemony is articulated may be located in Congo Rose's desire to have Jake physically mistreat her, a false consciousness that reflects the way that race and gender are coupled in attitudes of inferiority (112). Jake's decision to leave her because his disposition will not permit him to abuse her on a continual basis is an act against racist superiority (119). Though because it signifies black-white unity it may seem to be antithetic to Congo Rose's internalization of white hegemony, Zeddy's refusal to demonstrate commonality with all workers, black and white, is also a demonstration of manufactured consent. Early in the text, Zeddy objects to blacks giving away other black people to white authority (23). But near the end Zeddy realizes the wrong of his thinking and resumes his comradeship with Jake (333). Indeed, Zeddy, achieving Marxian universal consciousness, comprehends the meaning of Jake's desertion: "You ain't no moh slacker than me. What you done was all right, Jakey, and I woulda did it mahself ef I'd had the guts to" (334). In the black over white, anarchistic, sexually inverted world of *Home to Harlem*, Jake's act of desertion is an act of heroism, just as his act of deserting Congo Rose is an act of resistance against right-wing hegemony. The bond between black workers—and all workers—is made resilient by the realization of the necessity for common cause against white nationalist power. The emancipation for black working bodies lies in liberty from imperialist hegemony in all its forms.

Although necessarily a didactic text, *Home to Harlem* is interested in instructing its readers in revolutionary thought at an even deeper level. Inherent in its revolutionary dialogism is the potential for understanding how all categories of identity are oppressive, formed under the same conditions as race and nation. *Home to Harlem*'s truly radical act is to release a critique of all binary thinking, a critique that will find its ultimate expression in *Banjo* and *Romance in Marseille*, and it goes about attending to this cultural work in multiple ways, beginning with characterization. Now and then the reader is presented with the lingering query over whether Jake is exclusively heterosexual. In the beginning of *Home to Harlem*, Jake dreams of making his way home to Harlem, and his dreams of black women, articulated through a pun on the word *pansy*, resemble images of transvestites: "Brown girls rouged and painted like dark pansies" (8). In addition, there is the "big friendship" between Jake and Ray. Billy Biasse, for one, questions the nature of their relationship. When Ray decides to quit his job with the Pennsylvania Railroad, Jake says, "Why, ef you quit, chappie, I'll nevah go back on that there white man's sweet chariot." Hearing this, Billy says, "Whasmat? . . . Kan't you git along on that theah without him?" Following this remark, Billy says, "Git you'self going quick and come on down to mah place, son. The bones am lonesome for you" (240). Billy is a gambler, and "the bones" are his dice, so he wants Jake to come to his place to shoot craps. But the remark has another meaning whereby Billy is suggesting that his own "bones" yearn for Jake. Finally, when Ray decides that the best thing to do is leave the United States and go to sea, Jake "gripped Ray's shoulder" and tells his friend that he wishes he was "edjucated mahself," a comment that puzzles Ray, given the Haitian's ambivalence about being cultured. He says, "Christ! What for?" The reader knows that Jake is ready to "try anything once" (149), so it should not be surprising when, described as being "like a black Pan out of the woods [who] looked into Ray's eyes with frank savage affection," he meaningfully utters, "'Becaz I likes you'" (272). Like Ray's Onanistic dream novel, *Home to Harlem* smears "dark desire all over [its] pages" (228).

In the beginning of the narrative, the story is almost exclusively Jake's, and part of the narrative shows how the African American protagonist, admirable as a natural, instinctual, masculine being, carries narrow views of women, views that are a consequence of his being a *natural, instinctual, masculine* being. When Jake meets Ray, *Home to Harlem* doesn't make Ray the sidekick, as criticism has generally represented Ray—*Home to Harlem* as the original black buddy story.

Nor does the narrative only shift its focus to the Haitian or just shuffle back and forth between the two characters, though in parts the novel seems to do just this. Ultimately McKay's narrative creates a third space where the two comrades may share the position of the conventional protagonist, thus dialogizing the traditional western idea of the protagonist's solitary inner voice, an act that radicalizes not only McKay's narrative but the idea of the modern novel itself. One black male without the other would not make Harlem *home*. The two characters merge into a dialectical materialist exchange, forming a black Marxist bivocality, each filling the other's lack so that he may grow as a black subject. In other words, they attempt to *become* together, Ray's existential alienation and isolation and Jake's deficiency of "letters" nearly surmounted by a mutually formed coming into being, with Ray bringing the high (culture) for Jake, Jake the low (the primitive) for Ray. Without Ray's intellectual striving, Jake's instinctual primitive incapacity for being inhibited and repressed alone cannot lead to revolutionary reform. And without Jake's primitive acceptance of the natural state of things, Ray's culture and knowledge is incomplete, an insomniac intellectualism that cannot "feel" his comrade humanity, the first order necessary under Leninist vanguardist Marxism, the second point from which McKay's novel departs radically from Van Vechten's *Nigger Heaven*. Even when Jake finally finds his "little brown," Felice, their heterosexual union is linguistically figured by and interlaced with Ray's queer black anarchist dream: "They wove an atmosphere of dreams around them and were lost in it for a week" (314).

Finally, it is useful to consider the term *diaspora* and its relation to McKay's indispensable identity marker, *Negro*. While the identity classification *Negro* may be articulated by white racist communicative acts, in McKay's queer anarchist logic Negro is neither a secure linguistic taxonomy nor stable identity category. As *Home to Harlem*'s Negro is always situated in dispersion, always scattered beyond the boundaries, always already situated in the incertitude of diaspora, he or she may benefit from a kind of self-conferred emancipation, a form of independence that occurs culturally, politically, and sexually. It is in this dynamism of black self-determination that one may locate McKay's controversial primitivism, the one attribute of his thinking that has made those who study black literature, beginning with Du Bois, accuse him of perpetuating racist ideology. In *Home to Harlem*, as well as being a figure of Laurentian "blood-knowledge," paradoxically the Negro is a signifier for modern change, for insurgency—a revolutionary who naturally cannot adapt to supremacist law, a counterhegemonic agent that immanently cannot cede to modern capitalist and nationalist domination. In *Home to Harlem*, the *modern* is most radically enacted in the *Negro*.

The "Rude Anarchy" of "Black Boys" in *Banjo*

[T]he vagabond lover of life finds individuals and things to love in many places and not in any one nation.

Banjo

The more Ray mixed in the rude anarchy . . . of the black boys . . . and came to a realization of how close-linked he was to them in spirit, the more he felt that they represented . . . the irrepressible exuberance and legendary vitality of the black race. And the thought kept him wondering how that race would fare under the ever tightening mechanical organization of modern life.

Banjo

IN 1929, the same year that Alexander "Sasha" Berkman spelled out the *ABC of Anarchism*, Claude McKay published his second primer of transnational black queer permanent revolution, *Banjo: A Story without a Plot*. My interest is in expanding the critical discussion of McKay's second novel beyond its importance as a fundamental influence on négritude, as critics have customarily classified it. I am interested in *Banjo* as a queer négritude Marxist text. *Banjo*'s narrative holds an intriguing conversation with *Home to Harlem* (1928), then surpasses its comrade manifesto to portray the experience of the transnational black subject creating black modernity at the edges of the diaspora. In this way, McKay's strategic, contingent négritude envisages the rhetorics for Édouard Glissant's radical adjustment of négritude, as *Banjo*'s articulation of creolization demonstrates that the phenomenological condition of coming into being, of *coming out* beyond race, creates the potential for new emergences. *Banjo* wages a queer black anarchist plot, an even more radical conspiracy than its antecedent. Integrated with its radical intrigue, its lack of a narrative plot makes it possible to stage its revolutionary scheme. Through its freedom gained by way of narrative plotlessness, in other words, its Trotskyist (anti)plotting, *Banjo* writes its own black militant modernist aesthetics, uniting its black proletarian characters to perform a leftist négritude modernism. *Banjo*'s narrative collectivity, its "rude anarchy" of "black boys," achieves the dissemination of the agency of subjectivity that engenders a black anarchist polyvocality. The proliferation of the novel's subjectivity effects a revolutionary awareness of the significance of a protagonist in a novelistic narrative, revealing the immanent deconstruction of the isolated hero in the western novel. But *Banjo* does more than that. Although his second published novel is a black Trotskyist manifesto, *Banjo*'s modernism also articulates McKay's variety of Gramscian counterhegemony. McKay bares the cultural manifestation of blackness as manufactured consent in racist and imperialist ideology, as black distinction faces becoming absorbed by and subsumed into capitalist discourses. *Banjo* is a European-imported queer anarchist little black bomb clandestinely constructed to be chucked into the works, into the Imaginary, of international capitalism and imperialism, nationalist racism and fascism. Ultimately, *Home to Harlem* and *Banjo* collectively execute an organic intellectual artistic counterdiscourse in order to expand modernist notions of subjectivity, thus performing a Gramscian "rearticulation" of the formalism of identity, and immanent in this is the integrated imposition of whiteness and heterosexuality as a means for social control. These brother in arms fictions, *Banjo* and *Home to Harlem*—both employing McKay's fictional self-representation, Ray—expropriate the rhetoric of bohemianism and black sexual agency, thereby deconstructing the speech act intended to be performed by a white chimera on authentic black queer sexuality.

To begin to understand the import of *Banjo*, it is necessary to investigate the record of its relatively disappointing reception. Following nimbly on his popular if critically bruised first novel, *Home to Harlem*, McKay published *Banjo*, a book that fared far less well than his 1928 best seller. It is interesting that Michael Gold deemed *Banjo* insufficient in political terms. Writing in *New Masses*, Gold praised *Banjo's* critique of bourgeois values, but criticized it as inadequate as a proletarian novel. When McKay returned to the United States in the early 1920s, the Jamaican poet served as coeditor with Gold of the leftist journal *Liberator*, then left the position after a dispute, he says, over the kind of literature that the journal should publish (Maxwell, *New Negro* 95–124). He claims that Gold believed the *Liberator* "should become a popular proletarian magazine, printing doggerels from lumberjacks and stevedores and true revelations of chambermaids," while McKay argued in favor of the periodical publishing "good stuff that could compare with any other writing" (*Long Way* 139). For Gold to accuse McKay's novel of struggling black proletarian characters of not satisfactorily upholding proletarian principles indicates how little of McKay's purpose was expressed. Set in Marseilles during the early 1920s and portraying the exploits of an assemblage of black diaspora characters, *Banjo* didn't have the public that the first novel had, but the difficulty it faced went deeper than its unclassifiability. Due to having to follow *Home to Harlem*, *Banjo* was burdened with excess critical baggage. Even *Banjo's* favorable reviews reflected the lingering debate about McKay's first novel.

The vogue of attaching a subtitle during the Harlem Renaissance, moreover, offers an illuminating way into McKay's second novel. The subtitle affixed to a book title by a black writer denotes the slave narrative's need to attach authenticity: the subtitle "written by himself," as in Equiano and Douglass, with the case of Harriet Jacobs being the most instructive example of questioning the legitimacy of black authorship. During the New Negro Renaissance, book subtitles tended to be satirical of the need to verify black authorship, making wry comments on the requirement for the solemn subtitles of slave narratives. In the same year that he published *Banjo: A Story without a Plot*, Jessie Fauset released *Plum Bun: A Novel without a Moral* (1929), whose subtitle cleverly satirizes the public's need for black novels that articulate an earnest probity. Even the subtitle of Wallace Thurman's first play, *Harlem: A Melodrama of Negro Life in Harlem* (1929), mocks the ostensible necessity for additional verification.

In her *Opportunity* review, Gwendolyn Bennett points out that like *Home to*

Harlem, Banjo is a book that does not much resemble other novels. Bennett's review essentially focuses on the problem posed by *Banjo*'s subtitle, "a story without a plot." She acknowledges that most readers don't get McKay, whereas she, a devotee, recognizes that his novels are better understood as black modernist manifestos than conventional storylines: narratives devoid of plots. Implicit in Bennett's sympathetic review is an acknowledgment that the general faultfinding with McKay's fiction was the leftover disapprobation of *Home to Harlem*, a novel that critics imputed cashed in on the white Harlem Renaissance writer Van Vechten's unwisely titled *Nigger Heaven* (1926). With the soreness of Van Vechten's impertinence as well as a few other egregious instances of white portrayals of southern migrant black folk persisting, black reviewers generally reproached McKay's first novel for its favorable representation of illicit booze and drug use, "primitive" and violent behavior, and saucy blues lyrics. The title, or subtitle, of *Banjo* also drew some captious attention among its detractors (Edwards 189). Critics zeroed in on the supplementary title as an excuse to assail *Banjo* for other reasons, its plot lacuna evoking its lack, like *Home to Harlem*, of decency. The problem with *Banjo* was with what the novel was *without*.

While the historic critical link with Van Vechten's novel shows the accrual of a residual controversy, *Banjo* does carry on a more intimate relationship with another full-length fiction, René Maran's *Batouala: A True Black Novel* (1921). As its own subtitle suggests, *Batouala* laid claim to a kind of authenticity formerly unachieved, a legitimacy that, of course, a book like *Nigger Heaven* would not be entitled to claim. Winner of the French Prix Goncourt prize in 1922, *Batouala* was the first novel by a black author to take the view of an African protagonist: the title character, an African chief. *Banjo* resembles *Batouala* in that each narrative consists of Negro characters who compel the European imagination to grant black presence, although *Banjo* does not resemble *Batouala*'s arrival, as McKay's did not win the acclaim that Maran's novel enjoyed. A Martinican writer, Maran lived in both Africa and France for many years. Maran wrote for a French readership, and he set *Batouala* in western Africa, focusing on the struggle of indigenous people faced with European colonialism and the loss of indigenous ways. Such a narrative meant much to the young expatriate modern primitive Ernest Hemingway, who wrote a glowing review of *Batouala* for the *Toronto Weekly Star* in 1922, because it told the story of *l'autre côté*, the world where the primitive, the modern's Manichean Other, manifestly dwelled (Herdeck 2). McKay was likewise wild about the novel, though for another reason, regarding *Batouala* as dangerous because it was alleged to be outlawed in the French colonies. Indeed, the allegedly notorious *roman nègre* makes an appearance in *Banjo*, when Ray meets a creole student from Martinique, a mimic man who denies his own *creolité*: "Ray asked him if he had ever heard of René Maran's *Batouala*. He replied that the sale of *Batouala* had been banned in the colony and sniggered approvingly. Ray wondered about the truth of that; he had never heard any mention of it" (199). Whether or not McKay was certain that the novel was truly banned in Maran's own country, such precarious celebrity was precisely the sort of distinction the black Trotskyist and anticolonialist author would like to see for his second novel, though when this kind of attention actually materialized, he became alarmed. When McKay was living in Morocco, his second time in the Arabic country, and the French colonial police in Fez detained him in 1930, he was convinced that *Banjo* "had something to do with it!"—probably with justification.[1] *Banjo* may not have had the readership that *Home to Harlem* had, but evidently some of those who did read it understood only too well its anarchistic, antinationalist import.

As it differed from his first novel, McKay's second fictional narrative, though also named after its black protagonist, was markedly different than Maran's. *Banjo* places blacks from various points of the compass smack in the middle of the French urban-industrial environment, albeit compelled to live as habitués of the social perimeter, making the socially marginalized Africans, African Americans, and West Indians, sojourning a far cry from Africa, the restless, rootless, alienated expatriates. Situated at the other edge of the map from Maran's narrative of the tragically failed attempt at preserving black integrity, McKay's novel explores the other effects of modernity on black people, what happens as the result of the mingling of blacks scattered throughout the metropolitan center. Paradoxically, though located in the metropolitan core of western culture, France, black Marseilles of the early 1920s, a long step further than Harlem, was one of the outermost zones of the diaspora, one of the far-flung reaches of Garvey's *Negro World*. The southern French seaport marked the cartography of the existential black international, not the discrete fields of the American Imaginary of the 1920s, where blacks, whether African or African American, inhabit a relatively insulated homogeneity. Through this way of seeing the world, practically all-black Harlem has more in common with Dakar than it does with Marseilles. Is it any wonder that few American reviewers, black or white, knew how to respond to McKay's second novel, and why a modern primitive expatriate like Hemingway could rave about *Batouala* yet overlook *Banjo*?

But *Banjo* had another readership, one that American readers would not have considered. *Banjo*'s circulation on the Continent may have been small, but this slim reading circle is of enormous historical importance for the tidal waves of revolutionary ideas it set off in the black Atlantic: the négritude intellectual sphere situated in Paris in the early 1930s. Aimé Césaire, Léon-Gontran Damas, and Léopold Sédar Senghor were as passionate about *Banjo* as McKay was about *Batouala*, placing the Jamaican's novel next to the Martinican's as a canonical négritude text. And *Banjo* foregrounds its négritudist claim. The Senegalese Communist organizer Lamine Senghor materializes twice in the novel, unambiguously manifesting the négritude "*présence africaine*" (207, 267). *Banjo* was translated and published in the influential magazine *Légitime Défense* only three years after its American appearance, and its publication caused quite a stir among the black intellectuals who were initiating the anticolonialist artistic and political movement, as the American-published novel demonstrated excellently the budding notion among black Francophone intellectuals of a modernist black diaspora internationalism. By way of accentuating how important McKay's book was among the négritude intellectuals, Césaire identified *Banjo* as "truly one of the first works in which one saw an author speaking of the *nègre* with a certain literary dignity" (qtd. in Edwards, 187). Indeed, Césaire said that he could recite verbatim passages of the novel. McKay's Continental readership for *Banjo*, though small and ironically not American, was historic, as *Banjo* served as a key négritude manifesto. This is ironic because, though ardently critical of the United States, since he had left Jamaica McKay saw himself always as a writer vying in the American literary field. It is important to add that as well as admiration for *Banjo*'s performance of diaspora, the African and West Indian intellectuals in France appreciated its staging of black proletarianism. Like many French intellectuals in the late interwar period, including such Left Bank lights as Simone de Beauvoir, Albert Camus, and Jean-Paul Sartre, the négritude writers were committed members of the Communist Party. McKay was friendly with the sisters Jane and Paulette Nardal, passionate Communists, who with Suzanne Lacascade and Suzanne Roussy-Césaire were among the leading figures of négritude (Cooper 215, 290).[2]

But the Afro-French négritudists were not the only national separatist group to claim McKay as a fellow warrior. I would re-present an artifact that, as A. L. McLeod says, "has remained esoteric": the translation of McKay's story "Near-White" into Catalan, accompanied by a commentary for the Catalan reader by the eminent literary figure Josep Miracle in 1938, as the Spanish Civil War raged in Miracle's city, Barcelona: "The Black Soul Rises: Claude McKay's 'Near-White.'" "Near-White" was published first in the magazine *Europe* in 1931 and then collected in his 1932 short story collection, *Gingertown*. Miracle's remarks implicitly indicate a political relationship between the effort of black folk in

America and the struggle of Catalan nationalism and leftism against Falangist nationalism and transeuropean fascism, effectively joining Popular Front leftism in Spain with the American Cultural Front. As late as 1938, one year after his American-published autobiographical repudiation of Communism, McKay was seen in Loyalist Spain as a black brother in "*la lucha*," the struggle for leftist international revolution and preservation of the Second Republic.

In view of his ostensible break with radical politics by the time he wrote it, McKay's second novel therefore poses problems. I am particularly interested in what McKay means when he affixes to his main title the proviso "a story without a *plot*" (emphasis added). In 1927 E. M. Forster published his prolegomenon on modernist fiction, "The Plot." Forster's thesis is that since the modern novel's interest is in investigating the depths of human psychology, the Aristotelian notion of plot is an intrusive anachronism. Indeed, plot "is a fetish, borrowed from the drama, from the spatial limitations of the stage" (228). Fiction, Forster says, should invent its own motivating device, "suitable to its [own] genius" (228). The modernist prototype of plotlessness was James Joyce's dreamlike novel *Ulysses* (1922), a text of such European sophistication that it was banned in the United States as pornography and the FBI assembled a file on Joyce (Law 219–39; Culleton 46). The federal case against Joyce's novel relied on U.S. postal laws—regulations against using the U.S. mail to send and deliver pornographic material, as if the mail could be used to post little black anarchistic sex bombs. In view of the Feds' anxiety about what exists under the cover of a creative text, it is useful to revisit the fact that in the early 1920s, federal agents kept track of McKay because they thought he was a Bolshevik agent, and then in the mid-1930s resumed their surveillance when he returned to the United States. It is useful to reexamine the piece of evidence that while writing for the *Workers' Dreadnought*, a militant Socialist journal in London in the early 1920s, he composed under several assumed names, something he had done twice before (Cooper 123), and that in 1922 the Bureau of Investigation believed that the Russians had given him another alias, or code name, Sasha, when he was recruited as a courier. A politically engaged writer may use a nom de plume for several reasons, among them being the employing of a nom de guerre. Like his model, the ancient black Arab poet Antar, McKay saw himself as something of a warrior poet (*Long Way* 89), yet he did not want to be linked by the authorities to a subversive piece of his own writing.

Consequently, it is interesting to consider the other denotation of the word *plot*, how one may understand his "impish"[3] sense of humor and how such a signifier may apply to the study of a writer like Claude McKay. The black radical author was no stranger to political plots, and it is useful to review his implication in such activities. He was mixed up in a conspiracy involving the various leftist organizations during the early 1920s transition period in England. The scheme took place during the time when the Communist Party, or the British Section of the Third International, was attempting to establish itself in Britain, an act which involved a good deal of conflict among not just the Left and Right but also between radical factions, as Socialism in Britain was a loose confederation of clannish parties and secret societies up until the early 1920s (*Long Way* 73–85). As a result of this wrangle, the London police arrested *Workers' Dreadnought* publisher Pankhurst for sedition, and after being questioned by the authorities about his connection to her, McKay fled London back to the shores of Manhattan (*Long Way* 86–87; Cooper 123–26). But he also escaped from England because he was caught in the imbroglio between the leftist factions in London, one that could have led, he implies, to becoming a casualty of the internal radical struggle if he had remained. He made his way to Russia later that year to participate enthusiastically in the Third Communist International, his magic pilgrimage to the Soviet Union. My point is that dismissing the possibility that he may have acted as some sort of intelligence agent may be a form of denying the black Marxist his due, his act of secret black *agency*. How many black diaspora authors may have acted as left-wing spies? To follow up on evidence I examined in chapter 1, rather than continually accused wrongly, it is just as instructive to consider how he may have indeed served as a subversive agent of some sort, a kind of négritude Kim Philby, a black Red Graham Greene, and how this question relates to *Banjo: A Story without a Plot*.

What does it mean that "*Tovarish* McKay,"[4] whose life had been transformed by his magic pilgrimage to Moscow, designated *Banjo* "a story without a plot" and that the curious appendage attracted unpleasant critical attention to the novel? What does it mean that some critics laid into the endeavor ostensibly for its absence of plot but really for its lack of propriety? Black critics did not pounce on the novel for being politically treasonable; they attacked it for being culturally seditious, as McKay, a known black author, had composed yet another novel that perpetuated crude stereotypes of black folk—blacks are primitive and natural in both novels. This situation is ironic if his intention in using the subtitle was to draw right-wing attention away from his subversive work. Indeed, McKay's life does resemble that of an undercover agent. To inventory once again these elements of his spylike doings, on occasion he employed pseudonyms, now and again carried a weapon, and seemed to be escaping from somewhere his entire life. He enjoyed relating sly escapades in his autobiography, moreover, and sometimes went out of his way to mislead even his readers about his actions. It may be too much to suggest that McKay added the supplementary title to deceive British and French agents. Yet, like *Home to Harlem*, also a story without a plot, *Banjo* is less a conventional novel and more of a queer black anarchist manifesto. McKay's blueprint for Negro writing, its pages staging dialectical materialist intellectual and intelligence work, exposes racism, colonialism, and imperialism and posits in their stead a black Trotskyist counterhegemony informed by a bohemian, or queer, dissidence.

Banjo may be designated a story without a plot, but it nevertheless stages a queer black *Communist plot*, or more precisely, a queer black anarchist conspiracy. It is intriguing to consider the moment in *Banjo* when Goosey, the African American who exists under a kind of "race pride" false consciousness, accuses Ray, the co-protagonist of the novel, of lacking racial self-respect because the exiled Haitian is "a man without a country" (183). Ray cannot return home because the United States took possession of Haiti, imprisoning his activist father and executing his brother in the street, as *Home to Harlem* explains (138). McKay was also a colonial without a country, in that he could not return to the United States for fear of being imprisoned by the federal authorities as a Communist agent. And it is just as likely that among the reasons he was laying low in Morocco was to avoid becoming a target of Stalin's merciless campaign to eradicate the anarchist cells, Trotsky's cohorts. Still, if McKay was a spy in Morocco, the time during which he finished his "story without a plot," he was a secret agent *without* agency, whose secret was all too well known. Though during the early 1920s he almost certainly did serve in some sort of capacity as an intelligence gatherer and information courier, if through no other means than by generating his radical journalism, by the late 1920s McKay probably was not an undercover agent for a country or organization. But he was an *agent provocateur*, inciting black proletarian agency through his novels, written for consumption by black readers in the United States. This is how through its accentuated, vitalizing license of plotlessness, its formal anarchy, *Banjo* establishes its own radical modernist aesthetic principles. *Banjo* may be lacking a plot in Aristotelian terms, but it does, as its supplemental title also suggests, have a *story*. Two central characters unite to demonstrate a Marxist *dialectic of modernism*, to use and adjust Michael North, in the narrative. As with *Home to Harlem*'s sharing of the position of protagonist, along with its inclusiveness of "black boys," the distribution of the agency of the subjective center gives the novel's narrative a black polyvocality. *Banjo*'s multivocality instigates a decentering of subjectivity, thus generating a second sense of the complexion, the role, as well as the meaning of a protagonist in a novelistic narrative. *Banjo* is a queer anarchist little black explosive device constructed to be flung into the machinery of world capitalism and international imperialism, nationalist racism and national socialism: the brutal, material expression of self-interest. As the chapter titled "White Terror" says, "Business! Prejudice and business! In Europe, Asia, Australia, Africa, America, those were the two united terrors confronting the colored man" (193). McKay's potentially explosive device, a product with Marxian "use value," is aimed also at what he saw as the complacent black middle class.

By the late 1920s, Harlem Renaissance authors were moving toward composing literature that united the struggles of the hard-pressed black urban and migrant populace with those of the American proletariat and internationalist fight against imperialism. A year after McKay published "The International Spirit" in the pages of Du Bois's *Crisis*, Alice Dunbar-Nelson published the poem "The Proletariat Speaks" (1929) in the NAACP organ. Such renaissance lights as Du Bois (Robinson 185–98), Countée Cullen (Wald 83), Sterling Brown (Wald 263), and even Alain Locke, who in identifying the renaissance ethos in 1925 would assert that the New Negro was not radically disposed, would progress toward the black Marxist position (Locke later became conservative) (Wald 277–79). But of the renaissance writers, Langston Hughes most passionately enlisted in McKay's vanguard. In 1930 Hughes published the anti-imperialist "Merry Christmas" in *New Masses*, a poem whose blunt rage would set the tenor for such poetry of the 1930s as "Good Morning Revolution" (1932), "One More 'S' in the U.S.A." (1934), and "Let America Be America Again" (1936). His Marxist agitprop dramas, like *Scottsboro Limited* (1933), *Don't You Want to Be Free?* (1938), and *De Organizer* (1939), engages in the same cultural work. Although critics have universally ignored the transparently radical leftist communication of his short fiction, most of his Depression-period short stories, beginning with the black Marxist creation myth "Cora Unashamed" (1933), also demonstrate Hughes's political point of reference. Coming along at the end of the 1920s, *Banjo* was intended to be a book that both the black proletariat and black Marxist cultural workers could use.

Although the text is politically Trotskyist and aesthetically anarchist, moreover, the modernist principles that *Banjo* articulates better resemble the second-stage Marxism of Antonio Gramsci's overturning of Marx's base-superstructure model by focusing on culture as a site of struggle and hegemony. Blackness is the cultural expression of ideology that McKay exposes as manufactured consent in racist and imperialist power relations, as William Maxwell suggests in his analysis of McKay's *Negroes in America* (1923), a text that Maxwell designates a nascent form of black cultural studies (*New Negro* 87). Published six years later,

Banjo enacts black cultural studies in the form of the novel. *Banjo*'s Marxism, moreover, with its metanarrativistic permeability, its insertion of a self-reflexive appearance of Jake Brown and even that "one strutting fool" Jerco (160) from *Home to Harlem*, as well as freely sampling from the author's life, articulates a black modernism, another intonation of diaspora cruising. *Banjo* does self-reflexively carry baggage from his prior outing. The two novels articulate a counterculture of modernity, a form of black dialectical materialism that liberally samples from the first stage Marxist focus on commodity fetishism (the black body as commodified fetish) and the Lukacsian theory of reification (the objectification of racial oppression and subordination under imperialism as immanent) with the cultural materialist interest in identity: class, sexuality, gender, and nationality as capitalist structures of feeling. *Banjo*'s Marxist sex anarchism ransacks both sides of the base-superstructure binary, contingently putting into use the late first-stage Leninist-Trotskyist permanent revolution thesis while articulating a cultural materialist critique of identity and hegemony, being particularly interested in exposing the construction of blackness. It then subjects the Marxist hybrid to black struggle: the emergence of a black revolutionary nationalism that is at once Marxist internationalism as well as an anticolonial Pan-African transnationalism.

Banjo begins with the coming ashore of the African American title character. No matter how far he roams, the very dust of America clings to Banjo's selfhood, as he is described as "a great vagabond of lowly life. He was a child of the Cotton Belt, but he had wandered all over America. His life was a dream of vagabondage that he was perpetually pursuing and realizing in odd ways, always incomplete but never satisfactory" (11). Restless Banjo, always anxious to move on, relocates to Canada and serves in the Canadian military during the Great War. Stuck working on a factory assembly line after the war, he then decides to quit Canada. But instead of returning to the United States, he concocts a curious scheme to be sent across the black Atlantic at Canadian expense: "Seized by the old restlessness for a sea change while he was working in an industrial plant, he hit upon the unique plan of getting himself deported" (11). Banjo's ploy reflects the fact that McKay was nearly always on the verge of being expelled from wherever he dwelled. Banjo's scheme to be deported is obvious to the Canadian authorities but works anyway. Not only is Banjo's black Americanness apparent to all; even his regional makeup is transparent: "Everything about him—accent, attitude, and movement—shouted Dixie" (11–12). Banjo's lack of suffering due to the imposition of national identity demonstrates McKay's response to the predicament of Du Bois's concept of double consciousness, the theory that a kind of attenuation inheres in being "African American" because America categorically excludes from its ontological construction the African side of the hyphenated ethnic-national identity. An embodiment of one possible resistance to double consciousness, Banjo's insistence that he is "foreign" (12) illustrates that his national identity is not a constitutive part of his personal selfhood. Banjo's rejection of the American side of the hyphenated identity is made more dramatic because his "Africanamericanisms" are scored on his tongue (12). As soon as Banjo opens his mouth, everyone knows that he is African American, even the Canadian officials who have no choice but to send him away, to *repatriate* him—in an ironic, playful spin on popular Pan-Africanist, black pan-nationalist reveries of "returning" to Africa—back to Europe. Banjo is indeed a kind of *internationalist* by way of an elaborate joke, though a thought-provoking one: insisting on being repatriated to a nation one has never seen and to a speech community whose language one does not speak. Once again the reader encounters a McKay character who is a "bad nationalist" (*Long Way* 300), an Althusserian bad subject, the human subject who is incapable of being interpellated by the linguistics of the nation.

When Banjo eventually finds his way to Marseilles, "the most international place" in France (135), he experiences a kind of traveler's ecstasy of the *arrivant*, as Bajan poet Kamau Brathwaite terms Caribbeans who cruise against the current: "It was Banjo's way to take every new place and every new thing for the first time in a hot crazy-drunk manner. He was a type that was never sober, even when he was not drinking" (13). In Marseilles Banjo is delighted to encounter a black Bacchic Babel of "Senegalese, Sudanese, Somalese, Nigerians, West Indians, Americans, blacks from everywhere, crowded together, talking strange dialects, but, brought together, understanding one another by the language of wine" (36). He meets a group of black itinerants inhabiting the Marseilles Ditch, the seamy seaport. "The shining black big-boned lad who bore such a contented expression on his plump jolly face" is the West Indian "leader and inspirer of the group" Buchanan Malt Avis, known as "Malty" (5). Another is Ginger, the fittingly named Jamaican, a "chestnut-skinned fellow with drab-brown curly hair," a black diaspora itinerant who exists literally—and contentedly—without identity, indeed without country: "He had lost his seaman's papers. He had been in prison for vagabondage and served a writ of expulsion [from France]. But he had destroyed the writ and swiped the papers of another seaman" (5). The Senegalese Dengel, who as a French African colonial speaks little English, "preferred the company of Malty and his pals"—the diaspora vagrants—to that of his countrymen" (6). Dengel is a character who also demonstrates *Banjo*'s comment on national identity and state chauvinism. Finally, among Malty's ragtag band is another African

American, Bugsy, a "small, wiry, dull-black boy who . . . sardonically [reminds] Banjo of his [own] recent high-flying" (6). Bugsy is "always aggressive of attitude. The fellows said that he was bughouse and he delighted in the name Bugsy that they gave him" (6). A black American, Bugsy carries a name that imprints onto his identity a criminal or *lumpen* subcultural selfhood, an externalization he relishes.

The resistance against state national identity enforcement and the unselfconscious embodiment and vocalization of blackness are tied to resistance against acceptable forms of survival under an industrial capitalist system. Sex workers and gay characters populate *Banjo* as plentifully as they occupy *Home to Harlem*. Latnah, an African woman Banjo takes up with, earns her living through sexual commerce. And around the middle of the novel, the black boys of the Ditch encounter "a troop of painted [white] youths who, holding hands, danced around them with queer gestures and queerer screams, like fairy folk in fables" (196). Yet black women are evidently not the only sex workers in the Ditch, and made-up white fairies are not the only queers. The black male characters who dwell on the waterfront of Marseilles from time to time work in the sex trade: "Often they [the black male vagabonds] traveled devious and separate routes in pursuit of a 'handout,' and sometimes had to wander into strange culs-de-sac to obtain it" (32). Employing the travel trope is the most appropriate means of depicting black-white male sexual commerce in *Banjo*. A risky undertaking, diaspora cruising can lead to keeping strange trysts. It sometimes means finding oneself in newly imagined locations, surviving in *les tristes tropiques* of the diaspora.

Banjo assembles its critique in several ways, including a criticism of the "racial renaissance." Ray insists that the "educated Negroes" from the North, in their top-down, ostensibly pragmatic philosophy of striving to join the white middle-class and capitalist economy, contribute to the very ideology they believe they oppose. Following the Marxist elevation of the proletariat as politically conscious and the Bolshevik Tolstoy-inflected exaltation of the purity of the peasant, Ray articulates the need for organizing an emergent black revolutionary socialism that looks to the common people. The black southern folk have retained the African origins, the traces of authenticity, as Leninist Communists promoted the purity of the masses before the advent of the Stalinist social democracy period, while the black middle class in its single-minded aim to achieve according to the standards of the majority has abandoned its foundations: "It's the common people . . . who furnish the bone and sinew and salt of any race or nation. In the modern race of life we're merely beginners. If this renaissance we're talking about is going to be more than a sporadic and scrabby thing, we'll have to get down to our racial roots to create it" (200). The passage demonstrates his capacity for uniting an ostensible antithetic cultural chauvinism with proletarian internationalism, for articulating a diaspora intelligence that cruises fluidly between cartographically recognized compass points.

The black Trotskyist Ray of *Banjo*, indeed the anarchy of the novel itself, tactically selects and deploys portions of social-economic and cultural philosophies for black underclass usage. Ray argues that "race" is not the problem—or *a* problem—for black people. Race is the advantage for blacks: "many Negro intellectuals . . . are bellyaching about race" (200). Both drawing on and modifying Du Bois, McKay articulates the *problematic* as education. *Banjo*'s intertextuality with *Home to Harlem* emerges as Ray, as in the previous novel taking the role of teacher, repeats the companion novel's critique of "education" as Marxian false consciousness. The following also prefigures Du Bois's thesis of "history" being the property of white supremacy in *Black Reconstruction in America* (1935): "What's wrong with you-all is your education. You get a white man's education and learn to despise your own people. You read biased history of the whites conquering the colored and primitive peoples, and it thrills you just as it does a white boy belonging to a great white nation" (*Banjo* 200–201). To be black and *engagé* is to identify the link between the oppression of domestic racism and that of international imperialism—the strategy Trotsky and McKay brought into being in Moscow when they articulated *collectively* a permanent revolution that positioned blacks at the vanguard of transnational insurgency (*Long Way* 208–9).[5] The metonymic "white boy" who mystically identifies with the "great white nation" is less able to perceive his role in the hegemonic structure, how his consent is invisibly manufactured. Ray also refers to comments he made in *Home to Harlem* about "civilization": "Once in a moment of bitterness he had said in Harlem, 'Civilization is rotten.' And the more he traveled and knew of it, the more he felt the truth of that bitter outburst" (163). Like Ray in *Home to Harlem*, Ray in *Banjo* regrets the effects of "civilization" on his natural black selfhood: "He hated civilization because its general attitude toward the colored man was such as to rob him of his warm human instincts and make him inhuman" (163).

Ray's reiterations of *Home to Harlem*'s unresolved issues indicates that blacks are best disposed to occupy the front line because the black subject is constantly reminded of his or her subclass position in the exclusionist hegemony. The black proletarian is therefore, with a bit of cultural education supplied by advance guard cultural educators like Ray, better positioned to perceive the function of and to resist nationalist ideology. McKay later both relies on and reverses Du Bois further by articulating the Negro as not a problem but a "challenge" to western civilization and its functions (273). As Du Bois challenged B. T. Washington's adaptationist philosophy, essentially arguing the blacks were not the problem—indeed, institutionalized racism was—McKay's dialectical materialist critique of Du Bois amends the color line theory to recognize the revolutionary potential in the black proletariat. This anarchist *dis-position* lies at the center of his radical philosophy: the Negro, compelled to inhabit the margins of the diaspora, is a kind of inheritor of resistance, possessed of the faculty, if educated adequately, to effect revolutionary change.

Lincoln Agrippa "Banjo" Daily's natural incapacity to be fabricated into the American nationalist identity formation is signed by his compound appellation, his string of names pointing to the multiple faces of his Negro newness, his one-man revolutionary *nature*. Although his *given* name seems to suggest the imposition of white signing on a black subject, he is first "Lincoln" because he enunciates his own emancipation. His middle name suggests Marcus Agrippa, which is a name that calls up Marcus Aurelius Garvey. Linked in a curious way to this—as middle-class American and Caribbean blacks often named their children after western classical figures (like Festus Claudius McKay), consciously giving names that suggested authority—Agrippa helped Augustus transform Roman society. Banjo's middle name of Agrippa points to his friendship with Ray, the "revolutionist" (270) cultural worker. However, an irony exists in the two being black, as their race signs them as antithetic to imperialism's model couple, particularly of Rome, which saw itself as the binary opposite of everything African, as propagated by the Roman origin myth, Virgil's *Aeneid*; indeed, they are contrary to the origins of imperialism. His family name of Daily underscores his existential ethos: "I'm just a right-there, right-here baby, yestiday and today and tomorraw and forevah" (33).

Most important, the assumed name Banjo repudiates the presumed *instrumentality*, the dehumanization, of the human subject under modern existence, where one's human agency is typed, like the typist in *The Waste Land*, in accordance with one's essential somatic function: "Banjo caressed his instrument. 'I nevah part with this. . . . It is moh than a gal, moh than a pal; it's mahself'" (6). Banjo does not suffer from modern alienation from origin; his body and soul are not disengaged. Banjo's psyche is not fragmented, like the emasculated, shell-shocked hollow men of Eliot's postwar scorched terrain. Onanistic imagery arises regularly in McKay's writing, so it is apposite to find that the phallus-shaped, literally African-American musical instrument is like an appendage of Banjo's body, a phenomenal articulation of his selfhood. In ideological terms, the banjo differs radically from the typewriter. The metonymically assembled typewriter, extending even further the remoteness of referentiality, signifies modernity's mechanization and instrumentality of the human subject, the subordination of flesh to machine, the death of the human, in modernist terminology. In contrast to death in the form of modern industrialization, "Jungle jazzing" can "Shake down Death and forget his commerce, his purpose, his haunting presence in a great shaking orgy. Dance down the Death of these days, the Death of these ways in shaking that thing" (57). Jazzing is a "Sweet dancing thing of primitive joy, perverse pleasure, prostitute ways, many-colored variations of the rhythm, savage, barbaric, refined—eternal rhythm of the mysterious, magical, magnificent—the dance of divine life" (57–58). With its African drum torso and neck strung for melodic play, the banjo is the primal connection to Africa brought to America, its authenticity fortified by its link to slave times and then implementation as a jazz instrument. Where the typewriter is pure instrumentalism, a remote signifier of industrial-age terminology, empty of soul, the banjo is essence itself, a vigorous reminder of origin that has been adapted to the condition of diaspora, Banjo's "magic companion" (229), a singing west African *chi*.

Although his assumed name suggests a primordial link with derivation, Banjo does not see the musical instrument as a referent of the past. That is, Banjo refuses to see his instrument as a referent of slavery, a tool of racist ideology. The Ditch dweller "flute boy," Goosey, challenges Banjo's choice of musical instrument:

> "Banjo is bondage. It's the instrument of slavery. Banjo is Dixie. The Dixie of the land of cotton and massa and missus and black mammy. We colored folks have got to get away from all that in these enlightened progressive days. Let us play piano and violin, harp and flute. Let the white folks play the banjo if they want to keep on remembering all the Black Joes singing and the hell they made them live in." (90)

Significantly, Banjo, with his multiple names adding layer upon layer to his agency, gives "Goosey" his nickname, as a result of the young man's nervousness. Banjo feels anything but enslaved, rejecting the idea that the musical instrument he plays, with its jubilant tonal luster and its proletarian ease of transport, denotes and thereby on some level sustains the memory of slavery. He does not play "black-face coon stuff" (91), the white "theft," to use Eric Lott's term, of minstrelsy. Banjo's art, his lively jazzing—like movement—is the expression of freedom itself, in both its personal as well as political senses. Indeed, the title points to freedom, proletarian union, and radical struggle. Five years after the appearance of *Banjo*, the pseudonymous "Richard Frank" published an article in the *New Masses* on "Negro Revolutionary Music," which took for granted that "since whites were fascinated by Black music and often sang Black songs, Black music was truly the route to Communist politicization of the entire working class" (Wald 291).

Banjo's counterpart and comrade, the Haitian Ray, a character who cruises practically unaltered from *Home to Harlem*'s distant shores—if more conscious of his sexual difference—is the title character's antonym in every way except the one that counts most in a world where race is the first order of business. Banjo reminds Ray of Jake, from *Home to Harlem*: "Banjo's rich Dixie accent went to his head like old wine and reminded him happily of Jake" (64). The binomial is recognizable to readers of *Home to Harlem*, the splitting of the modern immanent in the characterization of Jake and Ray. Where Banjo is formally unschooled, Ray is educated; where Banjo is a primitive, Ray is a modern; where Banjo seeks his pleasures of the flesh with the opposite sex, Ray is same-sex oriented. *And both are black.* The two protagonists, if that is the best locution for the male lead dispersion, appear to construct an absolute binary opposition. Such a view, however, would not take into account the formality of the novel. United with a party of black vagabonds from various diaspora sites, Banjo, Ray, and the "rude anarchy" of "black boys" (324) form a collective subjectivity, a kind of pack animal assemblage, to use Deleuze and Guattari. The pluralism of the quay boys also takes a communal socialist economic shape, as they form what amounts to a vagabond collective: "Dividing up was a beach boys' rite. It didn't matter what share of the spoils the lucky beggar kept for himself, so long as he fortified the spirit of solidarity by sharing some of it with the gang" (158). Collectively in textual terms, Ray and the boys (including the nominally straight Banjo) form a diaspora multivocality that unites through class and race commonality as well as sexual difference, their connections bisecting at several critical if circuitously arrived at points—like the meandering nomadic vagrants they are. When the Haitian Ray says, "*Vive la révolution*," he also says, "Vive la différence." "The most precious thing about human life is difference. Like flowers in a garden, different kinds for different people to love" (208).

While he disparages the "bohemian high brows" (128) of the Left Bank and other "well-to-do poseurs plumbing low-down bohemian life" (138), Ray is identifiably proletarian-bohemian, in other words, queer, which suggests that he lives a life free of bourgeois claims to his selfhood, but paradoxically he is the least "free" and most in need of belonging to the assemblage. Like McKay, who struck primal attitudes in the buff for a living, Ray worked as a nude model in Paris, posing for modern artists. The "fierce moderns" discuss African art with

Ray (130). The fact that the modern artists make a fetish commodity of the body of African art, and therefore his own black flesh, causes a personal crisis for the model, as the object of the gaze is compelled to gaze on his own reification and evidently doesn't like what he sees. At one point Ray forgets that he is posing as a primitive and is transported home to "Harlem, right there in the Sheba Palace, in a sea of forms of such warmth and color that was never seen in a Paris studio" (130). The dream of authenticity causes Ray to give up nude modeling. Indeed, *posing* is a predicament posed to Ray on another level: "Ray had undergone a decided change since he had left America. He enjoyed his rôle as a wandering black without patriotic or family ties. He loved to pose as this or that without really being any definite thing at all" (136). "Sometimes" hiding behind the mask of a pretense permits Ray to perceive in ways that presenting oneself ingenuously would not, yet on the downside, posing, being a poseur, "deprived an emotion of its significance" (136). Despite his recognizable emancipation from the bondage of bourgeois morality, that is, McKay communicates an irony in the queer Ray's envy of the straight Banjo's authenticity and spontaneity, the African American's absence of the infliction of the intellect. However artful his pretense, and re-ally because of his intellectual affect, Ray suffers from the consequent modern alienation: "he felt deep down in his heart that Banjo's way was the better one and that he would rather lose himself down that road and be happy even to the negation of intellect" (242).

Though representative polarities in terms of the split between body and soul, the pair of Janus-faced protagonists converge in their incapacity to submit to the imposition of nationalist structures of feeling. Despite his obvious American-ness, Banjo is able to effect his own repatriation to a nation he has never seen, flouting national identity and thereby articulating an ironic, eccentric response to double consciousness. Ray's repudiation of the modern identity of national-ism, however, articulates itself on another level, through the intellect:

> The sentiment of patriotism was not one of Ray's possessions, perhaps because he was a child of deracinated ancestry. To him it was a poisonous seed that had, of course, been planted in his child's mind, but happily, not having any traditional soil to nourish it, it had died out with other weeds of the curricula of education in the light of mature thought.
>
> It seemed a most unnatural thing to him for a man to love a nation—a swarming hive of human beings bartering, competing, exploiting, lying, cheating, battling, suppressing, and killing among themselves; possessing, too, the faculty to organize their villainous rivalries into a monstrous sys-tem for plundering weaker peoples.

Man loves individuals. Man loves things. Man loves places. And the vagabond lover of life finds individuals and things to love in many places and not in any one nation. Man loves places and no one place, for the earth, like a beautiful wanton, puts on a new dress to fascinate him wherever he may go. A patriot loves not his nation, but the spiritual meanness of his life of which he has created a frontier wall to hide the beauty of other horizons. (137)

The "vagabond lover of life finds individuals and things to love in many places and not in any one nation": engaging in queer cruising, being a "vagabond lover" who finds "individuals and things to love in many places," is tantamount to revolutionary Marxist internationalism, the mass proletarian response to the "monstrous system for plundering weaker peoples." Both black protagonists refuse to accept the imposition of the modern state nationalism, in its material and metaphorical forms, on the individual human subject: Banjo because national identity will not fit the natural movement of his body; Ray because it will not correspond to the restless motility of his mind. Bhabha's "Third Space," or liminality, functions at the level of nationalist discourses as well as linguistic structures. Bhabha's in-between or "liminal" space persists in the "locations of culture":

> It is in the emergence of the interstices—the overlap and displacement of domains of difference—that the intersubjective and collective experiences of nationness, community interest, or cultural value are negotiated. How are subjects formed "in-between," or in excess of, the sum of the "parts" of difference (usually intoned as race/class/gender, etc.)? (2)

Indeed, the condition of dwelling between clear national borders is not reserved only for Banjo and Ray. Some of the anarchic black boys who reside in the Ditch have lost their papers and are therefore unable to prove their identities. The French government identifies a colonial without papers by the unhyphenated term "nationality doubtful" (313).

At the beginning of the third part of *Banjo*, the narrative presents a description that recalls the coal miner imagery of Lawrence's *Sons and Lovers* (1913), darkened further by racial politics: "Blackened from head to foot, clothes, hands, neck, face, a stream of men from the coal dock filed along the Quai des Anglais, across the suspension bridge, and into the Place de la Joliette. There was no telling blond from dark, yellow or brown from black" (227). But whose narrative is this? In part 2, Ray is unable to write the poem and story he longs to get down: "For weeks he had been purposely boozing and lazing and shutting his mind against the poem in his heart and the story in his head, both clamoring to be heard" (220). Banjo barges in to inform Ray that he is leaving, suspending indefinitely the idea of organizing a jazz "orchestry" (221), to take off with a group of white swells who have taken up the black musician as their current form of entertainment. In part 3, the reader learns that at last Ray, with Banjo gone, has begun to write, his feelings of inadequacy in *Home to Harlem* finally overcome while dwelling in the Ditch. Being in Marseilles—removed from America's insistence on hierarchal binary thinking, its double consciousness both in race as well as nationalist terms—permits Ray the freedom to write: "It was a solitary delight of the spirit, different from and unrelated to the animal joy he felt when in company with the boys of the Ditch" (260). The description of the coal dockers, the workers, as racially indistinguishable is Ray's narrative, the prose redolent of Hemingway's and Stein's minimalist, sensual lyricism: "Just then he was beginning to do some of the scenes of the Ditch and he felt lifted out of himself with contentment to sit by a sunny open window and work and hear sparrows chirping in the garden below" (260). Most important, Ray portrays the proletariat as unified as workers, as impossible to differentiate in racial terms.

Ray's Marxism, however, is not an idealistic philosophy. In one of the many debates in the narrative, debates that give voice to the novel's enactment of post-Hegelian dialectical materialism, the "sentimental radical" Crosby accuses Ray of not supporting the proletarian cause. Although Ray is a self-avowed "revolutionist," his Marxism does not seem to resemble what one would expect to hear coming from the hero of a proletarian novel:

> I hate the proletarian spawn of civilization. They are ugly, stupid, unthinking, degraded, full of vicious prejudices, which any demagogue can play upon to turn them into a hell-raising mob at any time. As a black man I have always been up against them, and I became a revolutionist because I have not only suffered with them, but have been victimized by them—just like my race. (270)

Ray, like McKay, the former Wobbly, is a Trotskyist, the term *revolutionist* indicating McKay's own turn toward anarchism and away from party politics. Organic intellectual Ray is a realist who articulates a cultural work that seeks to seize the hegemony without idealizing the aims of revolution: "I should like to see the indecent horde [the proletariat] get its chance at the privileged things of life, so that decency might find some place among them" (271). The solution to the problems of the proletariat is an anarchist revolution that incurs a cultural education of the proletariat.

It is instructive to consider the events that transpire immediately following the breakthrough moment when Ray is finally able to start writing about the Ditch—to start writing the lyrical négritude novel that the reader is reading, *Banjo*. Banjo, Malty, Dengel, and a "British West African" they pick up have a lunch date with an Egyptian merchant sailor and the ship's African American steward onboard an American steamer. When they reach the vessel, a white American officer refuses to let them board, telling his white seamen: "Don't let any of them niggers on here" (261). The boys become angry, and the English-speaking African says "he would show him [the officer] what 'niggers' could do if he came on the dock," adding, "[Y]ou're not in America. This is France" (262). The British West African's comment proves to be ironic. The officer calls the Marseilles *gendarmerie*, who seize the black men: "The boys were taken to the police station on Quai de Lazaret and given a merciless beating. Each of them was taken into a separate room by the policemen, knocked down and kicked. Then they were turned loose" (262). The action of the police reflects the European enforcement of brutal colonial policies, tactics that also evoke the rising fascism, as Banjo remarks to Ray: "[T]hey know their business so damn good you'd have to use one a them magicfying [*sic*] glasses to find the marks" (262).

Not long after, following his conversation with the white radical poet Crosby, Ray is walking home at a late hour, and for no evident reason he is detained by two gendarmes, one of whom clubs him on the back of the neck while he is reaching for his papers. His arrest recapitulates a grim scene of bondage: "The handcuff was a special chain kind that could be tightened and loosened at will, and the policeman took great pleasure in torturing Ray on the way to the jail" (264–65). At the police headquarters no charge is made against the Haitian. Outraged, Ray demands to know why he was handled so appallingly and for no apparent cause. He finds that the reason is as grim as his treatment. The police inspector informs Ray that "all the Negroes in Marseilles [are] criminals" (266). In Toulon, France, in 1924—an incident that would be repeated in Morocco in the late 1920s and early 1930s—the French police questioned McKay as a Communist agitator, and he recognized that he was in danger of expulsion when he was asked if he was a Communist (*Long Way* 260). Questioning McKay about being an internationalist, then accusing him of being an infiltrator and propagandist, the French colonial police in Morocco finally ordered him to leave Fez (*Long Way* 300). It is useful to recall that McKay was convinced that *Banjo* "had something to do with" his being detained and then effectively ejected (Cooper 270). *Banjo*'s depictions of police violence, unjustified detention, and a frank expression of institutional racism indicate more than merely a narrative device in this "story without a plot." The passages point to McKay's identity in his own fiction as a black intellectual plotting revolutionary change. Rather than merely a romantic radical like Crosby who—like Michael Gold, McKay insists in his memoir—idealizes the proletariat, Ray is a practicing "revolutionist."

In the novel's final pages, Ray comes to understand his own black diaspora restlessness in terms of race, nation, and modernity. Ray wants "to hold on to his intellectual acquirements without losing his instinctive gifts" (322–33). His "instinctive gifts" make it possible for Ray to mix "in the rude anarchy of the lives of the black boys—loafing, singing, bumming, dancing, loving, working," and the black intellectual "came to a realization of how close-linked he was to them in spirit, . . . the irrepressible exuberance and legendary vitality of the black race" (324). With this thought comes another, how the "race would fare under the ever tightening mechanical organization of modern life" (324). Ray contemplates "the great intellectual and social movements of his age" and the "growth of international feelings and ideas," manners of thought Ray "had dreamed" for "his race" (324). The intellectual and social movements include both modernism and Communist mass movements. As any true Marxist intellectual who belongs to a minority group should, Ray is ruthlessly interrogating the viability of international socialism for his own people, Negroes, querying the applicability of the most modern mode of "scientific" thinking, dialectical materialism, to the condition of diaspora and African peoples. But the passage also points to Ray's self-discovery and his ability at last to start writing prose. Ray realizes that the estrangement between self and Other, the anguish of the modern condition, is artificial, a discord he has internalized as a result of being exposed to western notions of education, striving, and intellectualism. At this moment Ray overcomes the angst he suffers at the end of Home to Harlem when he must take flight from America for European shores, taking on for himself the lonely life of the black expatriate. It is only through the act of locating the black diaspora proletarian enclave in Marseilles, distant from the black bourgeoisie who visit Paris like white tourists looking for "culture," that he is finally able to discover his own "rude anarchy," his "penchant for exotic sins" and "heathenish atavistic propensities" played out in his "dark . . . artistic urge," writing (209).

The novel's self-reflexivity is its most radical, anarchic feature. Like Ray, Jake Brown also makes his way from Harlem to Marseilles, making a meta-appearance in Banjo, his sudden, tardy materialization underlining the idea that diaspora is of necessity an itinerant environment: "The boys went into the Seaman's Bar and there was Home to Harlem Jake drinking with a seaman pal at the bar. He and

Ray embraced and kissed" (291–92). The cameo role appearance of "*Home to Harlem* Jake" reinforces the radical diaspora internationalism of McKay's second novel, the playful irony and self-reflexivity demonstrating how the supplemental *Banjo* moves further into the outer reaches of the black Atlantic than even its companion source text. Jake, "a good black American," indeed, "Too American" (296), shows up after seven years of being separated from Ray to convey that even the most American of black proletarians has crossed over—and the act of *crossing over* works on several levels. Near *Home to Harlem*'s own ending pages, Jake, "a black Pan out of the woods[,] look[s] into Ray's eyes with frank savage affection" and makes his unambiguous statement: "I likes you" (272). As in *Home to Harlem*, Jake's natural sexual tendency toward Ray arises once again, a queer double entendre revolving around their meeting in a bar full of "seamen": "The fust time I evah French-kiss a he, chappie," Jake says, "but Ise so tearing mad and glad to meet you this-away again" (292). The *cultural work* on Jake that Ray engaged in back in Harlem has had the desired effect. And the freedom to kiss a man is encouraged by the environment Jake is now in, Ray suggests: "That's all right, Jakie, he-men and all. Stay long enough in any country and you'll get onto the ways and find them natural" (292).

Jake's explanation for going back to work as a merchant sailor reflects the incapacity of McKay's black male protagonists, like the author himself, to adapt to marriage. In the lengthy, autobiographical short story "Truant," published in *Gingertown* (1932), a Pullman car waiter named Barclay Oram, persuaded that matrimony functions as a form of social control through the imposition of "the cold white law," abandons his spouse and child: "Spiritually he was subject to another law. Other gods of strange barbaric glory claimed his allegiance and not the grim frock-coated gentlemen of the Moral Law of the land" (157). In *Home to Harlem* Jake and Felice married in Chicago, but after two years of connubial life he returned to Harlem and then to sea. Jake found that a change of setting, returning to Harlem, was not enough, so "I just stahted up one day and got me a broad," a steamer, and set sail; going back to the sea makes Jake happy to be with his spouse and son, named after Ray, when he is home (292–93). And still envying his friend's education and intellectual ability, Jake expresses his hope that his son will also grow up to be a poet, evidently one reason he named his child after his friend. Through Ray's learning that Jake has named a son after him, the reader learns that, like McKay and like Barclay in "Truant," the Haitian has left behind a child: "I leave more things than I want to remember," Ray comments (293). Ray's predicament resembles Barclay's, who recognizes that the road less traveled by is not easy: "his true life lay in eternal inquietude" (162). Indeed, diaspora for McKay is a site of exploration, both material and spiritual, and the seafaring life taxes the traveler's tranquility.

But Ray is not alone among the novel's characters who wrestle with double consciousness. Even Banjo suffers from the effects of a Fanonian neurosis, and the "illness" is played out through a narrative on his musical instrument. In the final section of the text, Banjo loses his stringed instrument when some Senegalese trick him out of it. The Senegalese taking "his magic companion" (229) from the African American jazz musician is a comment both about Africans retrieving origins after slavery as well as African Americans in danger of abandoning their roots. After losing his banjo, he gets involved with a group of rich white tourists looking for the *divertissement du jour*. Banjo becomes deathly ill (243), then recovers and buys a "second-hand instrument," but "the old spontaneous, carefree happiness" cannot be recaptured (257), and Banjo goes "missing" once again (302). When Banjo makes his union with Ray at the novel's end, he returns to his true self, resisting the various forms of enslavement that civilization poses (325–26).

The intertextual conversation between *Home to Harlem* and *Banjo* is pervasive in the second novel, including the likelihood that straight Banjo, like hetero Jake, has it in him to veer queer with Ray. The reader knows early in the novel that Ray is infatuated with Banjo, a passion that is related to his fixation on Jake in the previous novel, stirred up by hearing the black southern dialect: "Banjo's rich Dixie accent went to his head like old wine and reminded him happily of Jake" (64). So it is not surprising to find that in the final pages of *Banjo*, the title character, like Jake, is attracted to his Haitian comrade. The difference between *Home to Harlem* and *Banjo*, however, is that whereas in the first novel Ray leaves his pal and Jake eventually finds Felice and heterosexual contentment, in the second novel Banjo returns to Marseilles and invites Ray to be his companion, having jettisoned Latnah from his life: "'Well, what you say, pardner?' demanded Banjo. 'Why you jest sidown theah so long studying ovah nothing at all? You gwine with a man or you ain't?'" (325). Banjo adds: "'Now wese bettah acquainted, theah's a lotta things befoh us we'll have to make together,'" and Ray remarks: "It would have been a fine thing if we could have taken Latnah along, eh?" (326). Banjo's comment is forthright: "Don't' get soft ovah any one wimmens, pardner. Tha's you' big weakness. A woman is a conjunction. Gawd fixed her different from us in moh ways than one. And theah's things we can git away with all the time and she just kain't. Come on, pardner. Wese got enough between us to beat it a long ways from here" (326). Their black male proletarian comradeship functions on at least two levels, the political and the personal.

As a means toward conclusion, it is instructive to consider another translation of the second volume of McKay's black queer manifesto trilogy, one that is in all ways antithetic to the négritude adaptation. In the same year that he published his memoir, a British film company made *Big Fella* (1937), a movie that was based on *Banjo*, with McKay's friend Paul Robeson playing the title role. The film was essentially lost until the Library of Congress restored it in the late 1990s. The emergence of a film version of McKay's inimitable novel starring the majestic Robeson may strike some as too good to be true. The truth, however, is that the Hollywood-inflected idiom *based on* achieves its most comprehensive import in this case. Though like McKay's story without a plot, the movie ostensibly takes place on the Marseilles waterfront and follows the adventures of a black male protagonist who enjoys the underbelly café life, the movie's plot does not even dimly resemble the black author's angry, radical, self-reflecting and self-reflexive, imaginatively autobiographical scheme. In *Big Fella*, carefree, indolent African American expatriate Joe becomes the nursemaid of a runaway well-heeled white boy. The twosome form a kind of Huck and Jim relationship, with the black surrogate father playing subordinate to the precocious, adopted white son. That is to say, the movie is more a kind of distorted culture industry version of *The Adventures of Huckleberry Finn*—made into a film two years later with Rex Ingram as Jim—mixed up with the exploitation of the 1936 film version of *Show Boat*, than anything having to do with *Banjo*. Indeed, the black-and-white picture is really an occasion for exhibiting Robeson's baritone singing skills. His name clearly scrounged from *Show Boat*, "Joe" regularly breaks into song, belting tunes with titles like "Lazin'" and "My Curly Headed Baby." Eventually, Joe gets into trouble with the police—a singularly apposite plot twist if one bears in mind that the script is ostensibly derived from a novel by a writer who spent more than two decades trying to dodge police detention and intelligence community surveillance. The narrative's real aspirant kidnapper, a shady, clownish Cockney who has made his way intact from the English music hall stage, frames poor Joe for abducting the rich kid. But the movie ends cheerfully, and broadmindedly, with big Joe not only proving his innocence but also doing the manly and socially responsible thing: rescuing the little brat. Formerly a bachelor who prefers his independence to the constraints of wedlock, Joe also gets married to a black girl, making the world safe for white women while confirming his heterosexuality—an essential act as he inhabits the homosocial, seamy underground Marseilles world, where sexual degenerates cruise freely, as they do in *Banjo*. One curious, almost metaphysical scrap of detail is the director's name, J. Elder Wills, a handle that queerly iterates that most demanding of directors, J. Edgar Hoover.

The appearance of Robeson in *Big Fella* in 1937, the year of McKay's autobiography, presents an intriguing set of questions. In view of his representation of the black orphan lost in "America," it is interesting that the title of the memoir, *A Long Way from Home*, is taken from a slave sorrow song made famous by Robeson, "Motherless Child": "Sometimes I feel like a motherless child / A long way from home." Although McKay had nothing to do with the making of *Big Fella*, the cinematic minstrelization of *Banjo* nevertheless does depict in a curiously exemplary manner the predicament he faced during the mid- to late 1930s, the evidence of his novel past, a predicament that Robeson also faced. *Home to Harlem, Banjo*, and *Romance in Marseille* were channels for McKay's own deep vibrato, his manifestation of radically dissident literary art. It is singularly edifying that the self-determining black hero of *Big Fella*, Joe, in the end collaborates with authorities, acts unselfishly on behalf of white folks, and enters into matrimony. Five years after McKay published his memoir and one year after he was called before the Senate investigation into subversive activities, the commencement of FBI surveillance of Paul Robeson would begin. Because of his own visits to the Soviet Union in the 1930s and membership in the CPUSA, Robeson, indisputably the most famous and influential black personality in America in the 1930s and 1940s, would become one of the most ruthlessly persecuted leftists of the cold war period, largely because, unlike Joe, he refused to cooperate. The government seized his passport during the 1950s, making it impossible for him to earn a living at the height of his talent; Robeson was blacklisted in the United States and unable to travel outside of the country to perform (Duberman 381–402). The FBI finally ceased its investigation of him as a subversive in 1974, after over thirty years of harassment, and evidently only because Hoover finally died in 1972. Comparable in length to the likes of Woody Guthrie's 109-page dossier, McKay's file, 10 pages longer than Guthrie's, is a dismally respectable representation of his rank as a radical artist between the wars. Grimly underscoring his "Big Fella" status with the government, Robeson's FBI dossier is made up of more than three thousand pages of documents. The depressing narrative of the African American performer, All-American athlete, intellectual, polyglot, and progressive activist provides a chilling context for McKay's dealings with the FBI and practically inescapable experience with Senate investigators. By confiscating his passport and arranging to have him blacklisted, the federal government effectively erased Robeson from the cultural landscape, a deletion whose resultant deficit is still felt, as one may see by the effort of the New American Studies and leftist recovery historicism project to recover figures like Robeson. Only five years after publishing the last part of his queer black Marxist novel trilogy, *Romance in Marseille*, McKay produced his autobiography, *A Long Way from Home*, a literary performance that is compelled to do a song and dance. The gradual disappearance of Claude McKay began at this moment, and like Robeson, the genuine genealogy of McKay's life and work is still cloaked in obscurity. As a result, the Right achieved its aim of forcing McKay into the archival vaults, into history's shadows and the government's closet.

But the final irony is that the act of shutting up McKay would be undone by progressive labor—the forcing open of the closet door. The act of compelling the FBI to permit the act of peering into its closet now makes possible an understanding of McKay's achievement. Ultimately the revolution McKay teased into being transpires in language, in the poetry of diaspora, specifically as the term corresponds to its indispensable identity marker in McKay's black modernist idiom, *Negro*. Current scholarship on his transnationalism offers a valuable critical engagement with the diaspora author's négritudist point of reference. The black transnationalist criticism is valuable because, as a result of excavating a significant record of his years in France, such scholarship makes the radical critical move of repositioning McKay away from the Harlem Renaissance chronotope and into the milieu of African and Caribbean struggle during the 1920s and early 1930s. However, such scholarship makes its assertions by arguing that his art and politics were composed of an unambiguous form of transnational négritude and black nationalism. Arguing that McKay poses diaspora as *exclusively* a black nationalist alternative to leftist internationalism, thus setting diaspora and Marxism in binary opposition, overlooks the author's own lyrical assembling of not only blacks across the Marxist diaspora but also the unifying of "picturesque proletarians from far waters whose names were warm with romance: the Caribbean, the Gulf of Guinea, the Persian Gulf, the Bay of Bengal, the China Seas, the Indian Archipelago" (*Banjo* 67), the blending together of workers from a range of diasporas, primed, as colonized subjects, for radical action. The novel scholars do not discuss, moreover—and despite the convention of tying *Home to Harlem* and *Banjo*, just as intimate a companion to *Banjo*—*Romance in Marseille* unites the diversity of diasporas with black and white queer proletarian workers. *Banjo* sets the bearing for this course, Ray in *Home to Harlem* and *Banjo*, his self-fictionalization, being the exemplar of the black proletarian queer.

Although he never used the word *diaspora*, McKay did articulate the idea of racial-cultural dispersion through his use of the term *Negro*. In McKay's logic, Negro is an unstable linguistic unit or identity category; the racial identity classification Negro takes on a specific epistemological and phenomenological complexity. Cedric Robinson says in *Black Marxism* that the Negro is an identity articulated by white racist communicative acts. The racial, really racist category *Negro* is essentially the brainchild of imperialism, an identity arrangement imposed on the slave subject that instrumentally implements white mastery under racial nationalism and industrial capitalism. In McKay's revision of the racial classification, the Negro, or the New Negro, is neither a received stable signifier nor a circumscribed identity. The Negro for McKay, if he or she may evade a totalized manipulation of the civilizing process, is a signifier for revolution: an identity that inherently cannot accommodate, a counterhegemonic situatedness that is intrinsically incapable of capitulating, an emancipated subjectivity no longer able to consent to enslavement. McKay's Negro is the black *bad nationalist*, always situated in dispersion, scattered beyond the boundaries, thus incapable of being interpellated. The post-Rousseauist, Nietzschean-minded McKay must propose a radical idea of the primitive, of savagery, turning the modernist primitive into a being who does not submit to binary relations. In the early 1920s sonnet "On a Primitive Canoe," the primal-recalled tribal canoe is contrasted with the slave ship, thereby making possible an interrogation of who is savage and who is civilized: "Why does it thrill more than the handsome boat / That boar me o'er the wild Atlantic ways, / And fill me with rare sense of things remote / From this harsh life of fretful nights and days?" (ll.9–12, *CP* 169). And in "The White House," the "chafing savage" (l.7) is compelled to "keep" his "heart inviolate, / Against the poison of" white "deadly hate" (ll.13–14, *CP* 148–49).

The embodiment of whiteness, the meaning of being white, is to be enslaved by bourgeois capitalism and sold the manufactured consent of capitalist ownership, including the possession of human beings, in McKay's toppling, after the materialist logic of Karl Marx, of the Hegelian dialectic. But the Negro, an identity that white capitalist society perceives of as incapable of civilizing, paradoxically has been left alone, in McKay's view, to follow his or her own pleasure at the perimeters of the diaspora: thus the explosion of revolutionary African American arts like black dance and jazz music, modern versions of African cultural sources. The disadvantage to being black is the hazard of racism and imperialism; the benefit is primitivism—not being white! Ironically, the "primitive arts" are situated at the core of "the modern," their subversive power in danger of being commodified (the "Jazz Age") and through such commodification kept in check by capitalist, imperialist, white hegemony. The McKay New Negro is most meticulously delineated in his pivotal novel, *Banjo*: "Senegalese, Sudanese, Somalese, Nigerians, West Indians, Americans, blacks from everywhere, crowded together, talking strange dialects" (36). Published in 1929, *Banjo* is pivotal because it acts as the fulcrum between *Home to Harlem*, put out a year earlier, and *Romance in Marseille*, composed over a three-year period after the publication of *Banjo*.

McKay is faced with the predicament of diaspora identity in a time when the Negro cannot occupy any trouble-free idea of material existence because racism and colonialism, as Fanon suggests, necessarily decentralize the Negro. Paradoxically there is no Negro *there*, because as Fanon says in *Black Skin, White Masks* (1952), the Negro must *be* there for the colonial state as an *aide mémoire* for racial inferiority, and for the Negro the effect of the subjection is to be disappeared from state and social discourses, to exist without prescribed agency. Recognizing this predicament, he articulates a Negro who resists the Fanonian inferiority complex by eluding the internalization of inadequacy. McKay's Negro is, in phenomenological terms, always becoming, and the variable location his Negro occupies is the diaspora—the Third Space where the Negro may function as a black queer Marxist revolutionary condition. The following quotation from *Home to Harlem*, Ray's comment on "modern education," sheds light on where the Negro may shape a new selfhood:

> modern education is planned to make you a sharp, snouty, rooting hog. A Negro getting it is an anachronism. We ought to get something new, we Negroes. But we get our education like—like our houses. When the whites move out, we move in and take possession of the old dead stuff. Dead stuff that this age has no use for. (243)

The imagery of the *hog* appears throughout McKay's 1920s and early 1930s writing, taking on several skins, making nearly multiple, necessarily paradoxical meaning. Here it echoes "If We Must Die": "let it [the death of the New—radical—Negro] not be like hogs, / Hunted and penned in an inglorious spot." The Negro must endeavor not to live like a hog, content to be thrown the scraps of modernity, to receive "modern education" and *civilization* without interrogation. Paradoxically, only the new has value for the Negro—a *new* primitivism—the modern that always endeavors to fashion itself against the received identity. Where can this self-creation take place? The Negro requires an entirely new territory to discover his or her own modernity, or "this age." The discovery cannot take shape in "The White House," to use the title of McKay's 1922 poem. It is instructive that Locke, without McKay's permission, altered the title to "The

White Houses" when he published the poem in *The New Negro* in 1925. Locke feared, probably justifiably, that the title might offend the sensibility of white readers—not to mention alert the attention of white penal authorities—who inevitably would see in the black radical author's idiom the shattering of the emblematic nucleus of American national power, the presidential residence. Locke, McKay insists, missed the point. The imagery of the house—like the hog-dog imagery, another central motif in his prose, from *Home to Harlem* to *A Long Way from Home*—certainly metonymizes the material situation of blacks moving into the brownstones of Harlem, unoccupied by whites as the Great Migration grew. Most important, however, the imagery of the *black* house, the white house's implicit photonegative, the unuttered presence, represents an imagined deterritorialization, a location where the self-fashioning of the Negro may take shape. The location is the diaspora.

McKay's diaspora provides a Third Space, an interstitial region, an international zone where, once again, Bhabhaesque "ambivalence" is possible and circumstance authorizes radical aberration. Cultural hybridity must be understood in terms of the way in which "cultural statements and systems are constructed in" a "contradictory and ambivalent space of enunciation":

> The intervention of the Third Space of enunciation, which makes the structure of meaning and reference an ambivalent process, destroys this mirror of representation in which cultural knowledge is customarily revealed as an integrated, open, expanding code. Such an intervention quite properly challenges our sense of the historical identity of culture as a homogenizing, unifying force, authenticated by the originary Past, kept alive in the national tradition of the People. In other words, the disruptive temporality of enunciation displaces the narrative of the western nation that Benedict Anderson so perceptively describes as being written in homogeneous, serial time.
>
> It is only when we understand that all cultural statements and systems are constructed in this contradictory and ambivalent space of enunciation that we begin to understand why hierarchical claims to the inherent originality of "purity" of cultures are untenable, even before we resort to empirical historical instances that demonstrate their hybridity. (37)

McKay's tendency is for diaspora over existing within national limits, whether the imposition of nationalism takes the form of an imagined community like America *or* a restrictive stable form of ethnic essentialism like a black cultural chauvinism that lays down laws about who may enter the discursive field. Mc-

Kay's diaspora seeks the permanent revolution. Merged with—indeed informing—this interstitial notion of diaspora are conditional nodes of Trotskyist-
anarchist politics and queer dissidence. His comment in *A Long Way from Home*
about leaving America once again in 1922, years after abandoning his marriage
and immediately after walking out on his coeditorship of the *Liberator*, clarifies his valuation of flux as a means toward such ends. It is useful to return to
the following passage from his memoir, an iteration that echoes his short story
"Truant": "I had wandered far and away until I had grown into a truant by nature
and undomesticated in the blood. There were consequences of the moment I
could not face. I desired to be footloose, and felt impelled to start going again"
(150). McKay's anarchic wanderlust, his natural truancy, pursues a transoceanic
diaspora cruise, as the imagery of *a long way from home* suggests, a limitless
drifting in the black Atlantic, to cite and revise Gilroy's analogue. One may
thereby recognize in McKay's diaspora the shifting stage, a Passage against the
Middle, for a string of *preferences*—racial, existential, political, and sexual—and
none of these chains of signification may be sundered from one another. Diaspora cannot be pinpointed as a destination on the Mercator map of colonial and
white nations. Nor is it a substitute cultural transnationalist system, an alternative form that acts in binary opposition to leftist internationalism. Diaspora, in
McKay's most intensively realized works, is the phenomenological interzone, the
existential international quarter, the epistemological commonwealth. A mode
of creolization, it is the cruised outskirts that authorize a queer black anarchist-
proletarian *becoming-identity*.

Polished in a European colonial territory by a Caribbean négritude revolutionary, *Banjo* is a bohemian anarchist black letter bomb fashioned for dispatch
to the United States. From the mid-1920s to the early 1930s, McKay pursued a
Trotskyist dedication to the proposition of "permanent revolution" and anarchism, though *dialectically* translated in such a way that ethnic nationalism and
Marxist internationalism do not when paired up become mutually absolutist.
Culture and anarchy must be tactical languages, not absolute values; their dialects of modernism must be contingent to local dialectical materialist conditions.
When Ray admires "the black boys' unconscious artistic capacity for eliminating
the rotten-dead stock words of the proletariat and replacing them with startling
new ones" (321), *Banjo* indicates that the revolutionary potential of black Marxism not only inheres in the intellectual firmament of the black hierarchy but also
resides, indeed is best exemplified, in the cultural expression, the speech community, of the lowest strata. Moreover, essential to the anarchist revolution is the
necessity for recognizing the interleaving of distinctive "working" and different

"loving": "For Ray happiness was the highest good, and difference the greatest charm, of life" (325). Vital to McKay's most engaging fictional narratives is the predicament of the black diaspora proletariat and the way in which bodies in sexual commerce cannot be disentangled from the condition of the black worker under capitalist imperialism—the exemplar being the "rude anarchy" of "black boys."

"Swaying to the Music of the Moon"

Black-White Queer Solidarity in *Romance in Marseille*

I was struck by the moon,
I was smitten by the moon,
Crazy for the fairy moon,
It lighted my heart and it caused me to roam.

Romance in Marseille

THE AIM OF this final chapter is to tease *Romance in Marseille* (c. 1929–32) from its archival vault in order to discover the novel's role as the crucial third text in McKay's queer black Marxist trilogy. McKay's merging of black proletarian being and revolutionary black queer becoming make *Romance in Marseille* a vital document of twentieth-century Anglophone literature. Indeed, it is ironic—or perhaps fitting—that what is perhaps the most remarkable primary literary text of the black diaspora is unfamiliar to the world. I discuss the significance of the sexual underworld in McKay's narrative, with notice given to the opportunity of black anarchist queer nationhood in the text—the liminal space where the socially undesirable may surreptitiously pursue their passion and pleasure—at the crossroads of queer brotherhood and leftist cultural work. The "plot" of McKay's black proletarian prolegomenon gives voice to a queer radicalism whose deviant presence spreads the word, in the manner of Leninist vanguardism, of queer anarchy among black workers, thereby disseminating the liberating spirit of Trotskyist permanent revolution. Articulating a ground-breaking idiom against colonial discourse, *Romance in Marseille* reflects Édouard Glissant's revision of négritude. The novel's creolization voices a kind of postcolonial phenomenological condition of becoming, an emergence beyond race to culture built on the potential for revolutionary mergings. Grasping the importance of McKay's final queer black Marxist manifesto makes possible a new entrée into his radical aesthetic undertaking. I offer an extended, mostly sequential close reading of the text, blending analysis and description so that the reader may gain a sense of the storyline.

It is necessary to be familiar with the text's chronological context, however, before looking into its construction and content. In 1929, during a brief visit to Bilbao, Spain, to undergo an unlicensed and unsuccessful medical treatment for a sexually transmitted disease, McKay undertook the writing of his fourth novel.[1] Initially called "The Jungle and the Bottoms," the document's title would at times take shape as "Savage Loving," but ultimately as a rule he would refer to the 172-page manuscript as *Romance in Marseille*.[2] Like the novel he had just published, *Banjo: A Story without a Plot* (1929), the story is set in Marseilles and chronicles the doings of a small party of diaspora blacks who form a subculture on the waterfront. Indeed, the title for *Romance in Marseille* appears in a passage in *Banjo*, a sentence that encapsulates a good deal about his unpublished novel: "There was a barbarous international romance in the ways of Marseilles that was vividly significant of the great modern movement of life" (69). After on-again, off-again periods of labor on the manuscript, he finished it—or ceased working on it in 1932— just before his last, long, lean year spent mostly in Tangier, Morocco, a desperate period for the expatriate author. Not only was McKay financially distressed, but the French colonial authorities also engaged in an elaborate plot to remove him from the Tangier international zone, accusing him of being a Communist agitator.

Rather than being a black diaspora picaresque that, like his previous novels, sampled loosely from his life, *Romance in Marseille* was, like Richard Wright's *Native Son* (1940), derived from an actual incident, and the author himself played a part in the events that inspired the manuscript. McKay wrote to his literary editor, William A. Bradley, about the episode. In February 1928, "one of the Nigerian seamen upon whom [McKay] was basing the character Taloufa in *Banjo* returned to Marseilles minus both feet" (Cooper 237). Nelson Simeon Dede had stowed away on a French steamer headed for New York, and when he was discovered he was locked up in "an unheated water closet" for the duration of the crossing (Cooper 237, 408). After docking it was discovered that he had suffered frostbite, so his legs were amputated below the knees. A New York attorney represented Dede and secured a settlement of seventeen thousand dollars, taking five thousand as a fee. On his way back to Nigeria, the merchantman stopped off in Marseilles, and "two days before finally sailing for Africa, the double amputee was jailed by French authorities" for illegally embarking on the ship two years earlier. McKay in his capacity as a writer threatened to make a "*cause célèbre* of the case," thereby bringing about Dede's release (237). The black writer then decided to dilate on the incident through fiction.

The story of why *Romance in Marseille* never saw publication, however, is still obscure. After *Banjo*'s comparatively mediocre showing following *Home to Harlem*'s success, McKay's publisher, Harper & Brothers, was not persuaded that publishing another book set in Marseilles about a group of black *lumpen* vagabonds was a judicious course to take. Notwithstanding, the publisher was at first willing to take on the manuscript, with minor changes. *Banjo*, "a story without a plot," was taken to task critically for this very absence, although those critics who faulted the novel for being plotless generally applied this reproof as a justification for assailing it for other reasons (Edwards 189). With *Romance in Marseille* McKay included a relatively intricate plot, although again *Romance in Marseille* is like *Banjo* much more a novel composed of a series of conversations between various diasporic African, African American, Caribbean, and Afro-European men on the predicament of being black and male in the modern world. Indeed, *Romance in Marseille* does resemble *Banjo* in many ways. But what actually took place in the story of why *Romance in Marseille* never saw the light of day seems to be more complicated.

An awareness of the historical context of the *sex novel* milieu of the 1920s and early 1930s and the trend's attendant discourses provides an understanding of the ways in which various parties responded to McKay's manuscript. The "sex novel," promoted and distributed principally by Boni & Liveright, the consummate bohemian-radical Greenwich Village publishing house, made up the *comme il faut* reading vogue among sophisticated American readers of the 1920s (Gilmer 27, 80; Hutchinson 367–72). Though not disposed toward publishing "racy" literature, Eugene Saxton transformed the languishing Harper & Brothers into a business that better resembled the thriving Boni & Liveright, as well as such flourishing publishers as Alfred A. Knopf and Harcourt, Brace. Saxton's Harper & Brothers imitated the way that these publishing houses had adapted to new trends in American literary tastes. As well as remodeling the old *Harper's* magazine to resonate with new tastes, Saxton modernized the publishing house of Harper & Brothers, expanding the catalogue to include more voguish authors. But Saxton's Harper & Brothers was not as progressive in sensibility as Boni & Liveright; Saxton himself was known to be "squeamish" about sexually suggestive books (Hutchinson 378). McKay was already painfully acquainted with a publisher's queasiness over promoting a book with an openly voluptuous subject matter. His first attempt at a novel during the mid-1920s was "Color Scheme." He hoped that Knopf would add his novel to their catalogue, but the manuscript was turned down because, as McKay's biographer says, "its explicit sexual references would almost certainly be judged obscene by the courts" (Cooper 221). One need only turn to the author himself to verify such a depiction of "Color Scheme." Faced with justifying the manuscript's subject matter, McKay offers one of his characteristically blunt remarks: "I make my Negro characters . . . fuck like people the world over."[3] Finally, frustrated with the reaction against his first novel, he burned the sole manuscript of "Color Scheme" in 1925.

As for frustrations over his fourth attempt at extended fiction, after Harper & Brothers at last decided in 1932 against publishing *Romance in Marseille*, McKay decided to shelve his novel and turn his attention toward producing another project. He believed that he could once again capture the attention of the literary world by publishing in a form he had not yet generated: a collection of short fiction. (Actually, the new book would be the first collection of short fiction he produced outside Russia, as he had published *Trial by Lynching: Stories about Negro Life in North America* with a Soviet press in 1925.) Also, he needed to make money, as he was running out fast. Although Saxton wasn't much more excited about this idea than he had been about *Romance in Marseille*, his publisher permitted McKay, whose name still possessed public currency, to proceed. This swiftly assembled book of short fiction was *Gingertown* (1932), a publication that would do no better than *Banjo*. After he had sent off the manuscript of *Gingertown*, he returned to the problem of *Romance in Marseille*.

Desperate for advice and hoping to recoup several years' worth of work, he sent *Romance in Marseille* to his old *confrère* and comrade, Max Eastman. Apparently recognizing that what McKay needed most was the advice of someone who worked on a daily basis with the publishing industry, Eastman suggested that yet another party appraise *Romance in Marseille*, so he asked the editor Clifton Fadiman to look at it. In a dispatch dated September 12, 1933, three days before McKay's forty-fourth birthday, Fadiman wrote to Eastman concerning "Savage Loving," or *Romance in Marseille*. Fadiman, even less enthusiastic than Saxton about the book, dismissed the manuscript as "sex hash." What catches my attention is the evocative turn of phrase—*sex hash*—as the locution strikes a conspicuous note if one bears in mind the common if notorious vogue of the *sex novel*. *Romance in Marseille* was essentially suppressed because of its sexual candor, censored because it dealt frankly with the abject class of black society: procurers, sex workers, and wharf-rat itinerants. Along with the usual tribulations associated with selling *literary* books, the publisher of racy novels potentially faced arrest for printing pornography, an act that was in the mind of the Right tied to political subversion. Censorship often acted obliquely, as McKay knew too well:

> The story of modernism is the story of censorship, too. Writers as diverse as James Joyce, James Baldwin, Claude McKay, Theodore Dreiser, Thomas Wolfe, Djuna Barnes, Sherwood Anderson, Zora Neale Hurston, D. H. Lawrence, Richard Bruce Nugent, Max Eastman, John Dos Passos, Floyd Dell, Ernest Hemingway, Langston Hughes, Radclyffe Hall, and countless others were at some point in their careers tormented by their unsuccessful efforts to see their work published. (Culleton 166)

This controversy, however, is not so simply resolved as a matter of a publisher, fearful of the government's menacing attention, censoring an author, in that additional, mitigating circumstances contributed to the novel never seeing print. Most important was McKay's response to Fadiman's dismissive comment, and even more categorical was Eastman's inferred deference to Fadiman's judgment. Fadiman's rejection and Eastman's implicit confidence in Fadiman's verdict dispensed the decisive one-two punch against *Romance in Marseille*, as far as McKay was concerned. Although he fortunately didn't burn it, as he did with "Color Scheme," he put aside the manuscript and never seemed to have given it another thought. Almost certainly he could have eventually published his novel, if not with Harper & Brothers, then with a more liberally disposed house like Boni & Liveright. In other words, as well as the near certainty that his novel met with such hostility because of its sexual frankness, among the biggest obstacles in the way of *Romance in Marseille*'s seeing the light of day was the author himself. The fact is, as one of the foremost impediments in the way of *Romance in Marseille* seeing print, McKay was the ultimate author of his own absence.

Another vital consideration is the novel's use of "plot" and the question of how this convention relates to McKay's political activity. I bring this up initially because, although critics have conventionally paired his 1928 best seller *Home to Harlem* with *Banjo*, the novel that most resembles *Banjo* is *Romance in Marseille*. Indeed, *Romance in Marseille* is something of an attempt to go beyond Banjo. Where *Banjo* is "a story without a plot," the narrative of *Romance in Marseille* does contain a plot; in fact, it carries out several intersecting plots. This difference between the two otherwise similar texts, I believe, may be tied to McKay's political work, his anarchist *agency*. William Maxwell considers the fact that federal agents broadly assumed McKay must be a Communist agent, a Bolshevik spy ("F.B. Eyes" 41). Maxwell then conjectures whether McKay may have been an agent of some kind, an intelligence gatherer or courier or both. Indeed, the proposition that he served as a covert agent furnishes a fresh illumination on at least part of the reason for the black Atlantic author's wanderlust. It certainly places a different light on the French Moroccan colonial administration's accusation against him as "a Bolshevik agent" (Cooper 252), "a radical propagandist" (*Long Way* 302). According to *A Long Way from Home* (1937), he is grilled by the French authorities in Morocco about his activities and about his habit of describing himself as an "internationalist" and "bad nationalist." The prospect that he was in fact an undercover agent of some obscure sort avails my study of a unique opportunity for analysis. As he was seduced by the black diaspora culture of Morocco, the queer society in Tangier and other sites in Morocco enticed him to remain in North Africa for three years. I am convinced that a third reason could exist for his three-year sojourn in Morocco: McKay's ambiguous intelligence work. Unquestionably the intrigue of Tangier was part of its allure for the radical writer.

Here we see the intersections of McKay's queer black proletarianism in a new light. It is not within the purview of my analysis to settle the question of whether he was in fact a black secret agent. My interest lies in how an intimate analysis of *Romance in Marseille* may be read through the Bureau of Investigation's well-wrought urn, as Maxwell articulates the circumstances, the bureau's own fastidiously rendered literary theory composed in order to analyze the black radical's texts. McKay designated *Banjo* "a story without a plot," and it may be too much to suggest that the author, known for numerous cunning exploits, appended the subtitle to throw off enemy agents. However, *Romance in Marseille* not only consists of several parallel running plot lines but is, as well, copious with plotting in the locution's collateral though related meaning: scheming, calumny, betrayal, rumor peddling, threats against security, intelligence gathering, attempts at blackmail, character assassination—in summary, the stock inventory of espionage conduct. Characters undertake cabals, intrigues, and machinations against one another in order to procure some mastery over their corner of the sexual commerce in the Marseilles waterfront slum. Even the structure of the narrative reinforces this notion. The composition of the story drifts to and fro, like the greasy quayside breakers, between characters plotting conspiracies and voices interacting in dialectical materialist dialogues. In other words, *Romance in Marseille*'s modulation iteratively shifts between the politically hazardous environment of conspiracy and intelligence collection and the conceptual, conditional, rationally disposed world where human beings may exchange views in order to build a consensus of Marxian consciousness without fear of being indicted by the police, denounced by the party, or executed by an assassin. At the end of this chapter, I will consider the full implications of the plot of *Romance in Marseille*.

The opening utterance of the novel expatiates on the protagonist's amputated legs, thus establishing the protracted figurative shape of the text: "In the main ward of the great hospital Lafala lay like a sawed-off stump and pondered the loss of his legs" (1). The autobiographical link is significant, not only because the manuscript's first chapters delineate the experience of a black protagonist undergoing medical treatment, like McKay himself when he started the book, but also because the hospital and illness constitute a fusion of the metaphorical and the existential that orders his oeuvre. The canto-like 1923 poems collected as "The Clinic" articulate perfectly his insalubrious distress. The most familiar poem among the "Clinic" cycle is "The Desolate City" (1926), but the Baudelaire-inflected "Mummy" expresses more intimately McKay's condition in the sanatorium, his loss of skin and therefore casualty of surface identity. The "sappers," McKay's detractors, both political and aesthetic, finally inflict their retribution on the harm caused by the unruly poet by bringing about his deadly illness. Is McKay suggesting that American, British, or French (or Stalinist) agents are responsible for his infirmity?

All of his flesh has fallen away
Between the skin and the bone,
Muscle and blood dried up in decay,
Leaving the skeleton.

And out of that skeleton has leaked
The last reserve of marrow,
The sappers unseen their vengeance have wreaked,
There is nothing left to harrow. (*CP* 198)

It is correspondingly significant that much of McKay's medical trouble was due to chronic sexually contracted illness. *Romance in Marseille* also registers that the hospitalization of its proletarian protagonist must be understood as a discourse in institutional terms. Foucault's discussion of the discourses of discipline and punishment is useful here. The hospital is an illegal alien immigrant deportation holding prison, McKay's narrative says (18), where the alignment of modern bodies seems perfectly normal. Like all of McKay's fiction and much of his poetry, the novel takes pains to draw out the binaries of natural bodies abutting institutionalized bodies, inverting, in the way of négritude poetry, the hierarchy of the civilized (institutionalized) body over the savage (natural) body.

Consonant with 1920s and 1930s Socialist Realist literature, and symmetrically consistent with the discussion above, the beginning of the story fills out a tabloidlike narrative, as if fleshing out newspaper clippings. The first part of the manuscript focuses on Lafala's troubles with the law and his struggle to gain financial independence—two difficulties with which McKay was intimately conversant. In Marseilles, Lafala stows away on an American ship bound for New York. Lafala desires to see Harlem, the New Negro Mecca, the heart of the black diaspora. When he is discovered, he is locked in "a miserable place" (4), a room with no heating, an image recalling the slave's experience of the Middle Passage. Eventually Lafala's legs are frozen, and when he arrives in the United States he is taken to the immigration hospital where doctors, probably acting rashly, amputate. The truncation of Lafala's legs registers a multileveled lacuna in his existence. While growing up as an African, Lafala experienced "joy" in "having a handsome pair of legs" reaching back to his "native" beginnings in the "bush with naked black youth" (1). Lafala "was baptized in a flood of emotion re-tasting the rare delight the members of his tribe felt always by the sight of fine bodies supported by strong gleaming legs" (1). Lafala's lower limbs bore his anamnesis, his bond with the past, personal and primordial: "He remembered lying down naked under the moon and stars while his playmates traced his image with pieces of crockery. And when they were finished they all held hands and dancing around it singing: 'The Moonshine Kid'" (1–2). Lafala's unimpaired, uncovered male body was traced, outlined by his tribe, ritualized as a kind of complete text, a body of laws unto itself: a representation of traceable male ancestry. Lafala was encircled, whole within the traditions and history of his patriarchal culture, with no boundaries beyond the lines of his trace and race. And he was the "Moonshine Kid," an African Wordsworthian child of the body and moon, the Césairian négritudist birth of the Blakean dark rejected twin. Indeed, the title *Romance in Marseille* inspires a primal mythology, as Romantic poets like Goethe and Shelley attempted for the first revolutionary age.

Accordingly, the imagery of *being cut off* is recognizable as the hazardous inescapable consequence of the modernist condition. For Lafala, an African of "primitive" origin, which in McKay's valuation of "savagery" grants an affirmation of the self that is inaccessible to those who toil exclusively under the modern, the human body and the subject's consciousness are one and the same. As *Home to Harlem* riffs on *The Sun Also Rises* (1926), so does *Romance in Marseille*: Hemingway's protagonist has lost his genitalia; McKay's central character has lost the appendages on which he strutted his stuff. However, a singular difference inheres between the two texts' representation of the loss of biological appendages. Jake Barnes's castration signifies the already present absence, the modernist loss of species regeneration and spiritual renewal. But Lafala's complete body was the material expression of his noumenal self. His loss is not symbolic of the already present modernist alienation because he does not suffer from the modern condition until he loses his legs. Upon entering the United States—in its totalizing nationalism, the modern world's most complete manifestation—Lafala's total self is disunited, his corporeal totality is rent from his noumenal wholeness, his own otherness enacted. Indeed, Lafala's sudden corporeal shortage upon entering New York harbor—the twinned concrete essence, Manhattan, and the abstract symbol, America, of nationalism and modernity, as in the sonnet "America" (1921)—portrays a modernist truncation of connection, a cutting off from a link to the past, the primitive, the authentic, the premodern, the communal, the origin. And as the image of Lafala being locked up in "a miserable place" evokes the Middle Passage, the novel points to the de facto enslavement of black bodies under nationalism and capitalism, the means by which black flesh is colonized by the modern enforcement of immigration and property laws. In Lafala's loss one may locate the accretion of manifestly competing yet somehow unified discourses of longing and lack, the merging of the modern with its repressed Other, in a multiple chain of signifiers. One of Homi K. Bhabha's discussions of Fanon and colonial ambivalence provides a terminology for reading McKay's mutilated black bodytext: "In the ambivalent world" of the "not quite/not white," on the margins of metropolitan desire,

> the *founding objects* of the western world become erratic, eccentric, accidental *objets trouvés* of the colonial discourse—the part-objects of presence. It is then that the corpus and the text lose their part-objects of presence; the body and book lose their representational authority. Black skin splits under the racist gaze, displaced into signs of bestiality, genitalia, grotesquerie, which reveals the phobic myth of the undifferentiated whole white body. (92)

Lafala's tangible shortcoming is metonymic of his blackness, thus his corporeal absence/presence performs "the myth of the whole white body." The body and the book are the demonstration in other words of western power, the unstated, unnecessary to iterate, link between the white body and the book, the "romance." Indeed, Lafala's bodytext is a "lost object" on the modernist landscape, a physical specimen that through double negation takes on entitlement.

Yet it seems that Lafala's legs embody another anamnesis as well—no less primordial, and ostensibly set in contradistinction with that of the *losses* of the Middle Passage and modernist nationalism. This recollection of the past is his introduction to European society: "As a kid boy, the missionaries brought him from the bush to the town where they lived and taught. And there his legs were put in pants and soon, soon he learned among other things the new delight of legs" (2). The reader of McKay may at first assume that Lafala's introduction to western society via the missionaries' enactment of Christian colonization would have an entirely deleterious effect, but this is not the case. Functioning as psychologically inflected synecdoche, Lafala's legs "learned" the "intimate chamber music of life." That is, he mastered a new dance, the modern cultural choreography of the western Other, through interaction with the missionaries. And among white society he felt as transported through what his legs "learned" as he had in the instinctive leg-play of his "bush" home: "Legs of ebony, legs of copper, legs of ivory moving pell-mell in columns against his imagination." Experiencing through his legs, Lafala's body became a cultural-organic hybrid, a traveling commonwealth among and between the binaries of black and white, the primordial and the neoteric, the traditional and modern. In another of his ruminations on Fanon, this time contemplating the logics and networks of anticolonialist liberationist politics, Bhabha articulates the way that difference breaks down the polarities of the traditional and modern, "the need to think the limit of culture as a problem of the enunciation of cultural difference" (34):

> The enunciative process introduces a split in the performative present of cultural identification; a split between the traditional culturalist demand for a model, a tradition, a community, a stable system of reference, and the necessary negation of the certitude in the articulation of new cultural demands, meanings, strategies in the political present, as a practice of domination, of resistance. . . . The enunciation of cultural difference problematizes the binary division of past and present, tradition and modernity, at the level of cultural representation and its authoritative address. (35)

Lafala's immigrant bodytext tentatively occupies Bhabha's "Third Space," in "the disjuncture between the subject of a proposition (*énoncé*) and the subject of enunciation, . . . in the passage through a Third Space"(36). Bhabha stresses that it is essential to "understand that all cultural statements and systems are constructed in this contradictory and ambivalent space of enunciation" in order "to understand why hierarchical claims to the inherent originality of 'purity' of cultures are untenable, even before we resort to empirical historical instances that demonstrate their hybridity" (37).

Using the Derridean deconstructive technology as well, Stuart Hall rearticulates the West Indian diaspora identity, saying that the Caribbean immigrant must negotiate the space between culture and diaspora. Bhabha traces the deconstructive binary in Hall's articulation of black diaspora identity; however, Hall's theory of culture and diaspora is useful for my purposes, along with and in tension with Bhabha's Third Space, in theorizing Lafala's presence as signifier in *Romance in Marseille*. Lafala is both linked to the traditional, the home culture, the source, as well as positioned to enter a state of coming into being, shifting between cultural-being and diaspora-becoming, occupying, like Bhabha's performative speech act, a third space: "Lafala's dancing legs had carried him from Africa to Europe, from Europe to America" (2). Lafala's capacity for movement makes him a kind of Derridean instrument of deconstruction—a desiring machine, to use Deleuze and Guattari, operating between and among. Indeed, the metaphoric structure of is apt. Through his legs Lafala is, or was, able to make such a move both materially and figuratively. Without his legs, he is culturally paralyzed, incapable of "dancing" across the black diaspora, severed not precisely from origin as from the independence to trip among two antithetic and fundamentally joy-giving worlds—the original and the encountered. Lafala suffers under western racist and colonialist oppression; therefore, the environment he inhabits circumscribes whatever freedom and pleasure he may have the opportunity to experience in the modern western world. Yet Lafala's two worlds are his two spheres as much as such worlds may be, offering joy because he is able, following Bhabha's theory of the emancipatory attributes of the nonwestern immigrant's cultural hybridity, to choose between. Emancipation is not the freedom to return to the *pays natal* or regain one's essential, premodern identity. It is not a destination reached and then attained and therefore fixed on a map, like the pins the child presses into the Mercator global plan once he or she has mastered a location in reference to its Others. In McKay—who read his Rousseau and in ways holds a metaconversation with his contemporary, Heidegger—the emancipatory is the freedom to move and in doing so to continue becoming. The image of cultural hybridity is in fact the ruling symbolic law of the narrative, a mechanism that functions on several levels, particularly with respect to the politicized black body and the predicament of black Marxism.

Questions respecting cultural-being and diaspora-becoming in *Romance in Marseille* are entangled with issues of revolutionary politics and socioeconomics. While laid up in the New York hospital, Lafala is approached by a proletarian-class African American patient, Black Angel, who urges Lafala to talk to a lawyer that the black man works for: "You oughta get some good money with you laigs chopped off and throwed away like trash" (8). The lawyer is a white Jew, and through Black Angel the narrative accentuates the class divide within black society and the way that white racist ideology permeates black socialization: "I don' trust no nigger lawyers," Black Angel says. "They'll sell you out everytime" (9). The political condition embodied in Lafala's loss is portrayed in Marxist terms, and this aspect of the text is central to McKay's early 1930s black proletarian literary purpose. Although *and because* he is legless, Lafala reaps a benefit from his loss. The sole material profit available to a colonized subject like Lafala is the prospect of trading a portion of his own flesh and bone, for Lafala's body is his only asset in an imperialist-capitalist society where the black subject serves solely as a labor commodity. McKay's novel shares in the popular discursive formation of the early 1930s in several ways, one of which is adapting charged black-white legal-political confrontations. The depiction of a white Jewish lawyer representing a young black man who because he is poor and black needs assistance demonstrates the historical imprint onto the text of the Scottsboro case, a hot racial incident that took place while McKay was working on his manuscript. In March

1931, nine black teenagers were accused of raping two white sex workers in Ala-
bama, then in record time eight were sentenced to death. The case of the Scotts-
boro boys represented the legislated institutionalization of lynching, the state of
Alabama's attempt to insert white civilian violent punitive control practices into
Jim Crow South legal structures. When the NAACP leadership, about which
McKay felt at best "ambivalence" (Cooper 142), heard that the CPUSA's International Legal Defense council was coming to the aid of the Scottsboro boys, the
African American civic organization refused to become involved in the cause.
Not so much worried about white appropriation of black causes, the NAACP
leaders in fact mimicked the right-wing capitalist-imperialist white American
hegemony's hostility for Red incursion. The ILD was popularly and laudably
identified among African Americans as a group of white Jewish lawyers; despite
the NAACP's condemnation of the CPUSA, thousands of African Americans
felt indebted to the "Jewish Communists" for their intervention.[4]

Just as significant, in order to convey to his proletarian-class client how he
must proceed, the lawyer likens Lafala's legal action to union labor organizing
activities, marking the initial affirming signifier for black and white radical socialist interaction in the narrative: "a lawsuit of that kind was like a strike," the
lawyer tells Lafala. "The employers will go their limit to compromise a strike,
but once it is on and the works dislocated, they don't care if the workers starve"
(15). Robin D. G. Kelley's work on black southern Communists, *Hammer and
Hoe: Alabama Communists during the Great Depression* (1990), offers assistance
toward realizing the metaphor of a lawsuit being like a union strike in an early
Depression period manuscript. In January 1931, some five hundred sharecroppers
organized a labor uprising in England, Arkansas; this action caused southern
Communists to begin thinking of ways in which black workers might be organized throughout the South. Party leaders set up Relief Councils and organized
hunger marches in support of the Arkansas sharecroppers. Suddenly poor black
farmers in Alabama who had heard of the "Arkansas example" wanted more information on how the Communists could assist them in their own desperate
situation. The Alabama farm workers also saw how the Communist Party swiftly
and efficiently intervened on behalf of the Scottsboro boys—the grave situation of the Scottsboro boys exemplified the general desperation of the Alabama
sharecroppers. In February, the CPUSA dispatched the Atlanta black Communist organizer Angelo Herndon to Alabama, Kelley says, "to address a group
of sharecroppers who had begun meeting regularly under the leadership of a
local black minister" (38). At this moment, Herndon "began organizing a union
under the auspices of the United Farmers' League" (38). In February 1931, im-

mediately preceding McKay's most intensive work on *Romance in Marseille*, the Alabama black Communist labor union movement was sensationally launched. *Romance in Marseille*'s early pages demonstrate the black Trotskyist-anarchist's approval of black Communist politics when strategic and successful.

Indeed, the entire early 1930s manuscript dilates on the importance of radical socialist even Communist Party organizing and teaching among the black proletariat. What's more, the distinction between Lafala's situation and those of the Scottsboro boys and the Alabama sharecroppers is significant. Another irony is at work in the text: the employment of a Jewish apparently left-leaning lawyer aiding a poor black man whose situation is not as immaculate as the signifiers within the discourse McKay elaborates in his fictionalized version. The lawyer also is not the heroic figure of the ILD or "De Organizer," to use the designation from Langston Hughes's agitprop one-act jazz musical in the late 1930s, a pageant about a figure like Herndon. Lafala's "case" verges on being a swindle, in fact, though certainly the Shipping Company's cold misconduct and their surgeons' negligent haste may be judged far worse than trying to make a marginally corrupt buck off a pitiless corporate holding. What is most impressive here is that McKay shows how the common oppression of blacks under capitalist, racist society may be a more entangled, difficult, complex matter than the most celebrated causes and divisive cases seem to be. Despite the lack of heroism in his story, Lafala's situation demonstrates how racist society would mangle and cast away the black body. And the lawyer, limited in the way he can pursue legally because of the open anti-Semitism among the legal community and juridical structures during the 1920s, must make his way as well as he can against shabby corporate dominions like the Shipping Company.

Lafala's lawyer asks the Shipping Company for one hundred thousand dollars in recompense for his client's loss. Because Lafala has no assets for a retainer's fee, the lawyer's stipulation is that Lafala pay him half of whatever the ultimate award may be, and Lafala eagerly accepts the lawyer's offer (13). The lawyer shows shrewdness in his campaign to win Lafala's case, in effect availing himself of early twentieth-century publicity technology; he photographs Lafala's stumps and acquires from his client a photo of himself before the accident. The lawyer then gets a tabloid newspaper to carry an account of Lafala's accident, "written in pointed modern sentimental sentences," accompanied by the two photographs: before and after (14). The same photos, picked up from the wire services, appear in another newspaper accompanied by a story that, though presented as original reporting, has been copied nearly verbatim from the primary text. McKay dem-

onstrates his antipathy toward the yellow journalistic style of the black press a
few pages later:

> At last the Negro newspapers caught up with Lafala and front-paged
> him with a blast so big and so black that such permanent front-pagers as
> the pretender to the throne of Africa [Marcus Garvey] and his titled en-
> tourage and all other personages of the moment were buried beneath it.
> The "Bellows of the Belt" shouted:
> AFRICAN DAMAGED FIFTY THOUSAND DOLLARS
> But it was outdone by the "United Negro" which ran:
> AFRICAN LEGS BRING ONE HUNDRED THOUSAND DOL-
> LARS (24)

McKay shows that real political commitment across cultural boundaries,
Lafala's bond with the white lawyer, may be contrasted with crude assumptions
respecting cultural nationalist identity politics. While in the hospital, Lafala receives pleas from various individuals and organizations for financial aid: "One
letter came from a youth, accompanied by his photograph. He had written a
book in which he had shown how the Negro Problem could be eliminated by the
Negro himself by means of psychic" (apparently instead of organized political)
"development" (24–25). "'It would be wonderfully appropriate,' [the correspon-
dent] wrote to Lafala, 'if a pure-blooded African should be the instrument by
which my sublime opus was brought to light'" (25). This comic bit of communication embodies the scrap of a meta-analogue; McKay was corresponding with
his editor and other parties about publishing his story of a "pure-blooded African"—with frustrating results. Another letter indicates how nationalist identity politics is used to defraud blacks. A letter comes from "the directress of the
Nubian Orphanage, asking a contribution. Black Angel explained to Lafala that
it was common knowledge in the Black Belt that black babies were not made
welcome in that orphanage" (25). Thus is the wretched condition of black people
employed for profit by whites. But by far the most extravagant, eccentric bit of
raillery in McKay's manuscript is that of the letter from the Christian Unity of
Negro Tribes, "asking Lafala to communicate with the association if he needed
any spiritual assistance in the handling of his affairs" (25). The acronym used by
the Christian Unity of Negro Tribes, the momentarily Rabelaisian text imparts,
is "the C.U.N.T."! McKay's rough joke demonstrates his aversion to both the
NAACP as well as its antithesis, the Universal Negro Improvement Association
(UNIA), Garvey's massive social movement organization—a plague on both

houses. What the three correspondences have in common is their enforcement of an absolutist racial politics from both ends of the spectrum. The white orphanage cynically exploits the sort of racist practices carried out by such institutions as the white orphanage itself. The Negro author and the CUNT capitalize on popular beliefs in the mystical unity of black folk, eliding the universal struggle of blacks, whites, and Asians. All three rely on essentialist identity politics, making reductive the complexity of international struggle.

Lafala and his lawyer develop a "pretty friendship" (16), and the African weaves a "hemp girdle," a garment worn by tribeswomen of his Senegalese culture, and sends it to the lawyer as a present (16). The girdle represents the only memory Lafala has left of motherhood in his culture, his link to biological origin. And though his legs are lost, Lafala's ability to weave such articles represents his histological link with his past, the memory of his African culture that still lives in his hands. The lawyer's response to Lafala's gift exhibits what amounts to a personal-political solidarity with the black man: "It [the girdle] carried me back to very ancient times," the lawyer says. "I mean the times when my people were also divided into tribes and wore girdles just as your people do today" (16). The lawyer's comment echoes the view of philanthropist Julius Rosenwald, who linked Jews and African Americans as a result of analogous histories (Lewis, *When Harlem* 102), a commonly expressed notion during the 1920s as black intellectuals generally saw themselves as closer in kind to Jews than to "Nordics" (148). In a single gesture, McKay links Jews and blacks in both the recovery of historical memory as well as oppression under western imperialism and dangerous nationalist movements. When the Shipping Company moves to have Lafala hastily removed from the immigration hospital and deported (McKay himself in fact always faced expulsion from Morocco), the lawyer moves Lafala into his apartment for protection. But at the moment when a form of insurgent solidarity is possible between the black and the Jew, the alliance across racial boundaries collapses. Realizing that the lawyer will likely win his case, the Shipping Company executives manage to intervene between Lafala and his legal counsel by having a colonial "official" assigned to "represent" him (26). How the Shipping Company may do this is traceable to Lafala's politically indeterminate, nationally interstitial colonial identity: Lafala "belonged to one of the parceled [that is, colonized] regions and was therefore either a colonial subject or a protected person" (26). (This is precisely the same kind of "national" identity McKay carried while living in international zone Tangier, Morocco, a site where he and other expatriates were protected and in McKay's case policed by their respective colonial representatives.) In one of the narrative's observations on class disparity, the de facto representative of the Shipping Company behaves toward the lawyer like "a lord condescending to a vassal." The official maneuvers to intercede between Lafala and his legal representative through a stratagem aimed at Lafala's dread of once again being "manipulated" by whites. That is, white doctors have already mangled Lafala's body, almost certainly operating rashly and without legitimate cause. And Lafala's weakness is mingled with his incapacity to maintain a resolute solidarity with a white class comrade—because the white doctors and the representatives of the Shipping Company mutilated his body. The official says that Lafala "is entitled to more money," and the lawyer and the official argue while the phrase "entitled to more money," like the mythical Siren, is "singing" in Lafala's ears. The official effectively intends to implant in Lafala's mind the idea that the lawyer is conning him, and therefore the African requires the "protection" of the Shipping Company (27). Lafala knows that this isn't true, however, and in fact he permits himself to be deceived by the official because he can hear only the clarion call of capital.

Not directly appealing to Lafala, the official tells the lawyer that the company has entrusted him with the protection of "this man's rights." The lawyer's acrid response amounts to Marxist ideology critique: "Protect him! . . . Why didn't you and your protecting kind give him protection before he stowed away to get frozen on the boat? Why didn't you find out about him before his legs were sawed off? . . . Fine protection you all give to these sort of people" (27–28). This speech falls on deaf ears, both the official's as well as Lafala's: "More money. That was the slogan of life. . . . Why should a little contract stand in the way when there was something more to gain which was legally awarded him. . . . Let the big white men battle it out over him. All he wanted was to come out from under it with what was left of his skin and all that he could possibly get" (28–29). Capital drives a wedge through legal union, the duty of solidarity, even personal fellowship. Lafala sees himself as "put . . . into the hands of the" official, in effect participating in a betrayal of both his agreement and friendship with the lawyer. McKay's narrative confirms that what has prevailed is not a black individual's triumph over white interference, from two sides of the class divide, as Lafala's interior monologue misleadingly suggests. Lafala desires to disentangle himself "with what was left of his skin," and this is understandable, but he fails to see that it is his "skin" which will not allow him to be free of complications. The lawyer says to the official: "You're a company man yourself, only the Company you work for is bigger than the one that maimed [Lafala].[5] But you all belong to the same Big Brotherhood" (30). The lawyer speaks from the position of the radicalized, articulating that capitalist and imperialist interests are one and that the aim of such interests is to locate the means for neutralizing such threats to its ascendancy as black and white solidarity. Later in the novel, Lafala, imprisoned once again, will learn the importance of this lesson. But at the end of the first part, Lafala travels "first class" across the ocean again, back to Marseilles (35).

The second part of the novel locates the narrative on the quayside of Marseilles, where the sexual economy and even the physical, natural world itself metonymically mirror the global capitalist order, a system whose metaphorical referent is the physical issue of penile erection: "Port of the fascinating, forbidding and tumultuous Quayside against which the thick scum of life foams and bubbles and breaks in a syrup of passion and desire" (36). As in *Banjo*, *Romance in Marseille* includes an assembly of black vagabonds, Lafala's cohorts, who collect in the section of Marseilles called "the Ditch." Also, as in *Banjo*, Lafala's comrades collectively represent a kind of microcosm of the black diaspora: an aggregate of African American, African, and West Indian. A pivotal character is the "huge West Indian from a British island," Babel, Lafala's old friend (106). Babel is both idler and worker, depending on his situation. Indeed, among the notable differences between *Banjo* and *Romance in Marseille* is that the latter concerns itself more directly with the plight of black laborers and questions of Marxist political work as such matters relate to sexuality and the pleasures of the flesh.

This section of the manuscript introduces two black sex workers: Aslima, with whom Lafala was romantically linked before leaving Marseilles; and La Fleur Noire (The Black Flower), who moves in on Lafala because he has returned prosperous. Aslima dropped Lafala and filched his money, producing an inflamed wound in his still impassioned thoughts about her. The reader finds that Lafala carries a flame for Aslima, a fixation he cannot shake no matter how he tries. The narrative also acquaints its reader with the community of denizens who frequent an aptly named café, dubbed the Tout-va-Bien, a "rendezvous of the colored colony and owned by a mulatto" (39). Rock is an African American, thus named because he "made his nest between the blocks way down the extreme end of the breakwater" (39), and Diup is a Senegalese who also lives on the streets. Aslima and La Fleur, once friends, have become embittered enemies, locked in commercial competition for the title of "queen of Quayside" (39). Animal imagery acts as an extended metaphor throughout the narrative, and the Deleuzian condition of *becoming-animal* is joined to transgressive sexuality. Rock and Diup are like "two mischievous monkeys" (49), but the prevalent untamed figuration in the text is McKay's familiar pig/hog imagery. The porcine trope appears several times in *Banjo*, used in the conventional sense to describe those in a privileged position "hogging" what should be more evenly distributed (221, 271). As Diup and Rock attempt to "do the split," a recent dance from America, Aslima enters "swinging herself as always from side to side most tantalizingly" (50). She sees Diup on the floor and "playfully kicked hi[s] behind,"[6] saying, "Always monkeying, you and that Rock" (50). Aslima then sees Lafala and "ostentatiously" begins "to vamp him," promising to "dance the jolly pig" (50). The narrative describes her pig dance: "If you have ever seen a pig dancing before rain, Aslima's movement was an exact imitation. She struck an attitude as if she were on all-fours and tossing her head from side to side and shaking her hips, like an excited pig flicking and trying to bite its own tail, she danced round and round the little circle of the café" (50–51). Later the African thinks about Aslima's dance: "his eyes without and within could see nothing but Aslima as the 'jolly pig,' while his ears were humming with the music of her honey-dripping words: 'I'll be a sweet pig to you'"(52). McKay insists that as a consequence of blacks living without being subjected to racism in Moroccan society, he felt culturally nourished in the Arabic country: "For the first time in my life I felt myself singularly free of color-consciousness. I experienced a feeling that must be akin to the physical well-being of a dumb animal among kindred animals, who lives instinctively and by sensations only, without thinking" (*Long Way* 300).[7]

Residing in culturally and sexually uninhibited Morocco evidently informed the writing of *Romance in Marseille*. The porcine imagery relates directly to sexual difference. Diup and Rock are unsuccessful at doing the split, the capering that led to Aslima's pig dance: "It ain't natural to us.... The split is women's business. God made them natural to split," Diup says (49). Rock's response is, "A woman's business is anybody's business," and by "business," Rock means sex, in its openly financed as well as more economically ambiguous forms in a patriarchal society. Like the "black boys" of *Banjo*, who "traveled devious and separate routes in pursuit of a 'handout,' and sometimes had to wander into strange culs-de-sac to obtain it" (32), Rock expresses the view that sexual commerce is not circumscribed by gendered hierarchical structures: "Ain't nothing a woman do you can't find a man to do. If you haven't a way, make one they say. Every white, black and brown a man at Quayside knows that. And the womens know that too" (49). In other words, Rock openly communicates his own queer penchant. The proprietor of the Tout-va-Bien, a striving mulatto petty bourgeois, objects: "That's what's wrong with the whole world today. Women trying so hard to do men's stuff and men doing women's stuff. God made man and woman different to do different stuff" (49). Rock's rejoinder amounts to a sex radical proclamation: "I don't believe in laying down no laws for nobody, for the biggest law-makers are the biggest law-breakers under cover" (49). At the narrative's end, when Aslima defies her pimp in a fatal confrontation, the merging of sexual radicalism and *becoming-animal* recurs.

The narrative voice of *Romance in Marseille* moves freely in and out of various points of view, without much regard for conventional narrativity, inflecting the spongy multivocalism of the text, effecting the anarchic decentering of the single authoritative voice. The narrative shifts to Aslima's point of view when she takes Lafala to her digs and contemplates his injury: "as she looked at Lafala on the bed, the shrunken stumps tapering to the knobs where once were lovely feet, she was moved by a great pity and a great shame" (42). Lafala lashes out at Aslima, essentially blaming her for his loss, and Aslima frankly reminds Lafala of the reality of her economic situation: "You know all we girls treat a stranger like that when we can get away with it. It's the law of the Quayside" (42). When Lafala attempts to pay Aslima for sexual conversance and she refuses to take his money, the narrative denudes the power structure within the sex/gender commodification system. The connection between loss of legs and modernist castration is unmistakable, and this imagery's significance may be understood through a blend of Marxist socioeconomic terms and an understanding of the body in sexual-economic intercourse. Aslima, a sex worker, recognizes that now Lafala has lost his masculine totality, in that the male body is the manifestation of masculine power. Even if he doesn't see this himself, Lafala is now closer to the *lacuna* under which Aslima and other women on the quay must work merely because of their sexed/bodily positioning. Later in the narrative, the reader learns of Aslima's personal history, of her own blending of polarities: "Aslima was a child of North Africa out of Marrakech, that city of the plain where savagery emerging from the jungle meets civilization" (58). As Lafala carries a fragmentary recollection of his matrilineal heredity through his hands, Aslima, born a slave, carries an insubstantial memory of her mother: "Aslima's mother was a robust Soudanese who had been sold a slave to the Moors. . . . She retained a shadowy remembrance of her mother, remembered running by her side clutching at her voluminous skirt when she went upon errands" (58). The details of Aslima's life following her removal from her mother bear close review. Slavers kidnapped Aslima while still a child and sold her to "the house of a wise old courtesan," who "brought her up in a fine spirit of materialistic interest," that is, slave capital economics (60). The hetaera sold Aslima to "a colored sub-officer from one of the French West Indies," and the soldier took Aslima to Casablanca (60–61). After several sexual engagements "with native and black," Aslima met a "tout" who arranged for her to sail for Marseilles: "There he got her into a house of love and received money from her" (60).

Aslima's "pity and shame" respecting Lafala's corporal truncation may be understood in materialist, politically gendered terms. Aslima's pity for Lafala and shame in her own however collateral connection in his loss cause the system of capital exchange for sexual commerce to break down. Aslima's recognition that Lafala may no longer occupy an unquestioned position of masculinist power—standing on his own two legs—is a perception of the Kantian instrumentality for Marxist revolutionary social interaction at the personal level. Lafala now encounters a new "law," a new statutory arrangement, though he still thinks he may act under the old gender order, and he still regards the world as if his legs were there—a kind of phantom memory trace that reinforces the hierarchical gender economy. Indeed, though he takes pleasure in his newfound status as a prosperous denizen of the quay, Lafala is ambivalent about his new identity, his exchange of the most valuable part of his body for financial independence: "Sometimes a wave of regret swept over him dampening his heart when the music [of jazz playing in cafés on the quay] tickled his upper half and the lower could not respond to it. But that sadness soon vanished under the sensation of the new power that having money gave him" (46). In this case, the rupture between Lafala's body and the system of capital production is identified in terms of Marxian use and exchange values.

When he still "had" legs, Lafala enjoyed a form of use value, an authentic worth that capitalist-imperialist contact could not take away—or, to see his stumps as a form of synecdoche, his legs enjoyed a use value. After they are gone, his absent legs take on an absolute exchange value, where their only importance lies in their substitution for capital. They are pure commodity, whose sole profit may be located in the capitalist marketplace, the forum where bodies are assessed only according to their exchange value—as on the slave block. Despite and really because of his newfound wealth, Lafala suffers from a Marxist false consciousness. Whereas *Banjo* is designated "a story without a plot," *Romance in Marseille* is abundant with plotting, including Lafala's legal wrangle with the Shipping Company, his disappearance and run-in with the French authorities, and Aslima's plot to loot the protagonist's capital. So then, the central concealment of the novel inheres in Aslima's purpose. Will she follow her material interest, quite understandably pursuing the way she has had to survive under capitalist objectified commodification as an African woman born into slavery and the sex trade? Or will she break with this materialist regime because she sees her relationship with

Lafala as something that can be separated from the exchange of sexed/gendered fetish commodities—black bodies—in the marketplace?

Chapter 14 introduces the Communist Party retreat, the Seamen's Club: "situated . . . in the drabbest and least interesting proletarian and factory quarter of Marseille. It was a large place with barroom, recreation room, reading room and theatre. The atmosphere was right" (98).[8] However, the seamen aren't much interested in going to the club (98). The problem with the Seamen's Club is that it is too far away from the merchant sailors' hangouts, like the café Tout-va-Bien. "Quayside was more attractive," the narrative asserts. "Even though the sordidness of Quayside was stinking, there were broken bits of color in the dirt" (98). The Seamen's Club is a headquarters established to attract merchantmen and dockworkers to join the Communist Party, but those who founded it were unaware that they had placed it in too remote a location to entice the men. This breakdown in connection demonstrates, in McKay's narrative, the problem of Communist political organization and real proletarian life. While Communist organizers proceed from the position that unaligned workers need to learn how they are exploited and then how they may participate in social change, it is the party apparatchiks who must be educated in the actual lived experience of the proletariat before any real achievement is possible among the black rank and file. This chapter also introduces the Seamen's Club's most active black promoter, a Martinican mulatto, Etienne St. Dominique, who spends much of his time on the waterfront trying to persuade the seamen, chiefly the black sailors, to go to the club (99). St. Dominique's process of radicalization is recognizable in the black participation in Great War history. While doing his military service, St. Dominique "met comrades of radical ideas," and such ideas "that he assimilated" (99) are among the by-products of military duty—the kind of insurgent outgrowth as a result of modernization strategies that the government did not anticipate when it pressed into service its colonial masses. After St. Dominique is discharged, he takes up with "proletarian intellectuals" (99). St. Dominique pursues Lafala, hoping to recruit the young African for the Seamen's Club. Lafala, for his part, is "very much impressed by St. Dominique's cultivated accent and his refined manners," echoing the way that Jake and Banjo respond to Ray in McKay's previous two novels.

As the French West Indian St. Dominique occupies in *Romance in Marseille* the sort of stand-up compatriot position of Ray, one may proceed with the assurance that this black Martinican radical proletarian cultural worker is from the authority of the text's point of view a worthy personality indeed. The black Marxist's name crosses three divergent histories. The name Etienne is presumably an appreciation of Etienne Léro, who published the prelude to the négritude manifesto, *Légitime Défense*. Léro quoted *Banjo*, as the négritudists would later also take pleasure in doing, saying that McKay had successfully portrayed "the sensual imagination of the black man" (Cooper 290). St. Dominique's cognomen demonstrates how estimable he is, in that the appellation is resonant of the Haitian slave uprising of the late eighteenth century, the Santo Domingo rebellion. The spirit of the Santo Domingo slave revolution is more than a mere metaphorical device in McKay's narrative, however. In his chapters devoted to the Seamen's Club, he weaves the history of African slave insurrection into the discourses of Lenin's radical proletariat and Trotsky's permanent revolution thesis. This act reiterates the passages where *Home to Harlem*'s West Indian intellectual, Ray, enlightens that text's unlettered African American, Jake, about the buried history of the Haitian Revolution. The Marxist historical materialism is illustrated repeatedly in *Romance in Marseille*. St. Dominique resembles Lamine Senghor, the black Communist leader of the Comité de Défense de la Race Nègre, an organizer McKay talks about in *A Long Way from Home*. Indeed, it is interesting that the *this* at the beginning of the following quotation possibly acknowledges the distinction between Lamine and Léopold Sédar Senghor: "This Senghor . . . was a war veteran and a Negro leader among the Communists. He was a tall, lean intelligent Senegalese and his ideas were a mixture of African nationalism and international Communism" (278). The real "Senghor took [McKay] to the international building for seamen in Marseilles. It was newly opened by Communists—a vast place, complete with bar, kitchen, theater and recreation room." The place is identical to the Seamen's Club in *Romance in Marseille*: "In the reading room there were newspapers in nearly all of the occidental and oriental languages. There were a few seamen, . . . but no Negroes, present. Senghor talked to the manager and said it was their job to get the Negroes to come to the International Seamen's building." But the problem is the same as it is in McKay's novel: "the building was far out in the center of the town and the Negroes preferred the international beehive of the Vieux Port. . . . The Negroes complained against the unions: Senghor told them the unions were Socialist unions and that they should become Communists" (279). Much of McKay's openness of expression in his memoir concentrates on the constraints of Communism, mixed with the limitations for black participation. It is important that *A Long Way from Home*'s ideology critique, with its transnational compass reading, converges mostly on the effects on blacks outside of the United States, particularly when the narrative articulates its ambivalence about Communism. Part of the representation of blacks in Communism occurs in his take on the négritude movement and its relation to the Communist Party in France. Another feature of "this Senghor" relates him to *Romance in Marseille*: "Senghor was interested in my writing and said he wished I would write the truth about the Negro in Marseilles. I promised him that I would some day" (278–79).

It is useful to build on areas of recontextualization raised in this study. In *Romance in Marseille*, the black Communist organizer St. Dominique bears an undeniable resemblance to both McKay and Lamine Senghor, essentially blending autobiography with the Senegalese Communist's life. But in the context of his memoir of disavowal, the négritude Communist becomes the object of the autobiographer's denigration, a disparagement that the author of *Romance in Marseille* does not display. Indeed, St. Dominique is among the most sympathetic characters in McKay's unpublished novel, presented as a courageous Communist cultural worker, analogous to the autobiographical intellectual worker Ray in McKay's first two novels. One may ask what has changed in the five years between the writing of *Romance in Marseille*, which culminated in 1932, and the composition of *A Long Way from Home*, published in 1937.

The description of the Seamen's Club also complicates the narrative of McKay's alleged early abandonment of Marxist politics:

> As one entered the reading room one faced an impressive magnified photograph of Lenin on the right of which there was a smaller one of Karl Marx. Under them was a drawing of two terrible giants, one white, the other black, both bracing themselves to break the chains that bound them. And under the drawing was the exhortation: Workers of the World, Unite to Break your Chains! All over the walls there were drawings and photographs of workers and workers' leaders from many countries, Soviet Russia taking first place. There were piles of pamphlets and newspapers in several languages, European and Asiatic. (101)

McKay could be caustic about charitable activity when such activity is really just an artifice for an aim other than benevolence, as in the pleas for assistance Lafala receives in the immigration hospital. So it is worth considering whether the description above and what follows may turn ironic. In fact, such does not seem to be the case. *Romance in Marseille*, a book replete with odd comic situations, withering satire, and the occasional Rabelaisian raillery, is cautious with its use of irony when it comes to the value of social action. When the narrative engages in irony, the effect is to show ultimately the subtle difference between true radical understanding and its antithesis.

Consider the description of the president of the club, a former college professor: "He was in no way ambitious. All he cared for was the devoting of his life to Service—given a place where he could help serve the cause of ignorant workers as conscientiously as he had once instructed young students" (102). One detects obvious irony in this passage, and other passages also support such a view. While speaking to Lafala about the merits of Marxist revolution, for example, the president remarks that "Lafala's race represented the very lowest level of humanity, biologically and spiritually speaking" (102). But as the narrative continues, it becomes clear that though McKay may be ironic about the cast of mind and the discourses a white character like the president has available to him, the radical message that such characters as the president imparts is not ironized. The reader witnesses how Lafala and other constituents of the black lumpenproletariat clearly demonstrate that they *are* ignorant of political affairs. In *The Eighteenth Brumaire of Louis Bonaparte*, Marx describes the lumpenproletariat as the unorganized mass of pickpockets, tricksters, gamblers, brothel keepers, and beggars (75). Such characters in *Romance in Marseille* are therefore in need of *proletarianization*—being educated and organized to become informed, engaged, politicized members of the international working class. And it becomes clear from McKay's point of view that, outside of the educated class, Africans are tardy in the acquisition of modern political organizational skills and therefore must be educated in the struggle against racist and imperialist labor conditions. As Lafala has now fully entered the modern world, so must the masses of black peoples in Africa and the diaspora.

In fact, Communists in *Romance in Marseille*, organized as they are, have the responsibility to show blacks how their struggle is linked with other cultural work on the planet and how their struggles are linked to those of their class comrades. Although the black characters in *Romance in Marseille* are sensible to their condition of oppression, they are unaware of how their oppression is proscribed legally and politically. As Lafala did in his dealings with his American Jewish lawyer, the African demonstrates perfectly his incognizance of the mechanism of ideology. The president of the Seamen's Club is happy to see a black man present, because the Communist Party is "trying to help your people. . . . And we want you all to help us help yourselves" (102). The president explains that Lafala's "being there with his yellow and white comrades was a symbol of the all-embracing purpose of the new social ideal. . . . But that was no hindrance to its full participation in the coming social order. For it would be a universal order including all peoples without difference of race and religion" (102). Lafala's response is likened to the problem of facing limited foreign language skills, and it amounts to a frankly Marxist observation on the part of the narrative: "All this was like an unknown tongue to Lafala. . . . His civilized contacts had been limited to the flotsam and jetsam of port life, people who went with the drift like the scum and froth of the tides breaking on the shore, their thinking confined to the immediate needs of a day's work down on the docks or a trip on the boat or any other means of procuring money for flopping, feeding, loving" (102). The rumination on the values of a black Marxism is demonstrated amply when Lafala tells the president that he is returning to Africa. The president, now sounding like a Trotskyist because he promotes international revolution, says, "You must help us over there as much as you can. We need the cooperation of your people. For the white workers alone cannot create a new society if the Capitalists have vast reserves of ignorant black and brown workers against them" (103).

At this juncture, the suddenly introduced character Falope, as if embodying the sudden emergence and impatience of the New Negro, interjects himself into not only the conversation but also the narrative. Vexed by the president's remark about ignorant blacks, Falope demands an account of the "vast reserves of ignorant whites" (103). In other words, blacks may be politically in the dark, but what about whites? The president does not answer, but St. Dominique asserts the familiar Leninist doctrine of vanguardism: "There is no first and last in the class struggle. . . . We need advanced groups of workers everywhere regardless of race to be the vanguard of the class struggle" (103). The answer reflects St. Dominique's own situation, that of a black Marxist cultural worker. What follows is a brief, dialectical exchange between Falope, representing those blacks who are suspicious of "any working class having the absolute power," and St. Dominique, portraying the internationalist proletarian cause, imparted through a black perspective. Although he does admit that he gets "on better with the bosses than the workers every time," in effect acknowledging that he identifies more with the class that oppresses him than with those with whom he shares class oppression, Falope articulates a valuable criticism of the Communist movement's disposition to collapse all oppressed groups into the category of class struggle. However, such details of personality do not matter so much as the larger question of how blacks of varied political persuasions may respond to Communist policies. Understanding Falope's critical disposition lies in grasping the complexity of black Marxism, an untamable dialectical materialism that charges from the margins and therefore must from time to time challenge the doctrine at hand. In this way black Marxism is burdened with endeavoring to undergo change, as Cedric Robinson says, even if such change contests everything of value that leftism has advanced and accomplished for all, including blacks.

In this section of the novel, the reader also encounters Babel, Lafala's closest friend. It turns out that Lafala had a "partner in stowing away" (106) who though discovered by the Shipping Company nonetheless "came out . . . of his confinement skin-clean and foot-whole" (106). After his New York detainment, Babel returns to Marseilles looking for his friend only to discover that Lafala has disappeared. In other words, just as Lafala suddenly vanishes from both the quay and the general narrative, several new characters appear and take part in the temporary narrative aimed at locating Lafala. Babel heads for the Tout-va-Bien, Lafala's old haunt. Several theories about Lafala's sudden absence have been bandied about, and the mulatto café owner initiates his own speculation, stirring the habitués of the now ironically dubbed Tout-va-Bien against St. Dominique by suggesting that the black Communist activist betrayed Lafala to the police. The café proprietor sees St. Dominique and the Seamen's Club as competition, thus the genuine impetus for his accusation against the radical organizer. When St. Dominique visits the café, the proprietor accuses him of being "a traitor," of effecting Lafala's absence. St. Dominique was in fact the last to see Lafala, and he recalls that when the two were leaving the Seamen's Club, the police closely observed their movements. When St. Dominique begins to wonder aloud whether the police did indeed pick up Lafala, the café owner, shouting over St. Dominique's speculations, accuses the black radical of being "an agitator against the Government and Society. Such people are not to be trusted, Bandits, he called them" (121). This time the irony is directed at the Red-baiter. McKay ironically reports the proprietor's next comment, as the owner incites hostility against the Communist, a comment that sounds as if it came straight from the Epic Theater of Bertolt Brecht: "And he warned the little robbers and cut-throats of the Tout-va-Bien against St. Dominique whom he called a dangerous type" (121). The café owner's vehemence is effective because he may rely on an ideology of anxiety about radicals, even among the lumpenproletariat; the entire café is "worked up and shouting against St. Dominique" (121). Meanwhile, the narrative has already reported Aslima's disposition respecting Lafala's absence. Aslima and Titin "were in a state of chronic contention" over Lafala's disappearance, Aslima convinced that Titin has had something to do with it (114). Near suicidal over Lafala's disappearance and now heeding the owner's accusations against St. Dominique, Aslima is caught up in the collective rage, joining the owner in accusing St. Dominique. At this point Babel, also convinced that the Communist has done Lafala a misdeed, moves to assail St. Dominique physically, invoking black absolutist personal politics: "I'll break you' face, you yaller bastard!" St. Dominique is clearly the sympathetic character in this scene: "although [St. Dominique] was not a fighter of any skill he was determined to stand his ground" (121). "But at that moment a white Quaysider known as Big Blonde barged in" (122).

Big Blonde defuses the situation immediately, and his opening utterance says much about his character: "What you all have against this man [St. Dominique]. It's not fair. He's a good friend to all colored fellows" (122). How may a black man be the target of mob violence when the canaille is black? The answer lies in color politics among blacks: "The proprietor of the bar . . . never got into a fight himself. But he would stand quietly by and watch a quarrel, even quietly abetting it until the antagonists got to blows. Then he would step in and call the police to arrest the one he didn't like. The police would always take his word and arrest the one he indicated" (122). The bar owner likes neither St. Dominique for his "activities among the seamen in Quayside" nor Big Blonde, who, in contrast with the other denizens of the waterfront, does not sustain "a kind of sacred regard for the proprietors of Quayside and their establishments" (122). McKay's narrative indicates the problem faced by Communist organizers like St. Dominique, those radicalized blacks who face the peril of irrational passion whipped up against them when among black working-class people who are manipulated by whites. Or, in this case, a "colored" of mixed heritage, a character who is apparently motivated by an albeit misled consciousness of his own class position—an owner, a member of the petit bourgeoisie—over race solidarity. The owner employs race union as a discourse in order to manipulate the black customers of his business to act against another black, although in this case the black man, St. Dominique, himself is a mulatto.

Like the ILD and other "white Communists" who fought for black rights, however, Big Blonde stands up for St. Dominique; Big Blonde is not motivated by self-serving aims like the lawyer in part 1. Babel, happy to see Big Blonde, attempts to explain to his white friend why he was on the verge of giving the black Communist, St. Dominique, a beating. Big Blonde dismisses the allegation against St. Dominique: "All this talk about Lafala is just so much crap. The police will find out where he is—if the rats of Quayside didn't drag him into some hole" (122). Big Blonde rates as one of McKay's most elegantly drawn portraits, and though he is white and analogically identifiable in literary terms—the Conradian antihero reference—he emerges queerly and thus further complicates the companion argument about *Home to Harlem* and *Banjo*, like one of McKay's exemplars of black proletarianism, Jake Brown:

> Big Blonde was like a hero straight out of Joseph Conrad, an outstanding enigma of Quayside. A big firm-footed broad-shouldered man, splendidly built but with haunting eyes of a lost child. He worked on the docks, a

happy worker, active like a madman reckless with his strength, making it hard for his fellow workers to keep up the pace. But he had no interest in the workers' unions and in spite of his natural roughness there was a singular and foreign air of refinement about him.

It was gossiped that he had once held a respectable position in the merchant service, but he never talked about his past life. Because of his quixotic habit of getting into difficulties, he was often in *trouble* with the police. Sometimes he was jailed for a short term; sometimes he went into hiding. He knew the Seamen's Club and frequented it sometimes ostensibly to read, but really to hide from the police in that district after he had got into *trouble* at Quayside. And so Big Blonde had come to know St. Dominique and understand his work in which he was not interested. (123, emphasis added)

The sudden advent of the gay white American working-class character Big Blonde—whose "trouble," one may be assured, is related to his sexual difference—at the moment when the African Lafala has disappeared signals the narrative's unwillingness to be contained by any single conventional novelistic phylum. Big Blonde's presence signifies the perfect solidarity of the international working class, black and white, in that he is a white laborer among black workers who harbors none of the president's doctrinaire views of blacks. Yet the white proletarian-class exemplar is queer, so the text cannot be safely affirmed as simply a proletarian novel with its customary manly (that is, straight) worker as the protagonist. Big Blonde is not the protagonist; he almost literally enters from the margins. In fact, it is Big Blonde's sexual difference, his utter difference and the narrative's candid utterance of his difference—his gender "trouble," to cite Judith Butler—that enables his fellow feeling toward blacks. To paraphrase and adapt Butler, if one makes trouble, one gets into trouble; therefore, trouble is inevitable. The question is "how best to make it, how best to be in it" (vii). Butler's discussion of sexual performativity of identity offers a valuable insight into Big Blonde's "role" in the text: "When the disorganization and disaggregation of the field of bodies disrupts the regulatory fiction of heterosexual coherence, it seems that the expressive model [the stable, rather than performative speech act] loses its descriptive force. That regulatory ideal is then exposed as a norm and a fiction that disguises itself as a developmental law regulating the sexual field that it purports to describe" (136). What's more, Big Blonde is a large, manifestly masculine character, a "living" reproduction of the colossus of Socialist Realist proletarian-folk monumental Bolshevik art who is thus coupled in majesty with his black complement, Babel. Big Blonde and Babel actualize the two heroic/

homoerotic Marxist bodies locked in corporal union that figure prominently on the wall of the Seamen's Club/Proletarian Hall, "the two terrible giants, one white, the other black, both bracing themselves to break the chains that bound them" (101). However, the *e* at the end of Big Blonde's name manifests his feminization, capsizing society's, the government's, and even the Communist Party's capacity for interpellation, thus conferring an unambiguous queer imprinting onto Big Blonde's body. His arrival, in other words, stresses that McKay's Bakhtinian *roman carnivalesque*, though populated almost exclusively by black bodies—characters of wide-ranging political, linguistic, and national orientations who verbalize their condition without external mediation—embraces collective queer anarchist difference.

Babel, Big Blonde, and St. Dominique make their way to the "loving house," La Creole (123), an entirely different atmosphere than that of the Tout-va-Bien. Big Blonde patronizes the tavern because "a boy companion of his," Petit Frère, works there. La Creole is a café "much frequented by the colored Quaysiders" because the "proprietress, a European, [who] had a partiality for colored folk," maintains a stable of "seven girls" of diverse black heritage (124), a kind of sex worker diaspora community. The bantam *français* Petit Frère's description reveals his personal relationship with Big Blonde: "He was wearing a new blue cache-col knotted round his neck and pushed into the waist of his pants. It was a gift from Big Blonde and it matched well his pale color and expressionless eyes" (125). The "tall mulatress who claimed to be an Egyptian . . . began a belly-wobble with Babel[,] and Big Blonde danced with Petit Frère" (124–25). A metonymy that anticipates Glissantian creolization, La Creole is a safe house for those who do not feel as circumscribed by racist ideology as do the subjects of mainstream society, an intermediary space between the Tout-va-Bien, with its hazardous intrigues and dangerous "touts," and a café the reader encounters later in the text, the wholly transgressive Petit Pain. The rhetoric of La Creole makes possible "love," the safe coming together of new forms, both African/Caribbean and straight/gay, the emancipation of race and sex arrangements. The merging of various enunciations of négritude with queer articulates the way in which the two share the condition of being incapable of surrendering to received linguistic and biological orders. Evidently among the advantages of belonging to shunned social and national groups, assemblages that are shoved to the margins in a society where race, class, gender/sexuality, and language régimes prevent inclusion is the capacity for resisting, if only momentarily and conditionally, a totalizing Imaginary Order, an ideology of stability. The bar's name, indicating a Caribbean creolization of racial and linguistic frontiers, suggests racial mixing and the open-ended fusion of blacks and whites, the miscegenation of two groups that mainstream society deems forever-twained polarities, further indicates the possibility for the "natural" union of queer and straight.

Certainly, this section of the manuscript is among the most anarchic in terms of subject agency, the free movement of the body, and the self-reflexivity of the narrative. Big Blonde's profuse character completes the Kantian multiple subjectivity of the novel's autobio-fictional voice, its cubist assembling of McKay's warring-loving modernist fragments. It is worth gathering together the four best drawn characters in the narrative. Lafala is the natural lover, addicted to everything of the body, an impenitent inhabitant of the inside of the skin, of the sensual. His antithesis and therefore the woman with whom he is obsessed, Aslima, is the cautious navigator of the world of commerce and sexuality, yet a character who somehow still clings to the romance. St. Dominique is the proletarianized cultural worker, the idealist, "de organizer," whose romance is revolution. And Big Blonde is the queer *inconnu*, unaffiliated, persecuted by the authorities, and because of this he is dedicated to the socialist revolution if carnally incapable, like McKay, of being a disciplined follower. Yet these deterritorializations, to employ Deleuze and Guattari once again, form a rhizomatic structure. Lafala shares Aslima's austere, glacial esteem for money, and Aslima feels a warm tenderness for the body that Lafala occupies so naturally. Aslima and St. Dominique both perceive the world as it is, thereby verging on glimpsing the Real, although their understanding of the socioeconomic reality contradicts the other. Each therefore exists in a polarity of diametric difference, pitching the Real, shattered, in antipodal directions, thereby sundering the possibility of catching unawares the Real itself. St. Dominique and Big Blonde are leftist comrades and therefore correspondingly dedicated to radical change, though each devotes himself in ways antithetic to the other according to his sense of how best he may do such cultural work. And Big Blonde shares Lafala's ardor for the male body, though Lafala's love is self-absorbed, and Big Blonde's is same-sexed: Lafala concentrates on his own body, whereas Big Blonde focuses on another's. Lafala/Aslima/St. Dominique/Big Blonde—collectively these are the figures in the circuitry of McKay's mind, the black lines on the white page that shape McKay's consciousness and complexion with respect to the word, circa 1929–32.

Following the fête at La Creole, Babel is mysteriously arrested once again. Big Blonde goes to the police station and discovers that Babel has been sent to the local jail, and then St. Dominique takes up Babel's situation (126–27). Thus the document begins another of its interwoven, familiar, repeating plotted routes, this time about blacks imprisoned and a black Communist acting as their advocate. St. Dominique has an old white college chum "in an important position in a municipal department" who is able to help out (128). The story of how St. Dominique is able to learn about the nature of Babel's arrest is a narrative of the black subject positioned in modern society. The popular enthusiasm among the French for African primitive art during the 1920s makes St. Dominique's white acquaintance "curious about the Negroid colony in Marseille and St. Dominique's work" (129). The white art lover has "obtained a few pieces of African wood sculpture and carved masks and sticks" from St. Dominique, who has acquired these primitive artifacts from West African seamen. Resembling the Jewish lawyer in part 1, who treasures and somewhat fetishizes the hemp girdle that Lafala gives him, the white bourgeois Frenchman, institutionalized and modernized, carries a kind of nostalgia for the primitive. And through this longing for a past that never existed, he wishes to transcend the fetishism of commodities under which the modern capitalist world is regulated in order to locate a genuine feeling, the authentic relationship with the original. Yet he may only imagine such a connection if it is recycled through the experience of the black Other, an act of engaging in the Symbolic Order belonging to the "African," thus defeating any opportunity for a genuine, skin-close relationship to the authentic. Under the modern condition's compulsory abandonment of the Real and embrace of the Symbolic and the Imaginary, white society stands captivated before the archeology of the primordial, the relics and fragments of authenticity, where the alienation of meaning does not exist, modern society reasons, where unmediated sensation may be regained. Modern western culture is therefore enthralled by the idea of an Other-within, untouched by institutional forces, a kind of Africanized Virgin of the Real. Yet capitalist society, the socioeconomic instrument that acts on behalf of white western culture, incarcerates the material bodies of the living primitive bad subjects.

Modern society's substantiality takes the shape of the state, the nation, the material signifier of the modern that must therefore subject black bodies to discipline and punishment in an effort to regulate, secure, identify, classify, and enthrall the margins—and set limits on the boundaries. The structure of modern society, with its notion of the individual's split, fragmented psychology, prevents the possibility of gaining access to the very thing it strives for: the authentic, the Real. For to be in the modern is to live in the Symbolic, in the Imaginary, bathed in the system of signifiers, installed within the simulacra of remoteness from the ontological and aetiological. Locating modern culture, Eliot's *The Waste Land* (1922) is a *topos* where the disembodied voice says: "These fragments I have shored against my ruin." Such is modernist alienation. And such is why modern society, expressed tangibly through the national state, must police back into line the living flesh of its idea, its invention, of the Real—the African.

Eventually St. Dominique is able to ascertain why Lafala and Babel have been arrested. The police have picked up Lafala for having stowed away, and the Shipping Company is behind his imprisonment. Babel is being detained for hiding in the ship's hold, too, but in fact his confinement stems from the Shipping Company seeing him as a means to force Lafala to return his settlement. The officials want Babel to state that Lafala's legs were unsound before he stowed away, that the Company was not liable for his affliction, but Babel imparts to St. Dominique: "I couldn't admit no such thing, . . . for all I knowed them Lafala's feet was sound feet and he was one dancing fool at Quayside" (130). In any event, the case against Lafala and Babel is lawfully valid—they did stow away—and each could be imprisoned for six months, so the Shipping Company has the advantage in its conspiracy. How St. Dominique is able to effect their release takes on a quasi-reflexive, somewhat autobiographical, even metafictional cast, with St. Dominique presenting himself as a literary figure in order to gain a hearing before the Shipping Company's representative. Among the levels of irony at work in this part of the text is that St. Dominique is literally a literary figure. St. Dominique's "functionary friend," the white college pal who sustains a passion for everything African, suggests that his black friend pose as "a man of letters in the respectable fashion" (131). St. Dominique's past at first resembles his author's, then abruptly turns to the familiar McKay spleen-venting on a favorite antipathy, the mania for anything black and literary: "After the unhappy ending of his college days, St. Dominique had among other things flirted with the literary muse. And once he had written for a magazine called the *Aframerican*[9] a colorfully descriptive account of Quayside. As Negroid talent usually has an effect in the close colored world entirely out of proportion to its general significance, St. Dominique had been hailed as the dark star rising in the European literary horizon and achieved a full-sized photograph of himself in the *Aframerican* magazine" (131). St. Dominique's white friend, "aware of the respect of local public opinion for the literary mind," shrewdly encourages the black Communist to have some "visiting cards printed," then go to the Shipping Company and introduce himself as a writer. The white friend may be beguiled by the fantasy of the African Other, but, curiously as a result of this, he knows how to play the establishment's game in a way that St. Dominique does not know. St. Dominique meets the manager of the Shipping Company, who informs the intermediary that Lafala would have been "granted adequate compensation" for his loss, but the African had "preferred to institute proceedings against" the company, "which had cost them an enormous amount of money and trouble" (132). This account is, of course, a contemptible fabrication, and St. Dominique, whose sole interest lies in hope of securing Lafala and Babel's release, responds with just as disingenuous a defense of Lafala: "St. Dominique said that Lafala was an ignorant uneducated savage and that in the despairing condition in which he was after the amputation of his legs it should not be held against him that he permitted a lawyer to act for him!" (132). The usage of the word *ignorant* echoes the Seamen's Club president's comment to Lafala about the need for Africans to become intellectually conscious of their condition in the modern world—ironic because a black Communist exploits the very language the president uses. And St. Dominique is able to manipulate the situation by relying on the manager's racist assumptions about blacks being incapable of determining their own welfare and Jewish lawyers taking advantage of such benightedness. This is exactly how black Communists were portrayed in the popular press and mainstream political discourses of the time. The manager then shows an interest in St. Dominique's purported literary handiwork, and the black mediator produces the *Aframerican* article with his accompanying photo. The manager thereupon promises "to use his influence to have Lafala and Babel released," then in smiling farewell enjoins, "Now don't go away and write anything bad about the Company," and St. Dominique, also beaming, assures the executive, "I couldn't now" (133). Yet another irony: the manager unquestionably assumes that blacks are incapable of representing their own interests, but he is willing to placate when it comes to Lafala and Babel's predicament because he is fearful about negative press that would be generated by a black journalist.

The factual basis for this narrative poses an interesting contrast with McKay's fictional version. McKay, like St. Dominique, the character based on the author himself, fought for the release of the African, Dede, who had lost his legs in the very same fashion as Lafala. However, he did not say that his friend "was an ignorant uneducated savage" or argue that "it should not be held against him that he permitted a lawyer to act for him." Not needing like St. Dominique to *pose* as a writer, McKay threatened retaliation through the pen. Yet it is significant that the work he engaged in on behalf of an African brother appears in a novel of the early 1930s, particularly as McKay, a Trotskyist at this time, presents his fictional self as a Communist organizer.

Following this scene, Falope, who helped the black Communist acquire the professional calling cards, and St. Dominique engage in another of McKay's familiar dialectical materialist dialogues, exchanging amicable if nevertheless trenchant retorts over the true nature of black identity and entitlement. The conversation revolves around whether the predicament of blacks in modern society is an "economic problem" or a "psychological one," and inevitably the discussion focuses on the question of the mulatto (134). In view of how his smooth-tongued black Marxist friend handled Lafala and Babel's situation, Falope accuses St. Dominique of being "a Bolshy pig" who needs "a black kingdom with a vast court shaded with palms and ferns and a black king sitting on his ivory throne with people around him and you a mediator between the people and the king" (133). McKay is, of course, alluding to O'Neill's *Emperor Jones* (1920), a play that lampoons Marcus Garvey, and seems to be echoing Ray's "marble palace" dream in *Home to Harlem* (157–58). But the discursive conflation of Communist cultural work with an idealized African hierarchical civilization resides unmistakably in the recognition that though rival civic forces engaged in vying for black folks' loyalty, the CPUSA and Garvey's UNIA share discourses and have parallel goals. Moreover, though ostensibly antithetic in philosophy—the CPUSA offered collective international proletarianism against the rise of industrial capitalism while the UNIA promoted black cultural nationalism against the institutionalization of racism—Garvey's UNIA indirectly abetted the CPUSA in recruiting blacks to their ranks (Robinson 213). As the CPUSA was forming, Garvey's UNIA was the most popular form of African cultural nationalism of the period, if indeed a useful strategic essentialism at times. Its "back-to-Africa" movement by the early 1920s counted thousands of members, and by the time McKay was writing *Romance in Marseille*, the Garveyite movement had waned. In the wake of this dearth, the CPUSA seemed to many to be the only organized social movement that presented a warm welcome to black laborers, as the situation of the Arkansas example and the Scottsboro boys illustrates. The NAACP, on the other hand, was focused on the Talented Tenth, the striving black middle class. Ironically the UNIA made possible the rise of the CPUSA among black workers because the Garveyite flair for spectacle—military style uniforms and marching parades, the familiar exhibitions of dramatic display to all Americans, black and white, Communist and nationalist—effectively mobilized black workers for social action. Thus in some manner the UNIA paved the way for the Communists' proportionately spectacular mobilizing tactics: street-corner calls to arms, massive demonstrations, along with journalistic condemnations of the powerful, and the like. Falope's denunciation of St. Dominique as a black Marxist enacts the common mingling of conflicting yet paradoxically mutually informing sociopolitical discourses: "The Internationale unites the human race" and "Back to Africa."

St. Dominique's rejoinder to Falope's however facetious accusation acts as a kind of comprehensive statement for *Romance in Marseille*'s narrative: "I'd prefer this or any other Mediterranean port to any kind of black kingdom" (133). This ostensibly trifling remark, seemingly presented as an *ennuyé* reaction to Falope's facetiousness, must be recognized as a rejection of more than the mere assertion of a literal geographical preference. In other words, St. Dominique, unquestionably the character who is closest to McKay in intellectual *dis-position*, rejects the notion of a mythic black nationalist realm where ambiguity cannot exist, where absolutist notions of racial national identity must endure. St. Dominique refuses this in favor of a Third Space, where ambivalence is possible and therefore contingency enables organic deviation. In addition, St. Dominique's comment speaks for McKay's propensity for diaspora over Fatherland, the interstitial over the axial—his preference for drifting boundlessly in the black Atlantic, to being permanently fixed in Africa, or "black Africa," itself. This rendition signifies a string of *preferences*, racial, existential, political, and sexual, none of which may be disentangled from one another. St. Dominique may reside in Marseille, but he speaks, as it were, through innovative technologies of modern communication, via McKay in Tangier. Diaspora itself becomes something more emblematic than a physical part of the world, various locations on a black map of the white world. Diaspora becomes the interval territory, the border region, the international zone: an expanse that authorizes a becoming-identity. Falope's retort to St. Dominique's elegant extrication from everything stable, knowable, certain, ascertainable—phenomenological certitude, ideological reduction⊠is a resort to absolutist color politics: "You're no Negro anyway. You're half here and half there and never will be whole anywhere." The narrative informs the reader that Falope is being facetious, but the unmistakable assertion of identity politics is at work in his response. Nonetheless, Falope inadvertently has provided St. Dominique with the logic of his own argument, as St. Dominique says: "Although you're pure-blooded, I'm more Negro in feeling than you" (134). Like diaspora, the identity marker *Negro* here takes on an epistemological complexity, one that makes *Romance in Marseille* among McKay's most urgent texts. As Robinson says in *Black Marxism*, the "Negro" is fundamentally an invention of imperialist discourses, a necessary subaltern subject that instrumentally enables white supremacy under racial nationalism and industrial capitalism (81). St. Dominique understands this singular philosophical question and states his difference in epistemological terms. For St. Dominique, the Negro is not an identity received by and thus circumscribed by racist discourses. The Negro is radicalism itself: insurgency that cannot be institutionalized, counterhegemony that cannot be attenuated. Therefore, St. Dominique is more Negro, more radical in consciousness and sensibility, than the ancestrally, eugenically more African Falope, who, suffering from Marxian false consciousness, has internalized racism through class domination and a restrictive ethnic nationalism. Although aware of racial disparity, Falope is incapable of recognizing how racism and imperialism are the superstructural, ideological signifiers of capitalism, a form of hegemony that, qua Fanon, exploits as its most effective weapon the enunciative act itself, determining the Negro for him or her as a subordinate subject. At the chapter's end, St. Dominique, sounding like the cultural educator Ray in both *Home to Harlem* and *Banjo*, advises Falope to "go and read the histories of peoples of the world and then think it out for yourself" (136). And finally the black Communist, returning the narrative momentum to the book's central plot, insists that Lafala's case is as much about race as it is about class: "It's a stinking proletarian case, from Marseille across the ocean to New York and back" (136).

Like the verbal exchanges, dancing is an expressive action throughout the text, as one may see by Babel's earlier recognition that Lafala had been "one dancing fool" and therefore could not equivocate about the soundness of Lafala's legs even if he had been the sort who is tempted to betray a friend. In chapter 19, the party at the Tout-va-Bien is a celebration of the pluralized body in motion: "The Quaysiders turned out *in a body* to welcome" Lafala [emphasis added], including "the low-down gangs of old-and-hard youth, girls and men, white and brown and black, mingled colors and odors come together, drinking, gossiping, dancing and perspiring to the sound of international jazz" (140). And the music itself is a creolized blend, a hybrid "jazzing" of two continents and the Caribbean: "A Martinique soldier strolled in with his accordion and began playing beguin tunes. The craze of the Charleston and black bottom was about dead and buried. But the beguin was there, always living in this heady Martinique dance, blood cousin to the other West Indian folk dances, the Aframerican shuffle and the African swaying" (141–42). Where one character who is bodily able refuses to, another who is physically disabled longs to dance. The beguin music "took St. Dominique by the skin and penetrated into his marrow and bone, tickling his joints," but the black Communist refuses to dance in the Tout-va-Bien because of the mulatto owner's attempt to stir up a mob against him during Lafala's absence (142). Lafala, however, is unable to get up and take the floor on his own two feet, but he and Aslima sway with the beguin: "The beguin rhythm caught him by the middle, drop to drop. The music swelled up and down with a sweep and rushed him," figuratively to be sure, "off his feet" (143–44). Lafala once again experiences the phenomenon of phantom memory trace—and the desire to dance to creolized black music is the catalyst. Aslima dances with Lafala: "And Lafala stood up leaning on Aslima and did the beguin. He started in timidly, then found it was not so difficult after all with Aslima carrying him along. . . . Some of the crowd dropped out of the circle so that Aslima and Lafala should have more space and standing upon chairs and tables stacked with bottles and glasses applauded as they shuffled around" (143). The narrative circles back once again as the description of Aslima dancing with Lafala recirculates the text's early portrayal of Lafala's youthful, complete body encircled ritualistically by his tribe. A diaspora subject now and a male in the modern world, thus inherently incomplete, Lafala is completed, actualized by dancing with Aslima, as the circle around them formally favors their contingent, transitory fusion. Reinforcing the "kinship" of diaspora blending through the act of executing the indigenous vinculum with origin in ritual form, Aslima performs "a native dance" that nevertheless exhibits cultural harmonious union: "Her primitive flamenco went naturally well with the music, showing kinship and revealing the African influence of both" the West Indian beguin and the Spanish Romany diapason (143). The denizens of the Tout-va-Bien cheer on Aslima, snapping their fingers and hailing her as "The Queen! The Queen!"

La Fleur takes in this spectacle with "chagrin and envy" (144). Though not disposed toward "big and aggressive men" like Babel, La Fleur "maneuvered herself to his side and began teasing him to dance" (145). At first Babel is not interested in dancing. Distracted, Babel is anxious about Aslima's intentions toward Lafala, believing that now that his friend is a man of means, the African should become respectable and therefore terminate relations with such women as Aslima. But Babel eventually relents, and he dances with La Fleur. Aslima's rival is interested in Babel because she wishes to acquire information about Lafala, to "learn the exact relations existing between Lafala and Aslima" (145). Following this, La Fleur produces her own set of texts, designed to create discord between Lafala and Aslima:

> Late that night when she was all alone La Fleur wrote three notes, disguising her large round heavy and awkward handwriting as much as she could.
>
> The first was to Lafala and ran: Look out, they're trying to get you with your own plan. Take warning from
>
> INSIDER.
>
> The second was addressed to the office where Lafala was officially represented and read: Lafala is menaced by a dangerous gang.
>
> The third was to Titin and sent by hand to a special café: Attention! Aslima is deceiving you. (146)

Chapter 20 returns to Big Blonde and Petit Frère, and the opening utterance of the segment seems to indicate the direction of the narrative: "From the thought of having an irresponsible gay time in Quayside with Lafala, Babel turned to work" (147). The distinction between labor and pleasure is signed as the difference between being responsible and being "gay." By the early 1930s *gay* and *queer* were widespread idioms used by underground folk to designate homosexual society, so it is appropriate to find the word *gay* employed in the narrative to describe "irresponsible" behavior, or pleasure. However, as one follows the action of the scene, Babel discovers that a simple binary, where work is the privileged category and pleasure, or "being gay," the degraded signified is not supported as the plot unfolds and character-subjects become entangled in treacherous games of conspiracy.

After a day's work alongside a gang of Senegalese dockers, Babel looks up Big Blonde, barging in on him while his monumental white counterpart is putting on his best suit.[10] Babel wishes to invite his white friend to a party, along with Lafala, St. Dominique, and Falope; the big West Indian wants to celebrate his and Lafala's release from prison. Big Blonde declines, having made plans to rendezvous with Petit Frère, and he becomes "quite lyrical" in anticipation: "Nothing could make him break that engagement. Not for the love of a drinking party which always delighted him, nor the bouquets of the rarest wines, nor the music of the hymen though sweet with the honey of the queen bee and glorious like the songs of Solomon's loves, no not for the virgin stars of the sky nor a brighter shining moon" (148). Big Blonde's "lyricism" about preferring his "Little Brother" to "the hymen though sweet with the honey of the queen bee" may be ironic on the level of the communicative act. The use of the "lyrical" term *hymen*, standing as emblematic, even metonymic of the clinical sounding vagina, indicates a sense of expressive distance from female bodies that one comes across throughout McKay's writing, the use of "C.U.N.T." for the NAACP being perhaps the most obvious example. It is rather surprising to discover that Big Blonde may not be exclusively gay if one holds to any notion of absolute sexual difference. Or is he bisexual, to use another clinical term? Big Blonde's social-sexual orientation is inadequately accounted for in clinical categories of sexual preference. Rather, he is queer. That is, Big Blonde's sexuality is unstable, intangible, and unascertainable clinically. It is worth reiterating that to be queer is not to have a sexual preference or orientation, in any event. Queer is the incapacity to be institutionalized sexually and therefore necessitates the condition of sexual dissidence, of sex radicalism. Queer is not a sexual orientation; it is a revolutionary dis-position, a sexual signing of anarchism. This bears repeating because the importance of

Romance in Marseille lies in its articulation of the radical nature of queer dis-positionality. Big Blonde seems constitutionally incapable of being fixed to any identity formation, including homosexuality, and the same may be asserted for Big Blonde's black queer anarchist-proletarian author, Claude McKay, and his own sense of his sexuality. Big Blonde's homoerotic lyricism works in solidarity with his radicalism; his sexuality is as political as his class condition. His lyricism derives from the manumission of the body, in work as well as in pleasure.

So it is poetically harmonious expressively and performatively that "in the midst of [Big Blonde's] lyricism Petit Frère arrived, fascinating with his pale prettiness and challenging deep dark-ringed eyes and insolent mouth" (148). Moreover, Petit Frère brings "a story." At the Domino Café,[11] where he now works, he has overheard "a little conversation between Titin and the Grand Ma-quereau, who was also entitled Duke of Quayside"; not without his resources, Titin has sought the advice of the reigning pimp of Marseille. "The conversation was about Lafala and the scheme of Aslima to despoil him" (148), and the small hustler reports the information because he hates Aslima's tout. Titin arranged for Petit Frère to work at La Creole, and the Little Brother is regularly obliged to pay the black panderer a percentage of his net proceeds, even though he now is installed elsewhere. Babel is alarmed by this piece of intelligence and implores Big Blonde, the most responsible of the quay denizens, to talk Lafala out of con-tinuing his liaison with Aslima. Big Blonde doesn't believe, however, that Lafala would let himself be trapped, to which Babel quips "that it wouldn't be so hard to believe if Big Blonde were less interested in petit frères and more in petit filles" (149). And it is plausible that Big Blonde's disinclination toward intimate relationships with women makes him less capable of seeing how heterosexed political intrigues function, in that the very act of being "involved" in hetero society means engaging in a form of political intrigue for the quaysiders, with tangled liaisons and cabals. Big Blonde's response demonstrates one reason why he inclines as he does: "Big Blonde guffawed and excused himself from joining Lafala and the others that night for just that reason. He and Petit Frère were go-ing to dine together and afterward resort to a little café" (149).

In the next scene Lafala is dressing when his room is "invaded" by Babel, along with St. Dominique and Falope (150). Babel recounts Petit Frère's story of Titin and Aslima's intrigue. But Lafala isn't affected by this information, and further-more he is "displeased with Babel for revealing his plans to St. Dominique and Falope" because the more who know about his plan to return to Africa with Aslima, the better the chance that Titin will learn of Lafala's intentions. Mean-while, Falope intervenes to admonish Lafala for his scheme to take Aslima back to Africa with him, siding with Babel: "I can't understand you, Lafala," Falope says. "You must be spoiled by civilization. What you're planning to do isn't right at all. It isn't African. It's a loving white way" (151). Lafala defends himself, saying that he has "passed all through that already," that he has already flirted with civilization and now he knows better. St. Dominique interjects, broadening the material dialectical exchange, arguing against Falope; the black Communist understands Lafala's feelings because he has "been through the same experience" himself (151). Falope's response to St. Dominique is: "Now I know why you're a red." And when St. Dominique offers his encouragement to Lafala to "go right ahead if you love her," Falope exclaims: "Love! What is this thing called love?" After hearing Falope's argument, Babel is now convinced that Falope is out of line and cracks: "Jest a funny little word with four letters" (151). The interchange alludes to the 1929 Cole Porter Tin Pan Alley hit "What Is This Thing Called Love?" This is evident not just in Falope's likely unintentional reference to the popular song but also in Babel's witty riposte: "What is this thing called love? / This *funny thing* called love?" (emphasis added).[12]

This question resonates throughout the narrative, from Lafala's recondite, almost mystical passion for Aslima, a social pariah because she is a sex worker, to Big Blonde's fascination with his "Little Brother." The chapter ends with an accruement on the question of the unspanable divide between African nationalism and Marxist internationalism. After a comparative linguistic English-French exchange over how many "letters" it takes to spell *love*—four in English, five in French—St. Dominique says, "I prefer to think of love without letters" (152). St. Dominique's comment recapitulates the rejoinder to the question raised by the song: What is this thing called love? Love is without "letters," without absolute lexical denotation, in that love may take multiple guises in the modern, cosmopolitan world of the diaspora; love must be heterogeneous in form. The third line of the Tin Pan Alley tune reinforces this view: "Just who can solve its mystery?" Falope objects, punning on the expressivity of "letters": "You can't be primitive and proletarian at the same time. We can't go back again. We have studied our figures and learned our letters. Now we are civilized" (152). But the answer to this query must be postponed, as all dialectical inquiries must be deferred in the narrative, when the plot inserts itself once again, this time in the shape of a boy delivering a letter for Lafala. The letter is the note composed by "Insider," La Fleur's falsification to disable Aslima's relationship with Lafala. The chapter that follows stages a single scene: what takes place when the four black men seek out Big Blonde for his counsel.[13]

The café where Big Blonde and Petit Frère rendezvous, the Petit Pain, is "Big

Blonde's favorite place when he was in a sentimental mood and wanted to spend a quiet evening with his little friend" (*Romance* 153). It is important that Big Blonde spends much of his time at the Seamen's Club reading room: "He knew the Seaman's Club and frequented it sometimes ostensibly to read, but really to hide from the police in that district after he had got into trouble at Quayside" (123). The pair visits the Petit Pain when they wish to escape rather raucous haunts like La Creole and the Tout-va-Bien, when they seek out a tranquil atmosphere where they may be alone. One should recall that Petit Frère, for his part, hangs around first La Creole, where he was installed by Titin, then moves on to the Domino Café; the male hustler spends most of his time in cafés where he earns his trade. Certainly the two intermittently meet—their two spheres consequently intersecting—at Petit Pain so that they may pursue their mutual predilection in private. My point here is that Big Blonde, a queer proletarian, blends his sexual conduct with his political impulse. Indeed, his need to "hide out" from the police by *hanging out* at the Seamen's Club indicates that the two worlds he dwells in are permeable, that his same-sex praxis and his Marxist penchant are wrapped in the same impetus. Big Blonde's need to hide out also contains an autobiographical element to it, as McKay himself permitted Michael, the white queer hustler, to use his Harlem digs to go underground, and McKay himself disappeared from the gaze of any number of policing agents at various times of his life.

Before discussing what takes place between Big Blonde and the other characters in chapter 21, I would assert that it is necessary to examine the painterly setting of the scene. The café Petit Pain signifies the interstitial, anomalous Third Space of the narrative: "Like the street [on which the Petit Pain is located] there was something a little sinister and something very alluring in this café, but difficult to define. It was a quality *strangely balancing between* the emotions of laughter and tears, ribaldry and bitter-sweetness" [emphasis added] (153). In *Banjo*, it is possible to drink a "camouflage absinthe-and-water" at one of the bars in the "Ditch" (172). Although McKay does not identify the café as an absinthe bar in *Romance in Marseille*, the description of the scene resembles a mélange of painted images of such drinking holes, ranging from the early Belle Époque to the early twentieth-century avant-garde. Degas's cheerless *L'Absinthe* (1876) is among the first to depict the scene; in Degas's painting a frowzy couple sit glumly over their glasses of the lime-colored libation, the café's mood articulated by an olive-drab tint. The postimpressionists turned from Degas's detached photographic if blurry portraiture to images that expose the external, the surface, to the interior, emotional core of the subjects: the penúmbrul, spectral paintings of cabarets by Toulouse-Lautrec; the glowering self-portraits and flaming scenes of cafés by Van Gogh; and the greenish, slightly warped-looking compositions of bistros by Gauguin. Finally, there are the blue period and cubist depictions by Picasso. All of these paintings are peopled by freakish, obscure figures, as in McKay's description: "The bar was run by a rather young man and his middle-aged paramour. The man was tall and very thin and his bloodless skin was like parchment upon his flesh and looked as if it were drawn away from his mouth. The woman was a spreading type in happy relief against the sharp harshness of the man" (153–54). The visual disproportionate sketch of the pair intensifies the psychological asymmetry of the setting. The man's skin is likened to an out-of-date, brittle kind of paper, underscoring the textual character of his presence. But the male character—really more of a vaguely "drawn" figure—though a kind of text is ultimately illegible. His "flesh" takes on a distinctly cubist look, "as if *drawn away from* his mouth." Where the male figure is lanky and gaunt, the female body is horizontally extended, standing "in happy relief," as in Toulouse-Lautrec's grotesque chiaroscuro, "against the sharpness," the pointy verticality, of the male torso.

As for the patrons of the bar, the "few clients" (rather than customers) include two "men of middle-class respectability" who are "throwing dice for a game called 'Pigs' with three lads evidently of the slum proletariat" (154). Also, two "fine and handsome sailors were sipping cognac and sugar with a young man slickly dressed like a professional dancer" (154). These three "soaked the cubes of sugar in the cognac and ate them and the right cheek of the young man twitched at regular intervals like a poor fish out of water and gasping for breath" (154). The two middle-class men are of course slumming, furtively engaging with three street hustlers. The sailors are engaged with a man who has the appearance of an expert dancer, that is, a man in performance habiliments, therefore dramatizing the ludic character of surface identity. His being identified as a "professional" suggests his *métier* in the sex trade. The inclusion of the startling simile, "the right cheek of the young man twitched at regular intervals like a poor fish out of water and gasping for breath," reinforces the troubled air of the setting by way of a surrealist, even absurdist metaphor. The man's face takes on the look of a struggling fish, his visage externalizing an animal struggling inside the face of a human. In addition to a *soldat disparu* sitting "over a small beer," there is "a decrepit woman with a half a glass of coffee perfumed with cognac between her sad elbows stuck at a weary slant into the table, her fingers crossed over her eyes" (154). This portrait bears a striking resemblance to Picasso's blue period composition *Woman Drinking Absinthe* (1901).

Indeed, the description of the bohemian dive is consistent with literary and painterly representations of the outlawed absinthe bar of early twentieth-century France, from the particularity of the saturating of lumps of sugar in cognac to the general shadiness of the setting.[14] Although absinthe was banned in France in 1915, its consumption continued surreptitiously throughout the 1920s (Conrad 137). The "clients" act subdued rather than rowdy, in contrast to the way the customers behave in the Tout-va-Bien and La Creole. Moreover, the Petit Pain manifests the air of concealment, stealth, and discretion, all of which would be indispensable for the atmosphere of a legally prohibited club. As for the depiction of the cognac and sugar, the most familiar drink is a pale green concoction, recognizable today in the various legal licorice-flavored substitutes, brands that before the ban offered absinthe: Pastis, Ricard, and Pernod Fils. Dissolving a sugar cube into an absinthe-and-water solution to produce the familiar dim green liquid was practically ritualistic for the absinthe drinker during the late nineteenth and early twentieth centuries. However, various absinthe cocktail recipes required fortifying the potent, psychotropic wormwood drink with cognac. Toulouse-Lautrec's favorite recipe "was called *tremblement de terre . . .* and consisted of absinthe and cognac" (Conrad 55).

The name Petit Pain suggests multiple linguistic meanings, indeed, partly relating to transgressive sexuality, partially having to do with absinthe drinking, and sometimes uniting the two. On the literal level the name suggests a small bread or loaf, or bar of soap in French, yet even this apparent signification implies an alternative meaning, in that both possible translations are metaphorical of the male sexual reproductive organ. *Pain* can also indicate *en français* "lump"—that is, a "lump of sugar"—fortifying the idea that the Petit Pain is a clandestine bar that covertly serves absinthe. Near the end of the scene, the all-male party sings a song called "Moon-struck," which contains the line "Crazy for my fairy moon" (157). The "fairy" reference suggests the queer society of the environment, and among absinthe's aliases is "the green fairy": *la fée verte*. An English pun resides in the name "little *pain*," of course, suggesting the despondency of those who are compelled to patronize this hidden oasis, whether for the illegal alcoholic drink or for the illicit sexual conversance, or both. Or because of what the drink and sex do to the "client": the dangers of decadence—alcoholism and sexual disease (McKay himself suffered from syphilis). The café is the stage for a *little pain*. The sound of the bar suggests the general feeling of loneliness: "A phonograph at the end of the bar was wheezing out a popular bal musette song, but the music sounded plaintive as if it were asking why more attention was not being paid to it" (154). A *bal musette* number is a dance strain; therefore the music feels deserted because, as the woman sitting at the bar is forsaken, no one is dancing to it. Dancing isn't allowed in the Petit Pain because the proprietors don't have a "dancing license" (156). Moreover, imagining that music can ask why it is not being paid enough attention is the kind of fanciful, hallucinatory thought that sometimes materialized in the mind of the absinthe drinker. Oscar Wilde talked of seeing the "most wonderful flowers, tulips and lilies, and roses" springing up and making a garden in the café he took absinthe in (qtd. in Ellman 469).

The "pale atmosphere" of the Petit Pain is changed when Babel, Lafala, St. Dominique, and Falope intrude, "adding . . . a touch of that exotic color for which Marseille is famous" (154). White—and pale green—meet black, in other words, with more than a splash of red mixed in. Resembling a sort of quayside Ministry of Information, the black men ask Petit Frère whether he can add any intelligence to what he has already provided, but the young man is "a simple kid and knew nothing of the extent and ramifications of the métier by which he ate his daily bread" (155). Indeed, the phrase "ate his daily bread" accentuates, through McKay's persistent, eccentric, crawl-space linguistic humor, that Petit Frère is a male hustler. This double meaning is where the name of the underground bar and the male hustler merge linguistically. Both are petit: one a diminutive, small-time transgressor; the other a necessarily small, hidden subterranean dive. Moreover, the bread in the name of the bar—"Petit Pain"—implies the penis, the meal his patrons pay the little brother to "eat."[15] With little to go on after Petit Frère's explicit nescience, Falope tries "in every way to scare Lafala away from his infatuation" with Aslima anyway. But Lafala knows the world of "romantic" intrigue in a way that the striving Falope, who spends his time "between his office and a cheap, respectable pension" house, can never know (155). Lafala has himself rejected the opportunity "of being a protector or some approximate thing in well-kept ease." That is, "he had not taken advantage of" the chance to be pimp because he did not feel "equal to the job of remaining forever a black god consecrated to the worship of phallism" (155). So Lafala requests that they all just "forget the whole damned thing" and offers to treat the party to several bottles of Spumanti wine (155–56).

The scene shifts back to Big Blonde and Petit Frère and to Big Blonde's concession to what is a fait accompli: "Now that the lads had invaded his retreat, [Big Blonde] gave himself willingly to the enjoyment of the party. He didn't want to impose Petit Frère upon them when he was invited. But it was all right to have him in the crowd [within the current situation] since they had come themselves to find him" (156). Big Blonde inhabits two spheres, and though he does so comfortably, he perceives when it is possible for such worlds—the orbit of the proletariat and the place of the queer—to intersect and when such a convergence is not so favorable. Except for the solitary soldier and the deserted woman, the bar has cleared out, and Big Blonde and Petit Frère experience the second intrusion. Two cruising "little brunettes resembling twins and dressed alike in soiled black frocks" obtrude on the scene: "They were just out on a cruising from a little *bal musette* in a neighboring alley" (156). The two young women fuss over the delighted Petit Frère and invite him to join them when he is finished hanging around the drab Petit Pain. The dialogue that follows is worth quoting at length.

> "I never understood why the girls are so affectionate with their little brothers," said St. Dominique to Babel in English. "I should think they would be jealous."
>
> "Lawd no!" said Babel. "They are all young and jolly and working together at the same trade."
>
> "But the little brothers steal business away from them," said St. Dominique.
>
> "And their men too sometimes," Babel laughed. "That's why the little sisters keep on the good side of the little brothers[."]
>
> "In Quayside it's business above everything else," said Lafala. "Our little brothers are liked and tolerated, because they're good business."
>
> "You're right," said Babel, putting his hand round Petit Frère's shoulder.
>
> Big Blonde removed it playfully, saying: "Keep your hand off that, old man."
>
> Laughing, Babel said: "Lemme sing you all a little song. My song is entitled: Moon-struck."

> I was struck by the moon,
> I was smitten by the moon,
> Crazy for the fairy moon,
> It lighted my heart and it caused me to roam
> Far away from my loving wife waiting at home. (156–57)

At this point, the others hum along, and Big Blonde and Babel rise to dance to the chorus, reproducing the monumental Socialist Realist mural on the wall of the Seamen's Club, where beneath the photographs of Lenin and Marx is "a drawing of two terrible giants, one white, the other black, both bracing themselves to break the chains that bound them. And under the drawing was the exhortation: Workers of the World, Unite to Break your Chains!" "Boss," says Babel to Big Blonde, an ungainly dancer, "the police can't interfere for this ain't no dancing. We just swaying to the music of the moon" (157).

In the chapter that takes place in the Petit Pain, the distinction between the café society and the proletarian culture of the Seamen's Club becomes clear, with the assistance of McKay's previous novel manuscript, *Banjo*. Jake Brown voyages from Harlem to Marseilles to make a cameo appearance in *Banjo*, a part of the second novel that demonstrates evidence of Jake's sexual tendency toward Ray. Significantly, they are meeting in a bar full of "seamen," another example of McKay's singular humor. The conversation over how the physical economy of the sex trade functions with two ostensibly competing forms of sexual work—with both women and gay men focusing their attention on the male population— suggests that a kind of nascent form of socialist financial order operates on the quay. The Marxist St. Dominique would imagine that the competition between women and "their little brothers" would inspire hostility. But Babel and Lafala, who are experienced with all matters respecting life in the slum, comprehend the nuance of the situation: that a kind of understanding exists between the two groups so that the male rough trade are in a sense valued members of the sexual culture. Sex culture in the Marseilles quayside sounds as though it is in this way more collectivist than capitalist, in that the assemblage of bodies is respected over the individual body. It is important that the male hustlers are "little brothers" and the female sex workers are "little sisters," the locutions *brother* and *sister* denoting the discourses of proletarian comradeship. In this way female and male sex workers are both recognized as integrated into the capitalist economy as well as capable of claiming the right of solidarity with the proletariat that is not banished as *lumpen*.

Moreover, the song Babel sings, "Moon-struck," returns the narrative once again to its beginning, when Lafala was still in Africa: "baptized in a flood of emotion re-tasting the rare delight the members of his tribe felt always by the sight of fine bodies" (1). Lafala "remembered lying down naked under the moon and stars while his playmates traced his image with pieces of crockery. And when they were finished they all held hands and dancing around it singing: 'The Moonshine Kid'" (1–2). As the moon is universally symbolic of the feminine, in the concentrated narrative symbolism of *Romance in Marseille* the moon is the anti-masculine urge ancestrally abiding in the male body. It is the "fairy moon," an "ambivalence," to use Bhabha, that the nisus of state nationalism, modern socialization, racist supremacy, and sex-gender hierarchal binarization cannot entirely extinguish. In addition, Babel and Big Blonde finally actualize the imagined drawing on the wall of the Seamen's Club, breaking the chains through dance and song, uniting the "Workers of the World." Now most of the principal characters collectively partake of the hereditary absinthe-like "moonshine," though instead of tribal past and its stability of identity, the fairy moon melody vocalizes the permeability of spaces between the boundaries. Lafala playfully warns Babel, "Look out the moon madness don't get you too," to which Babel responds, "I'm crazy all ways bar none" (158). In other words, "Moon-struck" becomes a chorus of the proletarian and the urge toward the "primitive," the pre-civilized condition of sexuality, before the systems of gender and sex, policed by law, the modern obsession with classification and order, forms of social enforcement that provide the discourses for colonialism and imperialism. To sing "Moon-struck" is to versify the queer interstitial space where difference is adumbrated by bodies brought together under poetry. Babel jokes that the "police" cannot arrest him and Big Blonde for dancing, even though the Petit Pain doesn't have a dancing license. One reason for this is that what they are doing is so ungraceful it can't be called "dancing." In any case, Babel says that they aren't dancing; they are merely "swaying" (inclining to, tending toward) to the fairy moon tune. Most important, however, Babel identifies that the authorities would be unable to interfere with the two if the police caught them—the government can't police their ungainly proletarian fairy moon dance—because their dance is merely expressive of the illicit act rather than the transgressive act itself, disobedient both in radical political and sexually dissident terms.

Such homosocial harmony, accordingly, cannot last, as a female character disrupts the concord between the men at the Petit Pain. The "old woman" who enters the café selling "dolls and such baubles" is "prematurely grey and her skin was wrinkled and her mouth twisted and she looked like an old cocotte to whom time and people had been cruel" (158). Judging from her interaction with Petit Frère, she must have been a sex worker at one time. Indeed, the same woman shows up in *Banjo*, coming between a game of checkers Banjo and Ray are playing "in a little café of the quarter" (93). Until the *demimonde* shows up, a bottle of wine is the only thing "between them": "A demi-crone of the hole came in with a ready-made gladness which seemed like it might change at any moment into something poisonous" (93). The sex worker asks Ray to buy her an absinthe, and he complies, but when she leans over and caresses him, he moves away from her:

> Her touch imparted to him an unbearable sensation as of a loathsome white worm wriggling down his spine. And mingled with that was the smell of the absinthe on her breath. He detested the nauseating sweet-

garlicky odor of absinthe. In the thing bending over him he felt an obscene bird, like the pink-headed white buzzard of the Caribbean islands that also exuded an odor like absinthe-and-garlic. (93)

When the woman sees that Ray finds her repulsive, she cries: "*Merde alors!* Why? I am not rotten," to which Ray responds, meaningfully, that perhaps he is the one who is "rotten" (94). Ray's reaction to the woman mystifies his friend Banjo, but the reader recognizes from *Home to Harlem* the familiar theme of guarded sexual difference in the Haitian character. In this way all three novels of queer black anarchist proletarianism are linked.

In *Romance in Marseille*'s translation, Big Blonde feels sorry for the woman while wanting "to be rid of the poor hag," so he decides to buy something, "but Petit Frère stopped him with a nudge that she did not miss" (158). For his part, "Babel roughly told her that they didn't want anything, she was in the wrong place" (158). Babel asserts that she has intruded on a homosocial "place" that is "wrong" for the quondam *demimonde*. "Indeed I am," she says, "there's no doubt I am when you have that thing"—indicating Petit Frère—"between you." As his presence and being constitute the trace of male sexuality, Petit Frère is metonymic of a penis: "that thing between you." The men collectively form a single male body. Petit Frère verbally abuses the woman, observing that she is "too God-forsaken old and ugly" and a "useless and jealous has-been" (158). In other words, the woman is no longer economically viable. Whereas she has lost her looks and is now useless because she can no longer trade her body, he is still young and sexually attractive, still possessing an exchange value. The woman responds with bitterness; Petit Frère, she says, is a "Petit cul-cassé," a "little suckling pig" (158). After more bad-mouthing from Petit Frère, the woman leaves, agitated, and the men laugh "hilariously." Subsequent to "an interval" the woman returns and throws animal excrement in Petit Frère's face, at which point "Big Blonde jumped up and knocked her sprawling to the floor" (159). St. Dominique remarks, "Well, that's a pretty ending to your moon song, fellows," and the party begins to break up (159).

Petit Frère goes to the lavatory to clean up, and when he returns, "well-washed and looking none the worse for his ordeal," he utters the glacial threat: "If I ever run across that old sow again I'll cut her twat out and give it to the dogs" (159), another of the many iterations of the hogs-dogs imagery of "If We Must Die" (1919). Trying to revive the party, Babel attempts to get all to sing the "Moonsong" again, but Big Blonde, his head on the table, is "crying softly" (160). "He's drunk!" says Babel, and this observation is indisputable, though it is not precisely why Big Blonde is weeping. At the end of the scene, the four black men "went out leaving Big Blonde and Petit Frère alone" (160). Undeniably, the Petit Pain sustains "a quality strangely balancing between the emotions of laughter and tears, ribaldry and bitter-sweetness" (153). Indeed, it is useful to recall the acumen of Oscar Wilde's comment on drinking absinthe: "After the first glass you see things as you wish they were. After the second, you see things as they are not. Finally, you see things as they really are, and that is the most horrible thing in the world" (qtd. in Ellman 469).

Petit Frère and Babel cruelly abuse the "old woman," and even Big Blonde, the kind-hearted proletarian giant, issues a vigorous blow, pitching her across the café. Petit Frère's comment about cutting out her "twat" and feeding it to the dogs—the four black men chortle callously at this comment—exposes the feral being that the little brother has fashioned in order to survive as a male hustler in the dangerous waterfront slum. Why do Petit Frère and Babel hold such contempt for the woman? Petit Frère has absorbed the hegemony he lives under, where the hierarchy of domesticated mammalian bodies under capitalism visibly determines their worth. His body, like a "doll" (158), has financial viability because of its exchangeability in the marketplace; the woman's creature body, the ruined frame of a former sex worker, does not. Additionally and integrated with his false consciousness, Petit Frère denies his connection with the others. In *A Thousand Plateaus: Capitalism and Schizophrenia* (1987), Deleuze and Guattari articulate their theory of becoming-animal. For the human subject to "become animal," she or he must enter the collective, the pack-mentality, thus deterritorializing the "human" as different from, alien to, and special in the animal world. Petit Frère's enunciation of cutting out the woman's "twat" and feeding it to the dogs demonstrates his "animal" nature in spades, but this is the clotted condition of bestiality, *not* a state of becoming. It is a demonstration of a partisan "pack mentality," but of the brutal, vicious, callous subject position. It is a taste for blood without the consciousness of the collective, without a "sense" of the pack as related, commodious, and mutually invested, with respect for the role of the Other. Petit Frère is incapable of working for the collective good.

It is interesting to consider the two Marxist mythic worker giants in concert. Babel's response is also complex. Capable of clever punning humor and delicate understanding, Babel is occasionally brutal and easily roused to thoughtless acts, as in his move to pummel St. Dominique when urged by the café owner of the Tout-va-Bien. Babel reacts to the woman's intrusion at the moment when he is performing a sexual transgression: dancing with Big Blonde. Babel's reaction to the once *demimondaine* is a reaction against the threat of the sudden emergence of the Real, the female body that is no longer classifiable according to sexual worth. Babel embodies the anxiety of homosocial feeling, the dread of encountering, at the moment when he is experiencing the interior space of his own sexual variance, a tangible "twat." As for Big Blonde's puzzling attack on the woman—puzzling because he is such a responsible, reasonable character—the answer may lie in the last detail of the scene, Big Blonde's head on the table and Babel's discovery that he is "crying softly." The reader knows that Big Blonde has acted in this way before, reported in chapter 17, when the queer white proletarian is introduced: "Once Big Blonde broke up the furniture in a saloon of the loving house of La Creole, because a boy companion of his was insulted there" (123). Clearly Big Blonde, marked as feminine by lamenting "softly," is saddened because the romantic interlude he has so looked forward to is spoiled by the intrusion of the woman and her casting of shit. He is also dejected because the queer proletarian brotherhood cannot last. But I would aver that some ambiguity inheres in the scene's conclusion. Not given to senseless, brutal acts, Big Blonde, probably in an absinthe-drunk, slaps the woman across the room, a person for whom he has only moments before felt compassion. It is likely as well that Big Blonde is weeping because he has himself acted brutally, particularly toward such a pitiable human being. Therefore, the former merchantman Big Blonde has not only shipwrecked the purity of his tryst but has also entered into the irrational practice of those who would behave violently toward any social outcast, whether aged, sex worker, or queer.

Finally, what exactly is intruded on? What is encroached on is not so much Big Blonde and Petit Frère's date as it is a delicate moment when the boundaries between men, raised by modern social systems, begin to crumble. Babel and Big Blonde's dance recalls the monumental image of the proletarian union of black and white imprinted on the wall of the Seamen's Club. The painting is meant to indicate the solidarity available through Communism to black and white workers in their mutually motivated work against capitalism, class, racism, imperialism, and nationalism. Significantly, Babel has just gotten off work as a docker with a group of Africans. Babel and Big Blonde's dance shakes this image from the wall and interpolates it in the bodies of living workers. This awakening thereby materializes the abstract, though realizing it in song, through the sort of "lyricism" on which Big Blonde waxes earlier in his reverie of the rendezvous with his little brother. Although Petit Frère is the metonymic penis and the "old woman" is the synecdochal vagina, the scene capsizes such binaries by portraying all hierarchies as imposed. Essentially the scene ends by underscoring the near-connection and inevitable incapacity for boundary crossing. Nonetheless, it stages a beginning, as all permanent revolutionary acts must be beginnings and all acts of becoming must be persistent, of queer black-white anarchist community.

In the chapter that follows, Lafala meets with the official—evidently the same administrator who occasioned his arrest—and discovers that the bureaucrat has also received a letter from La Fleur. Horrified at learning about "the first case of a Negro" wanting to marry "a colored prostitute," the official advises Lafala to leave Marseilles without taking Aslima (161). The official books Lafala's passage to West Africa and stipulates that he will not help Lafala unless the African leaves Aslima behind. Although Lafala decides accurately that the letter writing must be a "hoax," the black man reluctantly consents (161–62). From the perspective of the "clear and sobering daylight, . . . the practical side of Lafala's nature had reasserted itself over the sensual and decided him to do as his agent wished," the narrative explains, the same sort of logic that comes to Lafala when he decides to cut the lawyer out of the action in part 1. In being logical, Lafala must abandon "the sensual" and embrace "the practical side," made manifest by the already present agent. The "agent" is an official who thinks for another, who assumes agency for the subject, therefore absolving the subject of making his or her own decisions, of facing the uncertainty of becoming, of becoming a reasoning subject.

When Aslima hears the news of Lafala's departure, Babel and La Fleur are present in the café, and both are sanguine about the tidings. Cruelly rejoicing, Babel, the singer of songs, croons a tune: "Oh the jolly gals in this good ole port, / Who'll remember me after I'm gone" (168). La Fleur at first beams in "malicious triumph," but "her manner underwent a sudden change as she observed the terrible expression upon Aslima's face" (168–69). Aslima turns away muttering to herself, repeating, "Mektoub! Mektoub! (Destiny! Destiny!)" (169). Meanwhile, Titin is hunting for Aslima. A final communication, another misplaced letter, contains lethal intelligence: "Lafala had left a hundred dollars with his agent for Aslima which she could claim by showing her papers of identification. She could use the money to return home" (169). Titin curses Aslima as a "hardhearted slut": "She had all that money saved up from me and there were days when I actually starved" (169). The proprietor of the Tout-va-Bien, always ready to stir up violence between his black clientele, reproves Titin for "trusting any woman," as his own "paramour's face grew sharp with anger but she said nothing" (169). Somewhat ironically though understandably, La Fleur is the one who "flew to Aslima's room to warn her about the letter and to implore her to escape" (170). But Aslima, acting according to a fatal impassivity ("Mektoub!"), "did not care about anything. She said she did not mind what Titin did now" (170). La Fleur breaks down and cries, atoning for her treatment of Aslima, and Aslima says that it is "all right for she had also been mean," then urges La Fleur to retreat because "it would be better for her if Titin did not find her there" (170). When La Fleur departs, Titin enters, finding a calm Aslima, and though he rages and threatens to kill her, he abruptly becomes "nonplussed" because Aslima coolly calls him on his threat: "Take it [her life] then and stop shouting" (170). So Titin turns his rage on Lafala: "Oh to be outwitted by a creature of the jungle! . . . A half helpless savage. . . . A mere black stump of humanity" (170). On the manuscript's final page, Titin says: "Better I had killed him like a dog!" (171), an utterance that in grammatical terms makes Titin the dog: "While round us bark the mad and hungry dogs, / Making their mock at our accursèd lot."

La Fleur wishes to help Aslima because she is a lesbian and has all along carried an abiding secret affection for her adversary. Now, as Aslima, a kind of négritude Aida, faces death, the female sex workers are united in solidarity through their banishment from acceptable society and their constraint to serve male masters and the quayside capitalist system. This is asserted by the indeterminacy of the pronoun usage: "Aslima quietly told her to leave her alone" and "it would be better for her if Titin did not find her there." The signification of *her* in the clauses fuses Aslima and La Fleur, breaking down the inert physics of solitary subject agency and being. The union of Aslima and La Fleur is thrown back inversely—refracted in a fractured linguistic speculum—by the male solidarity between the "chorean" Titin and the misogynous mulatto proprietor. Here Titin echoes other parts of the manuscript where white officials dehumanize Lafala because he is an African. This time, however, a black man engages in the rhetoric of racial supremacy as it is mixed with Lamarckian hierarchy: "Oh to be outwitted by a creature of the jungle! . . . A half helpless savage." Lafala is "a creature of the jungle," nothing more than a wild animal in the food chain. To Lafala's categorical inferiority Titin adds his disfigurement: "a mere black stump of humanity." The sex worker is indeed like a captured bird, a fetish commodity in the sex marketplace. Aslima and La Fleur must be caged animals, also kept from advancement, from motility; they cannot be free agents in the masculinist socioeconomic order. Finally, Aslima throws "up her hands" not in surrender but "like a bird of prey about to swoop down upon a victim." Titin damns Aslima to "Hell," but she already dwells in her own personal abyss. Though killed by Titin, Aslima is not mastered; she continues becoming animal, dying for the only thing worth struggling for in the brutal Marseilles underworld: *romance*. Although the male queer proletarian characters cannot ultimately get together, both politically and sexually (two conditions that are in any case inextricably bound), because of the limitations in the possibility of intercourse "between" them, Aslima and La Fleur unite in a struggle against sexual slavery and capital domination, if coming together, ironically, too late to save Aslima. The reader discovers in Aslima's courageous death—her resolve to die violently rather than carry on as a slave—that *Romance in Marseille* has been, after all, as much her story as any of the other major characters. Indeed, one could argue that it is more her legend than anyone else's.

The most important reason for treating *Romance in Marseille* as if it were not a mere "dead letter" is that it tells a story that though absent from the larger archive—the shelves of libraries for seven decades—is yet riotously present in the discursive order of the early 1930s. Though a deviation from the norm, the measure being the proletarian novel, while at the same time in every significant way conscientiously upholding the convention, *Romance in Marseille* is *not* gay clairvoyance, a same-sex notification that is "ahead of its time." It is not a *communiqué avant la lettre*. One shouldn't only care about *Romance in Marseille* because it was a suppressed text, though this is certainly reason enough. The most compelling reason that one should care about this novel is that it tells the tale that though never read *was* composed. Therefore, what is just as interesting as the question of the historical disposition of this singular manuscript is the existence of the narrative itself. The most engaging matter respecting the unread *Romance in Marseille* and why it should be unwrapped, disrobed, teased from its dark corner—its archival vault but also the doubled closeting acts of compelling it to social banning and political banishment—is its queer black anarchist-proletarian story, its merging of the primitive and the proletarian. McKay's sex novel fuses black proletarianism and dissident black queer rhetorics, bringing politics and the personal together in what is one of the most vital documents of twentieth-century diaspora literature, published or not.

Some Remarks on the Critical
Implications of Queer Black Marxism

IN MY INTRODUCTION, I said that one of my aims is to open McKay's critical closet door for a more expansive discussion than has been possible until now. For this conclusion, I would like to offer a few comments on the future of McKay studies as well as black literary studies, radical leftist historicism, and queer cultural studies and to map out the "worldliness," to use Edward Said's term, between such spheres. By *worldliness* I mean the way in which scholarship is inexorably caught up in the civic sphere. Existing in a world where survival dictated one's aims, McKay endeavored to control the level of how "out" he would be, and among the writerly acts of the black transnational author was an attempt to consume rather than be consumed, demonstrated by the imagery of consumption in "America" (1921). My task has been to trace McKay's lines of flight, to listen closely to both what the queer black Marxist author said and what he felt prevented from saying openly. I also articulated in my introduction the problem of how impediments between Black Renaissance, black Atlantic, black diaspora, queer, and radical recovery studies may prevent these critical modes from collaborating. But I would add here that a greater difficulty lies in the hazardous political situation that presides in present humanities studies. Today the Right is secure in its conviction that it has prevailed over the Left—formerly notorious black Communists and Trotskyists like McKay are apparently no longer a concern.

The Right's confidence that history, in other words Marxism and leftism, has achieved mortality is demonstrated vividly by a section of the FBI Web site set aside to release files made available through the Freedom of Information Act (FOIA). The FBI Web site prominently displays an FOIA "library," with an electronic "reading room," something like the bureau's online version of the reading room in the British Library, the place where Marx composed much of his most important work and McKay, on a borrowed membership card, first read Marx. Enacted in 1966, the FOIA lurched along toothless for a decade until the Watergate era in the mid-1970s, when Ralph Nader headed an effort forcing legislation that enabled the law (Foerstel 48–49). In the late 1970s, the bureau was finally constrained to release files on figures like McKay. The agency dragged its heels because they claimed that the FOIA files contained still sensitive material and that declassification would jeopardize national security (an argument the federal government still counts on, as other parts of the FBI Web site make clear). The FBI was justifiably worried about being revealed as an organization of Stasi-like fanatics, persecuting anyone who did not toe the line of narrow right-wing ideological beliefs—in other words, that the chief danger to the American public was, after all, not Communism but the United States' policing of Communism.

During the present time of obsession with international terrorism, however, the FBI apparently is no longer anxious about divulging classified information in the form of surveillance dossiers from the interwar period and even after. In fact, the FBI Web site readily avails the Internet surfer with formerly sensitive files through easy-access portable document format downloads, a prominent part of the bureau's site being devoted to easy access to many dossiers, including Claude McKay's. Because of the relative lengthiness of the file, the FBI's McKay PDF "file" download is separated into two parts. The page describes the author accurately:

> Claude McKay's roots were in Jamaica and he was never a United States citizen. He spent some time in Russia in the early 1920's and was expected to return to the U.S. in 1923. McKay was an editor of the "Liberator." He wrote several articles for the "Negro World," advocating the extension of "bolshevism" in the United States as a means of obtaining freedom for the Negro.

The accuracy of the succinct description isn't surprising because the FBI has nothing to lose, as the threat posed by formerly dangerous radicals like McKay is no longer viable.

I suppose I might be grateful to the FBI for making the files so easily accessible, considering that only a few years ago obtaining such files, as Claire Culleton hilariously relates in her introduction to *Joyce and the G-Men* (2004), was such a grueling undertaking, the FBI placing mind-boggling barriers in the way of the legal right to use. Culleton also talks about the fact that when she finally received the documents, most of the papers in Joyce's file were almost completely lined out. So I guess I might also show some sign of gratefulness that, unlike Joyce's twenty-page FOIA file, McKay's is legible. But as the reader can see, I don't include a note of thanks to the FBI and State Department in my acknowledgments. One reason I have no gratitude toward the bureau is because the FBI site indicates no sense that the agency regrets the mayhem and malevolence of its past (or its present, it is almost unnecessary to say). On the contrary, the Web page conveys an impression of the bureau being exceedingly pleased with itself—the evildoers were after all defeated.

Perhaps this demonstration of the certainty that material *history* is finished is best exhibited by the agency's separate section devoted to "Famous Persons," a celebrity file link to records kept on luminary targets of observation like Pablo Picasso and John Lennon. Beyond the general self-satisfaction of the FOIA notables page, with its collection of classified intelligence on such nefarious characters as Albert Einstein, César Chávez, and Martin Luther King Jr., the celebrity file communicates a sense of titillation, of pornographic thrill—the promise of access to the boudoir of JFK and Marilyn Monroe. As for the subject of this discussion, it is noteworthy that though Richard Wright succeeds in getting onto the site set aside for celebrated if disreputable personalities (as does Paul Robeson), understandably McKay, the most notorious black Red of the 1920s, does not make it onto the celebrity pages. Agents Brennan and Hurley and Director Burns would no doubt be simultaneously pleased and disappointed.

I find it instructive to surf the contents of McKay's FBI file one more time, to ascertain whether this black Atlantic leftist author's once obviously manifest clout is indeed no longer viable. As I discuss in chapter 1, the filers see in "America" all that is traitorous and transgressive about McKay. In kind, McKay's fascination with the meaning of American political and social intransigence continued, right on through his years as an exile. In 1926, five years after his initial critique of America in verse form, McKay wrote "America in Retrospect" (*CP* 215). The narrator of the poem, again a "keen child," views America like a compelling moving picture, a film: "Like vivid scenes stamped on a keen child's mind, / Your gorgeous pageants entertain my view" (ll.1–12). As in "America," again the metaphor of illumination appears, in both of its senses, though this time the light is cinematic, the white luminosity projected onto the movie screen, the birth of a nation's "great all-sweeping lights," the age of mechanical reproduction. Here the reader again sees McKay the black material cultural critic of cinematic artifacts, as the film is once again Griffith's masterpiece of Hollywood master race ideology, *The Birth of a Nation* (1915): the spectacular imagery and technology "blind / Your vision to the Shadow over you" (ll.3–4). Racism is equated with fatality, as the Angel of Death, Azrael, casts a shadow over the land. That is to say, America's dazzling brilliance—simultaneously America itself and the culture industry, to use Adorno's term, that *projects* America, both reflections of a destructive Symbolic Order—creates the conditions that make it blind to its own impassive darkness, or racism. The "Shadow" figuration is ironic, a black irony, not only because McKay would later be shoved into the shadows by both the capriciousness of the literary marketplace and the villainy of the U.S. State Department, but also because America, the white goddess, is blinded by the self-generating act of producing her own shroud of darkness: racism and fascism. As in the earlier anti-paean to America, the speaker is a black "child" who is "wistful," and despite being wronged feels "no hatred deep and wild" because America's harsh lesson made the narrator into "a stoic introvert" (ll.5–8), an organic intellectual worker fortified with cold, critical powers. Once more time is of the essence, as the speaker, his "purpose plain," must use his "creative hours severe and stern" to "write in freedom and in peace / The accumulations of the years that burn, / White forge-like fires within my haunted brain" (ll.9–14). Living in Europe and Africa, McKay wrote about the "accumulations of the years that burn / White forge-like fires" in his mind for as long as he could.

As a reading of such sonnets as "America in Retrospect" demonstrates, the black modernist author Claude McKay's literary skill lay in exposing the looking-glass reality present in American racial and nativist systems of the interwar period. So it is perhaps not ironic that a national memory loss persists during the present time that validates McKay's between-the-wars suspicions for future America. Still, irony is useful in these difficult times. Indeed, as the moderns refined the language of literary irony, it is fitting that in present-day modernist literary analysis a kind of thinking should be lodged in the critical mind that normalizes the act of manifestly disregarding the very intellectual inheritance that makes modern American literary studies possible. Namely, in spite of work by scholars working to recover discarded Old Left writing—notwithstanding high modernist doctrine, the most innovative literature of the American modernist phase—the everyday study, or absence of study, of this body of texts is still regulated by a cold war assessment instrument. What is most troubling is that black radical literature is subject to a mode of critical reading that is tied historically to postwar right-wing ideology—an apolitical mode of application that is allegedly uninfected by ideology. In other words, "Old Left" literature, "vulgar Marxist" and related revolutionary writing that is obviously undeserving of critical attention, remains misunderstood when read at all. In a review of Alan Wald's aptly titled *Exiles from a Future Time* (2002), Paul Lauter refers to this phenomenon as "cultural amnesia":

> How is it possible to recover the cultural world in which writers of the Left in the 1930s and beyond had their being and created their work? . . . How does one move past—or through—the Cold War critical mentality that continues to present "Communist poetry" as an oxymoron, that leads our students to disbelieve that anyone could voluntarily affiliate with the party, that conditions most anthologies and courses to fill the literary "void" between T. S. Eliot's "The Hollow Men" (1925) and Ralph Ellison's *Invisible Man* (1952) with, at best, a few random pieces by John Steinbeck, Nathanial West, and Allen Tate? (360–61)

The irony intensifies, moreover, when this contradiction is understood in terms of the rise of a new American nationalist supremacy. Presently the Right roundly calls for the recuperation of traditional educational values, an effort that must be recognized as a part of the state nationalist institutionalization of Homeland Security. Although linking such projects as the writing into law of the Patriot Act and ridding the universities of radicals doesn't require much brainwork, I believe that their historical trajectory has not been adequately mapped out. I trace these post-9/11 acts to a pre–Ground Zero origin. The current right-wing attempt to seize control of public educational institutions bears a conspicuous resemblance to the campus crackdown on leftist academics stretching from the Little Red Scare of the interwar period to the McCarthyism of the postwar phase. That is to say, it should not be written off as a regrettable coincidence that as reform-minded college professors during the interwar and postwar periods were portrayed by the Right as fanatics plotting to torpedo the Ship of State, progressive-minded academics now are linked, in the post-9/11 American panic narrative, semantically to terrorists.

The current right-wing campaign to control university curriculum and culture is exemplified by the state of Colorado's forced resignation of UC president Elizabeth Hoffman. As an article in *Revolutionary Worker* reports, Hoffman defended academic freedom when she asserted that law and university policy protect academic freedom—namely, Ward Churchill's controversial remarks related to the terrorist bombings of September 11. According to the Web site for "People for the American Way," the Students for Academic Freedom (SAF) want to force Colorado's regency universities to pass the "Academic Bill of Rights," to combat liberalism and Democrats on college and university campuses. David Horowitz, SAF's founder, claims that American colleges and universities are "indoctrination centers for the political left" and that many higher education workers "hate America." Charging that universities have a "blacklist" for conservative professors, naturally the SAF has put together a blacklist of liberal academics and universities. Using the controversy as a catalyst for right-wing conversion, representatives of the Colorado legislature demand that conservative professors be hired to compensate for the allegedly large number of leftist academics in the system. Currently, my state of residence, Kansas, is moving toward enacting its own version of the contemptuously dubbed "Academic Bill of Rights."

This Red Alert tactic normalizes the Right's current plan for curricular expropriation, the anticipated educational "outcome" being the necessity to sever the link to progressive educational origins. Among the most troubling aspects of the Right's aim to restore time-tested standards is the attempt to appropriate the language of progressive pedagogic approaches, specifically the recovery of a valuable, disregarded past, the act of historical revisioning. In view of the Right's lip service given to the obligation to revert to age-old values, the project of doing away with multicultural education and replacing it with its ostensibly sensible antithesis reflects a grimly ironic attempt at interdiction.

Even more strenuous to visualize is Laura Bush's vision of an *apolitical* (that is, right-wing) multiculturalism. As the war against Iraq heated up, the First Lady organized a multicultural celebration at the White House, "Poetry and the American Voice," a symposium that would honor the poets Walt Whitman, Emily Dickinson, and Langston Hughes. Her staff invited a number of the country's finest poets. When her staff got wind that poets were planning on using the event to protest the coming "Shock and Awe," she "postponed" it indefinitely. The shutting down of the opportunity to protest the war with poetry led to a Web site calling for poems against the war; over eleven thousand poets sent some thirteen thousand poems. This in turn brought about the publication of *Poets against the War* (2003), an international anthology of poetry, including work by Lucille Clifton, Rita Dove, and Yusef Komunyakaa. Laura Bush's response was that there is no place for politics in poetry. I would say that I am puzzled by her reading of Hughes, but sadly I can see how the librarian could fail to see—if she has actually read him—the temperament of even Hughes's least obviously leftist writing.

What the old school attempt to appropriate the rhetoric of Left historical recovery really signifies is a rough-and-ready, cynical, politically motivated attempt to bring to an end the very forward-looking pedagogical objectives that academics who practice progressive teaching and study strive to maintain. It is important for those working in American modernist studies to remember that multiculturalism came about through radical educational undertakings conceived during the 1920s and 1930s, the kind of intellectual work that "America in Retrospect" evinces. In an article in *Radical Teacher*, the late historian Shafali Lal traces multiculturalism to the 1930s work of Rachel Davis DuBois (no relation to W.E.B. Du Bois), who headed the Bureau for Intercultural Education. From 1934 to 1954, the BIE worked hard to understand the predicament of immigrant children, then articulated an intercultural national project to educate diverse peoples. As a result of Lal's vital work, it is evident that the underpinnings for promoting a consciousness of culturally diverse peoples originates in the 1920s writings of New Negro, transnational, leftist, sexually dissident authors like McKay, cultural workers whose prose as well as poetry articulated the multicultural views for the pedagogic advances that followed. A committed multiculturalism lies in an awareness of the history of both the Bureau of Investigation and the Bureau for Intercultural Education—America in retrospect.

Ironically, those who would become the targets of the old Red alert were the intellectuals who articulated and practiced the modern scholarly reform that laid the groundwork for multiculturalism. The dreary reality is that when it comes to the study of black modernist writing, the historicist location of this conclusion, the Right does not really need to fret about leftist bias in the academy. In this age of higher educational "assessment" and "competencies," most readers of revolutionary modernist literature, above all black radical writing, are still not sufficiently competent to comprehend what is on the page in front of them, including the majority of those who teach it—and, most disquieting, even most who anthologize and write about it.[1] Current reading skills are indeed lamentably inadequate to the task of engaging historically with the multitude of dissident voices found in American literary texts, particularly those of the Negro Renaissance. James Smethurst's late 1990s comments on the disregard for radical recovery studies among critics of modernist literary study still hold true: "despite the recent work of such scholars as Paula Rabinowitz, Cary Nelson, Michael Denning, Walter Kalaidjian, Barbara Foley, and Alan Wald, most scholars 'know' what the literature of the 1930s is like because they have internalized the narrative of the failure of 'proletarian literature'" (9). This critical failure has preserved old difficulties in apprehending black Marxist literature of the modernist period.

Now is to be sure the time for new competencies. Until those who write about, teach, and publish on such subjects as the Harlem Renaissance recognize the need for innovative skills, black writing of the modernist moment will continue to be misunderstood, and scores of the period's texts will be overlooked. Without a radical shift in the study of black modernist literature, the result will be a persistent failure to see how African American and Caribbean writers between the wars concentrated on the intersection of nationalism and racism through a kind of black dialectical materialist act of literary criticism. When understood through a materialist critical means, this largely misinterpreted and generally unread body of literature has the capacity to communicate crucial knowledge to readers in today's classroom, library, and reading room. The literary documents of the modernist phase in particular retain a cultural currency because the history of state nationalist and racist hegemony may be traced to the second birth of the nation. This nativist nativity is the emergence of modern American nationalism in collaboration with the partnered growth of international capitalism and world imperialism. My point is that the explosive effects of such historical trajectories are obviously still dreadfully visible, verified by the globalization policies of the World Bank, IMF, and WTO, as the essays collected in Amitava Kumar's challenge to the pedagogy of "world literature" (and postcolonial studies), *World Bank Literature* (2002), demonstrate. The history of modern America and the world it makes its home in is not over. Until those who participate in generating the critical language of modern American literary history cultivate a far-reaching awareness of how black radical interwar writing worked in partnership with leftist commitment to disrobe the intimate coupling of state nationalist and racist ideology, those studying modernist literature will be incapable of undertaking its fullest import. The ultimate aim of this book is to suggest a manner through which it is possible to think about ways to renovate, to *modernize*, the analytic faculty the reader needs in order to gain a better-informed sense of urgent critical knowledge. My objective has been to regenerate lost, dangerous intelligence, to revive the creative efforts of black Marxist modernist writing, to resume our conversations with the dead—these "priceless treasures sinking in the sand," to reiterate McKay's vision of "America"—and to ask what they may communicate to us even now:

> Her vigor flows like tides into my blood,
> Giving me strength erect against her hate.
> Her bigness sweeps my being like a flood.
> Yet as a rebel fronts a king in state,
> I stand within her walls with not a shred
> Of terror. . . .

Notes

Introduction: Manifesting Claude McKay

1. McKay's "lost" poetry is salvaged in Maxwell's editing of the *Complete Poems*, which contains an excellent prologue to McKay's verse as well as over one hundred pages of annotation. In terms of recovering and reexamining McKay and leftist politics, Maxwell's "F.B. Eyes: The Bureau Reads Claude McKay" examines McKay's FBI file, acquired through the Freedom of Information Act. Baldwin devotes a chapter to McKay's sojourn in Russia during the early 1920s, and Lowney traces the meaning of the U.S. occupation of Haiti in McKay's *Home to Harlem*. James's *A Fierce Hatred of Injustice* places McKay in the history of Caribbean radicalism (James plans another volume entitled *Claude McKay: The Making of a Black Bolshevik, 1889–1923*). As for McKay's role as a black diaspora author, Edwards presents a chapter on McKay's *Banjo*, locating the novel in Afro-French négritude, and Stephens considers McKay and masculinity in terms of the black diaspora. In *The Shadowed Country: Claude McKay and the Romance of the Victorians* (2006), Gosciak examines McKay in terms of his revival of a late Victorian "modern pastoral." On his sexuality, Schwarz includes a chapter on McKay's sexual difference in *Gay Voices of the Harlem Renaissance*, and my own "Diaspora Cruises: Queer Black Proletarianism in Claude McKay's *A Long Way from Home*" discusses McKay's complex blending of sexual dissidence, black radicalism, and Marxist praxis.

2. One may find this view asserted in Rascoe's review, and for a subtler appraisal by a white writer, see Parker's. The most damaging evaluation by a black author is Du Bois's review in the *Crisis* in June 1928, as I discuss in more detail in chapter 3.

3. For information on the American and British surveillance on McKay, I am indebted to Maxwell, "F.B. Eyes." For the biographical treatment throughout this study, I rely heavily on Cooper's indispensable *Claude McKay: Rebel Sojourner in the Harlem Renaissance* (1987).

4. According to Maxwell (*New Negro* 4), the likely source of the assertion that "white Communists" uniformly duped black intellectuals comes from Cruse.

5. *Caribbean Quarterly* 38.1 (1992) is a special issue devoted to reconsidering McKay in terms of the early 1990s' new Caribbean studies. More recently, Hathaway's scholarship "relocates" some of his poetry and fiction, and Paquet's work looks at his autobiographical writing through the critical framework of Caribbean studies.

6. Edwards's "Vagabond Internationalism: Claude McKay's *Banjo*" discusses him as diaspora writer. For two more studies that are related to this topic, see Gosciak and Stephens.

7. In his interpretation of *Banjo* in *The Practice of Diaspora* (2003) Edwards argues that McKay poses a "vagabond internationalism" as *exclusively* a black international alternative to Marxism: "*Banjo* would appear to mark a shift in McKay's political focus away from the proletariat, traditionally conceived. . . . The book's fascination with Marseilles's transient denizens points less to an interest in the expansion and unionizing of the port city's industrial maritime base than to the margins of that development" (199). Edwards's scholarship is sedulous and estimable, but even if *Banjo* may be somewhat accurately described as a text that demonstrates McKay's abandonment of traditional, organized Marxist cultural work, I would point out that Edwards exhibits no awareness of McKay's next novel, the unpublished *Romance in Marseille*, a text that is focused on black Marxist action among black port workers. McKay was both diaspora radical and Marxist revolutionary until the mid-1930s, when he composed *Banjo*, a fact that is made evident in *Romance in Marseille*, composed after *Banjo*.

8. The disapproval of McKay's leftism and sexual difference has pervaded critical literature on the Harlem Renaissance since its occurrence, as I discuss in various parts of this book, but I think that the disapprobation, if embodied in a single text, is typified by the representation of McKay in Lewis's *When Harlem Was in Vogue* (1981). I pick this text because of its unquestionable value to Harlem Renaissance studies. Though now over twenty-five years in print, Lewis's book, more than any other, is the appraisal that still gives shape to the general understanding of what the Harlem Renaissance was; all other studies of Harlem Renaissance figures must be assessed next to the measure of Lewis's accomplishment. Its authority, therefore, is the foremost reason for my singling it out as a representative text.

Lewis's treatment of McKay signifies the critical ambivalence scholars have demonstrated when it comes to his politics and sexuality. The protagonist of Lewis's historical narrative is Du Bois, and partly as a result of McKay's bitter disputes with and unwarranted personal criticism of Du Bois, Lewis's handling of him is generally rather harsh, focusing on his repeated demands for financial help, his personal attacks on friends and patrons, and other less than laudable features of McKay's sometimes mercurial personality. McKay's personal faults, however, seem to inform his greater failings in Lewis's narrative, like his unwise premature enthusiasm for Communist politics—proved injudicious by McKay's later repudiation—and, by implication, his bohemian degeneracy, as these two vices are coupled, if latently, in Lewis's analysis. Later Lewis reevaluated the black radical's commitment to Communism when he composed the second volume of the monumental biography *W.E.B. Du Bois: The Fight for Equality and the American Century, 1919–1963* (2000). And to be fair, Lewis altered his treatment of sexual difference among Harlem Renaissance personalities when he published the Viking *Portable Harlem Renaissance Reader* (1994), which shows sympathy for same-sex society among renaissance figures, even reprinting Nugent's bun-burying tale "Smoke, Lilies and Jade" (1926).

9. Of the major critical works that discuss McKay's radical politics, Tyrone Tillery's

seems to be least comfortable with talking about his sexuality, and Winston James essentially ignores the sexual difference of his subject. Instead, James discusses the importance of Jamaican revolutionary politics in McKay's Harlem-based radicalism of the 1920s. By way of fashioning its thesis, *A Fierce Hatred of Injustice* asserts that critics have overstated the influence of McKay's first benefactor, Walter Jekyll. James claims that U. Theo McKay, Claude's older brother, was most instrumental in the formation of the poet's early years, not his gay white *confrère* and benefactor in Jamaica, Jekyll (36–41). James's textually oriented historical scholarship seeks to be painstaking, yet his assertion that Jekyll must take a backseat to U. Theo gainsays McKay's own insistence of Jekyll's sway over his life in writings spanning his career. As early as 1918, at the urging of his second queer patron and publisher, Frank Harris, McKay published a piece in Harris's *Pearson's Magazine* that emphasizes Jekyll's influence; and as late as 1937, his memoir, *A Long Way from Home*, reiterates this. Moreover, if persuaded by James's removal of Jekyll in his initial intellectual and aesthetic growth, what is one to make of McKay's 1933 roman à clef, his final published novel, the queerly titled *Banana Bottom*? In consummate colonial fashion, Christian missionaries send Bita Plant—McKay's queerly inscribed self-fictionalization—to England. The missionaries want to prove that the European enlightenment they are attempting to impose on the black Jamaican hill country people may be modeled by Bita's mimicry of fine manners and feminine reserve. Bita's only genuine ally and confidant is the Englishman Squire Gensir, a character to which Jekyll is the unmistakable factual correlative. With Gensir's assistance, Bita rejects her metropolitan education and embraces her roots, her instinctual African selfhood, most insistent of which is an emphatically non-Victorian sexuality.

It is true that McKay's attitude toward the patronage of his "special friend," Jekyll, was complex, as my own chapter 2 explores. Yet throughout his life he also stressed repeatedly that his English sponsor performed a pivotal role in shaping his intellectual and artistic selfhood. McKay never imputes to U. Theo such penetrating influence, and it is clear why: Jekyll represents the bridging of art and sexual difference. The unease with Jekyll's sexual orientation that pervades James's thesis is disconcerting. At once fraternal and patriarchal, the hereditary and heterosexual U. Theo is the acceptable fountainhead for the black author, whereas Jekyll's role is abrogated. The persistence of McKay's same-sex inflected relationship with Jekyll, whether actually genital or otherwise, is exiled to the endnotes of James's scholarship. His banishment of McKay's sexuality from an analysis of the New Negro author's political trajectory discloses a ruling problematic in James's work. However, the supposition in James's work is not exceptional. His expulsion of Jekyll from the black queer author's labor demonstrates a central critical problem in McKay studies. As though being forced to pick between parents in an unpleasant divorce, choosing between McKay's gay patron and black older brother, both of whom influenced him in their fashion, is finally not an exceedingly productive undertaking when it comes to understanding the way that sexual subversion, political radicalism, and diaspora wandering intersected in McKay's writings. An exception to the radical school's handling of McKay is Maxwell's *New Negro, Old Left*, which applies queer theory to his writings.

10. An indispensable engagement with its subject is Schwarz's *Gay Voices of the Harlem Renaissance* (2003).

11. Articles by Cobham, Spencer, and Woods correspond with this representation.

12. Criticism on leftist writers of the between-the-wars decades is not a recent development; Aaron's key *Writers on the Left: Episodes in American Literary Communism* appeared in 1961. However, a new wave on leftist writing of the interwar period begins with Nelson's 1989 *Repression and Recovery: Modern American Poetry and the Politics of Cultural Memory, 1910–1945*. Nelson articulates the elided fact in modernist literary studies that many American writers—both ethnic and white—were committed leftists during the interwar period. Nelson contends that aesthetically privileging allegedly politically unaligned modernist poetry over what critics have dismissed as protest poetry like much of McKay's verse enlists in the preservation of a rigid hegemonic binary system. This aesthetic hierarchy unthinkingly maintains a reactionary ideology of literary art, in effect subordinating aesthetics to an imperialist historical narrative, the very mechanism that impartial principles of taste purport to rise above. Nelson's study exposes the received, immanently deconstructing binary: high modernist poetry/proletarian poetry, with high modernist occupying the privileged first position, and proletarian poetry inhabiting the inferior, peripheral location.

Until Nelson's study, the widely held belief among many literary scholars was that political poets like McKay were unworthy of serious study, even those like McKay who composed many poems that did not seem to manifest a political statement (a number of McKay's poems are homoerotic love lyrics). He remained unstudied, even in black studies curricula, because of the tar brush of his protest poetry. Critics mechanistically applied high modernist, New Critical aesthetic formulas, so it surprised no one when they deemed the quality of proletarian poetry paltry next to that of genuine modernist period verse. Some poets were dismissed and even demonized in political terms, particularly in the dreary myopia of an enduring cold war anticommunism. In *The Art of Protest* (2005), Reed discusses the significance of twentieth-century social movements in American cultural expression: the importance of collective cultural and social expression in the act of articulating an alternative nationalism. Reed discusses how social movements grow through subcultures and countercultures, how by artistic opposition to mainstream cultural expression—fiction, film, murals, music, painting, and poetry—political protest is articulated. Nelson's text shows how U.S. modernist poetry collectively expresses a multiform struggle against reactionary ideology, how leftist American poetry of the interwar period effectively articulates the cultural expression of social movement politics. McKay is one of numerous neglected authors accounted for in *Repression and Recovery*'s roll call of radical modernist period poets. Nelson disputes the received wisdom on McKay's poetry, the idea that only recognizably experimental vers libre may portray the black modernist aesthetic, posing that the black poet's application of traditional meter constitutes a revolutionary act on American poetry itself, as McKay seizes the textual field of white supremacy, the belongings of western literature, and compels it to speak with an insurgent voice, forcing American poetry to express the view of the subaltern (89–90).

Repression and Recovery's retrieval of leftist poetry played a crucial role in the articulation of what would become the "New American Studies," and my study of McKay's most crucial prose works is meant to participate in the current North American cultural studies move toward probing the effects of nationalist and racist ideology in American literature. New American Studies scholars argue in favor of a North American Studies that does not stop at the frontiers of the United States, both in geographical and ideological terms. The New American Studies must not repeat the mistakes of the old cold war exceptionalist American Studies, when the center of the Mercator map was "America": when the study of American culture put America at the hub, and the rest of the world was measured in terms of its relation to the center. American Studies must become "less insular and parochial, and more internationalist and comparative" (Rowe, *Post-National* 2). What could be designated the New African American Studies is a recently developed critical mode that considers black literary works in terms of transnationalism, a black postnationalist studies that examines how many African American writers traveled beyond a boundary, not only geographically, linguistically, and politically, but also through the literary act itself by staging and exposing American nationalist ideology. A regularly overlooked study, as Kelley discusses in his introduction to the University of North Carolina Press's reprint of the 1983 text, Robinson's *Black Marxism: The Making of a Black Radical Tradition* (2000), would assist in closing the space between the history of black intellectual work and Communist cultural work. Robinson's scholarship must be understood in historical terms. Nelson's poststructuralist revisioning of modernist poets has encouraged scholars from across the critical map to engage with *Repression and Recovery*'s radical, inclusive theory of modernist period leftist literature, bodies of work not previously given the attention they deserved.

Not only should his work be reviewed in terms of the New American Studies, but McKay's postnationalist literary productivity may be understood in terms of the development of American cultural studies itself. Denning's *The Cultural Front: The Laboring of American Culture in the Twentieth Century* (1996) argues that American leftist intellectuals during the Depression—decades before the cold war model of American exceptionalism—formed a dialogical set of critical voices under the heteroglossic Popular Front movement. The Cultural Front of the mid-1930s served as the artistic wing of the Popular Front. The cold war model of binary-thinking anticommunism that persisted in and insisted on an exceptionalist ideology of "American Studies"—*the* form of American Studies until the advent of the postnationalist "cultures of imperialism" North American Studies theory and method—cannot claim to be the authentic critical underpinning for American Studies. American Studies as an exceptionalist critical discourse unconsciously promoted right-wing political values through a veneration of the single representative American voice, commonly identified as transcendent and therefore apolitical. Denning's scholarship proposes that an earlier model for American Studies, effected through the Great Depression–period Cultural Front, brought about a Marxist polyvocality, a dialecticism where competing voices necessarily came into play, building coalitions, then fragmenting and reforming to suit existing needs. Discussing Denning's contribution to the New American Studies in her 1998 American Studies Association presidential address, "What's in a Name?" Radway examines the problematic of "naming" in critical discourses, concentrating on how the pre-1990s phase of American Studies analytical discourses tended to articulate little critical self-consciousness about the use of the term *American Studies.* American Studies under 1970s and 1980s critical discourses tended not to question what kind of study was "American" and what wasn't, knowing instinctively what American Studies were. In literary studies, for example, American Studies meant a concern with white, male, often politically conservative writers whom scholars identify as the framers of the canon. Radway identifies Denning's work in *The Cultural Front* as a seminal post-exceptionalist American Studies text. The 1930s emergence of American Studies exposed a U.S. history that was not uniformly democratic. The writers of the Cultural Front, an academically noninstitutionalized, primary form of American Studies, unflinchingly scrutinized the history of racism, sexism, and imperialism in the United States and beyond national borders toward, in Cuban Marxist poet José Martí's inclusive phrase, "*nuéstra américa.*"

While Denning's work on the mid- to late 1930s is observably beneficial to understanding the origins of North American Studies, the New American Studies would profit from the recognition that the groundwork for cultural materialist interdisciplinary work may be located even earlier than in the Popular Front period. That is, it may be traced to the 1920s, founded in such intellectual labor as McKay's 1920s writings. As Maxwell demonstrates in *New Negro, Old Left: African-American Writing and Communism between the Wars* (1999), the kind of *cultural* work Denning describes going on during the 1930s took place in the 1920s, specifically in the intersecting advent of the New Negro movement of 1919 and the forming of the CPUSA in 1920. Like Hutchinson's *Harlem Renaissance in Black and White* (1995), Maxwell's work takes up the problem of allegedly estranged black and white spheres and argues against the prevailing view, adding the essential, disregarded record of black Communism: "*New Negro, Old Left* is motivated by the belief that inseparability of these two histories qualifies among the least understood features of modern black writing" (2). Portraying African American writers of the New Negro movement as either solely outsiders among Marxist politics or, in exclusion of all else, exploited by the CPUSA machine, Maxwell insists, is not only an assumption that disregards what was really a pluralistic history but also an act of negating black agency:

> With its appetite for evidence of white seduction and betrayal of black mouthpieces, the cautionary history joins fifty years of red squads in assuming that black intellectuals were incapable of transforming their party or their white radical counterparts, save through denunciations issued after escape. Such his-

tory thus begins by denying African-American literary Communists what it would seem finally to prize: a historically consequential self-direction. (5)

Communism and the New Negro movement matured together, each mutually informing the other. The two movements borrowed linguistically, existentially, and phenomenologically from one another so extensively that separating them would be a willful act of historical blindness. *New Negro, Old Left* consequently interrogates the segregation of the 1920s from the 1930s, the desire to sequester the vestal Harlem Renaissance from the contamination of black (and white) Communism, from African American radical organized proletarianism. Maxwell argues, moreover, that the list of seminal black intellectuals found in Robinson's *Black Marxism* could be expanded by the centralizing of McKay as well, particularly in light of McKay's *Negroes in America*:

> With its chief emphasis on the pressure of race within U.S. capitalist development, *The Negroes* takes a place at the opening of Black Marxism, the theoretical articulation of European working-class radicalism and black resistance in the African diaspora that Cedric Robinson traces through Du Bois, C.L.R. James, and Richard Wright. McKay's pre-echo of more recent, more exclusively academic work in African-American history, whiteness studies, cultural studies, and a post-Soviet Marxism without guarantees is valuable for its challenges as well as its flattering symmetries. Yet the Marxism of *The Negroes in America* is to my mind most significant for its moments of unassimilability within contemporary dialogues and genealogies and for its honored place within currently unclaimed Soviet lineages. (88–89)

New Negro, Old Left, like Wald's scholarship, discredits the myth of a New Left that concentrates on culture as a site of struggle ousting an Old Left, a "vulgar" Marxism focused only on overturning the economic base. Although not his express objective, Maxwell's scholarship exposes the artificiality of drawing a line vertically through history to indicate that no shameful Old Left ancestors still lurk in New Left politics. Following the establishment of this concept, it becomes evident that McKay's 1920s and early 1930s writings articulate the sources for the New American Studies, a tracing of origin without which no clear understanding of the postnationalist critique in American Studies is complete.

In order to understand McKay's complex interaction with and response to the Left, it is necessary to interrogate what is meant by the dismissive New Left terms *Old Left* and *vulgar Marxism*. In historiographic terms, these are expressions of an empty idiom. These terms effortlessly write off Marxist struggle during the modernist period as obvious reductivist ideology. But even with the enforcement of party protocols, no stable, singular form of Communism existed during the modernist phase. What existed instead were multiple Marxisms, Deleuzian multiplicities, in their ways as inflected by what is ordinarily recognizable as the positioning of the "post" as New Left politics. As Wald illustrates in his comprehensive scholarship on modernist period American leftism, and as Nelson says in his recent return to the question of literary modernism and radicalism, *Revolutionary Memory: Recovering the Poetry of the American Left* (2001), "There were, in effect, numerous communisms and more than one set of Popular Front beliefs at work in the 1930s" (189).

The same may be asserted for the 1920s, and the competing yet choral voices express themselves in such contested—and supposedly failed—sites as the language of the New Negro movement. Recognizing that the term *vulgar Marxism* originates with Engels's critique of the way Marxism could become debased during the late nineteenth and early twentieth centuries, I mean to indicate the term's usage in New Left discourses. It is vital to perceive that *Old Left* and *vulgar Marxism* are terms that come after the fact, expressions uttered so that the New Left politics could clear away the loam of history in order to make for itself an uncontaminated "new" space. Really, since *Old Left* is locked in the lesser binary position after *New Left*, the gesture to reduce previous forms of leftist effort says more about New Left philosophy than much about leftism during the modernist moment. Because the formation comes later, articulated after the complex lived histories of leftists during the modernist period, shriveling the events of the earlier period into a solitary spectacle, *Old Left* freezes the past into a legible and reducible history. An ideologically construed chronotope, the New Left redaction *Old Left* cannot possibly account for the unstable, indeed combustible multiplicity of Marxist combinations ablaze during the 1920s, as McKay's memoir, *A Long Way from Home,* makes apparent. New Left, as its tidy "new" dehyphenated modifier-noun configuration indicates, generates a speech act that talks over its antecedent, Old Left, in order to conceal that in fact it comes close to providing the instrument for its own deconstruction.

Ultimately, the present discussion reaches back to my previous assertion that New American Studies may be located in the New Negro movement and the rise of Communism in the United States. That is, if the New American Studies, an assemblage of critical rhetorics that are transparently linked to New Left political discourses, may locate itself in the advent of the New Negro movement and the rise of the Communist Party, then the idea that the Old Left was nothing more than vulgar Marxism becomes fraught with discursive trouble. Perhaps the most crucial characteristic of Denning's and Maxwell's work is the simple fact that American Studies traces its dust tracks in the road to Marxist theory and practice. In other words, within the critical field of American Studies, no outside to Marxist principles exists.

13. A University of Exeter press edition has been pending since 1995 but remains unavailable. Although *Romance in Marseille* is listed in both the press's paper and online catalogs, Exeter has no plans to bring it to press.

Chapter 1. Code Name Sasha, "My Real Name"

1. Maxwell queries the memoir's narrative, probing McKay's portrayal of the discord between himself and Michael Gold when the two writers coedited the *Liberator*; Max-

well notes that McKay's depiction is inconsistent with the historical record. The reason for his departure from the *Liberator* was very likely not the result of a white Communist attempting to impose his will on a black intellectual, as McKay suggests in his memoir. See his chapter titled "The Proletarian as New Negro, the New Negro as Proletarian: Mike Gold Meets Claude McKay," in *New Negro, Old Left*, 95–124.

2. This oft-quoted phrase appears in Alfred Douglas's 1894 poem "Two Loves."

3. Cooper discusses Eastman's influence over McKay in various parts of his biography: "While Eastman often lacked McKay's subtlety, he dared (however awkwardly at times) to develop broad general positions that McKay fundamentally accepted, despite specific reservations" (279).

4. The "Cities" poems appear in entirety, along with comprehensive annotations, in Maxwell's recent edition of the *Complete Poems*.

5. Shipway discusses the distinction between parliamentarism and *anti*-parliamentarism in Britain during the forming of the Communist Party in the early 1920s. Pankhurst's Workers' Socialist Federation briefly assumed the name "Communist Party, British Section of the Third International," which was a misleading title, given its hostility toward the CP of Great Britain. Unlike the CPGB, the CP(BSTI) opposed parliamentarism. However, the two rival groups did merge, though the union was fleeting, as the CPGB leadership wanted Pankhurst to relinquish control of the *Workers' Dreadnought*. When she refused, she was expelled from the CPGB.

Chapter 2. The "Distilled Poetry" of Queer Black Marxism in *A Long Way from Home*

1. Hughes records his youthful voyage to Western Africa in part 2 of *The Big Sea* (101–22).

2. St. Clair Drake's introduction to the reissue of *A Long Way from Home* poses the question: "neither southern France nor North Africa was his [McKay's] home. He did not have a chance to travel below the Sahara in the ancestral homeland, which he romanticized in some of his poetry" (xv).

3. Finlayson's *Tangier: City of the Dream* (1992) chronicles the experiences of Orton and other queer writers who ventured into Tangier's world of sexual divergence.

4. The identification of McKay as an American, or African American, author is reflected by his Library of Congress cataloging number; the classification of his poetry and fiction is numbered PS3525.A24785, a sorting that locates the author in African American literature.

5. I have formed this opinion based on my experience of giving papers on McKay at academic conferences.

6. McKay's letter to Eastman, June 28, 1933, discusses this issue.

7. McKay's romantic poem "The Tropics in New York" (1920), often reprinted and anthologized, illustrates his yearning for Jamaica.

8. In *Banjo*, Ray, the character who resembles McKay so much that one may almost

see the Haitian as an autobiographical version of the author, recoils at the idea of going back to his Caribbean homeland: "the very thought of returning to the Caribbean made him jumpy" (317). In truth, McKay didn't seem to think much about returning to Jamaica until faced with the reality that he was barred against doing so.

9. The "literary artistic chronotope," Bakhtin says, is "the intrinsic connectedness of temporal and spatial relationships that are artistically expressed in literature":

> spatial and temporal indicators are fused into one carefully thought-out, concrete whole. Time, as it were, thickens, takes on flesh, becomes artistically visible; likewise, space becomes charged and responsive to the movements of time, plot, and history. The intersection of axes and fusion of indicators characterizes the artistic chronotope. (84)

The chronotope inevitably effects more difficulty, however, than its organizational value offers:

> the process of assimilating an actual historical chronotope in literature has been complicated and erratic; certain isolated aspects of the chronotope, available in given historical conditions, have been worked out, although only certain specific forms of an actual chronotope were reflected in art. These generic forms, at first productive, were then reinforced by tradition; in their subsequent development they continued stubbornly to exist, up to and beyond the point at which they had lost any meaning that was productive in actuality or adequate to later historical situations. (85)

For my purposes, the term is useful for describing the way that literary classification functions. As it functions now as a kind of literary text itself, the Harlem Renaissance may be understood as a kind of literary-historical chronotope.

10. As for the use of *queer* as a disparaging term for a homosexual, usage occurs as early as the first decade of the twentieth century. Its use among same-sex society in the United States was common during the 1920s and 1930s, as one may see in McKay's writings.

11. Maiwald discusses how *Home to Harlem* was influenced by Carpenter's theories on sexuality and socialism, asserting that McKay's articulation of sexual difference was linked to a commitment to utopianism and that his representation of same-sex society in the novel was a kind of coded male sentimentality.

12. Cooper points out this fact (30–31), but does not treat its significance with the weight it deserves.

13. Jekyll used the term "special friend" to describe to the colonial governor his relationship with McKay (Cooper 29).

Chapter 3. "Dark Desire All Over the Pages": Race, Nation, and Sex in *Home to Harlem*

1. For the possible vernacular bonds between blue laws, blue movies, and blues music, see the *Oxford English Dictionary*'s entry for the etymology of the word *blue*.

2. For the latest comment on Du Bois's remark, see Schwarz's comment on "The Burden of Representation: Writers' Positions and Critics' Responses" (35).

3. James Johnson uses the word *Mecca* to describe Harlem in his essay "The Making of Harlem."

4. To confuse things, however, the first time the reader of *Home to Harlem* encounters McKay's redaction of Smith's lines, *bulldyking* is misspelled as "bulldycking" and *faggoty* as "faggotty" (36). The second time, however, both are spelled correctly (129). Also, why McKay does not quote Smith's recording faithfully isn't known. Smith's recording appeared in 1927, over five years after McKay had left Harlem. Living in France when he wrote *Home to Harlem*, McKay probably did not have the record. So he was forced to recall it, or else he heard it played abroad.

5. For a detailed account of Bentley and other black lesbian performers during the New Negro Renaissance, see Garber.

6. Watson says that Harlemites designated Saturday night "Square's Night" because the floors of nightclubs were crammed with whites from downtown (124–44).

7. Hughes includes a sequence of "social whist" party invitations in his section on "When the Negro Was in Vogue," in *The Big Sea* (229–32).

8. For a full account of Smith's lesbianism, see Albertson.

9. McKay says in *A Long Way from Home* that he carried a revolver for self-defense while working as a Pullman waiter because "we trainmen . . . had to be on guard against the sudden aroused hostility of the [white] mob" when stopping over in alien cities (54).

10. Steele, editor of Lawrence's *Psychoanalysis and the Unconscious, and Fantasia of the Unconscious* (2004), discusses Lawrence's "blood-knowledge" philosophy in his introduction:

> Lawrence's philosophical writings accompanied his major works of fiction at crucial points in his career. When making the final revision of *Sons and Lovers* in 1913, he began to formulate his beliefs about mind and body, together with what he saw as the religious dimension of his art. In January 1913, in the exultant rhetoric of a letter to the artist Ernest Collings, he affirmed a basic distinction between the conscious mind and the unconscious the intellect and what he came to call the "blood-knowledge" or "blood-consciousness":
>
>> My great religion is in a belief in the blood, the flesh, as being wiser than the intellect. We can go wrong in our minds. But what our blood feels and believes and says, is always true. The intellect is only a bit and a bridle. . . . We know too much. No, we *think* we know such a lot. . . . And

we have forgotten ourselves. . . . We cannot *be*. "To be or not to be"—it is the question with us now, by Jove. And nearly every Englishman says "Not to be." So he goes in for Humanitarianism and such like forms of non-being. (i. 503–504)

Here he locates a non-mental consciousness in the blood; blood-knowledge precedes and is more reliable than intellectual knowledge. His use of "blood," probably derived from Genesis ix. 4 ("flesh with the life thereof, which is the blood thereof"), seems to be largely a metaphor for sensory or non-rational life which Lawrence is now to expound as the "unconscious": in "the blood we have the body of our most elemental consciousness, our almost material consciousness" (179:32–4) (xxi–xxii).

11. The title of McKay's second memoir, published decades after his death, maintains the ambivalent link to Hemingway's book on African "green hills," emphasizing who has the right to claim a black land: *My Green Hills of Jamaica* (1979).

12. For an extensive account of the lesbian memoirist Barney, see Rodriguez.

13. For a discussion of the significance of the U.S. intervention in Haiti in McKay's novel, see Lowney.

14. Using the title of one of McKay's formerly uncollected mid-1930s poems, "The Years Between," a poignant lyric about his American homecoming, Maxwell's *Complete Poems* organizes his poems from the mid-1920s to the mid-1930s.

Chapter 4. The "Rude Anarchy" of "Black Boys" in *Banjo*

1. McKay makes this comment to his agent, William A. Bradley, in a letter, December 10, 1930 (Cooper 270).

2. Sharpley-Whiting's *Negritude Women* (2002) challenges the misreading of négritude as a masculine movement.

3. Perhaps fittingly, an imp eventually gets the better of McKay. In *A Long Way from Home* McKay reports on his "Magic Pilgrimage" to Russia, and he is especially proud of a "magnificent cartoon in colors, picturing me sailing on a magic carpet over the African jungles to Moscow. . . . An imp swiped it" (170).

4. McKay is designated *tovarish* by Mayakovsky and other poets when he reads his poetry to audiences in Moscow in 1922 (*Long Way* 186).

5. See chapter 1 on McKay's interaction with Trotsky as their dealings are depicted in McKay's FBI file.

Chapter 5. "Swaying to the Music of the Moon": Black-White Queer Solidarity in *Romance in Marseille*

1. McKay's first reference to the manuscript appears in a letter to Max Eastman on December 7, 1929.

2. The dropping of the final *s* at the end of Marseilles was (and still is) the common

British variant during the early 1930s, where the American spelling typically adds the *s*. To make matters a bit complicated, however, McKay occasionally added the *s,* as on the title page of his own manuscript. Far more often, though, he rendered the name of the French city without the ultimate *s*. References to the manuscript typically use "Romance in Marseille" because McKay ultimately referred to the text with this title. Cooper supplies a detailed biographical narrative on McKay and *Romance in Marseille* (266–89). Moreover, I italicize the title rather than using quotation marks, as I see the manuscript as a public record, virtually a recognized document, rather than merely an archival fragment, a special collections anomaly. Also, the last page is identified as page 171, but in fact the manuscript contains two pages designated as 99, the second labeled as "99a."

3. This comment appears in a letter from McKay to Arnold Schomburg, April 28, 1925.

4. See Kelley's discussion of the NAACP's stance toward the Scottsboro case in *Hammer and Hoe: Alabama Communists during the Great Depression* (78–91). Related to this, see the extraordinary archival recovery by Andrew Lee, *Scottsboro Alabama: A Story in Linoleum Cuts*, a formerly lost pictorial narrative of the Scottsboro case written by Lin Shi Khan and cut by Tony Perez.

5. The manuscript contains the typographical error *mained* instead of *maimed*.

6. The original manuscript contains the error: "she went and playfully kicked him behind" (50).

7. For a discussion of McKay's representation of the African American–Caribbean immigrant situation in his late 1930s study of Harlem, see my article "The Harlem Renaissance, Caribbean Radicalism, and Black Liberation Struggle."

8. The first reference to this establishment is as "The Seamen's and Workers Club." Moreover, the manuscript of *Romance in Marseille* itself exhibits McKay's complex politics, in both what the draft shows as well as in what the extant document reveals through the text beneath editing marks. That is, the only draft of the manuscript contains several pages with lines crossed out and corrections appearing where the author has indicated a change to a typesetter. On page 101 the text contains a salient alteration. Whereas most of the typesetting indications are lined out with a series of lowercase X marks typed over prior characters, thus making what appears beneath the editing marks unintelligible, page 101 contains two readable revised portions, clearly lined out in pencil by McKay. The relatively thin strikethroughs do not completely cover up the original text. Twice the author has indicated that "Seamen's Club" should be inserted where "Proletarian Hall" served as his original designation for the merchantmen's socialist club, thus ~~Proletarian Hall~~, with "Seamen's Club" typed above the strikethrough. Moreover, on page 105, McKay evidently missed editing out one of his several inclusions of "Proletarian Hall," apparently neglecting to eradicate this one and indicate the need to replace it with "Seamen's Club."

9. McKay's manuscript does not underline the title of the fictional magazine, as I have done.

10. Male characters, in McKay's narratives, frequently intrude on other male characters while they are dressing.

11. McKay's naming of Petit Frère's new haunt appears to be another example of McKay's curious sense of humor. In his "Soviet Russia and the Negro," published in the *Crisis* in December 1923, he talks of spending many evenings at the Domino Café, an infamous refuge of amateur poets and writers in Moscow, and where young Anarchists and Menshevists came to read and discuss their writing.

12. The song was featured first in Porter's revue *Paris*, which opened in New York in October 1928 (Schwartz 94). Porter included the song as well in his musical *Wake Up and Dream*, which premiered in London in March 1929 and ran for a respectable 263 performances, then moved on to Broadway (Schwartz 103–4). Although the two revues were not smash successes, "What Is This Thing Called Love?" instantly became an enormous hit, among Porter's most popular tunes, second only to another number featured in *Wake Up and Dream*, the bawdy "Let's Do It, Let's Fall in Love" (Schwartz 103). Dozens of versions of "What Is This Thing Called Love" were recorded and distributed, from cast recordings to a rendition by James P. Johnson. The "father of the stride piano," Johnson was among the most celebrated jazz artists of the late 1920s and early 1930s; during the late 1930s Johnson sought out Hughes to collaborate on the Communist agitprop musical *De Organizer* (Duffy 163–76). Porter claims to have written the tune while sojourning in Marrakech, evidently during the period that McKay was living in Morocco, writing *Romance in Marseille*. It seems likely that, given his wide range of camaraderie while living in Morocco, including Charles Henri Ford and Paul Bowles, McKay was aware of Porter's presence there at the very least.

13. With the exception of Schwarz's *Gay Voices of the Harlem Renaissance* (2002), critics have paid scant attention to *Romance in Marseille*. Schwarz provides an accurate description of the chapter, as in the following quote: "McKay ends the scene almost with a plea as Big Blonde, frustrated and 'crying softly,' seems to despair because of the cruelty men like himself and Petit Frère have to endure" (106).

14. For an overview of absinthe culture, see Conrad's *Absinthe: History in a Bottle* (1997).

15. In *Home to Harlem*, Zeddy remarks that Billy Biasse, a queer "wolf," "eats his own kind" (92).

Conclusion: Some Remarks on the Critical Implications of Queer Black Marxism

1. I could cite any number of critiques and anthologies that perpetuate the fiction that black Marxist, Communist, Anarchist—allied radical—writing of the interwar period is undeserving of critical attention. Most eminent are the headnotes preceding the selections of writers like McKay, Hughes, and Du Bois in the *Norton Anthology of African American Literature* (1997, 2004). These otherwise helpful commentaries discount the dedication to radical collectivist politics that New Negro writers engaged in or present their radicalism as phases of careers, intervals that came before moving on to more en-

lightened periods and therefore more satisfying literary acts. But I think that the myth is best exemplified by novelist Terry McMillan's introduction to her popular anthology of African American short fiction, *Breaking Ice* (1990). McMillan contrasts the kind of more recent fiction she has collected with previous generations' "protest literature" (xx). She places the quotation marks around the phrase, which seems to contradict her dismissal of writing by earlier generations; quotation marks should indicate that the author wishes to refer to someone else's locution and therefore doesn't abide by the convention of the expression. In any case, though the anthology's dazzling selection marks a historic advance in recognizing the development of postmodern African American short fiction, McMillan's dismissive attitude toward "protest literature" typifies the convention that writing with clear political themes is inferior to the historical realization of African American literature, writing beginning in the 1980s (or perhaps with Ellison's *Invisible Man*). McMillan probably means to group together writing of the 1960s with literature of the 1930s—not, of course, the apolitical Harlem Renaissance! However, her point is plain: that protest literature offers little subtlety—that it is almost purely polemical and therefore a debased form.

Bibliography

Aaron, Daniel. *Writers on the Left: Episodes in American Literary Communism*. New York: Harcourt, Brace & World, 1961.

Adorno, Theodor. *The Culture Industry: Selected Essays on Mass Culture*. Introd. J. M. Bernstein. London: Routledge, 1991.

Albertson, Chris. *Bessie*. 2nd ed. New Haven: Yale University Press, 2003.

Aldington, Richard. *Some Imagist Poets: An Anthology*. Boston: Houghton Mifflin, 1915.

Althusser, Louis. *Lenin and Philosophy and Other Essays*. Trans. Ben Brewster. London: New Left Books, 1971.

Anderson, Benedict. *Imagined Communities: Reflections on the Origins and Spread of Nationalism*. London: Verso, 1991.

Baker, Houston. *Modernism and the Harlem Renaissance*. Chicago: University of Chicago Press, 1989.

Bakhtin, M. M. *The Dialogic Imagination*. Ed. Michael Holquist. Trans. Caryl Emerson and Michael Holquist. Austin: University of Texas Press, 1981.

Baldwin, James. "Everybody's Protest Novel." *Notes of a Native Son*. 1955. Boston: New Beacon, 1983. 13–23.

———. *Giovanni's Room*. New York: Dial Press, 1956.

Baldwin, Kate A. *Beyond the Color Line and the Iron Curtain: Reading Encounters between Black and Red, 1922–1963*. Durham: Duke University Press, 2002.

Benjamin, Walter. "Surrealism: The Last Snapshot of the European Intelligentsia." *Reflections: Essays, Aphorisms, Autobiographical Writings*. Ed. Peter Demetz. Trans. Edmund Jephcott. New York: Schocken, 1978. 177–92.

———. "The Work of Art in the Age of Mechanical Reproduction." *Illuminations*. Ed. Hannah Arendt. Trans. Harry Zohn. New York: Schocken, 1969. 217–52.

Bennett, Gwendolyn. "Our Book Shelf." *Opportunity* 7 (Aug. 1929): 254.

Bergson, Henri. "Creative Evolution." 1907. *Modernism: An Anthology of Sources and Documents*. Ed. Vassiliki Kolocotroni, Jane Goldman, and Olga Taxidou. Chicago: University of Chicago Press, 1998. 68–71.

Berkman, Alexander. *ABC of Anarchism*. London: Freedom Press, 1929.

———. *Prison Memoirs of an Anarchist*. New York: Mother Earth Press, 1912.

Berlant, Lauren. *The Queen of America Goes to Washington City: Essays on Sex and Citizenship*. Durham: Duke University Press, 1997.

Bhabha, Homi K. *The Location of Culture*. London: Routledge, 1994.

Black, George. *The Good Neighbor: How the United States Wrote the History of Central America and the Caribbean*. New York: Pantheon, 1988.

Boone, Joseph. *Libidinal Currents: Sexuality and the Shaping of Modernism*. Chicago: University of Chicago Press, 1998.

Bosworth, R.J.B. *Mussolini: The Biography*. London: Hodder Arnold, 2002.

Bowles, Paul. *The Sheltering Sky*. New York: New Directions, 1949.

———. *Without Stopping: An Autobiography*. New York: Putnam, 1972.

Boyd, Valerie. *Wrapped in Rainbows: The Life of Zora Neale Hurston*. New York: Scribner, 2003.

Brathwaite, Edward Kamau. *The Arrivants: A New World Trilogy*. Oxford: Oxford University Press, 1973.

———. *History of the Voice: The Development of Nation Language in Anglophone Caribbean Poetry*. Port of Spain, Jamaica: New Beacon, 1984.

Breton, André. *Manifesto of Surrealism*. 1924. *Manifestos of Surrealism*. Ed. Richard Seaver. Trans. Helen R. Lane. Ann Arbor: University of Michigan Press, 1969. 1–48.

Breton, André, Leon Trotsky, and Diego Rivera. "*Manifesto*: Towards a Free Revolutionary Art." 1938. *Theories of Modern Art: A Source Book by Artists and Critics*. Ed. Herschel B. Chipp. Berkeley: University of California Press, 1968. 483.

Burch, Francis F. "Millay's 'Not in a Silver Casket Cool with Pearls.'" *Explicator* 48 (Summer 1990): 277–79.

Burton, Richard. *Arabian Nights: Tales from a Thousand and One Nights*. 1850. Introd. A. S. Bryant. New York: Modern Library, 2001.

Butler, Judith. *Gender Trouble: Feminism and the Subversion of Identity*. New York: Routledge, 1990.

Callinicos, Alex. *Trotskyism*. Minneapolis: University of Minnesota Press, 1990.

Carby, Hazel V. "Policing the Black Woman's Body in an Urban Context." *Critical Inquiry* 18.4 (Summer 1992): 738–55.

Caribbean Quarterly 38.1 (1992).

Chauncey, George. *Gay New York: Gender, Urban Culture, and the Making of the Gay Male World, 1890–1940*. New York: Basic Books, 1994.

Chukovsky, Korney Ivanovich. *Diary, 1901–1929*. Moscow: Soviet Writer, 1991.

Cobham, Rhonda. "Jekyll and Claude: The Erotics of Patronage in Claude McKay's *Banana Bottom*." *Queer Diasporas*. Ed. Cindy Patton and Benigno Sanchez-Eppler. Durham: Duke University Press, 2000. 122–53.

Conrad, Barnaby. *Absinthe: History in a Bottle*. New York: Chronicle Books, 1997.

Cooper, Wayne F. *Claude McKay: Rebel Sojourner in the Harlem Renaissance*. New York: Schocken, 1987.

Cowl, Carl. Preface. *Harlem Glory: A Fragment of Aframerican Life*. By Claude McKay. Chicago: Charles H. Kerr, 1990. 5–7.

Cruse, Harold. *The Crisis of the Negro Intellectual*. New York: Morrow, 1967.

Culleton, Claire A. *Joyce and the G-Men: J. Edgar Hoover's Manipulation of Modernism*. New York: Palgrave Macmillan, 2004.

Davis, Angela Y. *Blues Legacies and Black Feminism: Gertrude "Ma" Rainey, Bessie Smith, and Billie Holiday*. New York: Vintage, 1999.

Delavenay, Emile. *D. H. Lawrence and Edward Carpenter: A Study in Edwardian Transition*. London: Heinemann, 1971.

Deleuze, Gilles, and Félix Guattari. *A Thousand Plateaus: Capitalism and Schizophrenia*. 1972. Trans. Brian Massumi. London: Athlone, 1987.

Dellamora, Richard. *Masculine Desire: The Sexual Politics of Victorian Aestheticism*. Chapel Hill: University of North Carolina Press, 1990.

D'Emilio, John. *Sexual Politics, Sexual Communities: The Making of a Homosexual Minority in the United States, 1940–1970*. Chicago: University of Chicago Press, 1983.

Denning, Michael. *The Cultural Front: The Laboring of Culture in the Twentieth Century*. New York: Verso, 1996.

Dos Passos, John. "Against American Literature." 1916. *Modernism: An Anthology of Sources and Documents*. Ed. Vassiliki Kolocotroni, Jane Goldman, and Olga Taxidou. Chicago: University of Chicago Press, 1998. 334–36.

———. *Manhattan Transfer*. New York: Houghton Mifflin, 1925.

Douglas, Alfred Bruce. "Two Loves." 1894. *Nineteenth-Century Writings on Homosexuality: A Sourcebook*. Ed. Chris White. London: Routledge, 1999. 54–56.

Douglass, Frederick. *Narrative of the Life of Frederick Douglass*. 1845. *The Frederick Douglass Papers, Series Two: Autobiographical Writings; Volume 1 Narrative*. Ed. John W. Blassingame, John R. McKivigan, and Peter P. Hinks. New Haven: Yale University Press, 1999.

Drake, St. Clair. Introduction. *A Long Way from Home*. By Claude McKay. San Diego: Harvest, 1970. ix–xxi.

Duberman, Martin Baulm. *Paul Robeson: A Biography*. New York: Knopf, 1988.

Du Bois, W.E.B. *Black Reconstruction in America: An Essay toward a History of the Part Which Black Folk Played in the Attempt to Reconstruct Democracy in America, 1860–1880*. New York: Harcourt, Brace, 1935.

———. "The Browsing Reader." *Crisis* June 1928: 202.

———. *Dark Princess: A Romance*. New York: Harcourt, Brace, 1928.

———. "Lady Nicotine." *Inter-State Tattler* 16 Mar. 1928.

———. "The Looking Glass: Literature." *Crisis* Aug. 1916: 182.

———. *The Souls of Black Folk*. 1903. Baltimore: Johns Hopkins University Press, 1989.

Duffy, Susan. "A Collaboration of Jazz, Poetry, and Blues: *De Organizer*." *The Political Plays of Langston Hughes*. Carbondale: Southern Illinois University Press, 2000. 163–76.

Dunbar Nelson, Alice. "The Proletariat Speaks." 1929. *The Crisis Reader: Stories, Poetry, and Essays from the N.A.A.C.P.'s Crisis Magazine*. Ed. Sondra Kathryn Wilson. New York: Modern Library, 1999. 38.

Eastman, Max. *Artists in Uniform: A Study of Literature and Bureaucratism*. New York: Knopf, 1934.

———. *Since Lenin Died.* New York: Boni & Liveright, 1925.

Edwards, Brent Hayes. "Vagabond Internationalism: Claude McKay's *Banjo.*" *The Practice of Diaspora: Literature, Translation, and the Rise of Black Nationalism.* Cambridge: Harvard University Press, 2003. 187-240.

Ellman, Richard. *Oscar Wilde.* New York: Knopf, 1988.

Emanuel, James A., and Theodore L. Gross. *Dark Symphony: Negro Literature in America.* New York: Free Press, 1968.

Fabre, Michel. *From Harlem to Paris: Black American Writers in France, 1840–1980.* Urbana: University of Illinois Press, 1991.

Fadiman, Clifton. Letter to Max Eastman. 12 Sept. 1933. James Weldon Johnson Papers. James Weldon Johnson Collection of Negro Literature and Art, American Literature Collection, Beinecke Rare Book and Manuscript Library, Yale University, New Haven.

Fanon, Frantz. *Black Skin, White Masks.* 1952. Trans. Charles Lam Markmann. New York: Grove, 1967.

———. *The Wretched of the Earth.* 1961. Pref. Jean-Paul Sartre. Trans. Constance Farrington. New York: Grove Press, 1968.

Fauset, Jessie Redmon. *Plum Bun: A Novel without a Moral.* New York: Stokes, 1929.

Federal Bureau of Investigation. Claude McKay file, no. 61–3497. Assorted documents dated 16 Dec. 1921 to 31 May 1940 obtained under provisions of the Freedom of Information Act. 119 pages.

———. FOIA Claude McKay file, no. 61–3497, Reading Room Index. Web site with PDF file downloads. http://foia.fbi.gov/foiaindex/mckay_claude.htm.

———. FOIA Famous Persons Listing, Reading Room Index. Web site with PDF file downloads. http://foia.fbi.gov/famous.htm.

Finlayson, Iain. *Tangier: City of the Dream.* New York: HarperCollins, 1992.

Foerstel, Herbert. *Freedom of Information and the Right to Know: The Origins and Applications of the Freedom of Information Act.* Westport, Conn.: Greenwood Press, 1999.

Ford, Charles Henri. Letter to Claude McKay. 1938? James Weldon Johnson Papers. James Weldon Johnson Collection of Negro Literature and Art, American Literature Collection, Beinecke Rare Book and Manuscript Library, Yale University, New Haven.

Ford, Charles Henri, and Parker Tyler. *The Young and the Evil.* New York: Obelisk Press, 1933.

Forster, E. M. "The Plot." *Aspects of the Novel.* New York: Harcourt, Brace, & World, 1927. Rpt. in *Approaches to the Novel: Materials for a Poetics.* Ed. Robert Scholes. San Francisco: Chandler, 1961. 219–32.

Foucault, Michel. *Discipline and Punish: The Birth of the Prison.* Trans. Alan Sheridan. New York: Vintage, 1979.

———. *The History of Sexuality, Vol. 1: An Introduction.* Trans. Robert Hurley. New York: Pantheon, 1978.

Frank, Richard. "Negro Revolutionary Music." *New Masses* 15 May 1934: 29–30.

Fryer, Jonathan. *André and Oscar: The Literary Friendship of André Gide and Oscar Wilde*. New York: St. Martin's, 1998.

Gallacher, William. *The Chosen Few: A Sketch of Men and Events in Parliament, 1936–1940*. London: Londres, 1940.

Garber, Eric. "A Spectacle in Color: The Lesbian and Gay Subculture of Jazz Age Harlem." *Hidden from History: Reclaiming the Gay and Lesbian Past*. Ed. Martin Bauml Duberman, Martha Vicinus, and George Chauncey Jr. New York: New American Library, 1989. 318–31.

Gates, Henry Louis, Jr., and Nellie Y. McKay, eds. *The Norton Anthology of African American Literature*. 2nd ed. New York: Norton, 2004.

Gayle, Addison. *Black Expression: Essays by and about Black Americans in the Creative Arts*. New York: Weybright and Talley, 1969.

Gilmer, Walker. *Horace Liveright: Publisher of the Twenties*. New York: Random House, 1977.

Gilroy, Paul. *The Black Atlantic: Modernity and Double Consciousness*. Cambridge: Harvard University Press, 1993.

Glissant, Édouard. *Caribbean Discourse: Selected Essays*. Trans. J. Michael Dash. Charlottesville: University Press of Virginia, 1989.

Gold, Mike. "Dark with Sunlight." [Review of *Banjo*.] *New Masses* July 1929: 17.

———. "Towards Proletarian Art." 1921. *Michael Gold: A Literary Anthology*. Ed. Michael Folsom. New York: International Publishers, 1972. 62-70.

Goldman, Emma. *Living My Life*. 1931. Introd. Candace Falk. Salt Lake City: Gibbs M. Smith, 1982.

Golomstock, Igor. *Totalitarian Art in the Soviet Union, the Third Reich, Fascist Italy, and the People's Republic of China*. New York: HarperCollins, 1990.

Gosciak, Josh. *The Shadowed Country: Claude McKay and the Romance of the Victorians*. Piscataway, N.J.: Rutgers University Press, 2006.

Gramsci, Antonio. *Selections from Cultural Writings*. Ed. David Forgacs and Geoffrey Nowell-Smith. Trans. William Boelhower. London: Lawrence and Wishart, 1985.

———. *Selections from the Prison Notebooks*. Ed. and trans. Quintin Hoare and Geoffrey Nowell-Smith. New York: International, 1971.

Griffith, D. W., dir. *The Birth of a Nation*. Perf. Lillian Gish. Triangle Film Corporation, 1915.

Grosz, George. *Ecce Homo*. 1923. Introd. Henry Miller. New York: Grove Press, 1966.

Hall, Stuart. "Cultural Identity and Diaspora." *Colonial Discourse/Postcolonial Theory*. Ed. Patrick Williams and Laura Chrisman. New York: Columbia University Press, 1994. 392–403.

Hamill, Sam, ed. *Poets against the War*. New York: Thunder's Mouth Press/Nation's Books, 2003.

Hare, Maud Cuney. "Antar, Negro Poet of Arabia." 1924. *The Crisis Reader: Stories, Po-*

etry, and Essays from the N.A.A.C.P.'s Crisis *Magazine.* Ed. Sondra Kathryn Wilson. New York: Modern Library, 1999. 293–303.

Hathaway, Heather. *Caribbean Waves: Relocating Claude McKay and Paule Marshall.* Bloomington: Indiana University Press, 1999.

Hemingway, Ernest. *Green Hills of Africa.* Decorations by Edward Shenton. New York: Scribner, 1935.

———. *The Sun Also Rises.* New York: Scribner, 1926.

———. *Winner Take Nothing.* New York: Scribner, 1933.

Hemphill, Essex. *Ceremonies: Prose and Poetry.* New York: Plume, 1992.

Herdeck, Donald E. Introduction. *Batouala.* By René Maran. Portsmouth, N.H.: Heinemann, 1987. 1–5.

Holcomb, Gary E. "Diaspora Cruises: Queer Black Proletarianism in Claude McKay's *A Long Way from Home." Modern Fiction Studies* 49.3 (Winter 2003): 714–41.

———. "The Harlem Renaissance, Caribbean Radicalism, and Black Liberation Struggle: McKay's *Harlem: Negro Metropolis." Journal of Caribbean Studies* 18:1–2 (Fall 2003/Spring 2004): 71–78.

———. "New Negroes, Black Communists, and the New Pluralism." *American Quarterly* 53.2 (June 2001): 367–76.

———. "Travels of a Transnational 'Slut': Sexual Migration in Kincaid's *Lucy." Critique: Studies in Contemporary Fiction* 44.3 (Spring 2003): 295–312.

Hones, Bridget. "With 'Banjo' by My Bed: Black French Writers Reading Claude McKay." *Caribbean Quarterly* 38.1 (1992): 32–39.

Hoyt, Edwin. *The Palmer Raids, 1919–1920: An Attempt to Suppress Dissent.* New York: Seabury Press, 1969.

Hughes, Langston. *The Big Sea: An Autobiography.* 1940. Introd. Arnold Rampersad. New York: Hill and Wang, 1993.

———. *The Collected Poems of Langston Hughes.* Ed. Arnold Rampersad. New York: Vintage, 1994.

———. "Cora Unashamed." 1933. *The Ways of White Folks.* New York: Knopf, 1934. 5–18.

———. "Good Morning Revolution." 1932. In *Collected Poems* 162–63.

———. "I, Too." 1925. In *Collected Poems* 46.

———. *I Wonder as I Wander: An Autobiographical Journey.* 1956. Introd. Arnold Rampersad. New York: Hill and Wang, 1993.

———. "Let America Be America Again." 1936. In *Collected Poems* 189–91.

———. "Merry Christmas." 1930. In *Collected Poems* 132.

———. "One More 'S' in the U.S.A." 1934. In *Collected Poems* 176–77.

———. *The Political Plays of Langston Hughes.* Ed. Susan Duffy. Carbondale: Southern Illinois University Press, 2000.

Hutchinson, George. *The Harlem Renaissance in Black and White.* Cambridge: Harvard University Press, 1995.

Isherwood, Christopher. *Goodbye to Berlin*. London: Hogarth, 1939.

James, C.L.R. *The Black Jacobins: Toussaint L'Ouverture and the Santo Domingo Revolution*. 1938. New York: Vintage, 1989.

———. *World Revolution, 1917–1936: The Rise and Fall of the Communist International*. 1937. New York: Prometheus Books, 1993.

James, Winston. *A Fierce Hatred of Injustice: Claude McKay's Jamaica and His Poetry of Rebellion*. New York: Verso, 2000.

———. *Holding Aloft the Banner of Ethiopia: Caribbean Radicalism in Early Twentieth-Century America*. New York: Verso, 1998.

Jameson, Fredric. *The Political Unconscious: Narrative as a Socially Symbolic Act*. Ithaca: Cornell University Press, 1981.

Jekyll, Walter. *Jamaican Song and Story: Annancy Stories, Digging Sings, Ring Tunes, and Dancing Tunes*. London: Folklore Society, 1907.

Johnson, E. Patrick, and Mae G. Henderson, eds. *Black Queer Studies: A Critical Anthology*. Durham: Duke University Press, 2005.

Johnson, James W. "The Making of Harlem." *Survey Graphic* (Harlem Number) 6.6 (Mar. 1925): 635–39.

———. Preface. *The Book of American Negro Poetry*. Rev. ed. 1922. New York: Harcourt, 1969. 9–48.

Joyce, James. *Ulysses*. 1922. Ed. Hugh Kenner. Baltimore: Johns Hopkins University Press, 1987.

Karenga, Ron. "Black Art: Mute Matter Given Form and Function." 1968. *New Black Voices*. Ed. Abraham Chapman. New York: New American Library, 1972. 476–82.

Kaufman, Bob. *Golden Sardine*. San Francisco: City Lights, 1967.

Kelley, Robin D. G. *Hammer and Hoe: Alabama Communists during the Great Depression*. Chapel Hill: University of North Carolina Press, 1990.

Khan, Lin Shi, and Tony Perez. *Scottsboro Alabama: A Story in Linoleum Cuts*. Ed. Andrew Lee. Foreword Robin D. G. Kelley. New York: New York University Press, 2002.

Kolocotroni, Vassiliki, Jane Goldman, and Olga Taxidou. Introduction. *Modernism: An Anthology of Sources and Documents*. Chicago: University of Chicago Press, 1998. xvii–xx.

Kozintsev, Grigorii. *The Eccentric Manifesto*. 1922. Trans. Marek Pytel. London: Eccentric Press, 1992.

Kumar, Amitava, ed. *World Bank Literature*. Pref. John Berger. Afterword Bruce Robbins. Minneapolis: University of Minnesota Press, 2002.

Lal, Shafali. "1930s Multiculturalism: Rachel Davis DuBois and the Bureau for Intercultural Education." *Radical Teacher* 69 (Spring 2004): 18–22.

Larsen, Nella. *Quicksand*. New York: Knopf, 1928.

Lauter, Paul. "Searching for Lefty." *American Literary History* 17.3 (Summer 2005): 360–68.

Law, Jules David. "'Pity They Can't See Themselves': Assessing the 'Subject' of Pornography in 'Nausicaa.'" *James Joyce Quarterly* 27.2 (1990): 219–39.

Lef [Left Front of the Arts]. *Bolshevik Visions: First Phase of the Cultural Revolution in Soviet Russia, Part II*. Ed. William G. Rosenberg. Ann Arbor: University of Michigan Press, 1990.

Lehmann-Haupt, Hellmut. *Art under a Dictatorship*. New York: Oxford University Press, 1973.

Lenin, V. I. *Collected Works*. Vol. 23. London: Lawrence and Wishart, 1960.

Lewis, David L. *Portable Harlem Renaissance Reader*. New York: Viking, 1994.

———. *W.E.B. Du Bois: The Fight for Equality and the American Century, 1919–1963*. New York: Henry Holt, 2000.

———. *When Harlem Was in Vogue*. New York: Knopf, 1981.

Lindsay, Vachel. *The Congo and Other Poems*. New York: Macmillan, 1914.

Locke, Alain, ed. *Four Negro Poets*. New York: Simon & Schuster, 1927.

———, ed. *The New Negro: An Interpretation*. New York: A & C. Boni, 1925.

Lott, Eric. *Love and Theft: Blackface Minstrelsy and the American Working Class*. New York: Oxford, 1993.

Lowney, John. "Haiti and Black Transnationalism: Remapping the Migrant Geography of *Home to Harlem*." *African American Review* 34.3 (Fall 2000): 413–29.

Maiwald, Michael. "Race, Capitalism, and the Third-Sex Ideal: Claude McKay's *Home to Harlem* and the Legacy of Edward Carpenter." *Modern Fiction Studies* 48.4 (Winter 2002): 825–57.

Maran, René. *Batouala: A True Black Novel*. 1921. Trans. Barbara Beck and Alexandre Mboukou. London: Heinemann, 1987.

Marx, Karl. *Capital: A Critique of Political Economy*. 1867–1895. Trans. Ben Fowkes. New York: Penguin, 1992.

———. *The Eighteenth Brumaire of Louis Bonaparte*. 1852. Trans. C. P. Dutt. New York: International, 1987.

Marx, Karl, and Frederick Engels. *The Communist Manifesto*. 1848. Introd. Eric Hobsbawm. London: Verso, 1998.

———. *The German Ideology*. 1845–46. Ed. and introd. C. J. Arthur. New York: International, 1988.

Maxwell, William J. "F.B. Eyes: The Bureau Reads Claude McKay." *Left of the Color Line: Race, Radicalism, and Twentieth-Century Literature of the United States*. Ed. Bill V. Mullen and James Smethurst. Chapel Hill: University of North Carolina Press, 2003. 39–65.

———. Introduction. *Complete Poems*. By Claude McKay. Urbana: University of Illinois Press, 2004. xi–xliv.

———. *New Negro, Old Left: African-American Writing and Communism between the Wars*. New York: Columbia University Press, 1999.

McKay, Claude. *Banana Bottom*. New York: Harper, 1933.

———. *Banjo: A Story without a Plot*. New York: Harper, 1929.

———. *Banjo. Légitime Défense*. Trans. Ida Treat and Paul Vaillant-Couturier. Paris: Reider, 1931.

———. *Complete Poems*. Ed. William J. Maxwell. Urbana: University of Illinois Press, 2004.

———. *Constab Ballads*. 1912. Rpt. in *The Dialect Poetry of Claude McKay: Two Volumes in One*. Pref. Wayne Cooper. Freeport, N.Y.: Books for Libraries Press, 1972.

———. *Gingertown*. New York: Harper, 1932.

———. *Harlem Glory: A Fragment of Aframerican Life*. Chicago: Charles H. Kerr, 1990.

———. *Harlem: Negro Metropolis*. 1940. New York: Harcourt Brace Jovanovich, 1968.

———. *Harlem Shadows: The Poems of Claude McKay*. New York: Harcourt, Brace, 1922.

———. *Home to Harlem*. New York: Harper, 1928.

———. "How Black Sees Green and Red." *Liberator* June 1921: 17–21. Rpt. in *The Passion of Claude McKay* 57–62.

———. "If We Must Die." *Liberator* July 1919: 21.

———. Letter to William A. Bradley. 10 Dec. 1930. William Aspenwall Bradley Papers. Columbia University Rare Book and Manuscript Library. Columbia University, New York City.

———. Letter to Max Eastman. 28 June 1933. Max Eastman Papers. Lilly Library, Indiana University, Bloomington,.

———. Letter to Max Eastman. 7 Dec. 1929. Max Eastman Papers. Lilly Library, Indiana University, Bloomington.

———. Letter to James Weldon Johnson. 30 Apr. 1928. James Weldon Johnson Papers. James Weldon Johnson Collection of Negro Literature and Art, American Literature Collection, Beinecke Rare Book and Manuscript Library, Yale University, New Haven.

———. Letter to General Secretary of the ECCI Vasil Kolarov. Moscow. 23 Dec. 1922. Comintern Archive, f. 515, op. 1, d. 93, l. 92–93.

———. Letter to A. A. Schomburg. 28 Apr. 1925. Arnold A. Schomburg Papers, Schomburg Center for Research in Black Culture. New York: New York Public Library.

———. *A Long Way from Home*. New York: Lee Furman, 1937.

———. *My Green Hills of Jamaica and Five Jamaican Short Stories*. Ed. Mervyn Morris. Kingston, Jamaica: Heinemann, 1979.

———. *The Negroes in America* [*Negry v Amerike*, 1923]. Ed. Alan L. McLeod. Trans. Robert J. Winter. Port Washington, N.Y.: Kennikat, 1979.

———. *The Passion of Claude McKay: Selected Poetry and Prose, 1912–1948*. Ed. Wayne F. Cooper. New York: Schocken, 1973.

———. "Right Turn to Catholicism." Ms, Miscellaneous Claude McKay Papers. Schomburg Center for Research in Black Culture, New York Public Library. 1945?

———. *Romance in Marseille*. Ms., Miscellaneous Claude McKay Papers. Schomburg Center for Research in Black Culture, New York Public Library. 1929–32.

———. "Socialism and the Negro." *Workers' Dreadnought* Jan. 1920: 1–2. Rpt. in *The Passion of Claude McKay,* 50–54.

———. *Songs of Jamaica*. 1912. Rpt. in *The Dialect Poetry of Claude McKay: Two Volumes in One*. Pref. Wayne Cooper. Freeport, N.Y.: Books for Libraries Press, 1972.

———. "Soviet Russia and the Negro." *Crisis* Dec. 1923: 61–65. Rpt. in *The Passion of Claude McKay* 95–106.

———. "Speech to the Fourth Congress of the Third Communist International, Moscow." ("Report on the Negro Question." *International Press Correspondence* 3 [Jan. 1923]: 16–17.) Rpt. in *The Passion of Claude McKay* 91–95.

———. *Spring in New Hampshire and Other Poems*. London: Grant Richards, 1920.

———. *Trial by Lynching: Stories about Negro Life in North America* [*Sudom lincha*, 1925]. Ed. A. L. McLeod. Trans. Robert J. Winter. Mysore, India: Centre for Commonwealth Literature and Research, University of Mysore, 1977.

———. "The White House." *Liberator* May 1922: 16.

———. "The White Houses." *The New Negro: An Interpretation*. Ed. Alain Locke. New York: A. & C. Boni, 1925: 134.

McMillan, Terry, ed. Introduction. *Breaking Ice: An Anthology of Contemporary African-American Fiction*. Pref. John Edgar Wideman. New York: Penguin, 1990. xv–xxiv.

Meeker, Martin. "Behind the Mask of Respectability: Reconsidering the Mattachine Society and Male Homophile Practice, 1950s and 1960s." *Journal of the History of Sexuality* 10.1 (Jan. 2001): 78–116.

Miller, D. A. *The Novel and the Police*. Berkeley: University of California Press, 1988.

Miracle, Josep. "The Black Soul Rises: Claude McKay's 'Near-White.'" Trans. Mireia Aragay. *Quasi Blanca*. Edicions de la Rosa Dels Vents. Vol. 62, 1938. Ed. A. L. McLeod. Rpt. in *The Literary Half-Yearly* 34.2 (July 1993): 48–56.

Mosse, George. *Nationalism and Sexuality: Respectability and Abnormal Sexuality in Modern Europe*. New York: Fertig, 1985.

Moten, Fred. *In the Break: The Aesthetics of the Black Radical Tradition*. Minneapolis: University of Minnesota Press, 2003.

Mullen, Bill V., and James Smethurst, eds. *Left of the Color Line: Race, Radicalism, and Twentieth-Century Literature of the United States*. Chapel Hill: University of North Carolina Press, 2003.

Naison, Mark. *Communists in Harlem during the Depression*. Urbana: University of Illinois Press, 1983.

Nelson, Cary. *Repression and Recovery: Modern American Poetry and the Politics of Cultural Memory, 1910–1945*. Madison: University of Wisconsin Press, 1989.

———. *Revolutionary Memory: Recovering the Poetry of the American Left*. New York: Routledge, 2001.

Nordau, Max. *Degeneration*. 1892. Trans. George L. Mosse. Lincoln: University of Nebraska Press, 1968.

North, Michael. *The Dialect of Modernism: Race, Language, and Twentieth-Century Literature*. New York: Oxford University Press, 1999.

[Nugent], Richard Bruce. "Smoke, Lilies and Jade." *Fire!! A Quarterly Devoted to the Younger Negro Artists* 1.1 (1926): 33–40.

O'Neill, Eugene. *Complete Plays, 1913–1920*. New York: Library of America, 1988.

Paquet, Sandra Pouchet. *Caribbean Autobiography: Cultural Identity and Self-Representation*. Madison: University of Wisconsin Press, 2002.

Parker, Dorothy. Review of *Home to Harlem*, by Claude McKay. *The Portable Dorothy Parker*. Ed. Brendan Gill. New York: Penguin, 1991. 352.

Pavlic, Edward M. *Crossroads Modernism: Descent and Emergence in African American Literary Culture*. Minneapolis: University of Minnesota Press, 2002.

People for the American Way. Web site. http://www.pfaw.org/pfaw/general/

Radway, Janice A. "What's in a Name?" Presidential address to the American Studies Association, 20 Nov. 1998. *American Quarterly* 51.1 (1999) 1–32.

Rascoe, Burton. "The Seamy Side." *Bookman* 68 (Apr. 1928): 183.

Reed, T. V. *The Art of Protest: Culture and Activism from the Civil Rights Movement to the Streets of Seattle*. Minneapolis: University of Minnesota Press, 2005.

Reid-Pharr, Robert. *Gay Black Man*. Foreword Samuel R. Delaney. New York: New York University Press, 2001.

Ricoeur, Paul. *Time and Narrative*. 3 vols., 1983–85. Trans. Kathleen McLaughlin and David Pellauer. Chicago: University of Chicago Press, 1984–88.

Robeson, Paul. *Here I Stand*. New York: Beacon, 1971.

Robinson, Cedric J. *Black Marxism: The Making of a Black Radical Tradition*. 1983. Rpt. Chapel Hill: University of North Carolina Press, 2000.

Rodriguez, Suzanne. *Wild Heart: A Life: Natalie Clifford Barney's Journey from Victorian America to the Literary Salons of Paris*. New York: Ecco/HarperCollins, 2002.

Rowe, John Carlos. *Literary Culture and U.S. Imperialism: From the Revolution to World War II*. Oxford: Oxford University Press, 2000.

———, ed. *Post-Nationalist American Studies*. Berkeley: University of California Press, 2000.

Rowley, Hazel. *Richard Wright: The Life and Times*. New York: Henry Holt, 2001.

Rubin, Gayle. "Thinking Sex: Notes for a Radical Theory of the Politics of Sexuality." *Pleasure and Danger: Exploring Female Sexuality*. Ed. Carole S. Vance. London: Pandora Press, 1992. 267–319.

Said, Edward W. *The World, the Text, and the Critic*. Cambridge: Harvard University Press, 1983.

Schulter, Daniel P. *Gay Life in the Former USSR: Fraternity without Community*. New York: Routledge, 2002.

Schwartz, Charles. *Cole Porter: A Biography*. New York: Dial Press, 1977.

Schwarz, A. B. Christa. *Gay Voices of the Harlem Renaissance*. Bloomington: Indiana University Press, 2003.

Schwitters, Kurt. *Kurt Schwitters: Poems, Performance Pieces, Proses, Plays, Poetics*. Ed. and trans. Jerome Rothenberg and Pierre Joris. Philadelphia: Temple University Press, 1993.

Scruggs, Charles. Review of *The Harlem Renaissance: The One and the Many,* by Mark Helbling. *African American Review* 35.2 (Summer 2001): 317–19.

Sears, James T. *Behind the Mask of the Mattachine: The Hal Call Chronicles and the Early Movement for Homosexual Emancipation*. New York: Harrington Park Press, 2006.

Sedgwick, Eve Kosofsky. *Between Men: English Literature and Male Homosocial Desire*. New York: Columbia University Press, 1985.

Selden, Raman, Peter Widdowson, and Peter Brooker. *A Reader's Guide to Contemporary Literary Theory*. 5th ed. New York: Pearson Longman, 2005.

Serge, Victor. *Memoirs of a Revolutionary, 1901–1941*. 1963. Foreword Adam Hochschild. Trans. Peter Sedgwick. Iowa City: University of Iowa Press, 2002.

Sharpley-Whiting, T. Denean. *Negritude Women*. Minneapolis: University of Minnesota Press, 2002.

Shaw, George Bernard. *Pygmalion: A Romance in Five Acts*. 1916. Ed. Dan H. Lawrence. New York: Penguin, 2001.

Shipway, Mark A. S. *Anti-Parliamentary Communism: The Movement for Workers Councils in Britain, 1917–45*. Basingstoke: Palgrave Macmillan, 1988.

Smethurst, James Edward. *The New Red Negro: The Literary Left and African American Poetry, 1930–1946*. Race and American Culture. Oxford: Oxford University Press, 1999.

Smith, Bessie. "Foolish Man Blues." 1927. *Bessie Smith: The Complete Recordings*. Vol. 3. Sony, 1992.

Somerville, Siobhan B. "Notes toward a Queer History of Naturalization." *American Quarterly* 57.3 (Sept. 2005): 659–75.

———. *Queering the Color Line: Race and the Invention of Homosexuality in American Culture*. Durham: Duke University Press, 2000.

Spencer, Suzette A. "Swerving at a Different Angle and Flying in the Face of Tradition: Excavating the Homoerotic Subtext in *Home to Harlem*." *CLA Journal* Dec. 1998: 164–67.

Stansell, Christine. *American Moderns: Bohemian New York and the Creation of a New Century*. New York: Metropolitan Books, 2000.

Steele, Bruce. Introduction. *Psychoanalysis and the Unconscious, and Fantasia of the Unconscious*. By D. H. Lawrence. Cambridge: Cambridge University Press, 2004. xix–li.

Stein, Gertrude. *Three Lives*. 1909. New York: Modern Library, 1933.

Stephens, Michelle. *Black Empire: The Masculine Global Imaginary of Caribbean Intellectuals in the United States, 1914–1962*. Durham: Duke University Press, 2005.

Stovall, Tyler. *Paris Noir: African Americans in the City of Light*. Boston: Houghton Mifflin, 1996.

Svoboda, Frederick J. "What Was That Black Man? A Note on Eugene Bullard and *The Sun Also Rises*." *Hemingway Review* 17.2 (Spring 1998): 105–11.

Thurman, Wallace. *Harlem: A Melodrama of Negro Life in Harlem*. 1929. *The Collected Writings of Wallace Thurman: A Harlem Renaissance Reader*. Ed. Amritjit Singh and Daniel M. Scott. New Brunswick, N.J.: Rutgers University Press. 313–69.

——. *Infants of the Spring*. New York: Macaulay, 1932.

Tillery, Tyrone. *Claude McKay: A Black Poet's Struggle for Identity*. Amherst: University of Massachusetts Press, 1992.

Topp, Michael M. *The Sacco and Vanzetti Case: A Brief History with Documents*. Bedford Series in History and Culture. Boston: Bedford/St. Martin's, 2004.

Trombold, John. "Harlem Transfer: Claude McKay and John Dos Passos." *Juxtapositions: The Harlem Renaissance and the Lost Generation*. Ed. Lesley Marx and Loes Nas. Cape Town: University of Cape Town Press, 2000. 4–20.

Trotsky, Leon. "Answers to Comrade Claude MacKay." *Izvestia* 15 Feb. 1923: n.p.

——. *Literature and Revolution*. 1923. Ed. William Keach. Chicago: Haymarket Books, 2005.

——. *Permanent Revolution and Results and Prospects*. 1928. New York: Pathfinder, 1969.

——. *The Revolution Betrayed: What Is the Soviet Union and Where Is It Going?* Trans. Max Eastman. Garden City, N.Y.: Doubleday, Doran, 1937.

Tuttle, William M., Jr. *Race Riot: Chicago in the Red Summer of 1919*. Blacks in the New World. Urbana: University of Illinois Press, 1997.

Tzara, Tristan, and Francis Picabia. *Seven Dada Manifestos and Lampisteries*. Trans. Barbara Wright. New York: Calder, 1981.

Vaidon, Lawdom. *Tangier: A Different Way*. Metuchen, N.J.: Scarecrow, 1977.

Van Vechten, Carl. *Nigger Heaven*. New York: Knopf, 1926.

von Sternberg, Josef, dir. *The Blue Angel*. Perf. Marlene Dietrich. Paramount, 1930.

——. *Morocco*. Perf. Marlene Dietrich and Gary Cooper. Paramount, 1930.

Wald, Alan M. *Exiles from a Future Time: The Forging of the Mid-Twentieth-Century Literary Left*. Chapel Hill: University of North Carolina Press, 2002.

Watson, Steven. *The Harlem Renaissance: Hub of African-American Culture, 1920–1929*. New York: Pantheon, 1995.

Weeks, Jeffrey. *Coming Out: Homosexual Politics in Britain from the Nineteenth Century to the Present*. London: Quartet, 1977.

Whitfield, James Monroe. *America and Other Poems*. Buffalo: James S. Leavitt, 1853.

Wills, J. Elder, dir. *Big Fella*. 1937. Perf. Paul Robeson. British Lion Film Corporation. Library of Congress Restoration. Kino on Video, 1998.

Wirth, Thomas H. Introduction. *Gay Rebel of the Harlem Renaissance: Selections from the Work of Richard Bruce Nugent*. By Richard Bruce Nugent. Durham: Duke University Press, 2002. 1–61.

Woods, Gregory. "Gay Re-Readings of the Harlem Renaissance Poets." *Journal of Homosexuality* 26.2–3 (1993): 127–43.

Woolf, Virginia. *Orlando: A Biography*. 1928. New York: Harcourt Brace Jovanovich, 1956.

Worth, Robert F. "*Nigger Heaven* and the Harlem Renaissance." *African American Review* 29.3 (Fall 1995): 461–73.

Wright, J. W., and Everett K. Rowson. *Homoeroticism in Classical Arabic Literature*. New York: Columbia University Press, 1997.

Wright, Richard. "I Tried to Be a Communist." *The God That Failed*. 1949. Ed. Richard Crossman. Foreword David Engerman. New York: Columbia University Press, 2001. 115–64.

———. *Native Son*. New York: Harper, 1940.

Index

Lightning Source UK Ltd.
Milton Keynes UK
UKHW011010070421
381574UK00001B/141